by W·H·AUDEN

Forewords
AND
Afterwords

Forewords
AND
Afterwords

BY

W·H·AUDEN

Selected by Edward Mendelson

Random House

NEW YORK

Library of Congress Cataloging in Publication Data

Auden, Wystan Hugh, 1907–
Foreworks and afterwords.
Selected by Edward Mendelson.
1. Literature—Addresses, essays, lectures.
I. Title.
PN511.A78   809   72-10230
ISBN 0-394-48359-6

Acknowledgments appear in "A Note on the Text,"
beginning on page 525.

Manufactured in the United States of America

Designed by Andrew Roberts

2   4   6   8   9   7   5   3

For HANNAH ARENDT

Contents

✳

Contents

] x [

Contents

Forewords

AND

Afterwords

*

THE GREEKS AND US

*

Once upon a time there was a little boy. Before he could read, his father told him stories about the War between the Greeks and the Trojans. Hector and Achilles were as familiar to him as his brothers, and when the Olympians quarreled he thought of his uncles and aunts. At seven he went to a boarding school and most of the next seven years were spent in translating Greek and Latin into English and vice versa. Then he went on to another boarding school which had a Classical Side and a Modern Side.

The latter was regarded by boys and masters alike in much the same way as, in a militarist country, civilians are regarded by officers, and with the same kind of degrees of inferiority: history and mathematics were, like professional men, possible; the natural sciences, comprehensively labeled Stinks, like tradesmen, were not. The Classical Side, too, had its nice distinctions: Greek, like the Navy, was the senior, the aristocratic service.

It is hard to believe now that this story is not a fairy tale but a historical account of middle-class education in England thirty-five years ago.

For anyone brought up in this way, Greece and Rome are so mixed up with his personal memories of childhood and classroom that it is extremely difficult to look at these civilizations objectively.

This is particularly so, perhaps, in the case of Greece. Until near the end of the eighteenth century, Europe thought of itself less as Europe than as Western Christendom, the heir to the Roman Empire, and its educational system was based on the study of Latin. The rise of Hellenic studies to an equal and then a superior position was a nineteenth century phenomenon and coincided with the development of European nations and nationalist feeling.

It is significant, surely, that when, today, an afterdinner speaker refers to the sources of our civilization, he always names Jerusalem and Athens, but rarely Rome, for the last is the symbol of a religious and political unity which has ceased to exist and the revival of which few believe in or desire. The historical discontinuity between Greek culture and our own, the disappearance for so many centuries of any direct influence, made it all the easier, when it was rediscovered, for each nation to fashion a classical Greece in its own image. There is a German Greece, a French Greece, an English Greece—there may even be an American Greece—all quite different. Had Hölderlin met Jowett, for instance, one suspects that neither would have understood a word the other said, and their parting would have been cold.

Even within a single country different Greeces coexist. For instance here are two English caricatures:

Professor X. Reade Chair of Moral Philosophy. 59. Married. Three daughters. Religion: C of E (Broad). Politics: Conservative. Lives in a small suburban house stuffed with Victorian knick-knacks. Does not entertain. Smokes a pipe. Does not notice what he eats. Hobbies: gardening and long solitary walks. Dislikes: foreigners, Roman Catholicism, modern literature, noise. Current worry: his wife's health.

Mr. Y. Classical tutor. 41. Unmarried. Religion: none. Politics: none. Lives in college. Has private means and gives wonderful lunch parties for favorite undergraduates. Hobbies: travel and collecting old glass. Dislikes: Christianity, girls, the poor, English cooking. Current worry: his figure.

To X, the word Greece suggests Reason, the Golden Mean, emotional control, freedom from superstition; to Y it suggests Gaiety and Beauty, the life of the senses, freedom from inhibitions.

Of course, being good scholars, both know that their respective views are partial; X cannot deny that many Greeks were attracted to mystery cults and addicted to habits upon which "the common moral sense of civilized mankind has pronounced a judgment which requires no justification as it allows of no appeal"; Y is equally aware that the Plato of the *Laws* is as puritanical as any Scotch Presbyter; but the emotional tie to the Greece of their dreams, formed in childhood and strengthened by years of study and affection, is stronger than their knowledge.

There could be no stronger proof of the riches and depth of Greek culture than its powers of appeal to every kind of personality. It has been said that everyone is born either a Platonist or an Aristotelian; but it seems to me that there are more contrasted and significant divisions than this, between, for instance, the lovers of Ionia and the lovers of Sparta, between those who are devoted to both Plato *and* Aristotle and those who prefer Hippocrates and Thucydides to either.

II

The days when classical studies were the core of higher learning have now passed and are not likely, in any future we can envisage, to return. We have to accept as an accomplished fact that the educated man of today and tomorrow can read neither Latin nor Greek. This means, I think, that, if the classics are to continue to exert any educational effect at all, a change must be made in the emphasis and direction of Roman and Hellenic studies.

If Greek literature has to be read in translation, then the approach can no longer be an aesthetic one. The aesthetic loss in translation from one language into another is always immense; in the case of languages and cultures as far apart as Greek and English, it becomes practically fatal; one can almost say that the better a translation is as English poetry, the less like Greek poetry it is (e.g., Pope's *Iliad*) and vice versa.

To begin with there is the prosodic difficulty; quantitative unrhymed verse and qualitative rhymed verse have nothing in common except that they are both rhythmical patterns. An English poet can have much fun attempting, as a technical exercise or an act of piety, to write quantitatively:

With these words Hermes sped away for lofty Olympos:
And Priam all fearlessly from off his chariot alighted,
Ordering Idaeus to remain i' the entry to keep watch
Over the beasts: th'old king meanwhile strode doughtily onward,
(Robert Bridges. Iliad, xxiv, 468–71)

But no one can read this except as a qualitative meter of an eccentric kind, and eccentricity is a very un-Homeric characteristic.

Then there are the problems of word-order and diction; Greek is an inflected language where the sense does not depend on the position of the words in the sentence as it does in English; Greek is rich in compound epithets, English is not.

Lastly and most important of all, the poetic sensibility of the two literatures is radically different. Compared with English poetry Greek poetry is primitive, i.e., the emotions and subjects it treats are simpler and more direct than ours while, on the other hand, the *manner* of language tends to be more involved and complex. Primitive poetry says simple things in a roundabout way where modern poetry tries to say complicated things straightforwardly. The continuous efforts of English poets in every generation to rediscover "a language really used by men" would have been incomprehensible to a Greek.

In his introduction to *Greek Plays in Modern Translation,* Dudley Fitts quotes a translation of a bit of stichomythy from *Medea.*

> MEDEA: Why didst thou fare to earth's prophetic navel?
> AEGEUS: To ask how seed of children might be mine.
> MEDEA: 'Fore Heaven!—aye childless is thy life till now?
> AEGEUS: Childless I am, by chance of some god's will.
> MEDEA: This with a wife, or knowing not the couch?
> AEGEUS: Nay, not unyoked to wedlock's bed am I.

This is, as he says, comically absurd, but what is the poor translator to do? If, for instance, he translates the last two lines into modern idiom, he must write:

> MEDEA: Are you married or single?
> AEGEUS: Married.

This is no longer funny, but it has completely lost an essential element of the original style, the poetic ornamentation of simple questions and answers by casting them in the form of riddles.

It is significant that, in spite of the familiarity with and enormous admiration for Greek poetry of many English poets in the past, very few indeed show any signs of having been influenced by it in their style of writing—Milton and possibly Browning by the tragedians, Hopkins by Pindar, are the only names I can think of.

The attempt to translate the poetry of one language into another is an invaluable training for a poet, and it is to be hoped that new versions of Homer, Aeschylus, Aristophanes, Sappho, etc., will continue to be made in every generation, but their public importance is likely to be small.

Even when he is reading the epics or the plays, the average modern reader is going to find that a historical and anthropological approach is more fruitful than an aesthetic one.

Instead of asking "How good a tragedy is *Oedipus?*" or "Is such and such an argument of Plato's true or false?" he will try to see all aspects of Greek activity, their drama, their science, their philosophy, their politics as interrelated parts of one complete and unique culture.

Accordingly, in selecting the material for this anthology, I have tried to make it an introduction to Greek culture rather than Greek literature. In a literary anthology it would be absurd to represent Greek tragedy by Aeschylus alone, omitting Sophocles and Euripides, but if one wishes to understand the form and idea of Greek tragedy, it is better to give a trilogy like *The Oresteia* than three separate plays by three authors; so too with all the other poetic selections which have been chosen for their representative character as literary forms rather than for their individual poetic excellences.

Again, in the extracts from the philosophers the intention has been not to give a comprehensive picture of Plato and Aristotle, but to show how Greek thinkers dealt with certain kinds of problems, for instance the problem of cosmology.

Lastly, Greek medicine and Greek mathematics are so essential parts of their culture, that they cannot be ignored even by a beginner.

The exigencies of space in a volume of this size exclude much important material, but I have only consciously excluded one author, for reasons of personal distaste. I believe, however, that I am not alone in finding Lucian, one of the most popular of Greek writers, too "enlightened" for a generation as haunted by devils as our own.

III

There is no single Greek literary work of art as great as *The Divine Comedy;* there is no extant series of works by a single Greek literary artist as impressive as the complete plays of Shakespeare; as a period of sustained creative activity in one medium, the seventy-five-odd years of Athenian drama, between the first tragedies of Aeschylus and the last comedy of Aristophanes, are surpassed by the hundred and twenty-five years, between Gluck's *Orpheus* and Verdi's *Otello,* which comprise the golden age of European opera: nevertheless, the bewildered comment of any fifth century Athenian upon our society from Dante's time till our own, and with increasing sharpness every decade, would surely be: "Yes, I can see all the works of a great civilization; but why cannot I meet any civilized persons? I only encounter specialists, artists who know nothing of science, scientists who know nothing of art, philosophers who have no interest in God, priests who are unconcerned with politics, politicians who only know other politicians."

Civilization is a precarious balance between what Professor Whitehead has called barbaric vagueness and trivial order. Barbarism is unified but undifferentiated; triviality is differentiated but lacking in any central unity; the ideal of civilization is the integration into a complete whole and with the minimum strain of the maximum number of distinct activities.

It is impossible to say, for example, of a harvest dance of a primitive tribe whether it is aesthetic play, undertaken for the pleasure it gives the participants in performing it well, or religious ritual, an outward expression of an inward piety towards the powers who control the harvest, or a scientific technique for securing the practical effect of a better harvest: it is indeed foolish to think in such terms at all, since the dancers have not learned to make such distinctions and cannot understand what they mean.

In a society like our own, on the other hand, when a man goes to the ballet, he goes simply to enjoy himself and all he demands is that choreography and performance shall be aesthetically satisfying; when he goes to Mass, he knows that it is irrelevant whether the Mass be well or badly sung, for what matters is the attitude of his will towards God and his neighbor; when he plows a field, he knows that whether the tractor be beautiful or ugly or whether he be a repentant or a defiant sinner is irrelevant to his success or failure. His problem is quite different from that of the savage; the danger for him is that, instead of being a complete person at every moment, he will be split into three unrelated fragments which are always competing for dominance: the aesthetic fragment which goes to the ballet, the religious which goes to Mass, and the practical which earns its living.

If a civilization be judged by this double standard, the degree of diversity attained and the degree of unity retained, then it is hardly too much to say that the Athenians of the fifth century B.C. were the most civilized people who have so far existed. The fact that nearly all the words we use to define activities and branches of knowledge, e.g., chemistry, physics, economics, politics, ethics, aesthetics, theology, tragedy, comedy, etc., are of Greek origin is proof of their powers of conscious differentiation; their literature and their history are evidence of their ability to maintain a sense of common interrelation, a sense which we have in great measure lost as they themselves lost it in a comparatively short time.

> "... as their forefathers were they,
> those old seapirates, who with roving robbery
> built up their island lordships on the ruin of Crete,
> when the unforbearing rivalry of their free cities
> wrec'd their confederacy within the sevenscore years
> 'twixt Marathon and Issus; until from the pride
> of routing Xerxes and his fabulous host, they fell
> to make that most memorable of all invasions
> less memorable in the glory of Alexander,
> under whose alien kingship they conspired to outreach
> their own ambition, winning dominions too wide
> for domination; and were, with their virtue, dispersed
> and molten into the great stiffening alloy of Rome."
> (Robert Bridges. *Testament of Beauty*, I, 758–70)

] 9 [

The geography of Greece, where barren mountains separate small fertile localities from each other, encouraged diversity, migration to new colonies, and an economy of exchange rather than production for use. In consequence, the Greeks, who, when they first invaded the Aegean, were not so very different from any other patriarchal military tribe—the kind of life described in the *Iliad* is much the same as that described in *Beowulf*—rapidly developed within a comparatively small area a great variety of forms of social organization, tyrannies and constitutional city-states in Ionia, feudal oligarchy in Boeotia, a militarist police state in Sparta, democracy in Athens, almost every possible kind, in fact, but one, the extended centralized state typical of major river-basin areas like Egypt or Babylonia. The initial stimulus, therefore, to comprehension, inquiry, speculation, and experiment was present; but this explains neither the extraordinary talent the Greeks displayed in these activities nor their capacity to absorb influences and make them their own: unlike the Romans, the Greeks never give the impression of being eclectics; everything they do and say is stamped with their distinctive character.

Greek culture, as a glance at the chronological table at the end of this introduction will show, had successively three centers, the Ionian seaboard, Athens, and Alexandria. Sparta remained outside the general cultural development in a fossilized state of primitivism, exciting in her neighbors a mixture of fear, repulsion, and admiration. Nevertheless, she made, indirectly through Plato, a contribution which for good or ill, has influenced the world as much as any other element in Greek culture, namely, the idea of a consciously planned education of its citizens by the state; indeed the very concept of the state as something distinct from the ruling class, from the individual, and from the community might be said to be derived from Sparta.

At the beginning of Greek literature stands Homer. If the *Iliad* and the *Odyssey* are better than the epics of other nations, this is due not to their content but to their more sophisticated imagination —as if the original material had been worked over into its present form under much more civilized conditions than existed among, say, the Teutonic peoples until their heroic age was too far behind them to seem real. It is difficult, however, to make objective comparisons, since the Teutonic epics had little further history; Homer became, through the Romans, one of the basic inspirations of European literature, without which there would be neither an *Aeneid,* a *Divine Comedy,* a *Paradise Lost,* nor the comic epics of Ariosto or Pope or Byron.

The next development after Homer took place largely in Ionia and for the most part in and around the courts of tyrants who were, of course, more like the Medicis than like a modern dictator.

The Ionian scientists and the Ionian lyric poets had one thing in common, a hostility to polytheistic myth. The former saw Nature in terms of law rather than arbitrary volition; the latter saw their feelings as their own, as belonging to a single personality, rather than as visitations from without.

Thales' guess that all things are made of water was wrong; but the insight behind it, namely, that however many different realms of Nature there may be they must all be related was a basic presupposition without which science as we know it would be impossible. Equally influential was the assertion of Pythagoras, as a result of his work in acoustics, that all things are number, i.e., that the "nature" of things, that by virtue of which they are what they are and behave as they do, is not a question of what they are made of but of their structure, which can be described in mathematical terms.

The great difference between the Greek conception of Nature and later ones is that the Greeks thought of the universe as analogous to a city-state, so that for them natural laws, like human laws, were not laws *of* things, descriptions of how in fact they behave, but laws *for* things. When we speak of a falling body "obeying" the law of gravitation, we are unconsciously echoing Greek thought; for obedience implies the possibility of disobedience. To the Greeks this was no dead metaphor; consequently, their problem was not the relation of Mind to Matter, but of Substance to Form, how matter became "educated" enough, so to speak, to conform to law.

The lyric poets were equally important in their own sphere; for it was through them that Western civilization has learned to distinguish poetry from history, pedagogy, and religion.

The most famous phase of Greek civilization is, of course, that associated with Athens. If he knows nothing else about them, every man in the street has heard the names of Homer, Aeschylus, Sophocles, Euripides, Aristophanes, Socrates, Plato, Aristotle, and, if he is a little better informed, of Pericles, Demosthenes, and Thucydides. All but Homer are Athenian.

The Athenian period divides into two; the first is preceded by the political and economic establishment of the Athenian state as a mercantile democracy by Solon and Cleisthenes, and the demonstration of its strength through its victory over the Persian Invasion; the second is the product of political defeat, first by Sparta, then by Macedonia. The typical expression of the first period is drama, of the second philosophy.

In comparison with the preceding Ionian culture, Athenian drama is marked by a revulsion from luxury and frivolity towards austerity and simplicity, and by a return to myth. Above all, for the first and last time in history, an art, drama, became the dominant religious expression of a whole people, the dramatist the most important figure in their spiritual life. Compared with the Greek tragedians, Homer and Pindar seem secular writers, of educational value certainly for a ruling minority, but still primarily entertainers, subordinate in importance to the priest and the oracle. Like modern drama, which grew out of religious festivals such as Easter and Corpus Christi, Athenian drama was associated with the festivals of the Wine Press and of the Greater Dionysus. But, whereas modern drama was at first subordinate to the religious rituals and then developed a secular life of its own, leaving the festivals to themselves, Athenian drama, while being definitely works of art, whose value can be judged by vote, became the dominant religious exercise, of greater importance than sacrifices or prayers. In the nineteenth century and in our own the individual artistic genius has sometimes claimed a supreme importance and even persuaded a minority of aesthetes to agree with him; but only in Athens was this a universal social fact, so that the genius was not a lonely figure claiming exceptional rights for himself but the acclaimed spiritual leader of society.

The nearest modern equivalent is not any work of the theater, but a ball game or a bull-fight.

Greek tragedy returned to myth, but it was no longer the Homeric mythology; the Ionian cosmologists had done their work.

The gods are no longer essentially strong and accidentally right-eous; their strength is now secondary, the means by which they enforce the laws which they themselves keep and represent. In consequence, the mythology is subjected to strain; for, the more monotheistic it becomes, the greater the importance of Zeus, the less individual, the more allegorical, become the other gods. Fur-thermore, behind Zeus himself appears the quite unmythological concept of Fate. Now either the personal Zeus and the impersonal Fate must coalesce as the Creator God of the Jews, a step which the Greek religious imagination never took, or, in the end, Zeus becomes a Demiurge, an allegorical figure for the order in nature, and Fate becomes the true God, either as Fortune or as an im-personal Idea or First Cause, in which case drama ceases to be the natural vehicle for teaching about the nature of God and is replaced by the science of Theology.

It is partly for such reasons, perhaps, that the development from the piety of Aeschylus to the skepticism of Euripides is so rapid, and the period of Greek tragedy so short. As Werner Jaeger has pointed out, Sophocles stands a little apart from the other two in that, while their interests are basically the same, his concern was more with human character than with religious or social problems. For Greek tragedy to have developed further, it would have had to go on from Sophocles, abandon its relation to myth and festival, and become a frankly secular art; perhaps its very triumphs tied it too firmly to myth and festival to allow it to make the break which the Elizabethan drama, for instance, made. Thus, greatly as the Greek tragedians have been admired by later writers, they cannot be said to have exerted much direct literary influence. The influence of the philosophers is in striking contrast to this, for Plato and Aristotle between them established the basic premises of an intellectual life, the unity and the diversity of truth; moreover, they are responsible for the particular kinds of divisions to which we are accustomed. If, for example, one tries to read Indian philos-ophy, the great obstacle to understanding what it means is that the joints of man and nature, so to speak, are carved differently. Our cuts, our carving are Greek; and we find it hard for us to believe that there can be any others.

The final period of Greek culture, the Hellenist, or Alexandrian, returns to Ionian hedonism and materialism but without its relation to political and social life. The important achievements are technological. The literature, as typified by the Greek Anthology, is highly polished, pretty, but on the whole boring, at least to the present age, because of its immense influence on minor poetry since the Renaissance. To it we owe all the worst "classical" properties, the little rogue of a Cupid, the catalogue of flowers, Celia's bosom, etc., etc.

Christendom was a product of Jewish historical religious experience and Gentile speculation upon and organization of that experience. The Greek mind is the typically Gentile mind, and it is at odds with the Jewish consciousness. As a Greek the Christian is tempted to a seesaw between wordly frivolity and a falsely spiritual other-worldliness, both of them, *au fond,* pessimistic; as a Jew he is tempted to the wrong kind of seriousness, to an intolerance which persecutes dissenters as wicked rather than stupid. The Inquisition was a product of a Gentile interest in rationality and a Jewish passion for truth.

The clearest historical example is the Crucifixion. In their book *Talking of Dick Whittington* Hesketh Pearson and Hugh Kingsmill report an interview with Hilaire Belloc in which he says of the Jews:

> "Poor darlings, it must be terrible to be born with the knowledge that you belong to the enemies of the human race . . . because of the Crucifixion."

I cannot believe that Mr. Belloc is an altogether stupid man. Nevertheless, his statement is on a par with Adam's "The woman beguiled me and I did eat." He can hardly be unaware that the Crucifixion was actually performed by the Romans, or, to make it contemporary, by the French (the English said, "Oh, dear!" and consented; the Americans said, "How undemocratic!" and sent photographers) for the frivolous reason that Jesus was a political nuisance. The Jews who demanded it did so for the serious reason that, in their opinion, Jesus was guilty of blasphemy, i.e., of falsely claiming to be the Messiah. Every Christian is, of course, both Pilate and Caiaphas.

IV

If there is any reaction to the Greeks which may be called typical of our age as compared with preceding times, it is, I think, a feeling that they were a very odd people indeed, so much so that when we come across something they wrote which seems similar to our own way of thinking, we immediately suspect that we have misunderstood the passage. It is the unlikeness of the Greeks to ourselves, the gulf between the kind of assumptions they made, the kind of questions they asked and our own that strikes us more than anything else.

Take, for instance, the following passage from the *Timaeus:*

"Such was the whole plan of the eternal God about the god that was to be, to whom for this reason he gave a body, smooth and even, having a surface in every direction equidistant from the centre, a body entire and perfect, and formed out of perfect bodies. And in the centre he put the soul, which he diffused throughout the body, making it also to be the exterior environment of it; and he made the Universe a circle moving in a circle, one and solitary, yet by reason of its excellence able to converse with itself, and needing no other friendship or acquaintance. Having these purposes in view he created the world a blessed god."

Surely this kind of thinking is as extraordinary to us as any habits of an African tribe.

Even those of us whose mathematical equipment is of the most meager, have so imbibed the modern conception of number as an instrument for explaining nature, that we can no more think ourselves back into a state of mind where numbers were regarded as physical or metaphysical entities so that one number was "better" than another than we can return to a belief in sympathetic magic. Nor is the Platonic assumption about the moral nature of godhead any less peculiar to us that his shape. We may or may not believe that god exists, but the only kind of god in which we can think of believing is a god who suffers, either involuntarily like the Christian god because he loves his creatures and suffers with them; the kind of god who is both self-sufficient and content to remain so could not interest us enough to raise the question of his existence.

It is impudent of me to trespass at all inside a field where so many great and good men have spent their lifetimes. I can only try to limit the offense by confining my remarks to one aspect of Greek thought of which I am less ignorant than I am of others, namely to a comparison of the various Greek conceptions of the hero with our own, as an illustration of the distance between our culture and theirs.

V

The Homeric Hero: The Homeric hero has the military virtues of courage, resourcefulness, magnanimity in victory, and dignity in defeat to an exceptional degree. His heroism is manifested in exceptional deeds which can be judged by others who are forced to admit "He achieved what we could not have achieved." His motive is to win admiration and glory from his equals whether they are on his side or the enemy's. The code by which he lives is a code of honor which is not a universal requirement like law but an individual one, that which I require of myself and that which in view of my achievements I have a right to demand of others.

He is not a tragic figure, i.e., he does not suffer more than others, but his death has exceptional pathos—the great warrior comes to the same end as the lowest churl. He exists only in the present moment when he comes into collision with another heroic individual; his future forms the past traditions of others. The closest modern equivalent to the Homeric hero is the ace fighter pilot. Because he is so often engaged in single combat, he gets to recognize individual pilots on the side of the enemy and war becomes a matter of personal rivalry rather than any political issue; in fact he has a closer relation to the enemy ace than he has to the infantry on his own side. His life is so full of risks and hairbreadth escapes, so almost certain to end in death, and the effects of good luck and bad luck, of a sudden engine failure or an unforeseen change in the weather, are so serious that chance takes on all the aspects of a personal intervening power. The sense of having good days when he is protected and bad days when he is being worked against and the conviction that he will die when Fate decrees but not before become almost necessary attitudes to life.

There is still however an essential difference between the fighter pilot and the Homeric hero; to make the analogy close one would have to imagine that all the countries of the world had been continuously at war for centuries and that being a fighter pilot had become a hereditary profession. For the assumption of the *Iliad*, as of all early epics, which is so strange to us, is that war is the normal condition of mankind and peace an accidental breathing space. In the foreground are men locked in battle, killing or being killed, farther off their wives, children, and servants waiting anxiously for the outcome, overhead, watching the spectacle with interest and at times interfering, the gods who know neither sorrow nor death, and around them all indifferent and unchanging, the natural world of sky and sea and earth. That is how things are; that is how they always have been and always will be.

Consequently, there can be no moral or historical significance about the result of any conflict; it brings joy to the victor and sorrow to the vanquished but neither could imagine raising the question of justice. If one compares the *Iliad* with, for example, Shakespeare's *Henry IV* or Tolstoy's *War and Peace,* one sees that the modern writers are deeply concerned first with historical questions: "How did Henry IV or Napoleon come to power?" "What were the causes of the civil or international war?" and secondly with general moral questions: "What is the moral effect of war on human beings?" "What virtues and vices does it encourage as contrasted with those encouraged by peace?" "Irrespective of the individuals on both sides, did the defeat of Hotspur and Napoleon promote or retard the establishment of a Just Society?" These are questions which to Homer would seem meaningless. He does, it is true, give a cause for the Trojan war, the Apple of Discord; but this is both a divine cause, i.e., outside human control, and a frivolous cause, i.e., Homer does not take it seriously but uses it as a literary device for beginning his tale.

He does make moral judgments about his heroes. Achilles should not have refused for so long to aid the Greeks because of his quarrel with Agamemnon nor should he have treated the body of Hector as he did, but these are minor blemishes which neither affect the outcome of the war nor the final proof of his heroism, namely that he vanquishes Hector.

The pathos of Hector's death is simple: the nobler character is defeated; the pathos of Hotspur's death is ironic: he is a much more sympathetic individual than Prince Hal, but he dies defending the wrong cause.

Further, in the Homeric world where war is the norm, there can be no criticism of the military hero as such. The wrath of Achilles could never be a tragic flaw in his character in the way that the wrath of Shakespeare's Coriolanus is in his. Homer might well have described Achilles taking a bath but it would have been simply a description of a hero taking a bath, not, as in Tolstoy's description of Napoleon being bathed, a revelation that the military hero is an ordinary mortal just as weak as any of the thousands for whose death he is responsible.

Though it would be unfair to describe the Homeric hero as a mere puppet of the gods, his area of free choice and responsibility is pretty circumscribed. In the first place he is born, not made (often he is the son of an immortal father) so that though he does brave deeds, he cannot be called brave in our sense of the word because he never feels fear; in the second the situations in which he displays his heroism are given him; he can, on occasion, choose to fight or not to fight this or that opponent, but he cannot choose his profession or his side.

The world of Homer is unbearably sad because it never transcends the immediate moment; one is happy, one is unhappy, one wins, one loses, finally one dies. That is all. Joy and suffering are simply what one feels at the moment; they have no meaning beyond that; they pass away as they came; they point in no direction; they change nothing. It is a tragic world but a world without guilt for its tragic flaws is not a flaw in human nature, still less a flaw in an individual character, but a flaw in the nature of existence.

The Tragic Hero: The warrior-hero of the Homeric epics (and his civilian counterpart, the athlete of the Pindaric odes) is an aristocratic ideal. He is what every member of the ruling class should try to imitate, what every member of the subject class should admire without envy and obey without resentment, the closest approximation to a god—the divine being conceived as the ideally strong—possible to man.

The Tragic Hero, on the other hand, is not an ideal but a warning, and the warning is addressed not to an aristocratic audience, i.e., other potentially heroic individuals, but to the *demos*, i.e., the collective chorus. At the beginning of the play he appears in glory and good-fortune, a man of pedigree and achievement who has already demonstrated *arete* in the Homeric sense. By the end he has been plunged into exceptional suffering, i.e., he suffers more than the chorus, who are average citizens who have achieved nothing remarkable. He suffers because he has come into collision, not with other individuals, but with the universal law of righteousness. As a rule, however, the actual violation of which he is guilty is not his own conscious choice in the sense that he could have avoided it. The typical Greek tragic situation is one in which whatever the hero does must be wrong—Agamemnon must either kill his daughter or betray his duty to his army, Orestes must either disobey the orders of Apollo or be guilty of matricide, Oedipus must either persist in asking questions or let Thebes be destroyed by plague, Antigone must violate her duty either to her dead brother or to her city, etc. But the fact that he finds himself in a tragic situation where he has sinned unwittingly or must sin against his will is a sign that he is guilty of another sin for which the gods hold him responsible, namely the sin of hybris, an overweening self-confidence which makes him believe that he, with his *arete,* is a god who cannot be made to suffer. Sometimes but not always he manifests this hybris in acts—Agamemnon walks on the purple carpet, Darius tries to bridge the Hellespont—but even if he does not, he must be assumed to be guilty of hybris, otherwise he would not be punished by being made guilty of other sins. Through witnessing the fall of the tragic hero from happiness to misery, the chorus learns that the Homeric hero is not the ideal man they should try to imitate or admire. On the contrary, the strong man is tempted by his strength into becoming the impious man whom the gods punish, for the gods are not gods because they are ideally strong but because they are ideally just. Their strength is only the instrument by which they enforce their justice.

The ideal man whom every member of the democracy should

try to become is not the aristocratic heroic individual but the moderate law-abiding citizen who does not want to be stronger and more glorious than everybody else.

Here again, as in Homer, we find ourselves in a world which is quite alien to us. We are so habituated to the belief that a man's actions are a mixed product of his own free choices for which he is responsible and circumstances for which he is not that we cannot understand a world in which a situation by itself makes a man guilty. Take the story of Oedipus, for instance. Here is a man who hears a prophecy that he is to kill his father and marry his mother, tries to prevent it coming true, but in vain. How would a modern playwright treat this? He would reason that the only way for Oedipus to make certain of escaping what is foretold is for him never to kill anybody and never to marry anybody. He would therefore begin by showing Oedipus leaving Thebes and making these two resolutions. He would then proceed to involve him in two situations, firstly, one in which he is done a mortal injury by a man, secondly one in which he falls passionately in love with a woman who returns his love, situations, that is, of *temptation,* in which he is torn between doing what he wants and breaking his resolve.

He yields to both temptations, he kills the man and marries the woman, excusing himself as he does so with a lie of self-deception, that is, instead of saying to himself, "There is a possibility, however slight, that they are my father and mother; therefore I must not risk it," he says, "It is quite impossible that they should be my father and mother; therefore I may break my resolve." Unfortunately, of course, the slight possibility turns out to be the actual fact.

In Sophocles nothing like this happens. Oedipus meets an old man on the road, they have a trivial quarrel, and he kills the old man. He comes to Thebes, solves the riddle of the Sphinx, and makes a political match. About these two deeds he feels no guilt nor is he expected to feel guilty. It is only when in fact they turn out to be his father and mother that he becomes guilty. At no time has he been conscious of being tempted to do what he knows he should not do, so that at no time is it possible to say, "That was where he made his fatal mistake."

The original sin of the Greek tragic hero is hybris, believing that one is godlike. Nobody can be tempted into hybris except one who is exceptionally fortunate. Sometimes he can manifest his hybris directly, but it does not change his character in any way, only he is punished for it by being made by the gods to sin unwittingly or involuntarily.

The original sin of the modern tragic hero is pride, the refusal to accept the limitations and weaknesses which he knows he has, the determination to *become* the god he is not. A man, therefore, does not have to be fortunate, to be tempted into pride; a misfortune like Richard of Gloucester's hunchback will do just as well. Pride can never be manifested directly because it is a purely subjective sin. Self-examination can reveal to me that I am lustful or envious but it can never reveal to me that I am proud because my pride, if it exists, is in the "I" which is doing the examining; I can, however, infer that I am proud because the lust and envy which I can observe in myself are caused by it and it alone.

The secondary sins of which our kind of tragic hero is guilty and which cause his fall are not, therefore, a divine punishment for his initial sin but its effects, and he is as responsible for them as he is for it. He is not an unwitting sinner but a self-deceiving one, who refuses his guilty conscience. When Orestes slays Clytemnestra he does not anticipate the arrival of the Furies; when the Macbeths plan their murders they try to persuade themselves that they will not suffer the torments of guilt which they really know in their hearts they are going to.

In Greek tragedy suffering is a visitation from Heaven, a punishment imposed upon the hero from without. Through enduring it he expiates his sins and ends reconciled to the law, though it is for the gods not him to decide when his expiation is complete. In modern tragedy, on the other hand, this exterior kind of suffering which humbles the great and erring and leads them to repent is not tragic. The truly tragic kind of suffering is the kind produced and defiantly insisted upon by the hero himself so that, instead of making him better, it makes him worse and when he dies he is not reconciled to the law but defiant, that is, damned. Lear is not a tragic hero, Othello is.

These two differences between Greek and modern tragedy in

their conceptions, first of the relation of the hero's original subjective sin of hybris or of pride to his secondary sinful acts, and secondly of the nature and function of suffering, produce different attitudes towards time.

Unity of time is not only possible but right and proper in Greek tragedy because the characters do not change, only their situation so that the dramatic time required is simply the time required for the situation to change. In modern tragedy, unity of time is possible as a technical tour-de-force but rarely desirable, since one of the dramatist's principal tasks is to show how his characters not only are changed by changes of situation but also play active parts in creating these situations, and it is almost impossible to show this in a single uninterrupted passage of time.

The Erotic Hero: About three-quarters of modern literature is concerned with one subject, the love between a man and a woman, and assumes that falling in love is the most important and valuable experience that can happen to human beings. We are so conditioned to this attitude that we are inclined to forget that it does not go back beyond the twelfth century. It does not exist, for instance, in Greek literature. There we find two attitudes. There are plenty of lyrics of the serenade type—the "In delay there lies no plenty, then come kiss me sweet-and-twenty" kind of thing, expressing a simple, good-tempered, and unserious sensuality. There are also, as in the poems of Sappho or the story of Jason and Medea, descriptions of serious and violent sexual passion, but this is not regarded as something to be proud of but as a disaster, the work of merciless Aphrodite, a dreadful madness which makes one lose one's dignity and betray one's friends and from which any sane man or woman will pray to be spared. Our romantic conception, that sexual love can transform the lover's character and turn him into a hero, was unknown.

It is not until we come to Plato that we find descriptions of something like what we mean by romantic love spoken of with approval, yet the differences are still greater than the resemblances. In the first place it is assumed that this kind of love is only possible in a homosexual relation; and in the second, it is only approved of as the necessary first stage in the growth of the soul. The ultimate

good is the love of the impersonal as universal good; the best thing
that could happen to a man would be that he should fall in love
with the Good immediately, but owing to the fact that his soul is
entangled in matter and time, he can only get there by degrees;
first he falls in love with a beautiful individual, then he can progress to love of beauty in general, then to love of justice, and so
on. If erotic passion can or ought to be transformed in this way,
then it was sound psychological insight on Plato's part and not
simply the cultural pattern of erotic life in Greece that made him
exclude the heterosexual relation, for the latter leads beyond itself,
not to the universal, but to more individuals, namely the love of
and responsibility for a family, whereas, in the homosexual case,
since the relation of itself leads nowhere, the love which it has
aroused is free to develop in any direction the lovers choose, and
that direction should be towards wisdom which, once acquired,
will enable them to teach human beings procreated in the normal
way how to become a good society. For love is to be judged by its
social and political value. Marriage provides the raw material, the
masculine eros the desire and knowledge to mold that material
into its proper form.

The two great modern erotic myths, which have no parallels in
Greek literature, are the myth of Tristan and Isolde, or the World
Well Lost for Love, and the countermyth of Don Juan, the seducer.

The Tristan-Isolde situation is this: both possess heroic *arete*
in the epic sense; he is the bravest warrior, she is the most beautiful woman; both are of noble birth. They cannot marry each other
because she is already the wife of his king and friend, nevertheless
they fall in love. In some versions they accidentally drink a love
potion but the effect of this is not really to make them fall in love
but rather to make them realize that they already have and to
accept the fact as predestined and irrevocable. Their relation is
not "platonic" in the conventional sense, but the barriers of marriage and circumstances give them few opportunities for going to
bed together, and on each occasion they can never be certain that
it will not be the last. The love they feel for each other is religiously
absolute, i.e., each is the other's ultimate good so that not only is
sexual infidelity inconceivable, but all other relations to other
people and the world cease to have any significance. Yet, though

their relation is the only value that exists for them, it is a torment, because their sexual desire is only the symbolic expression of their real passion, which is the yearning of two souls to merge and become one, a consummation which is impossible so long as they have bodies, so that their ultimate goal is to die in each other's arms.

Don Juan, on the other hand, is not an epic hero; ideally, his external appearance is that of the man who nobody notices is there because he is so utterly commonplace, for it is important to the myth that he, the man of heroic will and achievement, should look to the outward eye like a member of the chorus.

If Don Juan is either handsome or ugly, then the woman will have feelings about him before he sets to work, and the seduction will not be absolute, i.e., a pure triumph of his will. For that, it is essential that his victim should have no feelings of her own towards him, until he chooses to arouse them. Vice versa, what is essential for him about her is not her appearance but simply her membership in the class Woman; the ugly and the old are as good as the beautiful and the young. The Tristan-Isolde myth is un-Greek because no Greek could conceive of attributing absolute value to another individual, he could only think in comparative terms, this one is more beautiful than that one, this one has done greater deeds than that one, etc. The Don Juan myth is un-Greek, as Kierkegaard has pointed out, not because he sleeps with a number of women, but because he keeps a list of them.

A Greek could understand seducing a girl because one found her attractive and then deserting her because one met a more attractive girl and forgot the first one; but he could not have understood doing so for an arithmetical reason, because one had resolved to be the first lover of every woman in the world, and she happened to be the next integer in this infinite series.

Tristan and Isolde are tormented because they are compelled to count up to two when they long to be able only to count up to one; Don Juan is in torment because, however great the number of his seductions, it still remains a finite number and he cannot rest until he has counted up to infinity.

The great enemy of both is time: Tristan and Isolde dread it because it threatens change, and they wish the moment of intense feeling to remain unchanged forever, hence the love potion and the irremovable obstacle in the situation which serve as defense against change; Don Juan dreads it because it threatens repetition and he wishes each moment to be absolutely novel, hence his insistence that for each of his victims it must be her first sexual experience and that he only sleep with her once.

Both myths are dependent upon Christianity, i.e, they could only have been invented by a society which has been taught to believe *a*) that every individual is of unique and eternal value to God irrespective of his or her social importance in the world, *b*) that dedication of the self to God is an act of free-choice, an absolute commitment irrespective of feeling, made with infinite passion, and *c*) that one must neither allow oneself to be ruled by the temporal moment nor attempt to transcend it but make oneself responsible for it, turning time into history.

Both myths are diseases of the Christian imagination and while they have inspired a great body of beautiful literature, their influence upon human conduct, particularly in their frivolous watered-down modern versions, which gloss over the fact that both the romantic couple and the solitary seducer are intensely unhappy, has been almost wholly bad. Whenever a married couple divorce because having ceased to be a divine image to each other, they cannot endure the thought of having to love a real person no better than themselves, they are acting under the spell of the Tristan myth. Whenever a man says to himself "I must be getting old. I haven't had sex for a week. What would my friends say if they knew," he is re-enacting the myth of Don Juan. It is significant also—it might interest Plato though it would probably not surprise him—that the instances in real life which conform most closely to the original pattern of both myths are not, in either case, heterosexual; the Tristan and Isolde one actually meets are a Lesbian couple, the Don Juan a pederast.

The Contemplative Hero: The Ideal Man of Greek Epic is the strong individual; the Ideal Man of Greek Tragedy is the modest citizen with a reverence for the law of justice; the Ideal Man of Greek Philosophy has something in common with both: Like the latter he is one who keeps the Law but, like the former, he is an exceptional individual, not a member of the chorus, for to learn how to keep the Law has become a heroic task which is beyond the power of the average man. To the question "What is the cause of evil and suffering?" Homer can only answer, "I don't know. The caprice of the gods perhaps"; Tragedy answers, "The violation of the laws of righteousness and justice by arrogant strong men"; Philosophy answers, "Ignorance of what the Law is which leaves the minds of men at the mercy of their bodily passions."

The Homeric hero hopes by brave deeds to win glory before he dies; the tragic chorus hopes by living modestly to escape misfortune as long as they live; the contemplative hero hopes for ultimate happiness of soul when he has succeeded in learning to know the true and eternal good, and so delivering his soul from the entanglements of his body and the temporal flux; and beyond this he must teach society how to attain the same freedom from injustice.

In theory, the possibility of doing this should be open to all alike but in practice it is limited to those souls whom the heavenly eros has inspired with a passion for knowledge, and whom temporal circumstances allow them to devote their lifetime to the search for wisdom; the stupid who cannot, the frivolous who will not, and the poor who have no time to understand are debarred. They may have valuable social functions to perform but it is not for them to say what the laws of society should be. That is the duty of the philosopher.

This ideal is stranger to us than it looks at first sight. We are familiar with two kinds of contemplative men: First, with the religious contemplative as represented by the various orders of monks and nuns or by the individual mystic. His aim is to know the hidden God, the reality behind all phenomena, but he thinks of this God as a person, i.e., what he means by knowledge is not objective knowledge *about* something which is the same for all minds and once perceived can be passed on to others by teaching, like the truths of mathematics, but a subjective relationship which is unique for every individual. A relationship can never be taught, it has to be voluntarily entered into, and the only possible method of persuading another to do it is personal example. If B is a friend of A and C is not, B cannot make C a friend of A by describing A, but if B, as the result of his friendship with A has become the kind of person C would like to be and is not, C may decide to try and make A's acquaintance, too.

Objective knowledge is the field of another kind of contemplative, the intellectual, the scientist, the artist, etc, and the knowledge he seeks is not about any transcendent reality but about phenomena. The intellectual, like the religious contemplative, requires individual passion but in his case it is confined to the search for knowledge; towards the object of his search, the facts, he must be passionless.

What is puzzling to us about the Greek conception of the contemplative hero is that these two kinds of activity are inextricably mixed, sometimes he seems to talk of a transcendent God as if He were a passive object, at other times of observable phenomena, like the movements of the planets, as if they were persons for which one could feel personal passion. Nothing is more bewildering to us about Plato, for instance, than the way in which, in the middle of a piece of dialectic, he will introduce what he himself admits to be a myth but without any feeling on his part that it is a peculiar thing to do.

It is hard to say whether one should call the Greeks more anthropomorphic in their thinking than we or less. On the one hand, in Greek cosmology everything in nature is thought of as being alive; the laws of nature are not descriptions of how things actually behave, laws *of,* but, like human laws, laws *for,* laws which they ought to obey and can fail to obey properly. On the other, in Greek political theory, human beings are thought of as if they were merely the matter out of which through his *techne* the craftsman-politician fashions the good society as a potter makes a vase out of clay.

To the Greeks the essential difference between man and nature was that the former can reason if he wants to, whereas for us the essential difference is that man has a self, i.e., that he and, so far as we know, apart from God, he alone is conscious of existing, and this consciousness is his whether he wants it or not, whether he is intelligent or not. The Greeks therefore had no real conception of the will as distinct from desire, so that, though they had, of course, observed the psychological fact of temptation, that one can desire what one knows is wrong, they were at a loss as to how to explain it. The weakest point in Greek Ethics is its analysis of Choice. This is all the more serious because politics is not peripheral but central to Greek Philosophy; the formation of the Good Society comes first, the quest for personal salvation or for scientific truths about matter or imaginative truths about the human heart, second. Through identifying the active source of the Good with Reason not with Will, they doomed themselves to the hopeless task of finding the ideal form of society which, like the truths of reason, would be valid everywhere and for everyone, irrespective of their individual character or their historical circumstances.

A concept is either true or false. A mind which entertains a false concept may be brought through steps of argument to entertain the true one, but this does not mean that a false concept has grown into the true; there is always a point in the dialectic, like the moment of recognition in tragedy, when the revolutionary change happens and the false concept is abandoned with the realization that it always was false. The dialectic process may take time, but the truth it discovers has no history.[1]

To think of the political problem as a problem of finding the

1. I do not know whether there is any historical relation but when I read the Platonic Dialogues I am constantly reminded of the stichomythy of tragedy. There also seems a parallel between the role of the Socratic dialectic in the education of the intellect and the role of free-association in the psychoanalytic education of the emotions. Both are developed from the observation that virtue cannot be taught, i.e., the truth cannot simply be stated by the teacher and learned by rote by the pupil because the results of learning cannot be separated from the process of inquiry which each individual must live through for himself at first-hand.

Both the Socratic and psychoanalytic techniques, too, are open to the same objections. They require individual supervision and take a very long time which makes them too expensive for the majority, and they presuppose on the part of the pupil or patient a genuine passion for truth or health. When the passion for truth is lacking, dialectic becomes a technique for avoiding coming to any conclusion just as, when the passion for health is lacking, self-examination is used to justify neurosis.

Isocrates was unfair to the Academy and overestimated the value of his own brand of education but he was not altogether wrong, perhaps, in believing that his method was better adapted to the needs of the average student and the talents of the average teacher. At any rate it was his method rather than Plato's which was adopted by the Romans and inherited by the West.

true form of organization leads either to political despair, if one knows one has failed to find it, or, if one thinks one has been successful, to a defense of tyranny for, if it is presupposed that people living in the wrong kind of order cannot have a good will and people living in the right kind cannot have a bad one, then not only will coercion be necessary to establish that order but also its application will be the ruler's moral duty.

The *Republic,* the *Laws,* even the *Politics,* should be read in conjunction with Thucydides; only a political situation as desperate as that which the historian describes could have produced in the philosophers who were looking for cure at once a radicalism which would break completely with the past to build up society again *ab initio* and a pathological horror of disunity and change. Living as we do in an age of similar stasis on a world-wide scale, we have witnessed a recurrence on both the Right and the Left, at both the economic and the psychiatric epicenters, of similar symptoms.

Further, we have seen with our own eyes the theory of creative politics put into practice, and the spectacle is anything but Utopian. This experience by forcing us to take Plato's political dialogues seriously not as playful exercises in logic, has altered our attitude, I think, to the other dialogues. If there is an essential not an accidental relation between his metaphysics and his politics, and the latter seem to us disastrously mistaken, then there must be a crucial error in the former as well, which it is of the utmost importance that we detect, if we are to offer a positive substitute for the Platonic kind of solution to the political crisis.

The Comic Hero: "Comedy," Aristotle says, "is an imitation of men worse than the average; worse, however, not as regards any and every kind of fault, but only as regards one particular kind, the Ridiculous, which is a species of the Ugly. The Ridiculous may be defined as a mistake or deformity not productive of pain or harm to others."

The most primitive form of comedy seems to have been tales in which, firstly, Gods, and, secondly, heroes and rulers behave in an undignified and ridiculous manner, that is to say, no better than the average man who lacks their *arete,* but, indeed, rather worse. Such primitive comedy is associated with holidays of license, during which the resentments of the small and the weak against the great and the strong may be freely expressed, in order that on the morrow when the habits of respect are re-established, the air shall be clear.

When, as in Athens, a growing rationalism comes to think of the Gods as keeping their own laws, and political power comes to be concentrated in the hands of a few, comedy finds new victims and new themes.

It is no longer the rulers as a class, but particular public figures who are made butts of; it is not authority as such that is the subject but topical political issues. The laughter of the audience is not the compensatory outburst of the weak against those who are above the law, but the confident laughter of people who know their strength, that is, either the scorn of the normal majority for the eccentric or arrogant individual whose behavior is not so much above the law as outside it, or the polemical passion of one political party directed against its rival. The target of such comedy is the man who violates the ethical norm because he does not believe it is binding; he has, that is, no social conscience. As a result he comes into collision, not with the law itself—it would be beneath the dignity of the law to concern itself with those who do not recognize it—but with others as outside the law as himself. He suffers, but the audience do not because they do not identify themselves with him. His suffering, too, is educational; through it he is cured of his individualistic mania and learns to conform to the law, out of prudence, if not from conscience.

This second type of comedy was invented by the Greeks and developed in Europe into the comedy of humor, as in the plays of Ben Jonson, and the comedy of manners and problems plays. If one disregards their lack of genuine poetry, the Gilbert and Sullivan operas are the closest approximation in English to the Aristophanic type of comedy.

There is, however, a third type which the Greeks did not possess—the greatest example is Don Quixote—in which the comic figure is at the same time the hero; the audience admire the very man they laugh at. Such a kind of comedy is based on a sense that the relations of the individual and society to each other and of both to the true good contain insoluble contradictions which are not so much comic as ironic. The comic hero is comic because he is different from his neighbors; either, like Don Quixote, because he refuses to accept their values, or, like Falstaff, because he refuses to pretend, as they do, to one set of values while really living by another: at the same time he is a hero because he is an individual, and not to be an individual, to think and behave in a certain way simply because everyone else does, is equally a comic madness.

The tragic hero suffers, and the audience, because they identify themselves with him through admiration, suffers too; the comic butt suffers but the audience, since they feel superior, do not. The relations of the comic hero and the audience to suffering, on the other hand, are ironic; the audience see the hero thwarted and defeated, experiences which they would regard as suffering, but the whole point is that to the hero himself these experiences are nothing of the sort; on the contrary, he glories in them, either because he has no shame or because he regards them as proof of his being right.

The nearest approach to such a figure among the Greeks is, of course, Socrates. In his person he exhibits the contradiction, so disliked by Nietzsche, between his subjective *arete* of soul, and his manifest lack of objective *arete;* he, the best man, is the ugliest man. Further, he suffers death at the hands of society and does not regard his fate as a tragic one. To the Greeks, however, he is either, as he is to Aristophanes, a comic butt who is justly punished, or as he is to Plato, a tragic martyr who suffers because the wrong party was in power, the individual who represents the Right Society. The notion that any individual claim to be the exception is guilty of pride and that all societies and parties, good and bad, are in the wrong simply because they are collectives would have been incomprehensible to them, as would have been the Christian insistence that Jesus was either the Incarnate God or not a good man and that his condemnation was by due process of Roman law.

VI

I have stressed the differences between Greek civilization and our own, firstly, because it seems to me one possible approach to an inexhaustible subject and one cannot take them all, and, secondly, because I can think of no better way of indicating what we owe to

Greece than drawing distinctions, for, of all intellectual acts, that is, perhaps, the most characteristically Greek.

It is they who have taught us, not to think—that all human beings have always done—but to think about our thinking, to ask such questions as "What do I think?" "What do this and that other person or people think?" "On what do we agree and disagree. Why?" And not only did they learn to ask questions about thinking, but they also discovered how, instead of giving immediate answers, to suppose something to be the case and then see what would follow if it were.

To be able to perform either of these mental operations, a human being must first be capable of a tremendous feat of moral courage and discipline for he must have learned how to resist the immediate demands of feeling and bodily needs, and to disregard his natural anxiety about his future so that he can look at his self and his world as if they were not his but a stranger's.

If some of the Greek questions turned out to have been incorrectly put, if some of their answers have proved wrong, that is a trivial matter. Had Greek civilization never existed, we might fear God and deal justly with our neighbors, we might practice arts and even have learned how to devise fairly simple machines, but we would never have become fully conscious, which is to say that we would never have become, for better or worse, fully human.

AUGUSTUS TO AUGUSTINE

*

Since the appearance of the first edition in 1940, I have read this book* many times, and my conviction of its importance to the understanding not only of the epoch with which it is concerned, but also of our own, has increased with each rereading.

It is divided into three sections. The first, "Reconstruction," describes the attempt of the Principate to justify itself as the political form which could best realize the good life on earth as envisaged by classical philosophy. It traces the fortunes of the New Order, from its foundation by Augustus, attended by the hopes of all civilized mankind, to its collapse after the death of Diocletian. The second, "Renovation," beginning with the edict of Milan in 313 A.D. and ending with an edict of 403 which authorized private individuals "to exercise with impunity the right of public vengeance against criminals," describes the futile attempt, interrupted by the platonist Julian, of the last Caesars to give the dying empire a new lease of life by substituting Christianity for philosophy as a state religion. The last section, "Regeneration," is an exposition of the writings of St. Augustine, in particular of his views of the doctrine of the Trinity, the State and Divine Providence in history.

* *Christianity and Classical Culture: A Study of Thought and Action from Augustus to Augustine,* by Charles Norris Cochrane.

The distinctive mark of classical thought is that it gives no positive value to freedom, and identifies the divine with the necessary or the legal. It separates order and freedom, and presupposes two everlastingly opposite principles; on the one hand God, who is pure Mind, One, neuter, immobile, and on the other the World, which is Matter, many, in chaotic motion. God, as pure Order, is absolutely self-sufficient and does not need the World; the World, however, needs God, for in its free state it is a meaningless chaos which can only acquire meaning by giving up its freedom and obeying law. According to Aristotle, it wants to do this and imitates God in the only ways which it can, namely, by taking typical forms and acquiring regular motions; according to Plato, it is helpless, and requires an intermediary demiurge who loves the divine ideas and models the world after them. Plato does not make it clear whether this is a voluntary act of the demiurge or a duty imposed on him by his knowledge of the ideas, but, in any case, it is not the demiurge that man is to get to know but the self-sufficient ideas. Man also consists of two elements, a rational soul which is "a scintilla of the divine archetype," immortal, capable of recognizing the necessity of truth and so becoming incapable of error, and a finite body which is mortal, incapable of redemption, but on whose freedom the mind can impose a decent order.

The final note in Homer was one of despair: the evil in the world is due to the gods from whose whims men cannot escape. Classical idealism, on the other hand, identifies evil with the freedom of finite matter, and believes that men can escape by becoming conscious of the truth which compels obedience. It agrees with Homer that history is evil, but believes that man has a telos which is, by imposing the true order on his nature, to rescue himself from the temporal flux. The aim of paideia (Jaeger's volumes should be read in conjunction with this book) is the creation of a supra-historical society, in which succeeding generations shall be exactly like each other in their perfect obedience to eternal laws. Creation, whether political, educational or artistic, is a one-sided affair of imposing universal or typical meaning upon passive or reluctant meaningless individuals: all the initiative comes from the creator or the mind; the creature or the body obeys involuntarily. Classical idealism cannot therefore oppose tyranny on principle; it can only oppose a particular tyrant on the ground that his order is not the true order. Unable to give any meaning to individuality, it has no proper place for the individual who imposes law, and tends in consequence to give him a superhuman, demiurgic status.

Nor can it establish any intelligible connection between the natural affective bonds and the love of justice, for the characteristic feature of philia or of eros is that it is personal—families and lovers love each other, not each other's virtues; they pity and forgive each other, that is, they allow each other to escape the universal law of justice.

By Augustine's time, the attempt to build a society on these principles had completely failed; the introduction of Christianity had not arrested the collapse; if anything, it hastened it.

In his writings, he is not trying to offer a more efficient substitute, which can be guaranteed to make men healthy, wealthy and wise, but to show that the Christian faith can make sense of man's private and social experience, and that classical philosophy cannot.

To the classical doctrine of God as an impersonal, immobile Being, the object of phronesis, he opposes the Christian doctrine of God as a unity of three Persons who created the world out of nothing:

> The first hypostasis, Being, the creative principle properly so called is, strictly speaking, unknown and unknowable, except insofar as it manifests itself in the second and third; the second hypostasis, the principle of intelligence, reveals itself as the logos, ratio or order of the universe; while the third, the hypostasis of spirit, is the principle of motion therein. To assert that these hypostases are uncreated is simply to assert their existence as principles. As such they are not to be confused in person; being is not to be resolved into order, nor is order to be resolved into process. At the same time, as a substantial unity of substance, they do not admit of separation, i.e., they are not mutually exclusive or antithetic. In other words, the opposition between them is purely and simply one of internal, necessary relations.

The doctrine of the Trinity is the theological formulation of the Christian belief that God is Love, and that by Love is meant not Eros but Agape, *i.e.,* not a desire to get possession of something one lacks, but a reciprocal relation, not an everlastingly "given" state, but a dynamic free expression; an unchanging love is a continually novel decision to love. The formula is an offense to the will and a foolishness to the reason, because the will is only convinced by the necessity of superior power which all weaker objects must obey, the reason by logical necessity, like the timeless truths of geometry. The will could accept the idea of either one or three persons, "very big men with red hair," but not the trinity in unity; the reason could grasp the latter as a concept, like a triangle, but not the doctrine of three *persons.*

A monolithic monotheism is always a doctrine of God as either manic-depressive Power or schizophrenic Truth. As the first, it can account for the existence of the world, but not for the evil in it; as the second, it can account for the evil, once there is a world the existence of which it cannot account for.

It follows from the doctrine of the Trinity that to say God chose to create the world, and to say He had to create it, mean the same thing, for the love which is God is, by definition, a creative love. A God of power could create a world and perhaps love it, but he could not need it to love him, for to him reciprocity would have no meaning; a God of truth would be self-sufficient and to him creation would be meaningless. The Christian doctrine of creation asserts, among other things, that there is nothing intrinsically evil in matter, the order of nature is inherent in its substance, individuality and motion have meaning, and history is not an unfortunate failure of necessity to master chance, but a dialectic of human choice.

To the classical doctrine of Man as an immortal divine reason incarcerated in a finite mortal body, Augustine opposes the Christian doctrines of Man as created in the image of God, and Man as a fallen creature.

The contrast is not between body and mind, but between flesh, *i.e.,* all man's physical and mental faculties as they exist in his enslaved self-loving state, and spirit, which witnesses within him to all that his existence was and still is meant to be, capable of loving God in the same way that God loves him.

When a Christian, like Augustine, talks about ethics, therefore, he begins not with the rational act or the pleasant act, but with the *acte gratuite,* which is neither reasonable nor physically pleasant, but a pure assertion of absolute self-autonomy. As the hero in Dostoevsky's *Notes from Underground* says:

> You will scream at me (that is, if you condescend to do so) that no one is touching my free will, that all they are concerned with is that my will should of itself, of its own free will, coincide with my own normal interests, with the laws of nature and arithmetic. Good heavens, gentlemen, what sort of free will is left when we come to tabulation and arithmetic, when it will all be a case of twice two makes four. Twice two makes four without my will. As if free will meant that.

Man, that is to say, always acts either self-loving, just for the hell of it, or God-loving, just for the heaven of it; his reasons, his appetites are secondary motivations. Man chooses either life or death, but he chooses; everything he does, from going to the toilet to mathematical speculation, is an act of religious worship, either of God or of himself.

Lastly to the classical apotheosis of the Man-God, Augustine opposes the Christian belief in Jesus Christ, the God-Man. The former is a Hercules who compels recognition by the great deeds he does in establishing for the common people the law, order and prosperity they cannot establish for themselves, by his manifestation of superior power; the latter reveals to fallen man that God is love by suffering, *i.e.,* by refusing to compel recognition, choosing instead to be a victim of man's self-love. The idea of a sacrificial victim is not new; but that it should be the victim who chooses to be sacrificed, and the sacrificers who deny that any sacrifice has been made, is very new.

In his description of the earthly and the heavenly cities, Augustine draws from the Christian faith certain political conclusions. The human individual is to be envisaged

> not as a speck of cosmic matter, shooting up like a meteor through space, and for a brief moment lighting up the sky, before the darkness closes around it, nor yet as *anthropos tis,* a mere specimen in a biological, racial, occupational,

cultural or political group, but, in Tertullian's words, as the *vas spiritus,* the one real subject of volition, *i.e.,* of intelligent and deliberate activity.

At the same time, individuality is inconceivable except in relation to others; "his life and death are with his neighbors." Every society, from the smallest to the largest, is "a group of rational beings associated on the basis of a common tie in respect of those things which they love." Insofar as its members love themselves, a society is an earthly city in which order is maintained by force and fear of chaos, bound sooner or later to break down under the tension between freedom and law; insofar as they love God and their neighbor as themselves, the same society becomes a heavenly city in which order appears the natural consequence of freedom, not a physical or logical imposition.

> This may well be mysterious, but it is not mythical or hypothetical. For it means that the selfsame human wills have attached themselves, not to transcendental objects (that they leave to Platonism), but to a principle which gives the "object" world a wholly fresh complexion, thus making all things new.

To see this is to realize, first, that no power on earth can compel men to love; it can only compel them to conform till it is overthrown; all legislation and coercion, however necessary, has a negative function only; respectability can be a consequence of habituation, though not for long; love never becomes a habit. Second, there is no perfect *form* of society; the best form can only be the form through which at any given historical moment or in any given geographical location, love for one's neighbor can express itself most freely, *i.e.,* it is a practical not an ideological matter. There can, for the Christian, be no distinction between the personal and the political, for all his relationships are both; every marriage is a polis, every imperium a family; and he has to learn to forgive and sacrifice himself for his enemies, as for his wife and children.

He is to be neither an anarchist nor a non-political "idiot," but to act now, with an eye fixed, neither nostalgically on the past nor dreamily on some ideal future, but on eternity—"redeeming the time"—in the words of Sidney Smith, he is to "trust in God and take short views."

Our period is not so unlike the age of Augustine: the planned society, caesarism of thugs or bureaucracies, paideia, scientia, religious persecution, are all with us. Nor is there even lacking the possibility of a new Constantinism; letters have already begun to appear in the press, recommending religious instruction in schools as a cure for juvenile delinquency; Mr. Cochrane's terrifying description of the "Christian" empire under Theodosius should discourage such hopes of using Christianity as a spiritual benzedrine for the earthly city, which may use the words of the Lord's Prayer but translates them into its own classical meanings, admirably retranslated into the vulgar English by William Blake:

Our Father Augustus Caesar who art in these thy Substantial Astronomical Telescopic Heavens, Holiness to Thy Name or Title, and reverence to Thy Shadow. Thy Kingship come upon Earth first and then in Heaven. Give us day by day our Real Taxed Substantial Money bought Bread; deliver from the Holy Ghost whatever cannot be taxed; for all is debts and taxes between Caesar and us and one another; lead us not to read the Bible, but let our Bible be Vergil and Shakespeare; and deliver us from Poverty in Jesus, that Evil One. For Thine is the Kingship or Allegoric Godship, and the Power or War, and the Glory or Law, ages after ages in Thy descendants; for God is only an allegory of Kings and nothing else.

*

HERESIES

*

Seventy years ago, undergraduates in revolt against their respectable church-going parents used to chant exultantly in chorus:

> *Wilt thou yet take all, Galilean?*
>   *but these thou shalt not take,*
> *The laurel, the palms and the paean,*
>   *the breasts of the nymphs in the*
>   *brake:*
> *Breasts more soft than a dove's,*
>   *that tremble with tenderer breath:*
> *And all the wings of the Loves, and*
>   *all the joy before death.*

Alas, as these lectures* demonstrate, the tidy contrast in Swinburne's lines between jolly, good-looking, sexy, extrovert Pagans on the one hand, and gloomy, emaciated, guilt-ridden, introvert Christians on the other was a romantic myth without any basis in historical fact. During the period between the accession of Marcus Aurelius in A. D. 161 and the conversion of Constantine in 313, the writings of Pagans and Christians alike seem to indicate that "men

* *Pagan and Christian in an Age of Anxiety,* by E. R. Dodds.

were ceasing to observe the external world and to try to understand it, utilize it or improve it. They were driven in upon themselves . . . the idea of the beauty of the heavens and of the world
went out of fashion and was replaced by that of the Infinite."

Of his own attitude towards his material, Professor Dodds has
this to say:

> As an agnostic I cannot share the standpoint of those who
> see the triumph of Christianity as the divine event to which
> the whole creation moved. But equally I cannot see it as the
> blotting out of the sunshine of Hellenism by what Proclus
> called "the barbarian theosophy." If there is more about
> Pagans in these lectures than about Christians, it is not be-
> cause I like them better; it is merely because I know them
> better. I stand outside this particular battle, though not
> above it. I am interested less in the issues which separated
> the combatants than in the attitudes and experiences which
> bound them together.

As his reviewer, it is only fair that I should follow the author's
example and state mine. As an Episcopalian, I do not believe that
Christianity did triumph or has triumphed. Thus, while I consider
the fourth-century victory of Christian doctrine over Neoplatonism,
Manichaeism, Gnosticism, Mithraism, etc., to have been what school
history books used to call "a good thing," I consider the adoption
of Christianity as the official state religion, backed by the coercive
powers of the State, however desirable it may have seemed at the
time, to have been a "bad," that is to say, an un-Christian thing. So
far as the writers with whom Professor Dodds deals are concerned,
I like his Pagans much better than his Christians, but, in his determination to be impartial, he seems to me to overlook the fact
that only one of his Christians, Clement of Alexandria, can be
called an orthodox Christian as orthodoxy was to be defined in the
succeeding centuries. My favorite theologian of the period is Irenaeus, and I am surprised that Professor Dodds says so little about
him. He tells us that Irenaeus came to the defense of the Montan-
ists, not, surely, because he agreed with them but because, gentle
soul that he was, he disliked persecution, even of cranks. But there
is no discussion of his writings. Lastly, though not explicitly stated,
I think the moral of Professor Dodds's book is that, in any serious

controversy where it is impossible for both parties to be right, the points upon which they agree are likely to be just those upon which, to later generations, they will appear to have both been wrong.

In his first lecture Professor Dodds examines the attitudes of the period towards the phenomenal world and the human body, and the various theories put forward to account for the existence of evil; in his second the relations between men and the daimonic world, the world of spirits which were believed to act as intermediaries between the human and the divine; in his third he discusses mystical experience in the strict sense, that is to say, the direct encounter of the human and the divine.

However different in their conceptions of the relation between God and the Cosmos, orthodox Platonism and orthodox Christianity were agreed that the existence of the Cosmos is a good and in some manner a manifestation of the Divine goodness. The psalmist says: "The heavens declare the glory of God and the firmament showeth his handiwork." Plato says that the Cosmos is "an image of the intelligible, a perceptible god, supreme in greatness and excellence, in beauty and perfection, single in its kind and one." It was this agreement which permitted Christendom to accept the Cosmic Model of Aristotle and the Hellenistic astronomers, and for the poets of the Middle Ages to find in it a constant source of joy and inspiration, in spite of the disparity between the Aristotelian God the Model presupposes, the impassive One who is loved by his creatures but cannot return their love, and the Christian God who became flesh and suffered for man on a cross. (As C. S. Lewis pointed out in *The Discarded Image,* references to the Model, so common in medieval poetry, are for the most part absent from medieval devotional and mystical writings.)

Even during the prosperous years of the Antonine peace, radically dualistic theories which were neither Platonic nor Christian began to be propounded and their influence grew stronger as the political and economic conditions in the Empire grew worse. Some held that the Cosmos had been created either by an Evil Spirit, or by an ignorant one, or by "bodiless intelligences who became bored with contemplating God and turned to the inferior"; others concluded that it had somehow or other fallen into the power of star-demons. The incarnation of the human soul in a fleshly body, living and dying on earth, was felt by many to be a curse not a blessing, and accounted for as being either "the punishment for an earlier sin committed in Heaven, or the result of a false choice made by the soul itself." Consequently, to an increasing number the body became an object of disgust and resentment. "Plotinus appeared ashamed of having a body at all; St. Anthony blushed every time he had to eat or satisfy any other bodily function." Among some Christians—the Pagans seem to have been less afflicted—it was fornication, not pride, which came more and more to be regarded as the archetypal sin, and violent mortification of the flesh as the only road to salvation.

To judge from the documents it would appear that in the third century Christianity was in grave danger of turning into Gnosticism. It did not, which suggests that the most vociferous and articulate were not typically representative of their Christian brethren. Not all, not even the majority can have held Marcion's doctrine of the creation, or castrated themselves like Origen, or indulged in glossolalia like Montanus, or behaved like Simeon Stylites. Orthodox Christianity, it is true, did accept the existence of the Devil, but it denied that he could create anything. When the New Testament speaks of "The Prince of this world," it certainly does not mean the Prince of the Cosmos nor assert that, so long as they are on earth, human souls have no option but to obey the orders of the Devil. By *this world* is meant, I should guess, Leviathan, the Social Beast. One may or may not hold the Devil responsible, but, when one considers the behavior of large organized social groups throughout human history, this much is certain; it has been characterized neither by love nor by logic. As for the more repellent and exhibitionistic kinds of asceticism, it was not long before the Church authorities set limits to them, condemning, for example, those who abstained from wine and meat on feast-days for "blasphemously inveighing against the creation."

Much of Professor Dodds's second, and most entertaining, lecture is devoted to dreams, in particular to the dream book of a certain Aelius Aristides—a fascinating "nut" and an ideal subject, surely, for E. M. Forster—and to the dreams which Perpetua, a young Christian convert, had while she lay in prison awaiting martyrdom. Whatever the social conditions, in all ages the uneducated have considered dreams significant and it was only, I should imagine, during the eighteenth and nineteenth centuries that the cultured dismissed them as meaningless. Since Freud we are all again agreed that "dreams are purposive."

A fascination with the "occult," on the other hand, with astrology, spiritualism, magic, and the like, is generally, I suspect, a symptom of social alienation. In the third century, astrologers, oracles, and mediums were taken seriously by Pagans and Christians alike. The Christian "belly-talkers," male and female, called themselves *prophetes,* but nothing that Professor Dodds has to tell us about them convinces me that they had anything of value to prophesy. Genuine inspiration, whether in artistic or religious utterance, may be mysterious but it is always comprehensible. Of *The Third Testament,* a Montanist document, Professor Dodds says: "Only a few scraps have been preserved, and like most communications from the Beyond, these scraps, it must be confessed, are extremely disappointing." And he quotes Professor Greenslade's verdict on Montanus: "The Holy Spirit seemed to say nothing of any religious or intellectual value to him." In due time the *prophetes* were suppressed by the ecclesiastical authorities, but one must not allow one's natural dislike of stuffy bishops to deceive one into imagining that the suppression was a great spiritual loss.

Professor Dodds classifies mystical experiences as being either "extrovertive," conveyed to the subject through his physical senses, or "introvertive," reached by the *via negativa:* a training of the mind to empty itself of all sensory images.

The two typical extrovertive visions are the Vision of Dame Kind and the Vision of Eros. There is no record of either in the third century. Plato had described the Vision of Eros, but we find no more descriptions of it until those of the Provençal poets in the twelfth century. Of the Vision of Dame Kind, there are hints in the *Bacchae* of Euripides but no unmistakable description, so far as I know, before Traherne's in the late seventeenth century.

Of the introvertive, specifically religious, mystical experience, there are, rather oddly, no surviving Christian examples from the third century. The two men, Plotinus and Porphyry, whose writings were later to have a great influence upon Christian mystics, were both Neoplatonists. A problem posed by all descriptions of mystical experience is the impossibility of knowing to what extent the intellectual and theological presuppositions of the mystic modify the experience itself. To a Neoplatonist, the vision of the One must necessarily be one-sided: What he sees cannot see him. To a Christian, it must necessarily be felt as an encounter between two persons. To say, as some theologians have, that in the mystical vision it is "God who takes the *first* step" seems to me meaningless, unless all that is meant is that it is the Grace of God which causes such-and-such an individual to desire and seek to attain it through ascetic discipline and habits of prayer. If he fails, he can, of course, explain this by saying that God does not wish to reveal Himself to him. This the Neoplatonist cannot say; he is faced with the problem of explaining why, once he has discovered the correct technique of meditation, he cannot enjoy the vision at will: In the course of a lifetime, Plotinus experienced it four times, Porphyry once.

Professor Dodds says that he agrees with Festugière's dictum: "Misery and Mysticism are related facts." Are they always? I would agree that when mystical *theories* are fashionable, talked about at parties by people who have no intention of submitting themselves to the arduous discipline required for practice, society is probably not in a very healthy state, but most of the practicing mystics we know about do not seem to have been miserable persons; on the contrary, they were often not only jolly but active, practically-minded organizers.

In fact it now looks as if the cultivation of extrovertive mystical experience—the Vision of Dame Kind can, it seems, be induced by the hallucinogenic drugs—is more likely in practice to lead to a loss of concern for other human beings than the introvertive.

In his last lecture Professor Dodds discusses the ways in which Pagans and Christians thought about each other. From being an obscure sect, disliked by the crowds, as oddities always are, and suspected of horrid secret rites, but people no man of education would give a thought to, by the reign of Marcus Aurelius, Christians had become numerous and influential enough to be taken seriously both by the authorities and by intellectuals. Persecution, hitherto sporadic and incoherent, became under Marcus Aurelius,

Decius, and Diocletian a deliberate planned State policy. Intellectuals like Celsus and Porphyry felt that Christianity was a cultural threat dangerous enough to deserve attack and, on the Christian side, there were now converts like Tertullian and Origen educated enough to explain and defend their beliefs. To the authorities the obstinate refusal of Christians to pay formal homage to the god-emperor made them enemies of society. Today it seems strange that they should have made such a fuss, since nobody seriously believed that the Emperors were divine, but then it seems equally strange that the Emperors should have imagined a stable social order depended upon their subjects politely saying that they were. More understandably, their proselytizing zeal caused indignation: the more fanatic and tactless among them were quite prepared, for the sake of saving a soul, to wreck marriages and encourage children to disobey their parents.

To the educated Pagan, the importance they attached to *pistis,* or blind faith, their indifference to *logismos,* or reasoned conviction, seemed willfully irrational, though, as the century progressed, both sides shifted their ground. Tertullian might say defiantly *credo quia absurdum est,* but Origen and Clement recognized the value to apologetics of learning, literature, and philosophical argument, while the Neoplatonists came to realize that their position did not rest on logic alone, that they, too, held certain absolute presuppositions by faith. What strikes one now about the debates between them is that they seem to have been mostly concerned with minor issues. The fundamental doctrines on which they disagreed, the relation of God to the Cosmos, and the possibility of incarnate deity, were seldom seriously discussed. Instead, they argued endlessly about miracles and prophecies, a barren topic since both sides agreed that miracles could be wrought and prophecies made by evil spirits and men as well as good. They accused each other, probably justly, of reading meanings into texts which were not there, but both sides went in for allegorical interpretation, Christians of the Bible, Neoplatonists of Homer.

No certain or complete explanations can ever be given why one religion or *Weltanschauung* is accepted by a society in preference to its rivals, and Professor Dodds would be the first to say that his suggestions are tentative and partial. First, he thinks, there was the impression made by the Christian martyrs.

It is evident that Lucan, Marcus Aurelius, Galen and Celsus were all, despite themselves, impressed by the courage of the Christians in face of death and torture. . . . We know from modern experience of political martyrdoms that the blood of the martyrs really *is* the seed of the Church, always provided that the seed falls on suitable ground and is not sown too thickly.

Secondly, the Church was open to all men, without regard to social class, education, or their past lives. While, at most times, the Church has welcomed the intellectual, the artist, the mystic, it has never limited its membership to a cultural elite nor regarded mystical experience as necessary to salvation. Further, though organized hierarchically, high office has been open, in theory if not always in practice, to any man of talent and character irrespective of his birth. Thirdly, it was more successful than its rivals in giving its converts a sense of belonging to a community. Not only did it provide the essentials of social security by caring for widows, orphans, the old, the sick, the unemployed, but also to "the uprooted and lonely, the urbanized tribesman, the peasant come to town in search of work, the demobilized soldier, the rentier ruined by inflation, and the manumitted slave, it offered human warmth: Someone was interested in them, both here and hereafter."

I should like to venture a fourth suggestion. Despite appearances to the contrary, the Christian faith, by virtue of its doctrines about creation, the nature of man and the revelation of Divine purpose in historical time, was really a more this-worldly religion than any of its competitors, so that, when its opportunity came in the following centuries with the collapse of civil government in the West, it was the Church which took on the task of creating such social order and of preserving such cultural heritage as there was. On the evidence of its history, it would seem that Christianity has always been more tempted by worldliness, by love of money and power than, say, Islam or Buddhism. The charge which may justly be brought against the Church is, not that it has been unpractical or apolitical, but that it has so often been all too political, all too ready to make shady deals with any temporal power which would advance what it believed to be its interests.

For the majority of mankind life has always been uncertain and painful, but not every kind of uncertainty and suffering causes anxiety, only the unexpected kinds. Men can take most natural disasters like famine and flood in their stride because they know that harvests are bound to fail sometimes and rivers to overflow their banks. An epidemic of plague, however, can work psychological havoc because, although men have always known they must die, they are now suddenly faced by an unexpected kind of death.

Still deeper and more widespread is the anxiety caused when the techniques a society has invented for coping with life, which hitherto have been successful, no longer work. The Roman Empire had evolved legal, military and economic techniques for maintaining internal law and order, defending itself against external enemies, and managing the production and exchange of goods; in the third century these proved inadequate to prevent civil war, invasion by barbarians and depreciation of the currency. In the twentieth century, it is not the failure but the fantastic success of our techniques of production that is creating a society in which it is becoming increasingly difficult to live a human life. In our reactions to this one can see many parallels to the third century. Instead of Gnostics we have existentialists and God-is-dead theologians; instead of Neoplatonists, "humanist" professors; instead of desert eremites, heroin-addicts and Beats; instead of the cult of virginity, do-it-yourself sex manuals and sado-masochistic pornography. Now as then, a proper balance between detachment and commitment seems impossible to find or to hold. Both lead to evil. The introvert, intent upon improving himself, is deaf to his neighbor when he cries for help; the extrovert, intent upon improving the world, pinches his neighbor (for his own good of course) until he cries for help. We are not, any of us, very nice.

THE PROTESTANT MYSTICS

In his great book *The Mystical Element of Religion,* von Hügel defines a living religion as a tension-in-unity between three elements, the Institutional, the Intellectual and the Mystical. This holds in every sphere of human life. As individual members of an animal species, composed of living matter and mortal, we are all identically subject to the same physical and chemical laws. In this aspect of our being, the pronoun *We* is singular not plural, for the pronoun *I* has no meaning. It is meaningless to say *I* have a four-chambered heart. When the human species is compared with other species, the most conspicuous difference is that, aside from basic biological processes like breathing, digestion and physical growth, we seem to be born with no behavior-directing instincts; even the most elementary behavior required for physical survival and reproducing our kind has to be learned by each of us, either through imitation of or instruction by others. As Hazlitt said: "Without the aid of prejudice and custom, I should not be able to find my way across the room." This difference is particularly striking when one compares man with those creatures whose sociality rivals his, the social insects, for it is precisely among them that instinctive behavior is almost all-powerful and learning capacity almost nil. A bee or an ant society endures in time from one generation to another automatically; a human society can only endure by conscious effort, the passing on of a tradition from the older generation to the younger. Human society, that is to say, is always institutionalized, governed not by instinct or force, but by authority. As members of the human race, born without knowledge or sense of direction, the primary attitude of each individual towards authority must be one of faith; we cannot begin by doubting. A father points to an animal and says to his small son: "Look. A fox." It is conceivable that the father has never read any books on natural history and seldom been in the country so that he has mistaken a badger for a fox, but unless his son has faith in his father and believes that he knows the right names for all animals, if he begins by doubting, then he will never learn to speak.

All religions begin not with the present but the past for, when we ask a question about the meaning of the existence of ourselves and the universe, we and the universe are already in existence; all religions must therefore begin with cosmogonies, theogonies, creation myths. In addition, what we call, with detestable snobbery, the Higher Religions base their claims upon some event in historical time which has already taken place; each asserts that some divine revelation has been made, in and through such a person in such a place at such a time, and that this historical revelation is, for all future time, divine and redemptive. An institution which makes it its professional business to keep alive the memory of the event—otherwise later generations will be unaware that it occurred —and to assert its redemptive importance—otherwise later generations will take it as one historical event on a par with an infinite number of other historical events and devote no special attention to it—is essential.

The function of the Church as an institution is not to convert— conversion is the work not of men but of the Holy Spirit—but to make conversion possible by continuing to preach its good news in words and liturgical acts. She must go on repeating herself, no matter whether her repetition be passionate or, when faith is low, lifeless and mechanical, to preserve that possibility. Frost's lines are as true for peoples and generations as they are for the individual.

Our very life depends on everything's
Recurring till we answer from within.
The thousandth time may prove the charm.

In relation to any institution, ecclesiastical or secular, on all
matters of fact and theory concerning which we know ourselves
to be ignorant, and in all matters of conduct where uniformity is
obviously necessary or convenient, we are or ought to be catholics
(with a small c). To doubt for the sake of doubting, to differ for
the sake of being different is pride. Private judgment is a meaningless term, for no one is omniscient and omnipotent and every man
derives most of his thoughts, opinions and principles from others.
Obedience to some authority is inescapable; if we reject the
authority of tradition, then we must accept the authority of local
fashion.

We are created animals gifted with intelligence, that is to say,
we cannot be content merely to experience but must seek to make
sense of it, to know what is its cause and significance, to find the
truth behind brute fact. Though some individuals have greater
intelligence and curiosity than others, the nature of intelligence is
identical in every individual. It is impossible for something to be
true for one mind and false for another. That is to say, if two of us
disagree, either one of us is right or both of us are wrong.

In our relation to one another as intelligent beings, seeking a
truth to which we shall both be compelled to assent, We is not the
collective singular We of tradition, but a plural signifying a You-
and-I united by a common love for the truth. In relation to each
other we are protestants; in relation to the truth we are catholics.
I must be prepared to doubt the truth of every statement you make,
but I must have unquestioning faith in your intellectual integrity.

The basic stimulus to the intelligence is doubt, a feeling that
the meaning of an experience is not self-evident. We never make a
statement about what seems to us self-evidently the case. That is
why the positive content of a proposition, what it asserts to be
true, is never so clear as what it excludes as being false. Dogmatic
theology, for example, came into being more to exclude heresy
than to define orthodoxy, and one reason why theology must

continue to be and grow is that the heresies of one age are never the same as the heresies of another. The Christian faith is always a scandal to the imagination and reason of the flesh, but the particular aspect which seems most scandalous depends upon the prevailing mentality of a period or a culture. Thus, to both the gnostics of the fourth century and the liberal humanists of the eighteenth, the Cross was an offense, but for quite different reasons. The gnostic said: "Christ was the Son of God, therefore He cannot have been physically crucified. The Crucifixion was an illusion." The liberal humanist said: "Christ was physically crucified, therefore He cannot have been the Son of God. His claim was a delusion." In our own day, the stumbling block is again different. I think most Christians will find themselves in understanding sympathy with Simone Weil's difficulty: "If the Gospels omitted all mention of Christ's resurrection, faith would be easier for me. The Cross by itself suffices me."

Besides defending the Church against heresy, theology has another perennial task to perform, instructing the devout, both the institutional authorities and the mass of the laity, in the difference between the things of God and the things of Caesar. In addition to the absolute presuppositions which we consciously hold by faith as necessary to salvation, we all of us hold a large number of notions about what constitutes the beautiful in art, what is the just form of social structure, what the natural universe is like, etc., which we hold not by faith but by habit—they are what we are used to and we cannot imagine them otherwise. Along comes a new style of art, a social change, a scientific discovery, and our immediate reaction is to think that such changes are contrary to our faith. It is one of the tasks of the theologian to show that this is not the case, and that our fright is unnecessary. If this is not done, we shall presently find that we have changed either our faith or our God.

Whatever the field under discussion, those who engage in debate must not only believe in each other's good faith, but also in their capacity to arrive at the truth. Intellectual debate is only possible between those who are equal in learning and intelligence. Preferably they should have no audience, but if they do have one, it should be an audience of their peers. Otherwise, the desire for applause, the wish, not to arrive at the truth but to vanquish one's opponent, becomes irresistible. Never were the fatal effects of publicity in debate so obvious as in the sixteenth century. As Professor C. S. Lewis has written:

> The process whereby "faith and works" became a stock gag in the commercial theatre is characteristic of that whole tragic farce which we call the history of the Reformation. The theological questions really at issue have no significance except on a certain level, a high level, of the spiritual life; they could have been fruitfully debated only between mature and saintly disputants in close privacy and at boundless leisure. Under these conditions formulae might possibly have been found which did justice to the Protestant assertions without compromising other elements of the Christian faith. In fact, however, these questions were raised at a moment when they immediately became embittered and entangled with a whole complex of matters theologically irrelevant, and therefore attracted the fatal attention both of government and the mob. It was as if men were set to conduct a metaphysical argument at a fair, in competition or (worse still) forced collaboration with the cheapjacks and roundabouts, under the eyes of an armed and vigilant police force who frequently changed sides. Each party increasingly misunderstood the other and triumphed in refuting positions which their opponents did not hold: Protestants misrepresenting Romans as Pelagians or Romans misrepresenting Protestants as Antinomians.

In addition to being members of a species gifted with intelligence, each of us is created in the Image of God, that is to say, each is a unique person who can say *I,* with a unique perspective on the universe, the exact like of whom has never existed before nor will again. As persons, each of us has his biography, a story with a beginning, middle and end. As St. Augustine, following St. James, says: "Man was created in order that a beginning might be made." The dogma of the descent of all mankind from a single ancestor, Adam, is not, and should never have been imagined to be, a statement about man's biological evolution. It asserts that, insofar as he or she is a unique person, every man and woman, irrespective of race, nation, culture and sex, *is* Adam, an incarnation of all mankind; that, as persons, we are called into being, not by any biological process but by other persons, God, our parents, our friends and enemies. And it is as persons, not as members of a species, that we become guilty of sin. When we speak of being "born in sin," of inheriting the original sin of Adam, this cannot mean, it seems to me—I speak as a fool—that sin is physically present in our flesh and our genes. Our flesh, surely, is not in itself sinful, but our every bodily movement, touch, gesture, tone of voice is that of a sinner. From the moment consciousness first wakes in a baby (and this may possibly be before birth) it finds itself in the company of sinners, and its consciousness is affected by a contagion against which there is no prophylaxis.

The personal I is by necessity protestant (again with a small p), for no one else can have my experience for me or be responsible for my history. This I, though, exists only in the present instant: my past memories are never of myself alone. Towards my immediate experience, what is required of me is neither faith nor doubt but a self-forgetful concentration of my attention upon the experience which is only mine in the sense that it has been given to me and not to someone else. The *I* is only truly itself when its attention to experience is so intense that it is unaware of its own existence. I must not ask whether the experience is like or unlike the experience of others, a hallucination or objectively real, expected or unexpected, pleasant or painful. All these questions are to be asked later, for the answers are bound to be erroneous if, through distraction of attention, I fail to experience fully. When I do ask them, I shall usually find, of course, that however novel the experience may have been to me, most people have had similar experiences, and that the explanation and significance have long been known. But, occasionally, there may have been some element in it which is really novel. In that case, though I must beware of exaggerating its importance simply because it happened to me, I must neither deny it nor hug it as a private secret, but make it public though all the authorities on earth, administrative or intellectual, should laugh at me or threaten me with penalties. In any case, it is only through the sharing of personal experience, important or trivial, that our relation with others ceases to be that of one member of a social species to another and becomes that of one person to another. So, too, in my relation to God; it is personal experience which enables me to add to the catholic *We believe still* the protestant *I believe again.*

When von Hügel calls all that is not institutional or intellectual mystical, he obviously includes under this division many experiences which are not, in a technical sense, mystical. He includes any firsthand religious experience. But mystical experiences, whether concerned with God or with His creatures, have, of all experiences, the most right to be called firsthand, as owing least to either tradition or impersonal ratiocination.

II

There seem to be four distinct kinds of mystical experience:

> The Vision of Dame Kind
> The Vision of Eros
> The Vision of Agape
> The Vision of God

Before considering the differences between them one should consider what they have in common which makes comparison possible.

(1) The experience is always "given," that is to say, it cannot be induced by an effort of will. In the case of the Vision of Dame Kind, it can in some cases, it seems, be induced by chemical means, alcohol or the hallucinogenic drugs. (I have myself taken mescaline once and L.S.D. once. Aside from a slight schizophrenic dissociation of the I from the Not-I, including my body, nothing happened at all.) In the case of the Vision of God, it does not seem to be granted to anyone who has not undergone a long process of self-discipline and prayer, but self-discipline and prayer cannot of themselves compel it.

(2) The experience seems to the subject not only more important than anything he experiences when in a "normal" state, but also a revelation of reality. When he returns to a normal state, he does not say: "That was a pleasant dream but, of course, an illusion. Now I am awake and see things as they really are"; he says: "For a moment a veil was lifted and I saw what really is. Now the veil has fallen again and reality is again hidden from me." His

conclusion is similar to that of Don Quixote who in his bouts of madness sees windmills as giants, but when in his lucid intervals he sees them as windmills, says: "Those cursed magicians delude me, first drawing me into dangerous adventures by the appearance of things as they really are, and then presently changing the face of things as they please."

(3) The experience is totally different from that of "seeing things" whether in dreams or waking visions. In the case of the first three kinds which are concerned with visible creatures, these are seen with extraordinary vividness and charged with extraordinary significance, but they are not physically distorted; square objects do not become round or blue ones red, nor does the subject see objects which are not there when the vision fades. Again, one thinks of Don Quixote. He may see a windmill as a giant, but he doesn't see a giant unless there is a windmill there. In the case of the Vision of God, in which, whatever explanation one cares to make, what the subject encounters is not a visible creature, the mystics are unanimous in saying that they do not see anything in a physical sense. Thus St. Theresa says that in her true visions and locutions "she never saw anything with her bodily eyes, nor heard anything with her bodily ears." Sometimes they do "see and hear" things, but they always recognize these as accidental and irrelevant to the real experience, and to be regarded with suspicion. When his followers came to St. Philip Neri to tell him about their delightful visions of the Blessed Virgin, he ordered them the next time they had such a vision to spit in her face, and it is said that, when they did so, a devil's face was at once revealed.

(4) Though the experience is always given and surprising, its nature is never entirely independent of the subject. In the case of the Vision of Dame Kind, for example, it is commoner in childhood and adolescence than in maturity, and the actual content of the vision, the kind of creatures transformed and the hierarchy of importance among them seem to vary from person to person. To one color is the most significant, to another form, and so on. In the case of the Vision of God, the religious beliefs of the subject seem to play a part. Thus, when one compares the accounts given by Christian, Mohammedan and Indian mystics, it is impossible to say with certainty whether they are accounts of different experiences or accounts of the same experience described in different

theological languages, and, if the first, whether the differences are due to the mystic's beliefs. If a Hindu mystic, for example, were to become converted to Christianity, would his mystical experience show a change?

As an example of the difficulty of separating observation from interpretation of experience, let me take a trivial personal one. Many people have given accounts of what they experienced while having a tooth extracted under nitrous oxide, and these show close similarities. Thus William James says:

> The keynote of it is invariably a reconciliation. It is as if the opposites of the world, whose contradictions and conflict make all our difficulties and troubles, were melted into unity.

My experience, like his, was of two opposites, love in the sense of agape, and hate, but in my case they did not melt into a unity. I felt an absolute conviction about two things: (a) that, ultimately the power of love was greater than the force of hate; (b) that, on the other hand, however great any human being might estimate the force of hate to be, he would always underestimate it. The actual quantity of hate in the universe was greater than any human imagination could conceive. Nevertheless, the power of love was still greater. Would I, I ask myself, have had precisely *this* experience if I had not been brought up in a Christian home and therefore been a person to whom the Christian notion of agape was a familiar one, and I find myself unable to say yes or no with any certainty.

(5) From a Christian point of view, all four kinds of experience are, in themselves, blessings and a good; there is nothing in any of them that is contrary to Christian doctrine. On the other hand, all of them are dangerous. So long as the subject recognizes them as totally unmerited blessings and feels obligated by gratitude to produce, insofar as it lies in his power, works which are good according to their kind, they can lead him towards the Light. But if he allows himself either to regard the experience as a sign of superior merit, natural or supernatural, or to idolize it as something he cannot live without, then it can only lead him into darkness and destruction.

III : The Vision of Dame Kind

The objects of this vision may be inorganic—mountains, rivers, seas—or organic—trees, flowers, beasts—but they are all non-human, though human artifacts like buildings may be included. Occasionally human figures are involved, but if so, they are invariably, I believe, strangers to the subject, people working in the fields, passers-by, beggars, or the like, with whom he has no personal relation and of whom, therefore, no personal knowledge. The basic experience is an overwhelming conviction that the objects confronting him have a numinous significance and importance, that the existence of everything he is aware of is holy. And the basic emotion is one of innocent joy, though this joy can include, of course, a reverent dread. In a "normal" state, we value objects either for the immediate aesthetic pleasure they give to our senses —this flower has a pleasant color, this mountain a pleasing shape, but that flower, that mountain are ugly—or for the future satisfaction of our desires which they promise—this fruit will taste delicious, that one horrid. In the Vision of Dame Kind, such distinctions, between the beautiful and the ugly, the serviceable and the unserviceable, vanish. So long as the vision lasts the self is "noughted," for its attention is completely absorbed in what it contemplates; it makes no judgments and desires nothing, except to continue in communion with what Gerard Manley Hopkins called the inscape of things.

> Each mortal thing does one thing and the same:
> Deals out that being indoors each one dwells;
> Selves—goes itself; *myself* it speaks and spells
> Crying *What I do is me: for that I came.*

In some cases, the subject speaks of this sense of communion as if he were himself *in* every object, and they in him. Thus Wordsworth in *The Ruined Cottage:*

> . . . sensation, soul and form
> All melted in him. They swallowed up

> His animal being; in them did he live
> And by them did he live.

In his book *Mysticism, Sacred and Profane,* **Professor Zaehner** calls this the pan-en-henic vision, which he considers the definitive sign of the natural mystic; for him, an account which does not speak of this fusion of identities cannot be an account of a genuinely mystical experience. I think Professor Zaehner is mistaken. In their accounts of the Vision of God Christian mystics sometimes seem almost to say that they *became* God, which they cannot, of course, have believed; they are trying to describe, presumably, a state in consciousness so filled with the presence of God that there is no vacant corner of it detachedly observing the experience. The natural mystic who speaks in pan-en-henic terms does not really mean that he becomes a tree or that a tree becomes him. No one, for example, was more convinced than Richard Jeffries, who does speak in these terms, that "there is nothing human in nature." He would certainly say that in the vision he feels capable of imaginatively entering into the life of a tree, but that no more means he becomes a tree than imaginatively entering into the life of another human being means that one ceases to be oneself and becomes him.

The joy felt by the natural mystic may be called innocent. While the vision lasts, the self and its desires are so completely forgotten that he is, in fact, incapable of sin. On the other hand, unlike the religious mystic, he is unaware of sin as a past fact and a future possibility, because his mystical encounter is with creatures who are not persons, and to which, therefore, the terms moral good and moral evil do not apply. For the same reason, Eros plays no conscious role. No accounts of the Vision of Dame Kind ever use, as accounts of the Vision of God often do, the experience of sexual union as an analogy.

The interpretations of the Vision of Dame Kind and even the language in which it is described vary, of course, according to the religious beliefs of the subject, but the experience itself seems to be independent of them, though not entirely independent, I think, of either the personality or the culture of the subject. In our own culture, in various degrees of intensity, many persons experience it in childhood and adolescence, but its occurrence among adults is rare. In so-called primitive cultures it may persist longer. Colonel Van Der Post's account of the African Bushmen suggests to me that among them it may persist uninterrupted throughout life. Even in our Western culture, its frequency is not evenly distributed. It is to be observed that nearly all the accounts have been written by members of the Northern peoples—the Mediterranean countries have contributed very little—which means that in fact, though the fact may be irrelevant, most of them have been written by persons with a Protestant upbringing. My own, very tentative, explanation for this is that in the Mediterranean countries the individual experience of Nature as sacred is absorbed and transformed into a social experience, expressed by the institutional cults, so common around the Mediterranean, of the local Madonna and the local saint. Whether it is possible completely to Christianize in spirit what is plainly polytheistic in form, I shall not presume to say. If I have my doubts, it is because of the enormous aesthetic pleasure such cults give me and my nostalgic regret when I am in countries which lack them.

Though the Vision of Dame Kind is not specifically Christian, there is nothing in it incompatible with the Christian belief in a God who created the material universe and all its creatures out of love and found them good: the glory in which the creatures appear to the natural mystic must be a feeble approximation to their glory as God sees them. There is nothing to prevent him from welcoming it as a gift, however indirect, from God. To a Gnostic for whom matter is the creation of an evil spirit, it must, of course, be a diabolic visitation and to the monist who regards the phenomenal world as an illusion, it must be doubly an illusion, harmless, maybe, but to be seen through as soon as possible. To a philosophical materialist for whom the notion of glory has no meaning, it must be an individual delusion, probably neurotic in origin, and to be discouraged as abnormal and likely to lead the patient into the more serious and socially harmful delusion of some sort of theism. When such a staunch atheist as Richard Jeffries can speak of praying "that I might touch the unutterable existence even higher than deity," the danger of allowing people to take solitary country walks becomes obvious.

Believing Christians who have had the vision have always been explicit as to what it was *not*. Thus Wordsworth:

> He did not feel the God; he felt his works;
> Thought was not. In enjoyment it expired.
> Such hour by prayer or praise was unprofaned,
> He neither prayed, nor offered thanks or praise,
> His mind was a thanksgiving to the power
> That made him. It was blessedness and love.

And thus George Macdonald:

> I lived in everything; everything entered and lived in me. To be aware of a thing was to know its life at once and mine, to know whence it came and where we were at home —was to know that we are all what we are, because Another is what He is.

And they give thanks to God for it, not only for the joy that accompanies it, but also because it safeguards them, as even the Vision of God cannot, against a Gnostic undervaluation of the creaturely. Even in the Vision of God, the Christian must remember that, as Suso says:

> The being of the creatures in God is not that of a creature, but the creatureliness of every creature is nobler for it, and more useful, than the being it has in God. For what advantage has a stone or a man or any creature in its status as a creature, from the fact that it has been eternally in God?

To those who have never been Christians or, for one reason or another, have lost their faith, the very innocence of the experience can be an occasion of error. Since it involves neither the intellect nor the will, it is always possible for the intellect to misunderstand and the will to abuse it. The intellect can take the encounter with a numinous creature for an encounter with deity itself. Hence animism, polytheism, idols, magic and the so-called natural religions in which the non-human creation, including, of course, those physical and biological elements and forces which man shares with all other creatures, is the ultimate source of power and meaning and, therefore, responsible for man. Pantheism, as we find it in Goethe and Hardy, is really a sophisticated and sensitive form of humanism. Since man is, at present and so far as we know, the only creature in nature with consciousness, moral conscience, reason, will and purpose, a God (or Goddess) solely immanent in Nature must, unless He can create a new species, be at man's mercy; only man can tell Him what his will is or carry it out; one can pray to an idol, but it is difficult to see how one could *pray* to His Immanence, though one might revere Him.

The other temptation, more dangerous in a culture like ours than it was to the pagan world because in ours the experience is probably rarer and more temporary, is to idolize the experience itself as the *summum bonum* and spend one's life either gloomily regretting its loss and so falling into a state of accidie, or trying by artificial means, like alcohol and drugs, to recapture and prolong it. The hallucinogenic drugs are not, so far as we know, habit-forming, but no one has yet made a habit of taking them day after day for years. When this has been done, as it surely will be, I suspect that the law of diminishing returns will be found to apply to them as it applies to the more traditional artificial aids. If this should not turn out to be the case, if it should become possible for anyone to enjoy the Vision of Dame Kind whenever he wishes, the consequences might be even more serious. It is a characteristic of the world which this vision reveals that its only human inhabitant is the subject himself, and a continual indulgence in it could only lead to an increasing indifference towards the existence and needs of other human beings.

The vision of the splendor of creation, like all kinds, lays a duty upon one who has been fortunate enough to receive it, a duty in his turn to create works which are as worthy of what he has seen as his feeble capacities will permit. And many have listened and obeyed. It has been, I am quite certain, the initial cause of all genuine works of art and, I believe, of all genuine scientific inquiry and discovery, for it is the wonder which is, as Plato said, the beginning of every kind of philosophy.

IV : The Vision of Eros

Half the literature, highbrow and popular, produced in the West during the past four hundred years has been based on the false assumption that what is an exceptional experience is or ought to be a universal one. Under its influence so many millions of persons have persuaded themselves they were "in love" when their experience could be fully and accurately described by the more brutal four-letter words, that one is sometimes tempted to doubt if the experience is ever genuine, even when, or especially when, it seems to have happened to oneself. However, it is impossible to read some of the documents, *La Vita Nuova,* for example, many of Shakespeare's sonnets or the *Symposium* and dismiss them as fakes. All accounts of the experience agree on essentials. Like the Vision of Dame Kind, the Vision of Eros is a revelation of creaturely glory, but whereas in the former it is the glory of a multiplicity of nonhuman creatures which is revealed, in the latter it is the glory of a single human being. Again, while in the vision of Nature, conscious sexuality is never present, in the erotic vision it always is— it cannot be experienced by eunuchs (though it may occur before puberty) and no one ever fell in love with someone they found sexually unattractive—but physical desire is always, and without any effort of will, subordinate to the feeling of awe and reverence in the presence of a sacred being: however great his desire, the lover feels unworthy of the beloved's notice. It is impossible to take such accounts as a fancy poetization of any of the three kinds of unmystical erotic experiences with which we are all familiar. It is not simple lust, the detached recognition of another as a desirable sexual object, for in relation to anything one regards as an object one feels superior, and the lover feels inferior to the beloved. Nor is it sexual infatuation, the experience of *Vénus toute entière à sa proie attachée,* in which desire has invaded and possessed the whole self until what it craves is not sexual satisfaction only but a total absorption of the other self, body and soul, into itself; in this condition the dominant feeling is not of unworthiness but of anguish, rage and despair at not being able to get what one craves. Nor, again, is it that healthy mixture of mutual physical desire and *philia,* a mutual personal liking based on common interests and values, which is the securest foundation for a happy marriage for, in this state, the dominant feeling is of mutual respect between equals.

Moreover, all the accounts agree that the Vision of Eros cannot long survive if the parties enter into an actual sexual relation. It was not merely the social conditions of an age in which marriages were arranged by the parents which made the Provençal poets declare that married couples could not be in love. This does not mean that one must under no circumstances marry the person whose glory has been revealed to one, but the risk in doing so is proportionate to the intensity of the vision. It is difficult to live day after day, year after year, with an ordinary human being, neither much better nor much worse than oneself, after one has seen her or him transfigured, without feeling that the fading of the vision is the other's fault. The Vision of Eros seems to be much more influenced by social conditions than any of the others. Some degree of leisure and freedom from financial anxiety seems to be essential; a man who must labor ten hours a day in order not to starve has other matters to attend to: he is too occupied by practical necessities to think of more than his sexual need for a woman and his economic need for a good housekeeper and mother. And it would seem that the beloved must belong to a class of persons whom the lover has been brought up to regard as his social equals or superiors. One cannot, it seems, fall in love with someone whom one has been trained to think of as being less of a person, more of a thing than oneself. Thus Plato, though he came in later life to disapprove of homosexuality, can only conceive of the beloved as a male in his adolescence or early manhood because, in the Athens of his time, women were regarded as essentially inferior creatures.

The effect of the vision on the lover's conduct is not confined to his behavior towards his beloved. Even in his relations to others, conduct which before he fell in love seemed natural and proper, judged by his new standard of what he feels it should be to be worthy of her, now seems base and ignoble. Further, in most cases, the experience does not lead, as one might expect, to a sort of erotic quietism, a rapt contemplation of the beloved to the exclusion of others and the world. On the contrary, it usually releases a flood of psychic energy for actions which are not directly concerned with the beloved at all. When in love, the soldier fights more bravely, the thinker thinks more clearly, the carpenter fashions with greater skill.

The Church, whose institutional and intellectual concern in sexual matters is, and must be, primarily with marriage and the family, has always, very understandably, regarded the Vision of Eros with the utmost suspicion. Either she has dismissed it as moonshine, or condemned it offhand, without trying first to understand it, as idolatry of the creature and a blasphemous parody of the Christian love of God. Knowing that marriage and the vision are not compatible, she has feared that it will be, as it very often is, used as an excuse for adultery. Condemnation without understanding, however, is seldom effective. If the lover idolizes the beloved, it is not what we ordinarily mean by idolization, in which the worshipper makes his idol responsible for his existence. This kind of idolization can certainly occur in the relation between the sexes. Cases of men and women who shoot themselves and each other because the object of their affection does not return it, or loves somebody else, may be read of almost every day in the newspapers, but one knows at once that they cannot have been truly in love. The true lover would naturally rather his beloved returned his love than refused it, he would rather she were alive and visible than dead and invisible, but if she cannot return his love, he does not try to compel her by force or emotional blackmail, and if she dies, he does not commit suicide but continues to love her.

The two most serious attempts to analyze the Vision of Eros and give it a theological significance are Plato's and Dante's. Both agree on three points: (a) the experience is a genuine revelation, not a delusion; (b) the erotic mode of the vision prefigures a kind of love in which the sexual element is transformed and transcended; (c) he who has once seen the glory of the Uncreated revealed indirectly in the glory of a creature can henceforth never be fully satisfied with anything less than a direct encounter with the former. About everything else they disagree radically. One of the most important differences between them is obscured by the inadequacy of our vocabulary. When I say, "X has a beautiful profile," and when I say, "Elizabeth has a beautiful face," or "the expression on Mary's face was beautiful," I have to use the same adjective, though I mean two totally different things. Beauty in the first statement is a given public quality of an object; I am talking about a quality the object *has,* not about what it *is.* If (but only if) a number of objects belong to the same class, I can compare them and arrange them in order according to the degree of beauty they possess, from the most beautiful to the least. That is why, even among human beings, it is possible to hold beauty contests to elect Miss America, and possible for an experienced sculptor to state in mathematical terms the proportions of the ideal male or female figure. Beauty in this sense is a gift of Nature or of Chance, and can be withdrawn. To become Miss America, a girl must have inherited a certain combination of genes and have managed to escape any disfiguring diseases or crippling accident, and, diet as she may, she cannot hope to remain Miss America forever. The emotion aroused by this kind of beauty is impersonal admiration; in the case of a human being, it may also be impersonal sexual desire. I may want to sleep with Miss America, but I have no wish to hear her talk about herself and her family.

When I say, "Elizabeth has a beautiful face," I mean something quite different. I am still referring to something physical—I could not make the statement if I were blind—but this physical quality is not a gift from Nature, but a personal creation for which I hold Elizabeth to be responsible. The physical beauty seems to me a revelation of something immaterial, the person whom I cannot see. Beauty in this sense is unique in every case: I cannot compare Elizabeth and Mary and say which has the more beautiful face. The emotion aroused by it is personal love, and, again, this is unique in every case. To the degree that I love both Elizabeth and Mary, I cannot say which I love more. Finally, to say that someone is beautiful in this sense is never simply a favorable aesthetic judgment; it is always a favorable moral judgment as well. I can say "X has a beautiful profile but is a monster," I cannot say, "Elizabeth has a beautiful face but is a monster."

As creatures, human beings have a double nature. As members of a mammalian species which reproduces itself sexually, each of us is born either male or female and endowed with an impersonal need to mate with a member of the opposite sex; any member will do so long as he or she is not immature or senile. As unique persons we are capable of, but not compelled to, enter voluntarily into unique relations of love with other persons. The Vision of Eros is, therefore, double too. The beloved always possesses some degree of that beauty which is Nature's gift. A girl who weighs two hundred pounds and a woman of eighty may both have beautiful faces in the personal sense, but men do not fall in love with them. The lover is, of course, aware of this, but what seems to him infinitely more important is his awareness of the beloved as a person. Or so, at least, Dante says. What is so puzzling about Plato's description is that he seems unaware of what we mean by a person. By beauty, he always seems to mean impersonal beauty and by love impersonal admiration.

> [The lover] should begin by loving earthly things for the sake of the absolute loveliness, ascending to that as it were by degrees or steps, from the first to the second, and thence to all fair forms; and from fair forms to fair conduct, and from fair conduct to fair principles, until from fair principles he finally arrive at the ultimate principle of all, and learn what absolutely Beauty is.

The more I study this passage, the more bewildered I become, and I find myself talking to Plato's ghost and saying:

"(1) As regards earthly things, I agree that I can compare two horses, or two men, or two proofs of the same mathematical theorem, and say which is the more beautiful, but will you please tell me how I am to compare a horse, a man and a mathematical proof and say which is the most beautiful?

"(2) If, as you say, there are degrees of beauty and that the more beautiful should be loved more, then, at the human level, it must be the moral duty of all of us to fall in love with the most beautiful human being known to us. Surely, it is very fortunate for all concerned that we fail to do our duty.

"(3) It is quite true, as you say, that a fair principle does not get bald and fat or run away with somebody else. On the other hand, a fair principle cannot give me a smile of welcome when I come into the room. Love of a human being may be, as you say, a lower form of love than love for a principle, but you must admit it is a damn sight more interesting."

How different, and much more comprehensible, is Dante's account. He sees Beatrice, and a voice says, "Now you have seen your beatitude." Dante certainly thinks that Beatrice is beautiful in the public sense that any stranger would call her beautiful, but it would never enter his head to ask if she were more or less beautiful than other Florentine girls of her age. She is Beatrice and that is that. And what is the essential thing about her is that she is, he is absolutely certain, a "graced" person, so that after her death, he is convinced, as a believing Christian, her soul is among the redeemed in Paradise, not among the lost in Hell. He does not tell us exactly what the sins and errors were which had brought him near to perdition nor, when they meet again, does Beatrice, but both speak of them as acts of infidelity to her, that is to say, if he had remained faithful to his vision of one human creature, Beatrice, he would not have committed offenses against their common Creator. Though unfaithful to her image, he has, however, never completely forgotten it (the Platonic ladder makes the forgetting of an image on a lower rung a moral duty), and it is this memory, the fact that he has never completely ceased to love her, which makes it possible for Beatrice to intervene from Heaven to save his soul. When, at last, they meet again in the earthly paradise, he re-experiences, though infinitely more intensely, the vision he had when they first met on earth, and she remains with him until the very last moment when he turns towards "the eternal fountain" and, even then, he knows that her eyes are turned in the same direction. The Vision of Eros is not, according to Dante, the first rung of a long ladder: there is only one step to take, from the personal creature who can love and be loved to the personal Creator who is Love. And in this final vision, Eros is transfigured but not annihilated. On earth we rank "love" higher than either sexual desire or sexless friendship because it involves the whole of our being, not, like them, only a part of it. Whatever else is asserted by the doctrine of the resurrection of the body, it asserts the sacred importance of the body. As Silesius says, we have one advantage over the angels: only we can each become the bride of God. And Juliana of Norwich: "In the self-same point that our Soul is made sensual, in the self-same point is the City of God ordained to him from without beginning."

V : The Vision of Agape

The classic Christian example of this is, of course, the vision of Pentecost, but there are modes of it which are not overtly Christian. Since I cannot find a specific description among these selections, I shall quote from an unpublished account for the authenticity of which I can vouch.

> One fine summer night in June 1933 I was sitting on a lawn after dinner with three colleagues, two women and one man. We liked each other well enough but we were certainly not intimate friends, nor had any one of us a sexual interest in another. Incidentally, we had not drunk any alcohol. We were talking casually about everyday matters when, quite suddenly and unexpectedly, something happened. I felt myself invaded by a power which, though I consented to it, was irresistible and certainly not mine. For the first time in my life I knew exactly—because, thanks to the power, I was doing it—what it means to love one's neighbor as oneself. I was also certain, though the conversation continued to be perfectly ordinary, that my three colleagues were having the same experience. (In the case of one of them, I was able later to confirm this.) My personal feelings towards them were unchanged—they were still colleagues, not intimate friends—but I felt their existence as themselves to be of infinite value and rejoiced in it.
>
> I recalled with shame the many occasions on which I had been spiteful, snobbish, selfish, but the immediate joy was greater than the shame, for I knew that, so long as I was possessed by this spirit, it would be literally impossible for me deliberately to injure another human being. I also knew that the power would, of course, be withdrawn sooner or later and that, when it did, my greeds and self-regard would return. The experience lasted at its full intensity for about two hours when we said good-night to each other and went to bed. When I awoke the next morning, it was still present, though weaker, and it did not vanish completely for two days or so. The memory of the experience has not

prevented me from making use of others, grossly and often, but it has made it much more difficult for me to deceive myself about what I am up to when I do. And among the various factors which several years later brought me back to the Christian faith in which I had been brought up, the memory of this experience and asking myself what it could mean was one of the most crucial, though, at the time it occurred, I thought I had done with Christianity for good.

Compared with the other kinds of vision, the Vision of Agape has several peculiarities. In the Vision of Dame Kind, there is one human person, the subject, and a multiplicity of creatures whose way of existence is different from his. The relation between him and them is therefore one-sided; though they are transfigured for him, he does not imagine that he is transfigured for them. In the Vision of Eros two human persons are involved, but the relation between them is unequal; the lover feels unworthy of the beloved. If it should so happen that both experience the vision simultaneously in regard to each other, both will still feel unworthy. In the Vision of God, two persons are again involved, the soul and God, and the relation of creature to Creator is utterly unequal, but it is a mutual one; the soul is conscious of loving God and being loved by Him in return. Like the Vision of Dame Kind, the Vision of Agape is multiple, but it is a multiplicity of persons; like the Vision of Eros, it involves human persons only; like the Vision of God it is of a mutual relation; but unlike any of the others, this relation is a relation between equals.

Not the least puzzling thing about it is that most of the experiences which are closest to it in mode, involving plurality, equality and mutuality of human persons, are clear cases of diabolic possession, as when thousands cheer hysterically for the Man-God, or cry bloodthirstily for the crucifixion of the God-Man. Still, without it, there might be no Church.

VI : The Vision of God

No one could be less qualified than I to discuss what the bulk of these selections are concerned with, the direct encounter of a human soul with God. In the first place because I lead an ordinary sensual worldly life, so that I can scarcely be surprised if I have never seen the God whom no man has seen at any time, a vision which is reserved, the Gospels tell us, for the pure in heart. In the second place, because I am an Anglican. Of all the Christian Churches, not excluding the Roman Catholic, the Anglican Church has laid the most stress upon the institutional aspect of religion. Uniformity of rite has always seemed to her more important than uniformity of doctrine, and the private devotions of her members have been left to their own discretion without much instruction or encouragement from her. Her intellectual temper is summed up in a remark by one of her bishops, "Orthodoxy is reticence," and the frigid welcome she offers to any kind of religious "enthusiasm" in a sentence of C. D. Broad's: "A healthy appetite for righteousness, kept in due control by good manners, is an excellent thing; but to 'hunger and thirst' after it is often merely a symptom of spiritual diabetes."

It would be false to say that she has completely neglected the intellect: in the field of Biblical criticism, in particular, she has done great things, for the freedom of her scholars to inquire has not been hampered, as it has been sometimes in the Roman Church, by hierarchical fiats, and the atmosphere of spiritual moderation with which she surrounds her children has restrained them from the extravagant speculations in which German Protestant scholars have sometimes indulged.

Nor has she failed to inspire many men and women to a life of interior prayer. There is, as one can see in the writings of men like George Herbert, Lancelot Andrewes, Charles Williams, a characteristic Anglican style of piety, different from both Catholic and Evangelical piety, but nonetheless genuinely Christian. At its best, it shows spiritual good manners, a quality no less valuable in the religious life than in social life, though, of course, not the ultimate criterion in either, reverence without religiosity, and humor (in which last trait it resembles Jewish piety). Like all styles of piety it becomes detestable when the fire of love has gone out. It is no insult to say that Anglicanism is the Christianity of a gentleman, but we know what a tiny hairbreadth there is between a gentleman and a genteel snob.

In every sphere of life, when we read or listen to accounts of experiences which are completely strange to us, we tend either to be bored or, if they make us envious, to try and explain them away, and in reading the Christian mystics, Catholic or Protestant, I have, as a worldly man, to be constantly on my guard about this tendency. Then, as an Anglican with an Anglican's prejudices, I must not pretend that I do not have them, but I must pray that the evidence these writers present will refute them.

The first thing which disturbs me is the number of mystics who have suffered from ill-health and various kinds of psycho-physical disturbances. I am aware, of course, that many, perhaps the majority, of those whose achievements in this world, in art, in science, in politics, have earned them the right to be called great men, have suffered from physical and psychological abnormalities, and that to dismiss their achievements on that account as "sick" is the cheapest kind of philistine envy. I cannot help feeling, however, that there is a fundamental difference between a great man and a mystic. In the case of the latter, what matters, surely, is not what he or she outwardly "achieves"—the vision of God cannot be a "work" like a poem—but what they are. The vision is only granted to those who are far advanced in the practice of the Imitation of Christ. In the Gospels, there is no suggestion that, in his human nature, Christ was anything but physically and psychologically normal, no reports of any mental crisis such as we read of in the life of Mahomet. Even more importantly, since the God-Man is a unique case, the twelve Apostles whom he chose seem to have been equally healthy. The mystics themselves do not seem to have believed their physical and mental sufferings to be a sign of grace, but it is unfortunate that it is precisely physical manifestations which appeal most to the religiosity of the mob. A woman might spend twenty years nursing lepers without having any notice taken of her, but let her once exhibit the stigmata or live for long periods on nothing but the Host and water, and in no time the crowd will be clamoring for her beatification.

Then I am a little disturbed by the sometimes startling resemblances between the accounts of their experiences given by mystics and those given by persons suffering from a manic-depressive pychosis. The differences between them are, of course, obvious too. The inflated egoism of the manic-depressive is always conspicuous, whether, in his elated phase, he thinks that, unlike other folks, he is God, or, in his depressed phase, he thinks that, unlike other folks, he has committed the Sin against the Holy Ghost. The genuine mystics, on the other hand, always interpret their ecstasy as a gratuitous blessing from God which they have done nothing to deserve and their dark night of the soul not as evidence of their extraordinary wickedness, but as a period of trial and purgation. Thus, speaking of the two phases, the Arab mystic Qushayri says:

> There are cases of contraction the cause of which is not easily ascertainable by the subject . . . the only remedy for this condition is complete submission to the will of God until the mood passes. . . . Expansion, on the other hand, comes suddenly and strikes the subject unexpectedly, so that he can find no reason for it. It makes him quiver with joy, yet scares him. The way to deal with it is to keep quiet and observe conventional good manners.

A similarity, however, remains. This suggests to me two possibilities. Is it not possible that those who fall into a manic-depressive psychosis are persons with a vocation for the *via negativa* which they are either unaware of or have rejected? In the late Middle Ages there were, no doubt, many persons in monasteries and convents who had no business there and should have been out in the world earning an honest living, but today it may well be that there are many persons trying to earn a living in the world and driven by failure into mental homes whose true home would be the cloister. Secondly, though no one in this life can experience the Vision of God without having, through a life of prayer and self-mortification, reached a high level of spiritual life, is it not possible that certain psycho-physical human types are more likely to have such experiences than others who have reached the same level? Whether this is so or not, both the ecclesiastical authorities and the mystics themselves have always insisted that mystical experience is not necessary to salvation or in itself a proof of sanctity. St. John of the Cross, for instance, says:

> All visions, revelations, heavenly feelings, and whatever is greater than these, are not worth the least act of humility, being the fruits of that charity which neither values nor

seeks itself, which thinketh well, not of self, but of others.
. . . many souls, to whom visions have never come, are in-
comparably more advanced in the way of perfection than
others to whom many have been given.

Certainly, in reading accounts of the early life of those who
have chosen the *via negativa,* whether or not their choice was
later rewarded by visions, how often one comes across the same
kind of character, a man or woman who seems, both by talent and
temperament, born to command, to wield power either in the
temporal or the spiritual sphere, a person, that is, for whom the
Third Temptation of Christ can be, as it cannot for most of us, a
real temptation. (If Satan were to promise me all the kingdoms of
the earth on condition that I bowed down and worshipped him, I
should laugh because I should know that, given my limited capacities, he could not fulfill his promise.) Their rejection of what one
would have thought to be their natural destiny may have been
occasioned by an awareness that, in their case, their gift for power
and domination, if exercised, could only bring disaster to others
and themselves. As Goethe, who certainly felt no natural sympathy
for the *via negativa,* observed about St. Philip Neri:

> Only superior and essentially proud men are capable of
> choosing on principle to taste the enmity of a world which
> is always opposed to the good and the great, and empty the
> bitter cup of experience before it is offered to them.

In this selection of writings by Protestants, practicing or lapsed,
I can find little which a Catholic reader will consider alien to his
experience or contrary to faith and morals. (He may find Sweden-
borg rather hard to swallow but so, as a Protestant, do I.) Many
of them are concerned with visions of nature, at which level theological doctrine is irrelevant, though it is relevant to any interpretation of their significance. Among those directly concerned with
man's relation to God, more attention is paid, as one would expect,
to the Pauline conversion experience than one would find in a
similar collection written by Catholics, for it is this experience upon
which most of the Protestant churches have based their claims.
There are two kinds of conversion, the conversion from one faith
—it may be atheism—to another, and the transformation of an un-

thinking traditional faith into a personal conviction. Here we are only concerned with the second. It would be nonsense to say either that this experience does not occur among Catholics or that the Catholic Church, institutionally and theologically, does not pray that it shall occur and welcome it when it does: she certainly does not desire, and never has, that her children should go through their lives attending Mass and going to confession as she prescribes without this ever becoming more than a ritual routine in which they experience nothing for themselves. But she has been, perhaps, overly aware, as the Protestant churches have certainly been insufficiently aware, of the spiritual danger implicit in all firsthand experience, the temptation to imagine one is a special person to whom the common rules do not apply, the temptation intellectually to suppose that since an experience is new to oneself, it is new to the human race, the thinkers of the past cannot possibly throw light on it, and one must construct a new philosophy of one's own.

But, at least during her post-tridentine phase, now happily over, the Catholic Church seemed more or less to take the view that the proper place for her protestants, those who claimed firsthand experience, was the priesthood or the cloister where she could keep a sharp eye on them, and that no more could be asked of the laity than obedience to her rules. The Protestant churches, on the other hand, probably asked more of the average layman than is, humanly speaking, possible. Kierkegaard, himself a Protestant, put the difference neatly:

> Catholicism has the universal premise that we men are pretty well rascals . . . The Protestant principle is related to a particular premise: a man who sits in the anguish of death, in fear and trembling and much tribulation—and of those there are not many in any one generation.

Aside from this difference in emphasis, the main difference seems to be one of vocabulary. The language of the Catholic mystics shows an acquaintance with a whole tradition of mystical literature, that of the Protestant is derived almost entirely from the Bible. The former, living in monastic orders and, usually, under the spiritual direction of a confessor, have at their disposal a highly developed technical theological language, which the latter, except for the

Calvinists, have lacked. Consequently one might say that the Catholic writes like a professional, the Protestant like an amateur.

The virtue of the amateur is freshness and honesty, his defect a clumsiness in expression; the difficulty for a professional is that he may be unaware that the traditional language he has inherited is falsifying what he means to say. One sometimes comes across passages written by Catholic mystics which, taken out of the context of their whole writings and their lives, seem to be not Christian but monist or Manichaean, and I think the reason for this is probably the influence on the Catholic vocabulary of certain writers, in particular Plotinus and Pseudo-Dionysius, who were not Christians but Neoplatonists.

VII

Even among the most ignorant, there can be very few Protestants today who still think that Rome is the Scarlet Woman, or Catholics who think, like the officer Goethe met in Italy, that Protestants are allowed to marry their sisters. And among the more thoughtful, there can be few, no matter what church they belong to, who do not regard the series of events in the sixteenth and seventeenth centuries whereby the Western Church became divided into Catholics and Protestants with capital letters, hating and despising each other, as a spiritual tragedy for which all parties concerned must bear some of the blame. Looking back, there seems no *rational* reason why the habits of reading the Bible and family prayers from which Protestants have obviously derived so much strength and refreshment could not have been added to the sacramental habits from which Catholics have, as obviously, derived so much, instead of both parties regarding them as incompatible. There seems no *rational* reason why a return to St. Paul and St. Augustine could not have rescued theology from its sterile debate between Realism and Nominalism without leading to Calvinism and, as a defense reaction, to the adoption by Rome, understandably but still, to my mind, mistakenly, of Thomism as the official Catholic philosophy. But history, of course, it not rational nor repeatable. (For me the most mysterious aspect of the whole affair is not theological or political but cultural. Why was it that the peoples and nations who became Protestant were precisely those who, before Christ was born, had been least influenced by the culture of *pagan* Rome?)

That Protestant and Catholic no longer regard each other as monsters is a reason for thanking God, but also a reason to be ashamed of ourselves that we, as Christians, have contributed so little to this more charitable atmosphere. If we have learned that it is wicked to inflict secular penalties on heresy, to keep people in the faith by terror, we have learned it from skeptical rationalists who felt, like Earl Halifax, that "Most men's anger about religion is as if two men should quarrel for a lady they neither of them care for." Even after the burnings stopped, the religious minority, Catholic or Protestant, still continued to suffer sufficient civil disabilities to ensure that to a great extent religious boundaries would coincide with state boundaries and prevent the average Protestant and Catholic from ever meeting. Defoe says that in the England of his time "there were a hundred thousand fellows ready to fight to the death against popery, without knowing whether popery was a man or a horse," and the situation in Catholic countries can have been no better. Again, the campaign to make the secular authorities grant equal rights to all citizens, irrespective of their religious beliefs, was certainly not headed by Christians. Even when equality in law had been granted, class barriers remained which have only begun to disappear in my own lifetime. Among the English middle classes, thanks to the existence of old Catholic families whose social status was unimpeachable, it might be eccentric or immoral to be a Catholic, but it was not infra dig like being a Dissenter. When I was young, for an Anglican to "go over to Rome" was rather like having an illegitimate baby, an unfortunate event but something which can happen in the best families. But for an Anglican to become a Baptist would have been unthinkable: Baptists were persons who came to the back door, not the front. Once again, the part played by Christians in fighting against social injustice and snobbery has not been a conspicuous one. Lastly, whether we desire it or not, we are being brought closer together by simple physical fear. There are large areas of the globe where it is now a serious worldly disadvantage, and sometimes dangerous, to be a Christian of any kind, and these areas may very well increase.

When all fleshly and worldly circumstances favor a greater

mutual understanding, any failure of charity on our part becomes all the more inexcusable. As I write, it is but a few days to Pentecost, the Ecumenical Feast, in what the Pope has proclaimed an Ecumenical Year. As a preliminary we might start by thanking each other, and the modern secular culture against which we both inveigh, for the competition. It is good for Protestant minister and Catholic priest to know that there is a church of another persuasion round the corner and a movie-house across the way from them both, to know that they cannot hold their flocks simply because there is no other place of worship to attend, or because not attending some place of worship will incur social disapproval. I have often observed how much more vital, liturgically, both Catholic and Protestant services become in countries with religiously mixed populations than in countries which are overwhelmingly one or the other. Then, after this exchange of compliments, we might reread together the second chapter of Acts. The miracle wrought by the Holy Spirit is generally referred to as a gift of tongues: is it not equally a gift of ears? It is just as miraculous that those in the parts of Libya about Cyrene and strangers from Rome should be able to listen to Galileans, as that Galileans should be able to speak to them. The Curse of Babel is not the diversity of human tongues—diversity is essential to life—but the pride of each of us which makes us think that those who make different verbal noises from our own are incapable of human speech so that discourse with them is out of the question, a pride which, since the speech of no two persons is identical—language is not algebra—must inevitably lead to the conclusion that the gift of human speech is reserved for oneself alone. It is due to this curse that, as Sir William Osler said, "Half of us are blind, few of us feel, and we are all deaf." That we may learn first how to listen and then how to translate are the two gifts of which we stand most urgently in need and for which we should most fervently pray at this time.

GREATNESS FINDING ITSELF

Dr. Erikson is that happy exception, a psychoanalyst who knows the difference between a biography and a case history. As a therapy, the goal of psychoanalysis is to free the patient from the slavery of impersonal behavior so that he may become capable of personal deeds. A deed is an act by which the doer voluntarily discloses himself to others: behavior is involuntary and discloses, not a unique self, but either those natural needs common to all men or those diagnosable complexes which the patient shares with other sufferers of the same kind. Thanks to psychoanalysis, it is now a matter of public knowledge that, frequently, when we imagine we are acting as ourselves, we are really only exhibiting behavior, and it is one of the analyst's tasks to unmask this illusion in his patients.

Professionally, that is to say, what the analyst is concerned with and confronted by every day in his consulting room is behavior, not deeds. But a biographer is concerned with deeds, with those events in the life of his subject which distinguish it from the lives of all other human beings. Biographical studies of great men by psychoanalysts only too often leave the reader with the feeling: "Well, if that was really all there was to this life, where was the greatness?" Most great men who do deeds which influence the course of history or make words which outlive their own death have exhibited, at critical points in their lives, extremely neurotic behavior, but their greatness cannot be explained away in terms of their neuroses. Had Hölderlin, for example, not suffered from schizophrenia, his poetry would have been different—he might even not have written any—but his schizophrenia does not explain why his poetry is good and recognizable as written by Hölderlin and nobody else.

In his investigation of the psychological crises in Luther's life up to the age of forty-three, Dr. Erikson never allows his professional knowledge of neurotic behavior to obscure his awareness that Luther the historical person transcends Luther the patient. At the same time, quite rightly for him, he approaches Luther's history as a psychoanalyst, not as a theologian, a political economist, or a literary critic.

> This being a historical book, religion will occupy our attention primarily as a source of ideologies for those who seek identities. In depicting the identity struggle of a young great man, I am not concerned with the validity of the dogmas which laid claim to him, or the philosophies which influenced his systematic thought, as I am with the spiritual and intellectual milieu which the isms of his time—these isms had to be religious—offered to his passionate search. . . . In this book, Ideology will mean an unconscious tendency underlying religious and scientific as well as political thought: the tendency at a given time to make facts amenable to ideas, and ideas to facts, in order to create a world image convincing enough to support the collective and the individual sense of identity. . . . In some periods of his history, and in some phases of his life cycle, man needs a new ideological orientation as surely and as sorely as he must have light and air.

In the lives of those persons who merit a biography, there are normally, according to Dr. Erikson, three periods of psychological crisis: the crisis of Identity, the crisis of Generativity, and the crisis of Integrity. Roughly speaking, these occur in youth, middle age and old age, respectively, but they usually overlap and the intensity and duration of each varies from individual to individual.

In the Identity crisis, the young man or woman is trying to

find the answer to the question "Who am I *really,* as distinct from what others believe or desire me to be?" This is a crisis of consciousness. The Generativity crisis is a crisis of conscience. The question now to be answered is: "I have done this and that; my acts have affected others in this or that way. Have I done well or ill? Can I justify the influence which, intentionally or unintentionally, I have had on others?" Both the Identity and the Generativity crises are preoccupied with freedom and choice. The Integrity crisis of old age is concerned with fate and necessity. As Dr. Erikson puts it, it demands "the acceptance of one's one and only life cycle as something that had to be and that, by necessity, permitted of no substitutions, the knowledge that an individual life is the accidental coincidence of but one life cycle with but one segment of history."

In *Young Man Luther,* Dr. Erikson traces Luther's development up to the onset of his Generativity crisis which began to trouble him when he had become a husband, a father, and a world-famous public figure. One or two remarks which he makes suggest that he thinks Luther was less successful at solving this crisis than he had been at solving his Identity crisis, but he has limited his study to the latter.

In later life Luther used to refer to himself as the son of a poor peasant. This, as Dr. Erikson shows, was largely a fantasy. Hans Luder, it is true, was born a peasant, but left farming to become a miner.

> The life of a miner in those days was hard, but honorable and well-regulated. Roman law had not penetrated to it; far from being slave-labor, it had a self-regulating dignity, with maximum hours, sanitation laws, and minimum wages. By succeeding in it at the time when he did, Hans Luder not only escaped the proletarization of the landless peasant and unskilled laborer, he also made a place for himself in the managerial class of mine shareholders and foundry co-leaders. . . . To call Hans Luder a peasant, therefore, shows either sentimentality or contempt. He was an early small industrialist and capitalist, first working to earn enough to invest, and then guarding his investment with a kind of dignified ferocity. When he died he left a house in town and 1250 Gold-gulden.

Like most fathers who have begun to rise in the world, he was anxious that his son should rise still further. He made Martin go to Latin School and University, and hoped to see him become a jurist and, maybe, even a burgomaster.

Parents who are ambitious for their children are rarely permissive with them, and in a culture where corporal punishment is the normal method of discipline, they do not spare the rod. Hans Luder had a violent temper but there is no evidence that he was more sadistic than the average father. His son's account of his reaction to one paternal beating is revealing. "I fled him and I became sadly resentful towards him, until he gradually got me accustomed to him again." This sentence, Dr. Erikson points out, reveals two trends in the relationship between father and son. "Martin, even when mortally afraid, *could not really hate his father,* he could only be sad; and Hans, while he could not let the boy come close, and was murderously angry at times, *could not let him go for long.*"

Most modern books on bringing up children warn parents against projecting their own ambitions onto their children and demanding of them a high standard of achievement. It seems to me that this warning is merited only in cases where there is no relation between the parents' ambition and the child's actual endowments. If the child is stupid, it is obviously harmful to show anger or shame because he is not at the top of the class, just as it is wrong for a father to try to force a son with a talent for, say, engineering, into the family grocery business. But there are many cases in which a parent's ambition is quite justified—if his child *is* talented, talented in the way which the parent believes. From my own experience, I would say that, in the majority of cases, the children of parents who were ambitious for them are successful and, whatever the conflicts and mistakes may have been, they recognize in later life how much they owe their success to the high standard of achievement which was demanded from them at home. Hans was mistaken in believing that Martin should take up a secular career, but in all other respects he understood his son's character remarkably well. He knew, when Martin was convinced to the contrary, that the celibate life of a monk was not his vocation and, sure enough, in due time Martin left the monastery and married.

He hoped to see his son a successful figure in public life, and Martin succeeded beyond his wildest dreams.

The Protestant Era might be called the era of the Rebellious Son, but this rebellion was against the Fathers rather than a father. Protestantism set out to replace the collective external voice of tradition by the internal voice of the individual conscience which, since it is internal to the subject, is his contemporary. In religion, it shifts the emphasis from the human reason, which is a faculty we share with our neighbors, and the human body, which is capable of partaking with other human bodies in the same liturgical acts, to the human will which is unique and private to every individual.

Since this interiorization of the paternal conscience is a process that each person can only do for himself, the character and behavior of his actual father became more significant in deciding his development in the Protestant era than it had previously been when a man's father was one member among others of the Father class.

At a less conscious level, Protestantism implies a rejection— rejection is not the same thing as rebellion—of the Mother. The doctrine or Predestination which makes the actions of God's will arbitrary from a human point of view makes the notion of necessity meaningless and thereby denies any spiritual significance to the fact that we are born from the bodies of our mothers through the necessary processes of nature.

In its attitude towards the flesh, Protestant piety, even at its most puritanical, is less ascetic than Catholic piety precisely because it attributes less spiritual importance to the flesh. Whatever views one may hold for or against fasting and corporal penance, such practices indicate a belief that the body is a partner with the soul in the spiritual life.

The doctrine of justification by Faith implicitly denies this partnership, for the flesh, subject to natural necessity, can neither possess faith nor lack it, but it is by means of the flesh, and by no other means, that works are done.

Consciously, both during his Identity crisis, and in later life, Luther was preoccupied with his relation to his father and to an overmasculine God, but there are many things about him which suggest that his mother played a much more important role in his life than he himself realized. We know little about her except that she was imaginatively superstitious and a somewhat submissive character, who is reported to have sung to her young son a ditty: "For me and you nobody cares. That is our common fault." But, as Dr. Erikson says, it is extremely rare for a person to succeed in discovering his identity unless his relation to his mother in the years of infancy was one of basic trust. Luther's career suggests that his infancy must have been a happy and secure one, and that, like most fathers, Hans Luder left the care and training of Martin's early years to his mother. Later, however, when he took over the supervision and disciplining of his son, his wife was too passive a character to be able to stand between them or stand up for her child when Papa was unreasonable or unjust. If the Cranach portrait is a good likeness, the bond of identity between Luther and his mother must have been extraordinarily close, for in the picture Luther looks like a middle-aged woman. We know, too, that in later life he became obese, and an obese male always looks like a cross between a small child and a pregnant woman. Then, however opinions may differ about Luther's theology and actions, no one has ever denied his supreme mastery of his mother tongue, his ability, as a preacher, to offer "the milk" of the word. (Luther himself said: "You must preach as a mother suckles her child.") Of the three modes of human activity—labor, fabrication, and action—it may be said that labor is sexless, fabrication feminine, and action masculine. Preaching is an art, that is to say, a mode of fabrication, not a mode of action; and all "making" is imitative of motherhood, not fatherhood. It is fascinating to speculate about what Luther would have become had his father died during his early adolescence. My guess is that, instead of becoming a theologian and a religious leader, he would have turned into a great secular writer, probably a comic one, and that he would certainly not have become a Protestant. But Papa did not die, so the Pope became Antichrist, the Madonna a nonentity, and the only feminine ideal Luther could offer was, as Dr. Erikson wittily remarks, "women who wanted to be like parsons if they couldn't be parsons' wives."

The onset of Luther's identity crisis can be precisely dated. On June 2, 1505, when he was seventeen, he was caught in a thunderstorm. A lightning bolt struck the ground near him. Terrified, he cried out: "Help me, St. Anne! [the patron saint of miners] I want to become a monk." Presently, he told his friends that he felt committed to enter a monastery, but did not inform his father. This decision is a clear example of the adoption of an experimental mask (Dr. Erikson compares it to Freud's decision to become a research neurologist). In that age, entering a monastery was a quite ordinary thing for a young man to do.

> To become a monk meant merely to find an entrance, on a defined professional level, to the Catholic empire's hierarchy of clerical employees, which included in its duties diplomacy, the administration of social welfare in countries, counties, cities and towns, spiritual ministration, and the more or less ascetic cultivation of personal salvation. . . . When Martin joined the Augustinian order he became part of that clerical middle class which corresponded and overlapped with the class in which his father wanted him to find a foothold.

Nor was such a step irrevocable; it was always possible to leave, if this was done with discretion.

Rationally, his father's anger was unjustified, but intuitively Hans was right in guessing that his son was making a mistake and making it moreover to spite him.

> The final vow would imply both that Martin was another Father's servant, and that he would never become the father of Hans's grandsons. Ordination would bestow on the son the ceremonial functions of a spiritual father, a guardian of souls and a guide to eternity, and relegate the natural father to a merely physical status.

Once inside the monastery, trouble, of course, began. Consciously, Luther was determined to prove to himself and his father that he was in the right; subconsciously he knew that the monastic vocation was not for him. In consequence he tried to outdo all the other monks in piety and became that bugbear of the confessional, a scrupuland. In his middle twenties an event occurred which shows how near he came to disaster. One day in the choir of the monastery he suddenly fell to the ground, roaring with the voice of a bull: *"Ich bin's nit!"* [It isn't me!] Chance, or Divine Providence, saved him by transferring him to the monastery of Wittenberg and introducing him to the vicar-general of that province, Dr. Staupitz. Staupitz was not particularly remarkable in himself, but he loved Luther like a son, and for the first time in his life Luther found himself treated by an older man as someone of importance. Moreover, by encouraging Luther to lecture and preach, Staupitz released Luther's real talents. From whatever internal conflicts he might continue to suffer, henceforth his ego had the satisfaction of knowing that there was something he could do supremely well. Preaching to an audience also enabled him to objectify his personal problems, to view them not as peculiar to himself but as representative of the spiritual problems of his age.

A young man has discovered his true identity when he becomes able to call his thoughts and actions his own. If he is an exceptional young man, these thoughts and actions will be exceptional also, publicly recognizable as new and revolutionary. So Freud became Freud when he hit on the idea of the Oedipus complex, Darwin Darwin when he perceived that higher species must have evolved from lower, Luther Luther when he heard in St. Paul's phrase *The Just shall live by Faith* the authentic voice of God. That this revelation should have come to him in a privy is fascinating but not, I think, surprising. There must be many people to whom religious, intellectual, or artistic insights have come in the same place, for excretion is both the primal creative act—every child is the mother of its own feces—and the primal act of revolt and repudiation of the past—what was once good food has become bad dirt and must be got rid of. From then on, Luther's fate became his own.

Dr. Erikson's book is so full of wise observations not only about Luther but also about human life, that no quotations could do it justice: it must be read all through. To me, it is particularly illuminating and important because I believe that the Protestant Era, that is to say, an era in which the dominant ideology was protestant (with a small p) and catholic ideology the restraining and critical opposition, is now over, that we have entered a Catholic Era in which the relative positions of the two ideologies is reversed because today the nature of the identity crisis, individual and collective has changed, and changed precisely because of the success of protestantism in all its forms. A solution to our difficulties cannot be found by protestant approach because it is protestantism which has caused them.

In terms of religious history, Newman's conversion to the Roman Church in 1845 marks the beginning of our era. The Christian doctrine which Protestantism emphasizes is that every human being, irrespective of family, class, or occupation, is unique before God; the complementary and equally Christian doctrine emphasized by Catholicism is that we are all members, one with another, both in the Earthly and the Heavenly City.

Or one might say that, in conjugating the present tense of the verb *to be,* catholicism concentrates on the plural, protestantism on the singular. But authentic human existence demands that equal meaning and value be given to both singular and plural, all three persons, and all three genders. Thus, protestantism is correct in affirming that the *We are* of society expresses a false identity unless each of its members can say *I am;* catholicism correct in affirming that the individual who will not or cannot join with others in saying *We* does not know the meaning of *I.*

Whether one considers oneself, one's friends and neighbors, or the history of the last hundred years, it seems clear that the principal threat to a sense of identity is our current lack of belief in and acceptance of the existence of others. Hence the grisly success of various totalitarian movements, for the Evil One can only seduce us because he offers bogus solutions to real needs, one of which is the need for personal authority both to obey and to command (force is impersonal and altogether evil). The function of protestantism today is not to solve our problems but to warn against and oppose all solutions that are speciously, not authentically, catholic, to point out that the catholic community can only be realized by the will of each lutheran individual to create it. By catholic community I do not mean the Christendom of the thirteenth century, nor by lutheran individual, a Lutheran of the sixteenth: there is, as Lichtenburg observed, "a great difference between believing something *still* and believing it *again.*"

SHAKESPEARE'S SONNETS

Probably, more nonsense has been talked and written, more intellectual and emotional energy expended in vain, on the sonnets of Shakespeare than on any other literary work in the world. Indeed, they have become the best touchstone I know of for distinguishing the sheep from the goats, those, that is, who love poetry for its own sake and understand its nature, from those who only value poems either as historical documents or because they express feelings or beliefs of which the reader happens to approve.

It so happens that we know almost nothing about the historical circumstances under which Shakespeare wrote these sonnets: we don't know to whom they are addressed or exactly when they were written, and, unless entirely new evidence should turn up, which is unlikely, we never shall.

This has not prevented many very learned gentlemen from displaying their scholarship and ingenuity in conjecture. Though it seems to me rather silly to spend much time upon conjectures which cannot be proved true or false, that is not my real objection to their efforts. What I really object to is their illusion that, if they were successful, if the identity of the Friend, the Dark Lady, the Rival Poet, etc., could be established beyond doubt, this would in any way illuminate our understanding of the sonnets themselves.

Their illusion seems to me to betray either a complete misunderstanding of the nature of the relation between art and life or an attempt to rationalize and justify plain vulgar idle curiosity.

Idle curiosity is an ineradicable vice of the human mind. All of us like to discover the secrets of our neighbors, particularly the ugly ones. This has always been so, and, probably, always will be. What is relatively new, however—it is scarcely to be found before the latter half of the eighteenth century—is a blurring of the borderline between the desire for truth and idle curiosity, until, today, it has been so thoroughly erased that we can indulge in the latter without the slightest pangs of conscience. A great deal of what today passes for scholarly research is an activity no different from that of reading somebody's private correspondence when he is out of the room, and it doesn't really make it morally any better if he is out of the room because he is in his grave.

In the case of a man of action—a ruler, a statesman, a general—the man is identical with his biography. In the case of any kind of artist, however, who is a maker not a doer, his biography, the story of his life, and the history of his works are distinct. In the case of a man of action, we can distinguish in a rough and ready way between his private personal life and his public life, but both are lives of action and, therefore, capable of affecting each other. The political interests of a king's mistress, for example, may influence his decisions on national policy. Consequently, the historian, in his search for truth, is justified in investigating the private life of a man of action to the degree that such discoveries throw light upon the history of his times which he had a share in shaping, even if the victim would prefer such secrets not to be known.

The case of any artist is quite different. Art history, the comparison of one work with another, one artistic epoch with another, the study of influences and changes of style is a legitimate study. The late J. B. Leishman's book, *Themes and Variations in Shakespeare's Sonnets,* is an admirable example of such an enquiry. Even the biography of an artist, if his life as a man was sufficiently interesting, is permissible, provided that the biographer and his readers realize that such an account throws no light whatsoever upon the artist's work. The relation between his life and his works is at one and the same time too self-evident to require comment—

every work of art is, in one sense, a self-disclosure—and too complicated ever to unravel. Thus, it is self-evident that Catullus's love for Lesbia was the experience which inspired his love poems, and that, if either of them had had a different character, the poems would have been different, but no amount of research into their lives can tell us why Catullus wrote the actual poems he did, instead of an infinite number of similar poems he might have written instead, why, indeed he wrote any, or why those he did are good. Even if one could question a poet himself about the relation between some poem of his and the events which provoked him to write it, he could not give a satisfactory answer, because even the most "occasional" poem, in the Goethean sense, involves not only the occasion but the whole life experience of the poet, and he himself cannot identify all the contributing elements.

Further, it should be borne in mind that most genuine artists would prefer that no biography be written. A genuine artist believes he has been put on earth to fulfill a certain function determined by the talent with which he has been entrusted. His personal life is, naturally, of concern to himself and, he hopes, to his personal friends, but he does not think it is or ought to be of any concern to the public. The one thing a writer, for example, hopes for, is attentive readers of his writings. He hopes they will study the text closely enough to spot misprints. Shakespeare would be grateful to many scholars, beginning with Malone, who have suggested sensible emendations to the Q text. And he hopes that they will read with patience and intelligence so as to extract as much meaning from the text as possible. If the shade of Shakespeare has read Professor William Empson's explication of "They that have power to hurt and will do none" (Sonnet 94), he may have wondered to himself, "Now, did I *really* say all that?", but he will certainly be grateful to Mr. Empson for his loving care.

Not only would most genuine writers prefer to have no biography written; they would also prefer, were it practically feasible, that their writings were published anonymously.

Shakespeare is in the singularly fortunate position of being, to all intents and purposes, anonymous. Hence the existence of persons who spend their lives trying to prove that his plays were written by someone else. (How odd it is that Freud should have been a firm believer in the Earl of Oxford theory.)

So far as the sonnets are concerned, the certain facts are just two in number. Two of the sonnets, "When my love swears that she is made of truth" (138), and "Two loves I have, of comfort and despair" (144), appeared in *The Passionate Pilgrim,* a poetic miscellany printed in 1599, and the whole collection was published by G. Eld for T. T. in 1609 with a dedication "To.The.Onlie.Be-getter.Of.These.Insuing.Sonnets. Mr. W.H." Meres's reference in 1598 to "sugred Sonnets" by Shakespeare is inconclusive: the word *sonnet* was often used as a general term for a lyric, and even if Meres was using it in the stricter sense, we do not know if the sonnets he was referring to are the ones we have.

Aside from the text itself, this is all we know for certain and all we are ever likely to know. On philological grounds, I am inclined to agree with those scholars who take the word *begetter* to mean procurer, so that Mr. W.H. is not the friend who inspired most of the sonnets, but the person who secured the manuscript for the publisher.

So far as the date of their composition is concerned, all we know for certain is that the relation between Shakespeare and the Friend lasted at least three years:

> Three April perfumes in three hot Junes burned,
> Since first I saw you fresh, which yet are green. (104)

The fact that the style of the sonnets is nearer to that of the earlier plays than the later is not conclusive proof that their composition was contemporary with the former, because a poet's style is always greatly influenced by the particular verse form he is employing. As Professor C. S. Lewis has said: "If Shakespeare had taken an hour off from the composition of *Lear* to write a sonnet, the sonnet might not have been in the style of *Lear*." On the whole, I think an early date is a more plausible conjecture than a late one, because the experiences the sonnets describe seem to me to be more likely to befall a younger man than an older.

Let us, however, forget all about Shakespeare the man, leave the speculations about the persons involved, the names, already or in the future to be put forward, Southampton, Pembroke, Hughes, etc., to the foolish and the idle, and consider the sonnets themselves.

The first thing which is obvious after reading through the one hundred and fifty-four sonnets as we have them, is that they are not in any kind of planned sequence. The only semblance of order is a division into two unequal heaps—Sonnets 1–126 are addressed to a young man, assuming, which is probable but not certain, that there is only one young man addressed, and Sonnets 127–154 are addressed to a dark-haired woman. In both heaps, a triangle situation is referred to in which Shakespeare's friend and his mistress betray him by having an affair together, which proves that the order is not chronological. Sonnets 40 and 42, "Take all my loves, my love, yea take them all," "That thou hast her, it is not all my grief," must be more or less contemporary with 144 and 152, "Two loves I have, of comfort and despair," "In loving thee thou know'st I am forsworn."

Nor in the two sets considered separately is it possible to believe that the order is chronological. Sometimes batches of sonnets occur which clearly belong together—for example, the opening series 1–17, in which the friend is urged to marry, though, even here, 15 seems not to belong, for marriage is not mentioned in it. At other times, sonnets which are similar in theme are widely separated. To take a very trivial example. In 77 Shakespeare speaks of giving his friend a commonplace book.

> Look what thy memory cannot contain,
> Commit to these waste blanks.

And in 122, he speaks of a similar gift from his friend to him,

> Thy gift, thy tables, are within my brain.

Surely, it is probable that they exchanged gifts and that these sonnets belong together.

The serious objection, however, to the order of Sonnets 1–126 as the Q text prints them is psychological. Sonnets expressing feelings of unalloyed happiness and devotion are mixed with others expressing grief and estrangement. Some speak of injuries done to Shakespeare by his friend, others of some scandal in which the friend was involved, others again of some infidelity on Shakespeare's part in a succession which makes no kind of emotional sense.

Any passionate relationship can go through and survive painful crises, and become all the stronger for it. As Shakespeare writes in Sonnet 119:

> O, benefit of ill: now I find true
> That better is by evil still made better;
> And ruined love, when it is built anew,
> Grows fairer than at first, more strong, far greater.

But forgiveness and reconciliation do not obliterate memory of the past. It is not possible to return to the innocent happiness expressed before any cloud appeared on the sky. It is not, it seems to me, possible to believe that, *after* going through the experiences described in Sonnets 40 and 42, Shakespeare would write either Sonnet 53,

> In all external grace, you have some part,
> But you like none, none you, for constant heart.

or 105,

> Let not my love be called idolatry,
> Nor my beloved as an idol show,
> Since all alike my songs and praises be
> To one, of one, still such, and ever so.
> Kind is my love today, tomorrow kind,
> Still constant in a wondrous excellence.

If the order is not chronological, it cannot, either, be a sequence planned by Shakespeare for publication. Any writer with an audience in mind knows that a sequence of poems must climax with one of the best. Yet the sequence as we have it concludes with two of the worst of the sonnets, trivial conceits about, apparently, going to Bath to take the waters. Nor, when preparing for publication, will an author leave unrevised what is obviously a first draft, like Sonnet 99 with its fifteen lines.

A number of scholars have tried to rearrange the sonnets into some more logical order, but such efforts can never be more than conjecture, and it is best to accept the jumble we have been given.

If the first impression made by the sonnets is of their haphazard order, the second is of their extremely uneven poetic value.

After the 1609 edition, the sonnets were pretty well forgotten for over a century and a half. In 1640 Benson produced an extraordinary hodgepodge in which one hundred and forty-six of them were arranged into seventy-two poems with invented titles, and some of the *he*'s and *him*'s changed to *she*'s and *her*'s. It was not until 1780 that a significant critical text was made by Malone. This happened to be a period when critics condemned the sonnet as a form. Thus Steevens could write in 1766:

> Quaintness, obscurity, and tautology are to be regarded as the constituent parts of this exotic species of composition. . . . I am one of those who should have wished it to have expired in the country where it was born. . . . [A sonnet] is composed in the highest strain of affectation, pedantry, circumlocution, and nonsense.

And of Shakespeare's essays in this form:

> The strongest act of Parliament that could be framed would fail to compel readers unto their service.

Even when this prejudice against the sonnet as such had begun to weaken, and even after Bardolatry had begun, adverse criticism of the sonnets continued.

Thus Wordsworth, who was as responsible as anyone for rehabilitating the sonnet as a form (though he employed the Petrarchan, not the Shakespearean, kind), remarked:

> These sonnets beginning at CXXVII to his mistress are worse than a puzzle-peg. They are abominably harsh, obscure, and worthless. The others are for the most part much better, have many fine lines and passages. They are also in many places warm with passion. Their chief faults—and heavy ones they are—are sameness, tediousness, quaintness, and elaborate obscurity.

Hazlitt:

> If Shakespeare had written nothing but his sonnets . . . he
> would . . . have been assigned to the class of cold, artificial
> writers, who had no genuine sense of nature or passion.

Keats:

> They seem to be full of fine things said unintentionally—in
> the intensity of working out conceits.

Landor:

> Not a single one is very admirable. . . . They are hot and
> pothery: there is much condensation, little delicacy; like
> raspberry jam without cream, without crust, without bread;
> to break its viscidity.

In this century we have reacquired a taste for the conceit, as we
have for baroque architecture, and no longer think that artifice is
incompatible with passion. Even so, no serious critic of poetry can
possibly think that all the sonnets are equally good.

On going through the hundred and fifty-four of them, I find
forty-nine which seem to me excellent throughout, a good number
of the rest have one or two memorable lines, but there are also
several which I can only read out of a sense of duty. For the inferior ones we have no right to condemn Shakespeare unless we
are prepared to believe, a belief for which there is no evidence,
that he prepared or intended them all to be published.

Considered in the abstract, as if they were Platonic Ideas, the
Petrarchan sonnet seems to be a more esthetically satisfying form
than the Shakespearean. Having only two different rhymes in the
octave and two in the sestet, each is bound by rhyme into a closed
unity, and the asymmetrical relation of 8 to 6 is pleasing. The
Shakespearean form, on the other hand, with its seven different
rhymes, almost inevitably becomes a lyric of three symmetrical
quatrains, finished off with an epigrammatic couplet. As a rule
Shakespeare shapes his rhetorical argument in conformity with this,
that is to say, there is usually a major pause after the fourth, the
eighth, and the twelfth line. Only in one case, Sonnet 86, "Was it
the proud full sail of his great verse," does the main pause occur
in the middle of the second quatrain, so that the sonnet divides
into 6.6.2.

It is the concluding couplet in particular which, in the Shakespearean form, can be a snare. The poet is tempted to use it, either to make a summary of the preceding twelve lines which is unnecessary, or to draw a moral which is too glib and trite. In the case of Shakespeare himself, though there are some wonderful couplets, for example the conclusion of 61,

> For thee watch I, whilst thou dost wake elsewhere,
> From me far off, with others all too near,

or 87,

> Thus have I had thee as a dream doth flatter,
> In sleep a king, but waking no such matter,

all too often, even in some of the best, the couplet lines are the weakest and dullest in the sonnet, and, coming where they do at the end, the reader has the sense of a disappointing anticlimax.

Despite all this, it seems to me wise of Shakespeare to have chosen the form he did rather than the Petrarchan. Compared with Italian, English is so poor in rhymes that it is almost impossible to write a Petrarchan sonnet in it that sounds effortless throughout. In even the best examples from Milton, Wordsworth, Rossetti, for example, one is almost sure to find at least one line the concluding word of which does not seem inevitable, the only word which could accurately express the poet's meaning; one feels it is only there because the rhyme demanded it.

In addition, there are certain things which can be done in the Shakespearean form which the Petrarchan, with its sharp division between octave and sestet, cannot do. In Sonnet 66, "Tired with all these, for restful death I cry," and 129, "Th' expense of spirit in a waste of shame," Shakespeare is able to give twelve single-line *exempla* of the wretchedness of this world and the horrors of lust, with an accumulative effect of great power.

In their style, two characteristics of the sonnets stand out. Firstly, their *cantabile*. They are the work of someone whose ear is unerring. In his later blank verse, Shakespeare became a master of highly complicated effects of sound and rhythm, and the counterpointing of these with the sense, but in the sonnets he is intent upon making his verse as melodious, in the simplest and most obvious sense of the word, as possible, and there is scarcely a line, even in the dull ones, which sounds harsh or awkward. Occasionally, there are lines which foreshadow the freedom of his later verse. For example:

> Not mine own fears nor the prophetic soul
> Of the wide world dreaming on things to come.   (107)

But, as a rule, he keeps the rhythm pretty close to the metrical base. Inversion, except in the first foot, is rare, and so is trisyllabic substitution. The commonest musical devices are alliteration—

> Then were not summer's distillation left,
> A liquid prisoner pent in walls of glass   (5)

> Let me not to the marriage of true minds
> Admit impediments . . .   (116)

and the careful patterning of long and short vowels—

> How many a holy and obsequious tear   (31)

> Nor think the bitterness of absence sour   (57)

> So far from home into my deeds to pry.   (61)

The second characteristic they display is a mastery of every possible rhetorical device. The reiteration, for example, of words with either an identical or a different meaning—

> love is not love
> Which alters when it alteration finds,
> Or bends with the remover to remove.   (116)

Or the avoidance of monotony by an artful arithmetical variation of theme or illustration.

Here, I cannot do better than to quote (interpolating lines where appropriate) Professor C. S. Lewis on Sonnet 18. "As often," he says, "the theme begins at line 9,

> But thy eternal summer shall not fade,

occupying four lines, and the application is in the couplet:

> So long as men can breathe or eyes can see,
> So long lives this, and this gives life to thee.

Line 1

> Shall I compare thee to a summer's day

proposes a simile. Line 2

> Thou art more lovely and more temperate

corrects it. Then we have two one-line *exempla* justifying the correction

> Rough winds do shake the darling buds of May,
> And summer's lease hath all too short a date:

then a two-line *exemplum* about the sun

> Sometime too hot the eye of heaven shines,
> And often is his gold complexion dimmed:

then two more lines

> And every fair from fair sometime declines,
> By chance, or nature's changing course, untrimmed

which do not, as we had expected, add a fourth *exemplum* but generalize. Equality of length in the two last variations is thus played off against difference of function."[1]

The visual imagery is usually drawn from the most obviously beautiful natural objects, but, in a number, a single metaphorical conceit is methodically worked out, as in 87,

> Farewell, thou art too dear for my possessing,

where the character of an emotional relationship is worked out in terms of a legal contract.

In the inferior sonnets, such artifices may strike the reader as artificial, but he must reflect that, without the artifice, they might be much worse than they are. The worst one can say, I think, is that rhetorical skill enables a poet to write a poem for which genuine inspiration is lacking which, had he lacked such skill, he would not have written at all.

On the other hand those sonnets which express passionate

1. *English Literature in the Sixteenth Century.* Oxford: Clarendon Press, 1954, p. 507.

emotions, whether of adoration or anger or grief or disgust, owe a very great deal of their effect precisely to Shakespeare's artifice, for without the restraint and distancing which the rhetorical devices provide, the intensity and immediacy of the emotion might have produced, not a poem, but an embarrassing "human document." Wordsworth defined poetry as emotion recollected in tranquillity. It seems highly unlikely that Shakespeare wrote many of these sonnets out of recollected emotion. In his case, it is the artifice that makes up for the lack of tranquillity.

If the vagueness of the historical circumstances under which the sonnets were written has encouraged the goats of idle curiosity, their matter has given the goats of ideology a wonderful opportunity to display their love of simplification at the expense of truth. Confronted with the extremely odd story they tell, with the fact that, in so many of them, Shakespeare addresses a young man in terms of passionate devotion, the sound and sensible citizen, alarmed at the thought that our Top-Bard could have had any experience with which he is unfamiliar, has either been shocked and wished that Shakespeare had never written them, or, in defiance of common sense, tried to persuade himself that Shakespeare was merely expressing in somewhat hyperbolic terms, such as an Elizabethan poet might be expected to use, what any normal man feels for a friend of his own sex. The homosexual reader, on the other hand, determined to secure our Top-Bard as a patron saint of the Homintern, has been uncritically enthusiastic about the first one hundred and twenty-six of the sonnets, and preferred to ignore those to the Dark Lady in which the relationship is unequivocally sexual, and the fact that Shakespeare was a married man and a father.

Dag Hammerskjöld, in a diary found after his death and just recently published in Sweden, makes an observation to which both the above types would do well to listen.

> How easy Psychology has made it for us to dismiss the perplexing mystery with a label which assigns it a place in the list of common aberrations.

That we are confronted in the sonnets by a mystery rather than by an aberration is evidenced for me by the fact that men and women

whose sexual tastes are perfectly normal, but who enjoy and understand poetry, have always been able to read them as expressions
of what they understand by the word *love,* without finding the
masculine pronoun an obstacle.

I think that the *primary* experience—complicated as it became
later—out of which the sonnets to the friend spring was a mystical
one.

All experiences which may be called mystical have certain
characteristics in common.

1. The experience is "given." That is to say, it cannot be induced or prolonged by an effort of will, though the openness
   of any individual to receive it is partly determined by his
   age, his psychophysical make-up, and his cultural milieu.
2. Whatever the contents of the experience, the subject is
   absolutely convinced that it is a revelation of reality. When
   it is over, he does not say, as one says when one awakes
   from a dream: "Now I am awake and conscious again of the
   real world." He says, rather: "For a while the veil was lifted
   and a reality revealed which in my 'normal' state is hidden
   from me."
3. With whatever the vision is concerned, things, human beings,
   or God, they are experienced as numinous, clothed in glory,
   charged with an intense being-thereness.
4. Confronted by the vision, the attention of the subject, in awe,
   joy, dread, is absolutely absorbed in contemplation and, while
   the vision lasts, his self, its desires and needs, are completely
   forgotten.

Natural mystical experiences, visions that is to say, concerned with
created beings, not with a creator God, and without overt religious
content, are of two kinds, which one might call the Vision of
Dame Kind and the Vision of Eros.

The classic descriptions of the first are to be found, of course,
in certain of Wordsworth's poems, like *The Prelude,* the Immortal-
ity Ode, "Tintern Abbey," and "The Ruined Cottage." It is concerned with a multiplicity of creatures, inanimate and animate, but
not with persons, though it may include human artifacts. If human
beings do appear in it, they are always, I believe, total strangers

to the subject, so that, so far as he is concerned, they are not persons. It would seem that, in our culture, this vision is not uncommon in childhood, but rare in adults.

The Vision of Eros, on the other hand, is concerned with a single person, who is revealed to the subject as being of infinite sacred importance. The classic descriptions of it are to be found in Plato's *Symposium,* Dante's *La Vita Nuova,* and some of these sonnets by Shakespeare.

It can, it seems, be experienced before puberty. If it occurs later, though the subject is aware of its erotic nature, his own desire is always completely subordinate to the sacredness of the beloved person who is felt to be infinitely superior to the lover. Before anything else, the lover desires the happiness of the beloved.

The Vision of Eros is probably a much rarer experience than most people in our culture suppose, but, when it is genuine, I do not think it makes any sense to apply to it terms like heterosexual or homosexual. Such terms can only be legitimately applied to the profane erotic experiences with which we are all familiar, to lust, for example, an interest in another solely as a sexual object, and that combination of sexual desire and *philia,* affection based upon mutual interests, values, and shared experiences which is the securest basis for a happy marriage.

That, in the Vision of Eros, the erotic is the medium, not the cause, is proved, I think, by the fact, on which all who have written about it with authority agree, that it cannot long survive an actual sexual relationship. Indeed, it is very doubtful if the Vision can ever be mutual: the story of Tristan and Isolde is a myth, not an instance of what can historically occur. To be receptive to it, it would seem that the subject must be exceptionally imaginative. Class feelings also seem to play a role; no one, apparently, can have such a vision about an individual who belongs to a social group which he has been brought up to regard as inferior to his own, so that its members are not, for him, fully persons.

The medium of the Vision is, however, undoubtedly erotic. Nobody who was unconscious of an erotic interest on his part would use the frank, if not brutal, sexual image which Shakespeare employs in speaking of his friend's exclusive interest in women.

But since she pricked thee out for women's pleasure,
Mine be thy love, and thy love's use their treasure.

(20)

The beloved is always beautiful in the impersonal sense of the word as well as the personal.

The Petrarchan distinction, employed by Shakespeare in a number of his sonnets, between the love of the eye and the love of the heart, is an attempt, I think, to express the difference between these two kinds of beauty and our response to them.

In the Vision of Eros, both are always present. But, to the lover, the second is the more important. Dante certainly thought that Beatrice was a girl whose beauty everybody would admire, but it wouldn't have entered his head to compare her for beauty with other Florentine girls of the same age.

Both Plato and Dante attempt to give a religious explanation of the Vision. Both, that is to say, regard the love inspired by a created human being as intended to lead the lover towards the love of the uncreated source of all beauty. The difference between them is that Plato is without any notion of what we mean by a person, whether human or Divine; he can only think in terms of the individual and the universal, and beauty, for him, is always beauty in the impersonal sense. Consequently, on the Platonic ladder, the love of an individual must be forgotten in the love of the universal; what we should call infidelity becomes a moral duty. How different is Dante's interpretation. Neither he nor Beatrice tells us exactly what he had done which had led him to the brink of perdition, but both speak of it as a lack of fidelity on Dante's part to his love for Beatrice. In Paradise, she is with him up until the final moment when he turns from her towards "The Eternal Fountain" and, even then, he knows that her eyes are turned in the same direction. Instead of the many rungs of the Platonic ladder, there is only one step for the lover to take, from the person of the beloved creature to the Person of their common Creator.

It is consistent with Shakespeare's cast of mind as we meet it in the plays, where it is impossible to be certain what his personal beliefs were on any subject, that the sonnets should contain no theory of love: Shakespeare contents himself with simply describing the experience.

Though the primary experience from which they started was, I believe, the Vision of Eros, that is, of course, not all they are about. For the vision to remain undimmed, it is probably necessary that the lover have very little contact with the beloved, however nice a person she (or he) may be. Dante, after all, only saw Beatrice once or twice, and she probably knew little about him. The story of the sonnets seems to me to be the story of an agonized struggle by Shakespeare to preserve the glory of the vision he had been granted in a relationship, lasting at least three years, with a person who seemed intent by his actions upon covering the vision with dirt.

As outsiders, the impression we get of his friend is one of a young man who was not really very nice, very conscious of his good looks, able to switch on the charm at any moment, but essentially frivolous, cold-hearted, and self-centered, aware, probably, that he had some power over Shakespeare—if he thought about it at all, no doubt he gave it a cynical explanation—but with no conception of the intensity of the feelings he had, unwittingly, aroused. Somebody, in fact, rather like Bassanio in *The Merchant of Venice.*

The sonnets addressed to the Dark Lady are concerned with that most humiliating of all erotic experiences, sexual infatuation —*Vénus toute entière à sa proie attachée.*

Simple lust is impersonal, that is to say the pursuer regards himself as a person but the object of his pursuit as a thing, to whose personal qualities, if she has any, he is indifferent, and, if he succeeds, he expects to be able to make a safe getaway as soon as he becomes bored. Sometimes, however, he gets trapped. Instead of becoming bored, he becomes sexually obsessed, and the girl, instead of conveniently remaining an object, becomes a real person to him, but a person whom he not only does not love, but actively dislikes.

No other poet, not even Catullus, has described the anguish, self-contempt, and rage produced by this unfortunate condition so well as Shakespeare in some of these sonnets, 141, for example, "In faith I do not love thee with my eyes," or 151, "Love is too young to know what conscience is."

Aside from the opening sixteen sonnets urging his friend to marry—which may well, as some scholars have suggested, have been written at the suggestion of some member of the young man's family—aside from these, and half a dozen elegant trifles, what is astonishing about the sonnets, especially when one remembers the age in which they were written, is the impression they make of naked autobiographical confession. The Elizabethans were not given to writing their autobiographies or to "unlocking their hearts." Donne's love poems were no doubt inspired by a personal passion, but this is hidden behind the public performance. It is not until Rousseau and the age of *Sturm und Drang* that confession becomes a literary genre. After the sonnets, I cannot think of anything in English poetry so seemingly autobiographical until Meredith's *Modern Love,* and even then, the personal events seem to be very carefully "posed."

It is impossible to believe either that Shakespeare wished them to be published or that he can have shown most of them to the young man and woman, whoever they were, to whom they are addressed. Suppose you had written Sonnet 57,

> Being your slave, what should I do but tend
> Upon the hours and times of your desire?

Can you imagine showing it to the person you were thinking of? Vice versa, what on earth would you feel, supposing someone you knew handed you the sonnet and said: "This is about you"?

Though Shakespeare may have shown the sonnets to one or two intimate literary friends—it would appear that he must have —he wrote them, I am quite certain, as one writes a diary, for himself alone, with no thought of a public.

When the sonnets are really obscure, they are obscure in the way that a diary can be, in which the writer does not bother to explain references which are obvious to him, but an outsider cannot know. For example, in the opening lines of Sonnet 125,

> Were't aught to me I bore the canopy,
> With my extern the outward honoring.

It is impossible for the reader to know whether Shakespeare is simply being figurative or whether he is referring to some ceremony in which he actually took part, or, if he is, what that ceremony can have been. Again, the concluding couplet of 124 remains impenetrable.

> To this I witness call the fools of Time,
> Which die for goodness, who have lived for crime.

Some critics have suggested that this is a cryptic reference to the Jesuits who were executed on charges of high treason. This may be so, but there is nothing in the text to prove it, and even if it is so, I fail to understand their relevance as witnesses to Shakespeare's love which no disaster or self-interest can affect.

How the sonnets came to be published—whether Shakespeare gave copies to some friend who then betrayed him, or whether some enemy stole them—we shall probably never know. Of one thing I am certain: Shakespeare must have been horrified when they were published.

The Elizabethan age was certainly as worldly-wise and no more tolerant, perhaps less, than our own. After all, sodomy was still a capital offense. The poets of the period, like Marlowe and Barnfield, whom we know to have been homosexual, were very careful not to express their feelings in the first person, but in terms of classical mythology. Renaissance Italy had the reputation for being tolerant on this subject, yet, when Michelangelo's nephew published his sonnets to Tomasso de Cavalieri, which are much more restrained than Shakespeare's, for the sake of his uncle's reputation he altered the sex, just as Benson was to do with Shakespeare in 1640.

Shakespeare must have known that his sonnets would be read by many readers in 1609 as they are read by many today—with raised eyebrows. Though I believe such a reaction to be due to a misunderstanding, one cannot say that it is not understandable.

In our culture, we have good reason to be skeptical when anyone claims to have experienced the Vision of Eros, and even to doubt if it ever occurs, because half our literature, popular and highbrow, ever since the Provençal poets made the disastrous mistake of trying to turn a mystical experience into a social cult, is based on the assumption that what is, probably, a rare experi-

ence, is one which almost everybody has or ought to have; if
they don't, then there must be something wrong with them. We
know only too well how often, when a person speaks of having
"fallen in love" with X, what he or she really feels could be
described in much cruder terms. As La Rochefoucauld observed:

> True love is like seeing ghosts: we all talk about it, but few
> of us have ever seen one.

It does not follow, however, that true love or ghosts cannot exist.
Perhaps poets are more likely to experience it than others, or
become poets because they have. Perhaps Hannah Arendt is right:
"Poets are the only people to whom love is not only a crucial but
an indispensable experience, which entitles them to mistake it for a
universal one." In Shakespeare's case, what happened to his relations with his friend and his mistress, whether they were abruptly
broken off in a quarrel, or slowly faded into indifference, is anybody's guess. Did Shakespeare later feel that the anguish at the
end was not too great a price to pay for the glory of the initial
vision? I hope so and believe so. Anyway, poets are tough and
can profit from the most dreadful experiences.

There is a scene in *The Two Noble Kinsmen* which most
scholars believe to have been written by Shakespeare and which,
if he did, may very well be the last thing he wrote. In it there is a
speech by Palamon in which he prays to Venus for her aid. The
speech is remarkable, firstly, in its choice of examples of the power
of the Goddess—nearly all are humiliating or horrid—and, secondly, for the intensity of the disgust expressed at masculine sexual
vanity.

> Hail, Sovereign Queen of secrets, who has power
> To call the fiercest tyrant from his rage,
> And weep unto a girl; that hast the might
> Even with an eye-glance, to choke Mars's drum
> And turn th' alarm to whispers; that canst make
> A cripple flourish with his crutch, and cure him
> Before Apollo; that mayst force the King
> To be his subjects' vassal, and induce
> Stale gravity to dance; the polled bachelor—

Whose youth, like wanton boys through bonfires,
Have skipped thy flame—at seventy thou canst catch
And make him, to the scorn of his hoarse throat,
Abuse young lays of love: what godlike power
Hast thou not power upon? . . .
                . . . Take to thy grace
Me, thy vowed soldier, who do bear thy yoke
As 'twere a wreath of roses, yet is heavier
Than lead itself, stings more than nettles.
I have never been foul-mouthed against thy law,
Nev'r revealed secret, for I knew none; would not
Had I kenned all that were; I never practised
Upon man's wife, nor would the libels read
Of liberal wits; I never at great feasts
Sought to betray a beauty, but have blushed
At simp'ring Sirs that did; I have been harsh
To large confessors, and have hotly asked them
If they had mothers: I had one, a woman,
And women 'twere they wronged. I knew a man
Of eighty winters, this I told them, who
A lass of fourteen brided. 'Twas thy power
To put life into dust; the aged cramp
Had screwed his square foot round,
The gout had knitted his fingers into knots,
Torturing convulsions from his globy eyes,
Had almost drawn their spheres, that what was life
In him seemed torture: this anatomy
Had by his young fair pheare a boy, and I
Believed it was his, for she swore it was,
And who would not believe her? Brief, I am
To those that prate, and have done, no companion;
To those that boast, and have not, a defier;
To those that would, and cannot, a rejoicer.
Yea, him I do not love, that tells close offices
The foulest way, nor names concealments in
The boldest language. Such a one I am,
And vow that lover never yet made sigh
Truer than I. O, then, most soft, sweet Goddess,

] 107 [

Give me the victory of this question, which
Is true love's merit, and bless me with a sign
Of thy great pleasure.

*Here music is heard, doves are seen to flutter; they fall again
upon their faces, then on their knees.*

Oh thou, that from eleven to ninety reign'st
In mortal bosoms, whose chase is this world,
And we in herds thy game; I give thee thanks
For this fair token, which, being laid unto
Mine innocent true heart, arms in assurance
My body to this business. Let us rise
And bow before the Goddess; Time comes on.

Exeunt. Still music of records.

*

A CIVILIZED VOICE

*

It is not often that knowledge of an artist's life sheds any significant light upon his work, but in the case of Pope I think it does. Most of his best poems are "occasional"—that is to say, they are concerned not with imaginary persons or events but with the historical and contemporary, with Pope's political and literary friends and enemies, so that without some knowledge about them we cannot properly understand what he wrote and why. (Such knowledge, needless to say, does not explain why he wrote so well.) For example, in the concluding lines of a poem probably written before 1715, Pope (or so I used to think) describes Addison as

> Statesman, yet friend to Truth! of soul sincere,
> In action faithful and in honour clear;
> Who broke no promise, served no private end,
> Who gain'd no title, and who lost no friend;
> Ennobl'd by himself, by all approv'd,
> And prais'd, unenvied, by the Muse he lov'd.

I was, of course, in error. These lines of the "Epistle to Addison" were addressed to James Craggs, his successor as Secretary of State. However, the whole tone of the poem is friendly.

Then, sometime between that date and 1735, Pope changed
his opinion and described Addison thus:

> Shou'd such a man, too fond to rule alone,
> Bear, like the Turk, no brother near the throne,
> View him with scornful, yet with jealous eyes,
> And hate for Arts that caus'd himself to rise,
> Damn with faint praise, assent with civil leer,
> And without sneering, teach the rest to sneer.

In understanding this change, we must be informed about Addison's somewhat devious behavior at the time of the almost simultaneous publication of Pope's translation of the *Iliad* and Tickell's.

More mysterious and much sadder is the history of the relationship between Pope and Lady Mary Wortley. She was the one
great, passionate love of his life, and though she could not recipro-
cate, she was obviously very fond of him, at least in the beginning.
What caused their estrangement is not clear. Current gossip had
various explanations—that Lady Mary had borrowed a pair of
sheets from Pope's mother and thoughtlessly sent them back un-
washed, or that at an ill-chosen moment he had made fervent advances and she had burst into laughter—but these were almost
certainly false. Mr. Peter Quennell's explanation, in his *Alexander
Pope: The Education of Genius 1688–1728,* is probably as close to
the truth as we can get:

> Their quarrel, if a definite quarrel took place, probably
> originated not in any single episode, but in the very nature,
> the secret stresses and strains, of their curiously unequal
> friendship. For Lady Mary, it had been an amusing literary
> diversion: for Pope, an all-absorbing passion. Pope had the
> pride that goes with genius; Lady Mary possessed a con-
> siderable share of talent, and, to the self-esteem that usually
> accompanies talent, she added the strain of levity and light-
> hearted cruelty that she derived from her education as a
> woman of the world.

Their estrangement seems to have begun in 1722, and the
suffering it caused Pope may be guessed from a poem he wrote to
Gay:

Ah friend, 'tis true—this truth you lovers know—
In vain my structures rise, my gardens grow,
In vain fair Thames reflects the double scenes
Of hanging mountains, and of sloping greens:
Joy lives not here; to happier seats it flies,
And only dwells where WORTLEY casts her eyes. . . .

What are the gay parterre, the chequer'd shade,
The morning bower, the ev'ning colonade,
But soft recesses of uneasy minds,
To sigh unheard in, to the passing winds?
So the struck deer in some sequester'd part
Lies down to die, the arrow at his heart.

Such grief may not excuse the ferocity with which, years later, he was to attack her, but it makes it comprehensible.

Then, we cannot fully understand Pope and any other writers of his period without knowing something about the general climate of thought and opinion by which they were surrounded. It was one of the few historical periods in which one could with accuracy speak of an educated élite who, whether as writers or as readers, shared the same artistic tastes and general ideas about Nature, Man, and Society—a period, therefore, when "originality" and "alienation" were not regarded as the hallmarks of genius. Take the question of religious belief. The uneducated multitude was fanatically anti-Papist. Defoe said that there were a hundred thousand fellows in his time ready to fight to the death against popery without knowing whether popery was a man or a horse. Though not physically persecuted, Roman Catholics were penalized: they could not live within ten miles of London, or attend a university, or serve in public office. But the educated laity, whether Protestant or Catholic, saw no reason that their theological differences should impair their social relations. Pope was born and remained a Roman Catholic, but throughout his life most of his closest friends were Protestant, and had any of them been asked to define precisely the difference between their faiths they would have found it difficult to give an answer.

Pope's statement of faith and his opinion of medieval Catholicism would scarcely have been approved of in Rome:

Nothing has been so much a scarecrow to them [the Protestants] as the too peremptory and seemingly uncharitable assertion of an utter impossibility of salvation to all but ourselves. . . . Besides the small number of the truly faithful in our Church, we must again subdivide, and the Jansenist is damned by the Jesuit, the Jesuit by the Jansenist, the strict Scotist by the Thomist, &c. There may be errors, I grant, but I can't think 'em of such consequence as to destroy utterly the charity of mankind, the very greatest bond in which we are engaged by God to one another. . . .

I am not a Papist, for I renounce the temporal invasions of the Papal power. . . .

> With *Tyranny,* then *Superstition* join'd,
> As that the *Body,* this enslav'd the *Mind;*
> Much was *Believ'd,* but little *understood,*
> And to be *dull* was constru'd to be *good;*
> A *second* Deluge Learning thus o'er-run,
> And the *Monks* finish'd what the *Goths* begun.
> At length, *Erasmus,* that *great, injur'd* name,
> (The *Glory* of the Priesthood, and the *Shame!*)
> *Stemm'd* the *wild Torrent* of a *barb'rous Age,*
> And drove those *Holy Vandals* off the Stage.

The truth is, I think, that the religion of all educated persons at the time, whether they knew it or not, was not Christian but Deist. Their political passions ran stronger, but even in politics their love of order was greater than their ideological commitments. Pope and most of his friends were Tories who detested the Whig plutocracy that had come to power with William III. Pope himself may even have had secret Jacobite sympathies, but one cannot believe that the failure of the Jacobites in 1715 and 1745 caused him sleepless nights. What he wanted, he said, was a king who would be "not a King of Whigs or a King of Tories, but a King of England," which "God of his mercy grant his present Majesty may be."

Mr. Quennell's book is equally excellent as a biography of a poet whom he admires and as a history of a period he loves and understands. It is beautifully written, scholarly but readable. He has, I am thankful to say, no ugly little secrets to tell us. Though Pope was often devious and unscrupulous in his dealings, his life was surprisingly free from scandal. In his youth, he may sometimes have visited brothels—given his physical disadvantages, what more romantic sexual adventures could he have hoped to have?—but in fact he was much less of a rake than he liked to make others believe. Nor was his life full of exciting incidents. He had three narrow escapes from death:

> First, he had been saved from the horns of a maddened cow at Binfield; secondly, when he was a very young man, an imprudent coachman, negotiating a dangerous ford, had almost driven him and his party into a deep hole in the riverbed; last of all, he had nearly been plunged to destruction in Lord Bolingbroke's hurtling coach-and-six.

And Mr. Quennell has one or two amusing anecdotes to tell, such as of the time when Pope read parts of his translation of the *Iliad* in the presence of Lord Halifax. On four or five occasions, the noble Lord interrupted:

> "I beg your pardon, Mr. Pope," he would say, "but there is something in that passage that does not quite please me. Be so good as to mark the place. . . . I'm sure you can give it a better turn." Pope was both puzzled and mortified; and on the journey home in Dr. Garth's chariot, he complained that, having thought over the passages criticised, he could not understand the Minister's objections. Garth, however, laughed heartily. . . . "All you need do," says he, "is to leave them just as they are; call on Lord Halifax two or three months hence, thank him for his kind observations on those passages, and then read them to him as altered." Pope obeyed the Doctor's instructions and "his lordship was extremely pleased" to observe that his criticisms had proved so effective, exclaiming that the passages he had singled out were now everything they should be.

Then, there was Pope's socially unfortunate meeting with Voltaire:

> As the day drew on and the hour of farewells approached, Pope suggested that he should remain for dinner;

and at the dinner table he met Mrs. Pope, a plain, modest, round-faced old lady; now over eighty-four years old, who, in her motherly way (writes Owen Ruffhead) noticing that their foreign guest "appeared to be entirely emaciated" and seemed to have a weak stomach, "expressed her concern for his want of appetite," at which Voltaire gave her "so indelicate and brutal an account of the occasion of his disorder contracted in Italy that the poor lady was obliged immediately to rise from the table."

But Pope's life has little gossip-column interest; most of his days were spent, quietly and industriously, writing, translating, landscape gardening, painting, playing with his dogs and entertaining his friends. (I am curious to know how many of his paintings and drawings have survived. I have myself seen a self-portrait in oils which is first-rate.)

While we are on the subject of the private life of an artist, I must take the opportunity to say how wholeheartedly I approve of Pope's attempt—alas, a vain one—to revise his private letters before letting the public read them, for he pruned them, sometimes changed the name of his correspondent, and pieced together separate items to form a single, more impressive text:

> Like Byron, Pope believed that his letters were bound to interest posterity; and, even in his least studied messages, he clearly had a double purpose: besides communicating with the friends he loved, he was establishing a link between himself and unborn readers. But he had none of Byron's reckless indiscretion; and, as soon as he took up his pen, he assumed the vigilant attitude of the true creative artist. His sense of style, which was immediately brought into play, affected both his use of language and his general handling of his theme. Wherever he felt that the record needed improvement, he hastened to apply the proper touches.

If private letters are to be made public—in my will I have requested my friends to burn mine—it is no more dishonest to revise a letter than a poem.

Then, what a pleasant surprise it is in these days to read of a writer who was an affectionate and dutiful son to both his parents.

Mr. Pope Senior seems to have been the ideal father for a poet. He encouraged his son but insisted on a high standard of performance. "These are not good rhymes," he would often remark, severely, and send the boy away to turn them better. "Pope was never beaten for interrupting his father's and mother's evening conferences, or thoughtlessly and selfishly tumbling downstairs. . . . In other respects he allowed him to go his way, conduct his education as he pleased, and read the books that most amused him." I do not believe that the average child can educate himself without the imposition of some external discipline, but Pope was not an average child, and in his case such permissiveness succeeded admirably. He taught himself to read by copying printed books. A priest named Banister taught him the rudiments of Latin and Greek and, as his pupil was to say later:

> If it had not been for that I should never have got any language: for I never learned anything at the little schools I was at afterwards.

Thereafter he studied these languages in his own way:

> I did not follow the grammar; but rather hunted in the authors for a syntax of my own: and then began translating any parts that pleased me particularly, in the best Greek and Latin poets: and by that means formed my taste; which, I think, verily, about sixteen, was very near as good as it is now.

Dates are always interesting and can sometimes be startling. One thinks so automatically of Pope as *the* poet of the eighteenth century that one is surprised at being reminded that he died before the century was half over. One is also apt to forget not only how precocious he was but how soon his talents were recognized. That Wycherley, aged sixty-four, should have asked Pope, aged eighteen, to correct and improve his verses is astounding. If not quite as precocious as Rimbaud, Pope was only twenty-one when he composed an important long poem, the *Essay on Criticism,* and twenty-six when he published the second version of *The Rape of the Lock,* an undoubted masterpiece. (Unlike some prodigies, however, he did not peter out early. The "Epistles" and "Imitations of Horace," written toward the end of his life, are among his best works.) Only someone who was certain not only of his genius but of his contemporary fame could have started collecting his letters at the age of twenty-four and at twenty-five been confident that he could get sufficient subscribers to make it financially possible for him to devote six years to translating the *Iliad.*

To counterbalance the blessings of genius and a happy home, there was, of course, the curse of ill health. At the age of twelve, infected by milk from a tubercular cow, he developed Pott's disease —a tuberculosis of the spine, which turned the originally good-looking boy into an invalid, "the little Pope the ladies laugh at." When one tries to imagine the atrocious suffering and humiliation this must have caused him, one marvels not that he should have sometimes been irrationally suspicious and excessively malevolent but that he should have so often been kind and generous and shown such a gift for friendship. Very few people in his condition would have been brave enough to write an essay on "The Club of Little Men":

> A set of us have formed a society, who are sworn to *Dare to be Short,* and boldly beat out the dignity of littleness under the noses of those enormous engrossers of manhood, those hyperbolical monsters of the species, the tall fellows that overlook us. . . . If any member shall take advantage from the fulness or length of his wig . . . or the immoderate extent of his hat . . . to seem larger and higher than he is, it is ordered, he shall wear red heels to his shoes and a red feather in his hat, which may apparently mark and set bounds to the extremities of his small dimensions.

But what is really important is his poetry, and perhaps the best approach to that is through his views on landscape gardening. During the early part of the eighteenth century in England, the relation between Man and Nature seems to have been happier than ever before or since. Wild Nature had been tamed, but machines had not yet debased and enslaved her. Earlier generations had thought of Nature as a dangerous realm against which men must erect defenses; later generations were to think of Nature as a realm of freedom into which the individual could escape from the constraints of human society. The older view is exemplified by the Baroque gardens of Europe, with their geometrical patterns and topiary work designed to make them look as unlike the Nature outside as possible. But in England landscape gardeners like William Kent held the view that their proper function was "to brush Nature's robe," to confine themselves to adding the final, decisive touches, planting a term here, a sphinx or an obelisk there, or "improving" a corner of the landscape to recall a picture by Lorrain or Poussin. Pope was Kent's enthusiastic disciple. A man who could write "A tree is a nobler object than a prince in his coronation robes" was certainly not afraid of Nature, and he poured ridicule on the old Baroque formalities:

> His Gardens next your admiration call,
> On ev'ry side you look, behold the Wall!
> No pleasing Intricacies intervene,
> No artful wildness to perplex the scene;
> Grove nods at grove, each Alley has a brother,
> And half the platform just reflects the other.
> The suff'ring eye inverted Nature sees,
> Trees cut to Statues, Statues thick as trees;

But he also believed that Nature needed Man's help to realize her beauties to the full:

> Consult the Genius of the Place in all,
> That tells the Waters or to rise, or fall,
> Or helps th'ambitious Hill the heav'n to scale,
> Or scoops in circling theatres the Vale,
> Calls in the Country, catches op'ning glades,
> Joins willing woods, and varies shades from shades,
> Now breaks, or now directs, th'intending Lines,
> Paints as you plant, and, as you work, designs.
> Still follow Sense, of ev'ry Art the Soul,
> Parts answ'ring parts shall slide into a whole,
> Spontaneous beauties all around advance,
> Start ev'n from difficulty, strike from chance.

An equally apt description, surely, of what Pope was after in his poetry and, at his best, succeeded in realizing. Comparing Dryden and Pope, Mr. Quennell says:

> Whereas our first reading of a passage by Dryden is usually sufficient to display his genius, Pope, whenever we reread him, is apt to reveal some unexpected subtlety. Dryden's virtues lie on the surface; in Pope's verse, several layers of significance are compressed into a single image; and his imagery has a protean charm that constantly changes and grows beneath the reader's eye.

In his first published poems, the *Pastorals,* Nature is, to be sure, too subordinate to artifice, precision to euphony; the epithets are as abstract and conventional as the Romantics imagined was typical of all Augustan verse:

> Soon as the flocks shook off the nightly dews,
> Two Swains, whom Love kept wakeful, and the Muse,
> Poured o'er the whitening vale their fleecy care,
> Fresh as the morn, and as the season fair.

But already he is capable of writing a memorable couplet which is vivid as well as melodious:

> The moving Mountains hear the pow'rful Call,
> And headlong Streams hang list'ning in their Fall!

And from the *Essay on Criticism* to the last poems, Pope's lapses into conventional diction become very rare; his epithets are almost always both exact and original. The only technical defect I can find in his mature work comes from his ingrained habit of thinking in couplets which are self-contained units. As a result, he sometimes fails to notice that the rhymes of two successive couplets are too similar:

> With arms expanded Bernard rows his *state,*
> And left-legged Jacob seems to emu*late.*
> Full in the middle way there stood a *lake,*
> Which Curll's Corinna chanced that morn to *make.*

It was, naturally, necessary for the poets at the end of the century to get away from the heroic couplet, which by then had become a dead end, and to discover new forms for both long poems and lyrics, but if Wordsworth had Pope in mind as the enemy when he advised poets to write "in the language really used by men" he was singularly in error. Should one compare Pope at his best with any of the Romantics, including Wordsworth, at their best, it is Pope who writes as men normally speak to each other and the latter who go in for "poetic" language. When Wordsworth tries to write according to his theories, the result is nearly always flat; to write well, he has to forget them. In Pope, theory and practice are one. Compare

> Shut, shut the door, good *John!* fatigu'd I said.
> Tye up the knocker! say I'm sick, I'm dead.
>> (POPE)

> She went from Op'ra, Park, Assembly, Play,
> To morning walks, and pray'rs three hours a day;
> To part her time 'twixt reading and Bohea,
> To muse, and spill her solitary tea,
> Or o'er cold coffee trifle with the spoon,
> Count the slow clock, and dine exact at noon.
>> (POPE)

> To me the meanest flower that blows can give
> Thoughts that do often lie too deep for tears.
>> (WORDSWORTH)

> A voice so thrilling ne'er was heard
> In springtime from the Cuckoobird,
> Breaking the silence of the seas
> Among the farthest Hebrides.
>> (WORDSWORTH)

To find "natural speech" in the verse of the early nineteenth century, one must go to the least "romantic" and most Popean in spirit of the poets—to the Byron of *Don Juan* and the Tom Moore of *The Fudge Family in Paris.*

The only major poem of Pope's which seems to me a failure is *An Essay on Man*. Occasional lines of great beauty like

> Die of a rose in aromatic pain

do not compensate for the unconvincing and boring Deist theology.

About his translation of the *Iliad,* there will always be two opinions. Those who dislike it say, quite truly, that Pope sees Homer through Vergilian spectacles (his warriors have much more Roman *gravitas* than their Bronze Age originals), that what in Homer is tragic in Pope too often becomes merely grandiose, and that the movement and structure of the English heroic couplet are far removed from those of the Greek hexameter. But when these critics have done their worst, it still cannot be denied that Pope's "translation" is a magnificent English poem, and that no subsequent translator, despite all advances in philological and archeological scholarship, has produced one as readable. To the problem of the meter, there cannot, I believe, be a completely satisfactory solution. Some twentieth-century translators have claimed that the best equivalent is a free six-beat line, but I agreed with Mr. Carne-Ross when he wrote recently in *Delos:*

> The claims . . . have, I think, been granted a great deal too readily. It is about the same length, but its lumbering gait is at the furthest possible remove from the supply articulated line of Homer. Most of the time it is verse only by typographical courtesy and its movement is so ill-defined that it falls a ready prey to any other metre whose path it chances to cross.

Today I feel a little less enthusiastic about *The Dunciad* than I felt when I last wrote about it, eighteen years ago. The Second Book in particular I find repellent, as grubby as anything produced by our contemporary "underground." The best things in the first three books are nearly always addenda to the *Essay on Criticism,* passages in which Pope forgets about personalities and writes beautifully about bad writing:

> She sees a Mob of Metaphors advance,
> Pleas'd with the Madness of the mazy dance . . .

How Time himself stands still at her command,
Realms shift their place, and Ocean turns to land.
Here gay Description Ægypt glads with showers;
Or gives to Zembla fruits, to Barca flowers . . .
On cold December fragrant chaplets blow,
And heavy harvests nod beneath the snow.

The Fourth Book, however, is superb throughout, and prophetic of much that we must endure today. Pope had never seen a
"behaviorist" or a "social scientist," but he guessed exactly what
such creatures would be like:

"Be that my task (replies a gloomy Clerk,
Sworn foe to Myst'ry, yet divinely dark;
Whose pious hope aspires to see the day
When Moral Evidence shall quite decay,
And damns implicit faith, and holy lies,
Prompt to impose, and fond to dogmatize):
Let others creep by timid steps, and slow,
On plain Experience lay foundations low,
By common sense to common knowledge bred,
And last, to Nature's Cause thro' Nature led.
All-seeing in thy mists, we want no guide,
Mother of Arrogance, and Source of Pride!
We nobly take the high Priori Road,
And reason downward, till we doubt of God:
Make Nature still incroach upon his plan;
And shove him off as far as e'er we can:
Thrust some Mechanic Cause into his place;
Or bind in Matter, or diffuse in Space.
Or, at one bound, o'er-leaping all his laws,
Make God Man's Image, Man the final Cause,
Find Virtue local, all Relation scorn,
See all in *Self,* and but for self be born:
Of nought so certain as our *Reason* still,
Of nought so doubtful as of *Soul* and *Will.*"

If only one of Pope's poems could be preserved, my choice
would be *The Rape of the Lock,* and Mr. Quennell's account of

how it came to be written will fascinate anyone who is interested in the factors which enter into poetic composition. The first factor was a historical incident—a feud between two old Catholic families, the Fermors and the Petres, which had broken out because the seventh Lord Petre had stolen a lock of hair from the head of Arabella Fermor. Lord Petre was the ward of Pope's friend John Caryll, who suggested to the poet that he might write a comic poem about the incident which would reconcile the parties by making them both laugh. The second factor was a literary genre, the mock epic—works like *The War of the Frogs and the Mice* (at one time attributed to Homer), Tassoni's *Secchia Rapita,* published in 1622, and Boileau's *Le Lutrin,* finished in 1683, all of which Pope had almost certainly read. To call this a second factor is not to say that it came second in time. Given Pope's literary tastes and talents, it is much more probable that the idea of writing a mock-heroic epic was already in his mind, awaiting a suitable subject. The third factor was a contemporary social fashion. One of the most brilliant passages in the poem, the account of the card game between the Baron and Belinda, might not have been written had not ombre, the particular game Pope describes, introduced into England from Spain in the previous century, recently become all the rage. Lastly, there was an odd book, *Le Comte de Gabalis,* by L'Abbé de Montfaucon de Villars, which Pope happened to read, either in the original or in an English translation, and from which he took his Sylphs and other "lower militia of the sky." Since these did not appear in the first version, I would guess that he had not yet read the book when he began the poem. In any case, he had an extraordinary stroke of good luck, for the Sylphs, etc., were exactly what he needed to play the role in a mock epic played by the Gods in a serious epic. Moreover, as tiny creatures, they were ideally suited to Pope's imagination, fascinated as he always was by *littleness.*

Aside from its many beauties, *The Rape of the Lock* demonstrates that Pope's imagination was much odder than it is generally supposed to be. I have said that his poetry was like his landscape gardening. The general layout of his Twickenham garden conformed to the general good taste of his time, but it contained one very peculiar feature—the grotto of which Dr. Johnson said, rather severely, "Where necessity enforced a passage, vanity supplied a grotto."

> [Pope] encrusted the passage with a rough mosaic of luminous mineral bodies—Cornish diamonds, knobs of metallic ore, lumps of amethyst, spiky branches of coral, coloured Brazilian pebbles, crystals and quartzes, slabs of burnished flint, and rare and interesting "fossile" specimens, amid a rich embroidery of rustic shell-work and scraps of looking-glass cut into angular designs. On the roof shone a looking-glass star; and, dependent from the star, a single lamp—"of an orbicular figure of thin alabaster"—cast around it "a thousand pointed rays." Every surface sparkled or shimmered or gleamed with a smooth sub-aqueous lustre; and, while these corruscating details enchanted the eye, a delicate water-music had been arranged to please the ear; the "little dripping murmur" of an underground spring— discovered by the workmen during their excavations— echoed through the cavern day and night.

So, in his poems, Pope will suddenly indulge in a certain "zaniness" which reminds me of Lewis Carroll.

> Here living *Teapots* stand, one Arm held out,
> One bent; the Handle this, and that the Spout:
> A Pipkin there like *Homer's Tripod* walks;
> Here sighs a Jar, and there a Goose-pye talks.
> Men prove with Child, as pow'rful Fancy works,
> And Maids turn'd Bottles, call aloud for Corks. . . .
>
> More she had spoke, but yawn'd—All Nature nods:
> What Mortal can resist the Yawn of Gods?
> Churches and Chapels instantly it reach'd;
> (St. James's first, for leaden Gilbert preach'd)
> Then catch'd the Schools; the Hall scarce kept awake;
> The Convocation gap'd, but could not speak. . . .
> The Vapour mild o'er each Committee crept;
> Unfinish'd Treaties in each Office slept;
> And Chiefless Armies doz'd out the Campaign;
> And Navies yawn'd for Orders on the Main.

Since Mr. Quennell's book is primarily a biography, not a work of literary criticism, it is fitting that in conclusion I return to Pope as a human being. In a period when many writers were hired agents of the government, he showed an admirable integrity. Though not as poor as most of Grub Street, Pope, at least until after the publication of his *Iliad,* was by no means rich, and tempting offers, it seems, were made. In 1717, according to his own account, which there is no reason to doubt, James Craggs, then Secretary at War, offered him

> both a pension of three hundred pounds and complete freedom from all official ties, since he was ready to pay the pension from secret-service funds at his disposal, "without anyone's knowing that I had it." This offer he repeated several times, "and always used to insist on the convenience that a coach would be of to me."

How admirable, too, that, while wholly dedicated to the vocation of the poet, he never became an aesthete—never, that is, regarded his vocation as superior to all others. On the contrary, he wrote:

> To write well, lastingly well, immortally well, must not one leave Father and Mother and cleave unto the Muse? . . . 'Tis such a task as scarce leaves a man time to be a good neighbour, an useful friend, nay to plant a tree, much less to save his soul.

Poetry does not allow us to escape from life, but it does grant us a brief respite from our immediate problems, refreshment for tired spirits and relaxation for tense nerves. As I get older and the times get gloomier and more difficult, it is to poets like Horace and Pope that I find myself more and more turning for the kind of refreshment I require.

*

WERTHER AND NOVELLA

*

So far as I know, Goethe was the first writer or artist to become a Public Celebrity. There had always been poets, painters and composers who were known to and revered by their fellow artists, but the general public, however much it may have admired their works, would not have dreamed of wishing to make their personal acquaintance. But, during the last twenty years or so of Goethe's life, a visit to Weimar and an audience with the Great Man was an essential item in the itinerary of any cultivated young man making his Grand Tour of Europe. His visitors in his old age were innumerable, but most of them had actually read only one book of his, written when he was twenty-four. What Goethe felt about this may be guessed from his first version of the Second Roman Elegy.

Ask whom you will, I am safe from you now, you fair ladies and fine society gentlemen! "But did Werther really live? Did it all really happen like that? Which town has the right to boast of the lovely Lotte as its citizen?" Oh, how often I have cursed those foolish pages of mine which made my youthful sufferings public property! If Werther had been my brother and I had killed him, I could scarcely have been so persecuted by his avenging sorrowful ghost.

The biographers tell us that *Werther* was the product of Goethe's unhappy love for Charlotte Buff, but this is certainly an oversimplification. When writing a novel, an author naturally often makes use of his personal experiences, but a novel is not an autobiography. Goethe, for instance, did not, like his hero, commit suicide. Again, Goethe makes Werther an idle dilettante, who sketches a bit, reads a bit, but is incapable of seriously concentrating on anything. There is an element of self-portraiture in this: all his life, partly out of a temperamental impatience and partly because he was interested in so many things, he found it difficult to finish a work, but idleness was never one of his vices. When he wrote *Werther* he was probably in a disturbed state, for, a year after its publication, he wrote: "I am falling from one confusion into another." The novel seems to me to be one of those works of art in which the conscious and unconscious motives of the creator are at odds. Consciously, that is, Goethe approved of his hero, but his unconscious motive was therapeutic: by cultivating to the extreme, but only in words, the indulgence in subjective emotions typical of the *Sturm und Drang* movement, to get it out of his system and find his true poetic self, just as Byron, after *Childe Harold,* was able to put humorless gloom behind him and realize his true talent as a comic poet. Certainly, the admirers of *Werther* would have been bewildered by these lines written in Goethe's middle-age.

> *Vergebens werden ungebundne Geister*
> *Nach der Vollendung reiner Höhe streben.*
> *Wer Grosses will, muss sich zusammenraffen;*
> *In der Beschränkung zeigt sich erst der Meister,*
> *Und das Gesetz nur kann uns Freiheit geben.*

(Unfettered spirits will aspire in vain to the pure heights of perfection. He who wills great things must gird up his loins; only in limitation is mastery revealed, and law alone can give us freedom.)

Living in the twentieth century, not the eighteenth, and knowing, as most of his contemporaries did not, Goethe's later work, *Werther* can still fascinate us, but in a very different way. To us it reads not as a tragic love story, but as a masterly and devastating

portrait of a complete egoist, a spoiled brat, incapable of love because he cares for nobody and nothing but himself and having his
way at whatever cost to others. The theme of the egoist who imagines himself to be a passionate lover evidently fascinated Goethe,
for, thirty years later, he depicted a similar character in Edouard,
the husband in *Elective Affinities*.

Had Goethe, from the bottom of his heart, really wanted his
readers to admire Werther, why did he introduce the story of the
servant who is in love with his widowed mistress? After nursing
his love in secret for some time, he finally makes a pass at her, is
surprised in the act by her brother and, of course, fired. Shortly
afterwards, he shoots the servant who had taken his place, though
he has no grounds whatsoever for supposing that the latter had
succeeded where he had failed. Goethe not only introduces this
character but also makes Werther, the future suicide, identify the
murderer's situation with his own, thereby making it impossible
for the reader to think of suicide as "noble." Again, if Goethe
really wished us to be Werther's partisan in the erotic triangular
situation Werther-Lotte-Albert, one would have expected him to
make Albert a coarse philistine to whom Lotte is unhappily married, but he does not. Albert is, to be sure, a "square" who does
not appreciate Klopstock or Ossian, but he is presented as a good
man, affectionate, hard-working, a good provider, and Lotte as a
contented wife. Never once does she show any signs of wishing
she had married Werther instead. She is very fond of him, but
evidently thinks of him as a "brother" with whom she can have
interesting conversations. Her weakness, which is in part responsible for the final catastrophe, is a dislike of admitting disagreeable
facts: she keeps on hoping that Werther will get over his passion
and become just a good friend, when she should have realized that
this would never happen, and that the only sensible thing for her
to do was to show him the door.

To escape from his own emotional confusion, Goethe became
a civil servant at the court of Weimar, where he soon had important responsibilities. Similarly, in a moment of lucidity, aided by
the good advice of his friend Wilhelm, Werther realizes that the
only sensible thing for him to do is to give Lotte up, go away, and
take a job, also, apparently, as some sort of civil servant. The

society he now finds himself in is stuffy, snobbish, and conventional, but the Count, his boss, takes a great liking to him, and he seems all set for a successful career. Then a disagreeable but trivial incident occurs.

> [Count C.] had invited me for dinner at his house yesterday, on the very day when the whole aristocratic set, ladies and gentlemen, are accustomed to meet there late in the evening. I had completely forgotten this fact; and it also did not occur to me that subordinate officials like myself are not welcome on such occasions.

The "set" arrive and he senses that the atmosphere is chilly, but, instead of leaving, defiantly remains, is openly snubbed, and finally has to be asked by the Count to leave.

About this several things may be said. In the first place it is the professional duty of anyone in diplomacy or civil service not to forget the habits of the society in which he is living. Secondly, Werther is already well aware that the aristocratic set consider themselves superior to everyone else and, therefore, to himself, for he is not of aristocratic but bourgeois origins. Lastly, if a man thinks the social conventions of his time and place to be silly or wrong, there are two courses of behavior which will earn him an outsider's respect. Either he may keep his opinions to himself and observe the conventions with detached amusement, or he may deliberately break them for the pleasure of the shock he causes. He makes a scandal, but he enjoys it. Werther, by staying on when it is clear that his presence is unwelcome, defies the company, but his precious ego is hurt by their reactions, and he resigns from his post, returns to Lotte and disaster for all, destroying himself and ruining the lives of Lotte and Albert. What a horrid little monster!

Novella, published in 1828, four years before Goethe's death, is an excellent example of a literary genre, the idyll, at which German writers, more than those of any other language group, have always excelled. (I cannot think of a single English work which could be accurately classified as one.) It may be read as a postscript to one of his greatest masterpieces, the epic poem *Hermann und Dorothea,* published in 1798. Like the pastoral, the presupposition of the idyll is a harmonious relation between man and nature, desire and reason, but its descriptions of man and nature are much more realistic, less idealized, than those of the pastoral. An idyll, like a comedy, must end happily, but, unlike a comedy, it is always sober and serious.

In *Novella,* there are two significant locations, the town market and the old castle, and two types of human character, the huntsman and the trainer of wild animals. The market is an image for a good human society, peaceful, industrious, co-operative, prosperous.

> The Prince's father had lived long enough to see, and to put to good use, the day when it became clear that all the members of a state should spend their lives in the same industrious way; that everyone should work and produce according to his faculties, should first earn and then enjoy his living.

> There were mountain people, having come down from their quiet homes among rocks, firs and pines, and mixing with the plains people, who lived among hills, field and meadows; also tradespeople from small towns, and others who had assembled here. After having quietly surveyed the crowd, the Princess remarked to her companion how all these people, wherever they came from, used for their clothing more material than was necessary, more cloth and linen, more ribbon for trimming. "It seems to me that the women cannot pad themselves enough, nor the men puff themselves out enough to their satisfaction."
> "And we won't begrudge them that pleasure," said the old gentleman. "People are happy, happiest indeed, when they can spend their surplus money on dressing themselves up and decking themselves out."

The old castle, long a ruin and overwhelmed by the forest, is now being repaired, not, it seems, to make it rehabitable, but as a tourist sight. If I understand Goethe rightly, he is telling a parable about the relation between wild, that is to say untamed, nature and human craft, or *techne.* Man must respect Nature and not try to enslave her: on the other hand, Nature needs Man's help if she is to realize her full potentialities. The daemonic, destructive aspect of Nature is represented in the story by the fire which, for the second time, has broken out in the market and threatens to destroy it. It is to be noticed, however, that a fire in such a place is probably caused by human carelessness: it is not an "Act of God." Man can and should tame Fire, just as, if he will have the sensitivity and the patience, he can tame the lion and the tiger. All too often, however, he regards wild creatures as things to be killed and exploited for his own pleasure. Significantly, in describing the Prince's hunting expedition, Goethe uses a military metaphor.

> . . . the plan was to penetrate far into the mountains in order to harass the peaceful inhabitants of those forests by an unexpected invasion.

It is natural enough that the Princess should be scared when she sees the escaped tiger approaching and that Honorio should shoot it, though, as they are soon to learn, it would have done them no harm unless frightened. Honorio's second thoughts about his deed are more dubious.

> "Give it the finishing stroke!" cried the Princess. "I'm afraid the beast may still hurt you with its claws."
> "Excuse me, but it is already dead," the young man answered, "and I do not want to spoil its pelt which shall adorn your sledge next winter."

The same attitude is displayed by the castellan, who is annoyed that he cannot shoot the lion.

> "Why did I take my gun to town yesterday to have it cleaned! If I had had it handy, the lion would not have stood up again; the skin would be mine, and I would have bragged about it all my life, and justly so!"

The Prince, the Princess, Honorio are good people but they are in need of further education, of the lesson in reverence for Life which is given them by the humble family, man, wife and boy, to whom the tiger and the lion belonged. Because they are good people, they are willing to learn even from their social inferiors. It was a fine artistic stroke on Goethe's part to make the chief instructor the child, and let him deliver his message in song, not in prose.

*

ITALIAN JOURNEY

*

Everybody knows that the thrones of European Literature are occupied by the triumvirate referred to in *Finnegans Wake* as Daunty, Gouty, and Shopkeeper, but to most English-speaking readers the second is merely a name. German is a more difficult language to learn to read than Italian, and whereas Shakespeare, apparently, translates very well into German, Goethe is peculiarly resistant to translation into English; Hölderlin and Rilke, for example, come through much better. From a translation of *Faust*, any reader can see that Goethe must have been extraordinarily intelligent, but he will probably get the impression that he was too intellectual, too lacking in passion, because no translation can give a proper idea of Goethe's amazing command of every style of poetry, from the coarse to the witty to the lyrical to the sublime.

The reader, on the other hand, who does know some German and is beginning to take an interest in Goethe comes up against a cultural barrier, the humorless idolization of Goethe by German professors and critics who treat every word he ever uttered as Holy Writ. Even if it were in our cultural tradition to revere our great writers in this way, it would be much more difficult for us to idolize Shakespeare the man because we know nothing about him, whereas Goethe was essentially an autobiographical writer, whose life is the most documented of anyone who ever lived; compared with Goethe, even Dr. Johnson is a shadowy figure.

For those whose ignorance of German cuts them off from Goethe's poetry and who have an instinctive prejudice against professional sages, *Italian Journey* may well be the best book of his to start on. To begin with, there are hundreds and thousands of Englishmen and Americans who have made an Italian journey of their own and, to many of them, their encounter with Italy, its landscape, its people, its art, has been as important an experience as it was to Goethe, so that the subject-matter of the book will interest them, irrespective of its author, and they will enjoy comparing the post-World War II Italy they know with the pre-French-Revolution Italy which Goethe saw. (Speaking for myself, I am amazed at their similarity. Is there any other country in Europe where the character of the people seems to have been so little affected by political and technological change?)

Goethe did not go to Italy as a journalist in search of newsworthy stories, but some of the best passages in *Italian Journey* owe as much to journalistic good luck as they do to literary talent. While sketching a ruined fort in Malcesine he is nearly arrested as an Austrian spy; Vesuvius obliges with a major eruption during his stay in Naples; sailing back from Sicily, the boat he has taken is kind enough to get itself nearly shipwrecked on Capri; eccentric and comic characters cross his path, like the Neopolitan Princess with the outrageous tongue, the choleric Governor of Messina, or Miss Hart, the future Lady Hamilton, who seems—God forgive her!—to have invented the Modern Dance; a chance remark overheard leads to his meeting with the humble relatives of Cagliostro, the most famous international swindler of the time. Goethe is not usually thought of as a funny man, but his descriptions of such events reveal a real comic gift and, even more surprisingly, perhaps, they show how ready he was to see himself in a comic light.

To write a successful travel book, one must have an observant eye and a gift for description. Goethe held definite views about how things should be described, which are summed up in a letter he wrote in 1826 about a young writer who had consulted him.

> Up till now he has limited himself to subjective modern poetry, so self-concerned and self-absorbed. He does very well with anything confined to inner experience, feeling, disposition, and reflections on these; and he will deal suc-

cessfully with any theme where they are treated. But he has not yet developed his powers in connection with anything really objective. Like all young men, nowadays, he rather fights shy of reality, although everything imaginative must be based on reality, just as every ideal must come back to it. The theme I set this young man was to describe Hamburg as if he had just returned to it. The thread of ideas he followed from the start was the sentimental one of his mother, his friends, their love, patience, and help. The Elbe remained a stream of silver, the anchorage and the town counted for nothing, he did not even mention the swarming crowds—one might as easily have been visiting Naumburg or Merseburg. I told him this quite candidly; he could do something really good, if he could give a panorama of a great northern city as well as his feelings for his home and family.

Goethe's own practice is peculiar and reminds me in a strange way of the a-literature of some contemporary French novelists. The traditional method of description tries to unite the sensory perception of objects with the subjective feelings they arouse by means of a simile or a metaphorical image. This Goethe very rarely does. On the contrary, he deliberately keeps the sensory and the emotional apart. He makes enormous efforts, piling qualifying adjective on qualifying adjective, to say exactly what shape and color an object is, and precisely where it stands in spatial relation to other objects, but, in contrast to this precision, the adjectives he employs to express his emotional reactions are almost always vague and banal—words like *beautiful, important, valuable* occur over and over again.

The difficulty about this procedure is that, by its nature, language is too abstract a medium. No verbal description, however careful, can describe a unique object; at best, it describes objects of a certain class. The only media for showing an object in its concrete uniqueness are the visual arts and photography. Goethe, of course, knew this, and said so.

We ought to talk less and draw more. I, personally, should like to renounce speech altogether and, like organic nature, communicate everything I have to say in sketches.

He also knew, of course, that this was an exaggeration. There are certain characteristics of things which are every bit as "objective" as their visual appearance and with which only language can deal. A drawing can show what something is at a moment, but it cannot show us how it came to be that way or what will happen to it next; this only language can do. What gives Goethe's descriptions their value is not his "word-painting"—he cannot make us "see" a landscape or a building as D. H. Lawrence, for example, can—but his passionate interest in historical development—more than most writers he makes us aware of *why* things have come to be as they are. He always refused to separate the beautiful from the necessary, for he was convinced that one cannot really appreciate the beauty of anything without understanding what made it possible and how it came into being. To Goethe, a man who looks at a beautiful cloud without knowing, or wishing to know, any meteorology, at a landscape without knowing any geology, at a plant without studying its structure and way of growth, at the human body without studying anatomy, is imprisoning himself in that aesthetic subjectivity which he deplored as the besetting sin of the writers of his time.

Goethe is more successful at describing works of nature than he is at describing works of art. Indeed, the reader sometimes finds himself wishing he had more often practiced what he preached when he said: "Art exists to be seen, not to be talked about, except, perhaps, in its presence." One reason for this is, of course, that Goethe knew a lot about natural history and very little about art history. Another may be that the two kinds of history are different. Natural history, like social and political history, is continuous; there is no moment when nothing is happening. But the history of art is discontinuous; the art historian can show the influences and circumstances which made it possible and likely that a certain painter should paint in a certain way, *if he chooses to paint,* but he cannot explain why he paints a picture instead of not painting one. A work of nature and a great work of art both give us, as Goethe said, a sense of necessity, but whereas the necessity of nature is a *must,* that of art is an *ought.*

When, thirty years later, the first part of *Italian Journey* was published, the German artistic colony in Rome was outraged. Those whom he had not mentioned were offended, and the works he had failed to see and the judgments he passed on those he did made them say that he must have gone through Italy with his eyes shut.

This was unfair. Like everybody's, Goethe's taste had its limitations, owing in part to his temperament and in part to the age in which he lived. It seems that the Giotto frescoes in the Arena Chapel were not on view when he was in Padua, and we know that he tried to see them, but he deliberately refused to visit the Two Churches in Assisi. For Goethe there was no painting or sculpture between Classical antiquity and Mantegna.

Yet, when one considers how little painting and sculpture and architecture Goethe had seen before he came to Italy, one is astounded at his open-mindedness. Though Palladio, for example, is his ideal modern architect, he shows far more appreciation of Baroque than one would have expected, more indeed than most of his successors in the nineteenth century. He started out with a strong prejudice against Christian themes as subjects for paintings and overcame it. Though to him the Apollo Belvedere was the finest achievement in Greek art, he learned to admire works of the archaic period like Paestum, and though he professes to be shocked by the grotesque villa of the Prince of Pallagonia, the zest with which he describes it betrays his fascination. And, in any case, Goethe made no claim to be writing a guide to Italian art; he tells us what he looked at and liked, he makes no claim that his judgments are absolute, and though he may, in our view, have overpraised some pictures, I do not think that he condemned any which seem to us really good.

One reason why we enjoy reading travel books is that a journey is one of the archetypal symbols. It is impossible to take a train or an aeroplane without having a fantasy of oneself as a Quest Hero setting off in search of an enchanted princess on the Waters of Life. And then, some journeys—Goethe's was one—really are quests.

Italian Journey is not only a description of places, persons, and things, but also a psychological document of the first importance dealing with a life crisis which, in various degrees of intensity, we all experience somewhere between the ages of thirty-five and forty-five.

The first crisis in Goethe's life had occurred in 1775 when he was twenty-six and already famous as the author of *Götz von Berlichingen* and *Werther*. One might say, though it is a gross oversimplification, that the *Sturm und Drang* literary movement of which Goethe was then regarded as the leader stood for spontaneity of emotion as against convention and decorum, Shakespeare and Ossian as against Racine and Corneille, the warm heart as against the cool reason. Such a movement has often arisen in history and the consequences have almost always been the same; those who embrace it produce some remarkable work at an early age but then peter out if they do not, as they often do, take to drink or shoot themselves. An art which pits Nature against Art is bound to be self-defeating. What Kierkegaard called the aesthetic religion which puts all its faith in the mood of the immediate moment leads, first, to the "cultivation of one's hysteria with delight and terror," as Baudelaire put it, and, ultimately, to despair, and it brought Goethe to the brink of disaster. "I am falling," he wrote in April of 1775, "from one confusion into another." His father suggested a trip to Italy and he was making plans to go. At the beginning of November he was in Heidelberg; the young Duke of Weimar sent his coach and invited Goethe to join him. A day or two later Goethe did so.

One would not have expected a young poet, who was well enough off to do as he liked, to choose to become a civil servant at a small court when he could have chosen to go to Italy. That Goethe did so is proof of his amazing instinct, which he was to show all through his life, for taking the leap in the right direction. In the state he was in, what could rescue him from a meaningless existence was not freedom but a curtailment of freedom, that is to say, the curb upon his subjective emotions which would come from being responsible for people and things other than himself, and this was precisely what Weimar offered. With the exception of the Grand Duke and Duchess, who were only eighteen, Goethe was the youngest person at court, yet, a year later, he became a Privy Councillor and, in the course of the next ten years, found himself at one time and another responsible for the mines, the War Department, and the Finances of the Duchy. In addition to these duties and as a further defense against subjectivity, he began to study science seriously, and in March 1784, he made an important discovery: he was able to show that the inter-maxillary bone existed in man as well as in the other mammals.

Those first eleven years in Weimar were also the period of his platonic affair, conducted largely by notes and letters, with Charlotte von Stein, a rather plain married woman with three children and eleven years older than he. Again it seems strange that a man in his twenties and thirties should have been satisfied with such a "spiritual," uncarnal relationship; yet again, perhaps, it shows the soundness of Goethe's instinct. While, as a Privy Councillor, he was ready to take impersonal responsibility, he was not yet ready to take emotional responsibility for another person; what he needed at the time was emotional security without responsibility, and that is obtainable only in a platonic relationship, as to a mother or an older sister.

To an outsider, Goethe's life in 1786 must have looked enviable. He held an important position; he was admired and loved. Yet, in fact, he was on the verge of a breakdown. The stability which Weimar had given him was threatening to become a prison. Though it had enabled him to put *Werther* behind him, it had failed to give him any hints as to what kind of thing he should be writing instead, for, while he had come to Weimar to get away from *Werther,* it was as its author that Weimar had welcomed and still regarded him. His official life had had its remedial effect, but as public affairs were not his vocation, his duties were becoming senseless tasks which exhausted his energies without stimulating his imagination. His greatest gains had been in his scientific studies, yet here again Goethe was not a scientist by vocation but a poet; scientific knowledge was essential to the kind of poetry he wanted to write, but, so long as he remained in Weimar, his scientific researches and his poetry remained two separate activities without real influence upon each other. As for his Weimar friends, he was beginning—this is one of the misfortunes of genius—to outgrow them. Herder, to whom, since he was a young student in Strasburg, he had owed so much, had nothing more to teach him, and probably, Herder's schoolmaster temperament which liked to keep disciples was beginning to irk him. So far as Charlotte was concerned, Goethe seems to have been, like Yeats, a man in whom the need for physical sexual relations became imperative only relatively late in life; by 1786 it had.

When the idea of escaping from Weimar to Italy first occurred to him we shall never know. He tells us that the longing for "classic soil" had become so great that he dared not read the classics because they upset him too much, but his actual decision to go may have been taken at the very last moment. On August 28, he celebrated his thirty-seventh birthday in Carlsbad, where a number of the court were taking the waters. Two or three days later, all the party except Goethe and the Grand Duke returned to Weimar under the impression that Goethe was going on a short geological excursion into the mountains. After they had gone, Goethe asked the Duke for leave of absence and, at three in the morning on September 3, jumped into a coach with no servant and hardly any luggage, assumed the name of Möller, and bolted. He does not appear to have been very explicit about his plans even to his sovereign, for the Duke cannot have received his letter, dated September 2, until after he had left.

> Forgive me for being rather vague about my travels and absence when I took leave of you; even now I do not know quite what will happen to me.
>
> You are happy, you are moving towards an aim you wished and chose for yourself. Your domestic affairs are in good order and in a good way, and I know you will permit me now to think of myself. In fact, you have often urged me to do so. I am certainly not indispensable at this moment; and as for the special affairs entrusted to me, I have left them so that they can run on for a while quite comfortably without me. Indeed, I might even die without there being any great shock. I say nothing of how favourable these circumstances are at present and simply ask you for an indefinite leave of absence. The baths these two years have done a great deal for my health and I hope the greatest good for the elasticity of my mind, too, if it can be left to itself for a while to enjoy seeing the wide world.
>
> My first four volumes are complete at last. Herder has been a tireless and faithful helper; now I need to be at leisure and in the mood for the last four. I have undertaken

it all rather lightly, and I am only now beginning to see what is to be done if it is not to become a mess. All this and much else impels me to lose myself in places where I am totally unknown. I am going to travel quite alone, under another name, and I have great hopes of this venture, odd as it seems. But please don't let anyone notice that I shall be away for some time. Everyone working with or under me, everyone that has to do with me, expects me from one week to the next, and I want to leave it like that and, although absent, to be as effective as someone expected at any moment. . . .

The only person Goethe knew in Rome, and by correspondence only, was the German painter Tischbein. Through him Goethe was introduced to the German artistic colony, and, though he keeps telling Weimar how lonely he is, it is clear that he was soon leading quite an active social life. But in Rome he was free, as in Weimar he had not been, to choose his own company, and his anonymity, though it did not remain a secret for long, seems to have been respected. Whether by his own choice or because Italians were difficult to get to know, he stuck pretty closely to his fellow countrymen. Whereas in Weimar most of his friends had been older than he was, those of whom he saw most in Rome, with the exception of Angelica Kauffmann, were all younger. When Goethe was thirty-seven, Tischbein was thirty-five, Kayser, Kniep, and Schütz thirty-one, Moritz twenty-nine, Lipps twenty-eight, Meyer twenty-six, and Bury twenty-three. Only one of them, Moritz, was a writer and an intellectual, not one of them was a poet or a clergyman, and, again with the exception of Angelica, they were all poorer than he. For Goethe at this period in his life, such a company had many advantages. Before he came to Italy he had seen very little original architecture, sculpture and painting, Classical or Renaissance, and he had the common sense to realize that before he could understand and appreciate it properly, his eye would have to be educated. He also wanted to learn to draw, not so much for its own sake—he never fancied that he might become a serious artist—as for the discipline; drawing was the best way to train his mind to pay attention to the external world. To train his eye, to learn to draw, he needed the help of professional artists, which most of his Roman friends were. Secondly, if he were to develop as a poet, the best companionship for him at this point, failing a real literary equal like Schiller, was an unliterary one or, at least, a company whose literary judgments he did not have to take seriously. They all knew, of course, that he was a famous poet and Angelica was a sympathetic feminine audience, but they did not pretend to be expert judges of poetry, and if they objected to anything, he could disregard their criticisms in a way that he still found it difficult to ignore the criticisms which came from Weimar. He acknowledged a debt to Moritz's prosodical theories, but otherwise the fresh stimuli to his imagination came, not from conversations or reading, but from watching the behavior of Italians and living in the midst of Italian nature, the climate, shapes, and colors of which were so utterly different from the northern nature he had known hitherto. How necessary it was for Goethe to remove himself from the literary atmosphere of Weimar can be guessed from his letters about his new version of *Iphigenie* and *Egmont,* for it is clear that Weimar preferred the old versions and did not care for his new classical manner.

Lastly, an artistic, somewhat bohemian, foreign colony in a great city gave him a freedom in his personal life which would have been out of the question at a provincial German court. As he gives us only his side of the correspondence, we have to infer what the reactions of Weimar were to his whole Italian venture. It seems fairly clear that they were hurt, suspicious, disapproving, and jealous. If the reader sometimes becomes impatient with Goethe's endless reiterations of how hard he is *working,* what a lot of *good* Italy is doing him, he must remember that Goethe is trying to placate his friends for being obviously so radiantly happy without them. One of the reasons why his account of his time in Rome, particularly of his second stay, is less interesting than the rest of *Italian Journey* is that one feels much is happening to Goethe which is of great importance to him, but which he declines to tell. There is no reason to suppose that Goethe's life in Rome was anything like Byron's in Venice, but it is impossible to believe that it was quite so respectable, or so exclusively devoted to higher things as, in his letters home, for obvious reasons, he makes it sound. The difference between the over-refined, delicate, almost neurasthenic face of the pre-Italian portraits and the masculine, self-assured face in the portraits executed after his return is very striking; the latter is that of a man who has known sexual satisfaction.

If Goethe did not tell everything, what he did tell was true enough. He did work very hard and Italy did do him a lot of good. Any writer will find *Italian Journey* fascinating for what Goethe says about his own methods of working. He would compose with extraordinary rapidity and in his head—if he did not write it down at once, he often forgot it—and under any circumstances: there cannot be many poets who have been able to write while suffering from seasickness. His chief difficulty, partly out of a temperamental impatience and partly because he kept having so many ideas and was interested in so many things, was in finishing a work. He starts re-writing *Iphigenie auf Tauris* and becomes distracted by the thought of another play, *Iphigenie in Delphi;* he is walking in the Public Gardens of Palermo, planning a new play about Nausicaa, when suddenly he is struck by an idea about the Primal Plant, and Botany chases away the Muse.

And he has so many unfinished pieces. When at last he finishes *Iphigenie,* begun in 1779, there is *Egmont* waiting, begun in 1775. He finishes *Egmont,* and there are two old *Singspiele* to rewrite. These done with, he takes out the yellowed manuscript of *Faust,* which is eighteen years old, and adds a scene or two, and he departs from Rome with the nine-year-old *Tasso* to re-work while traveling. And he does all this in the midst of social life, sightseeing, collecting coins, gems, minerals, plaster casts, taking drawing lessons, attending lectures on perspective and making botanical experiments. If to read about such energy is rather exhausting, to read about a man who is so enjoying himself is enormous fun.

We* have tried to produce a translation, not a crib. A crib is like a pair of spectacles for the weak-sighted; a translation is like a book in Braille for the blind. A translator, that is to say, has to assume that his readers cannot and never will be able to read the original. This, in its turn, implies that they are not specialists in his author. On the one hand, they probably know very little about him; on the other, their appetite for scholarly footnotes is probably small.

The translator's most difficult problem is not *what* his author

* *Italienische Reise* was translated with Elizabeth Mayer.

says but his tone of voice. How is a man who thought and wrote in German to think and write in English and yet remain a unique personality called Goethe? To offer a translation to the public is to claim that one does know how Goethe would have written had English been his native tongue, to claim, in fact, that one has mediumistic gifts, and, as we all know, mediums are often rather shady characters.

The circumstances under which *Italian Journey* was written, put together and published present a special problem. Most of its contents are based upon letters and a journal written at the time, but it was not until twenty-five years later that Goethe set to work to make a book out of them, and the third part was not published until he was almost eighty. A compilation of this kind involves editing, and it must be admitted that, as an editor, Goethe did not do a very good job. If a man writes two letters at the same time to two different people, it is only to be expected that he will repeat himself a little, and if at the end of an exciting and exhausting day he hurriedly jots down the events in his journal, it is natural enough if there is some disorder in his narrative—what should have come first comes as an afterthought, etc.—but if he decides to make a book out of such material, one has a right to expect him to cut out what is repetitious, to rearrange what is chaotic and clarify what is obscure.

Even in the first two parts of *Italian Journey,* there are places where Goethe has been careless. For instance, he presents his visit to Cagliostro's relatives as a passage from his journal, dated April 13 and 14, 1787. But suddenly, without warning, the reader finds him referring to events which did not take place until 1789. What Goethe has actually done is to print, not his original journal, but a talk about Cagliostro based on it which he gave in Weimar in 1792. As for Part Three, one can only conclude that Goethe handed the material over to his secretary without re-reading it and that the secretary was too overawed by the great man to suggest any corrections.

We have seen fit to do some editing ourselves. One previous English translator, an Anglican clergyman, omitted all favorable references made by Goethe to the Roman Catholic Church; we have confined ourselves to stylistic matters. We have cut some passages which seemed to us unduly repetitious and some allusions to things which were known to his correspondents but would be unintelligible to a reader without a lengthy note, and, here and there, we have transposed sentences to a more logical position. We have also omitted the whole article *Concerning the Pictorial Imitation of the Beautiful.* Our official excuse is that the ideas in it are not Goethe's but Moritz's; our real reason is that it is verbose rubbish and sounds like a parody of "deep" German prose.

To those who regard such tinkering as sacrilege, we can only cite the authority of the Master himself (*to Streckfuss, 1827*).

If the translator has really understood his author, he will be able to evoke in his own mind not only what the author has done, but also what he wanted and ought to have done. That at least is the line I have always taken in translation, though I make no claim that it is justifiable.

*

MR. G.

*

This excellent compilation* happens to be dedicated to me, but I am not going to allow this honor to stop me from log-rolling.

Many authors, composers, and painters have become internationally famous during their lifetimes, but Goethe is the only one I can think of who became, and for the last twenty-five years of his life remained, an international tourist attraction. For anyone making a European tour, male or female, old or young, German, French, Russian, English, or American, "visiting" Goethe was as essential an item on their itinerary as "doing" Florence or Venice.

This seems all the odder when one remembers that, to most of his visitors, he was the author of a single book. *The Sorrows of Werther,* written when he was a young man. Even inside Germany, only a few of his later writings, *Hermann and Dorothea, Faust Part I,* had enjoyed great success: some of his best works, *The Roman Elegies* and the *West-Oestliche Divan* for example, were read by few and liked by even fewer, and when the Second Part of *Faust* was published posthumously, a reviewer said: "Just as this book has physically appeared after the end of Goethe's bodily life, so also its intellectual content has survived his genius."

* *Goethe: Conversations and Encounters.* Edited and translated by David Luke and Robert Pick.

How and why Goethe should have acquired the reputation, among people who knew so little about him, for being a sage and public oracle is to me a mystery, and it is not the only one. What I find really surprising about Goethe's character is, not that he should have treated some of his visitors with icy formality, that some who arrived, expecting to receive pearls of wisdom, came away with nothing better than an *Umph!* or a *Do you really think so?,* but that Goethe should have consented to see them at all. Now and again a stupid visitor might be accidentally entertaining, like the Englishman who, having misread *das ächzende Kind* (the sobbing child) as *das achtzehnte Kind* (the eighteenth child) told Goethe he was surprised "that the father in the Erlkönig ballad was described as being so excessively concerned about the boy, when after all he had been blessed with so large a family"; but how many of them must have been plain crashing bores.

How on earth did Goethe stand it, year after year? Perhaps a passage from *Dichtung und Wahrheit,* which Messrs. Luke and Pick quote in their Introduction, offers a partial explanation:

> When I was alone I would, in imagination, summon some person of my acquaintance into my presence. I would request him to be seated, and discuss with him the subject that I happened to have in mind. He would then occasionally reply or express his agreement or disagreement by the usual gestures. . . . The strange thing was that the persons whom I selected for this purpose were never those of my closer acquaintance, but others whom I hardly ever saw, indeed some who lived in an entirely different part of the world and with whom I had only fleeting contact. But usually they were persons of a receptive rather than productive nature, who were prepared to listen quietly, with interest, and with a mind free of prejudice, to things which lay within their scope; although occasionally, for these dialectical exercises, I would summon natures more given to contradiction.

It is clear from this confession that, for Goethe, conversation meant a monologue. What he did with an imaginary audience he could do equally well with a real one. Given a bottle of wine and an attentive audience, he would start to hold forth on whatever was preoccupying his mind, less for the sake of his listeners than for his own. With a real audience, there is always the danger, of course, that the questions or objections they raise may not be those the monologist would have invented for them, but it would seem that in practice, Goethe was seldom interrupted. It is refreshing, therefore, to discover that, on one occasion at least, not only did someone flatly contradict him, but also Goethe had the grace to admit, with an effort, to be sure, that he was wrong:

> . . . on one occasion, at the Duke of Weimar's dinner-table, he delivered a long lecture on the science of artillery and in particular on the most effective positioning of batteries . . . I said: "My dear Herr Legationsrat! with all due respect, may I take the liberty of replying to you with Pomeranian frankness? In our country there is an old proverb: Cobbler, stick to your last! When you talk about the theater and literature and many other learned or artistic matters, we are all delighted to listen to you. . . . But it is quite another matter when you begin talking about gunnery and even trying to instruct us officers in it; for if you will excuse my saying so, this is something about which you know absolutely nothing" . . . Goethe at first turned quite red in the face at my words, whether with anger or with embarrassment I do not know . . . but he soon regained his full presence of mind and said with a laugh: "Well, you gentlemen from Pomerania certainly believe in frankness, one might almost say in rudeness, as I have just heard for myself all too clearly. But let's not quarrel about it, my dear Lieutenant! You have just taught me a very downright lesson, and I shall take good care not to talk about gunnery in your presence again or try to teach officers their own business." So saying, he shook me very cordially by the hand, and we remained the best of friends; indeed, it even seemed to me that Goethe now sought my company still more than he had previously done.
>
> (*A Prussian Artillery-officer*)

What happens when two monologists meet? After his meeting with Madame de Staël, Goethe reported to his friends:

> "It was an interesting hour. I was unable to get a word in; she talks well, but at length, at great length."—Meanwhile

a circle of ladies demanded to know what impression our Apollo had made on his visitor. She too confessed that she had failed to get in a word. "But" (she is said to have re-marked with a sigh) "when anyone talks so well, it is a pleasure to listen to him."

(*Amalie von Helvig*)

As a conversationalist, Goethe was not, like Sydney Smith or Oscar Wilde, a maker of witty epigrams. "How dare a man," he once remarked, "have a sense of humor when he considers his immense burden of responsibilities towards himself and others. However," he went on to say, "I have no wish to pass censure on the humorists. After all, does one have to have a conscience? Who says so?" Moreover, there is good evidence that, when he felt in the mood, he could make people laugh. The historian Heinrich Luden reproduces from memory an anecdote as told by Goethe about an encounter with an eccentric old Austrian general: It is unlikely that he improved upon Goethe's actual performance, yet what he gives us is extremely funny.

Nor was Goethe, like Dr. Johnson, a master of the lapidary statement. Neither in his recorded conversation nor his written works will one find an isolated memorable sentence like—"Sunday should be different from other days: people may walk but not throw stones at birds." (In his prose, that is: many of his verse epigrams are concise enough.)

One might say that Goethe, like Henry James—who also, curiously enough, in later life dictated his literary work—talked like a book, only one must add, "like a good book." Goethe's spoken words, that is to say, while not sounding in the least arti-ficial and stilted, have certain characteristics which we normally expect to find in words written to be read. The thought unit is the paragraph rather than the sentence; the sentences issue from his lips without hesitation, each syntactically perfect, and succeeding each other in a logical order. Goethe is one of the very few persons in history whose talk one wishes could have been tape-recorded rather than reproduced from memory by others.

Of course, the records we possess cannot represent the full range of his conversation. The only person in Goethe's life who was both his friend and his intellectual equal was Schiller and, though we have their correspondence, we know nothing about how they actually talked to each other when they were alone together. Nor do we know how Goethe talked to his wife, Christiane, when they were alone together. Most of the accounts we have were written by people with whom, however well he may have liked them personally, Goethe must have been conscious of his intellectual superiority, aware that, if he were to tell them exactly what he thought on many subjects, they would find him unintelligible or shocking.

Among the posthumously published poems of Goethe, there are some upon sexual and religious themes of a startling frankness (plug: several of these may be found in the Penguin volume of Goethe's *Poems,* selected and edited by David Luke) and we know that he sometimes talked in a similar vein. Those who heard him on such occasions kept the experience to themselves, either because they were genuinely shocked or, which is more likely, because they belonged to a civilized generation which still recognized the difference, today almost wholly ignored, between what may be said in public and what should only be said in private. *Conversations and Encounters* includes a description of one occasion when Goethe set out to be *épatant.* The French-speaking Swiss, Soret, had suggested to Goethe that, if he had been born an Englishman, he would have been a political Liberal.

> "What do you take me for?" retorted Goethe, assuming the paradoxical and ironical tone of his Mephistopheles, and thus giving a fresh turn to the conversation, no doubt in order to avoid political discussion, which he dislikes. "If I had been born an Englishman—which thank God I was not! I should have been a millionaire duke or rather a bishop with an income of thirty thousand pounds a year."
>
> "Excellent!" I replied, "but supposing you had chanced to draw an unlucky number instead of the winning one? There are a great many unlucky numbers."
>
> "My dear fellow," replied Goethe, "not all of us are born for the winning draw. Do you really think I should have committed the *sottise* of drawing unlucky? . . . I should have lied and dissembled so hard and so long, both in verse and in prose, that my thirty thousand a year would have been a certainty. One must get to the top if one is not

to be crushed, and at the height of one's greatness one must bear well in mind that the mob is a collection of fools and imbeciles. One would only be increasing their number if one could not turn to one's own advantage the abuses which have been established thanks to their folly, and from which others would profit if we ourselves did not."

Messrs. Luke and Pick, while doing justice to the obvious sources, like Riemer and Eckermann—I am very glad to see that, in their introduction, they have the courage to stand up for the *Conversations* which it is now the fashion to decry—have unearthed many items which will be unfamiliar to most readers.

I myself was particularly interested by the extract from Count Alexander Stroganoff's diary. Stroganoff came prepared to dislike Goethe heartily, for he detested circles of literary adorers and had not enjoyed Goethe's writings very much, yet, in the end, he was completely won over by Goethe the man.

Again, I knew that Goethe hated men who wore spectacles, but I never knew the reason before.

> I always feel that strangers who wear them are treating me as an object to be carefully inspected, that their armed gaze is piercing the most secret recesses of my mind and searching my old face for its tiniest wrinkle. But in trying to get to know me this way they are destroying all just equality between us by preventing me from getting to know them in return.

What would poor Goethe have suffered if sunglasses had been invented in his day?

Goethe's well-known dislike of dogs is in itself a fact of no great significance, except insofar as it points to an area of relative unconcern, surprising in a man with such an extraordinary wide range of interests. Goethe was passionately interested in human beings, weather, stones, and vegetables, but, in the animal kingdom, although he made one important anatomical discovery, he showed, for Goethe, little curiosity. The reason he gave Riemer for this is rather odd: animals have no conversation.

> Animals only interested him as more or less close organizational approximations to man, provisional forerunners of

the eventually manifest lord of creation. He did not despise them, indeed he even studied them, but chiefly he pitied them as masked and muffled creatures unable to express their feelings intelligibly and appropriately.

Goethe once said that the only time in his life when he had been really happy was the months he spent in Rome. He may have been exaggerating, but it is certainly true that his sojourn in Italy was the only time in his grown-up life when he was a completely free man, with no obligation to do anything or see anyone unless he chose. In Weimar, whether as a Civil Servant, a theater *intendant,* or a social lion, he had many irksome obligations.

> My real happiness lay in my poetic meditations and creations. But these were very much disturbed and limited and hindered by my worldly position. If I had been able to withdraw more from my involvement in public affairs and business, and to live a more solitary life, I should have been happier and could have done much more as a writer.

His worldly position, however, was of his own choosing and, had he decided to withdraw into a more solitary life, nobody would have stopped him.

My own feeling is that Goethe probably suffered much more from melancholia than he was willing to admit to others, either in his conversation or his writings, and, for that reason, was afraid of being alone. Further, for all his dislike of fanaticism in party politics, in his own way Goethe, too, believed that a writer should be "committed," that a purely literary life was inadequate for a human being, since every man is, in the Greek sense of the words, "a political animal," with social responsibilities that he cannot ignore without stunting his nature.

Goethe was an extremely complicated character and, in most Englishmen and Americans at least, he arouses mixed feelings. Sometimes one feels that he is a pompous old bore, sometimes that he is a dishonest old hypocrite or, as Byron said, "an old fox who won't leave his hole, and preaches a fine sermon from inside it." Yet, grumble as one may, one is forced in the end to admit that he was a great poet and a great man. Moreover, when I read the following anecdote:

Goethe suddenly got out of the carriage to examine a stone, and I heard him say: "Well, well! how did *you* get here?"—a question which he repeated. . . .

I find myself exclaiming, not "Great Mr. G!" but "Dear Mr. G!"

PORTRAIT OF A WHIG

Sydney Smith was born in 1771, two years after the invention of Watt's steam-engine and one year after Goldsmith's *Deserted Village,* that vivid description of the effects of land enclosure. It was still dangerous to walk through the streets of London after dark, there were no waterproof hats, no braces, no calomel, no quinine, no clubs, no savings banks, the government was completely in the hands of great landowners, and, in the best society, one third of the gentlemen were always drunk. He died in 1845, which was also the year in which Engels' *State of the Working Classes in England* was published and Newman was received into the Roman Catholic Church. The American Revolution, the French Revolution, the Napoleonic wars, the Romantic Movement had all occurred, there was gaslight in houses, there were railways through the country, the Victorian proprieties were firmly established (Bowdler's *Shakespeare* appeared in 1818) and public opinion had forced Parliament to soften the rigors of pure laisser-faire (the first Factory Act was passed in 1833).

Sydney Smith's mother, Maria Olier, came of French Huguenot stock; his father, Robert Smith, was an eccentric unstable character who left his bride at the church door and departed to America for several years, spent the rest of his life in travel and unsuccessful speculations, and insisted on his family sitting over the dinner table in the half-dark for hours. His children, however, did better for themselves: three of his sons went to India (the only daughter stayed, of course, at home), where one died young and the other two made fortunes; Sydney, his second son, ended up as a Canon of St. Paul's and the most famous wit of his generation.

Physically, he was swarthy, sturdy tending to stoutness and suffering in later life from gout. Mentally, like so many funny men, he had to struggle constantly against melancholia: he found it difficult to get up in the morning, he could not bear dimly lit rooms —"Better," he wrote, "to eat dry bread by the splendour of gas than to dine on wild beef with wax-candles"—and music in a minor key upset him. Writing to a friend who was similarly afflicted, he gave his own recipe for combating low spirits.

1. Go into the shower-bath with a small quantity of water at a temperature low enough to give you a slight sensation of cold, 75° or 80°.
2. Short views of human life—not further than dinner or tea.
3. Be as busy as you can.
4. See as much as you can of those friends who respect and like you, and of those acquaintances who amuse you.
5. Attend to the effects tea and coffee produce upon you.
6. Avoid poetry, dramatic representations (except comedy), music, serious novels, sentimental people, and everything likely to excite feeling and emotion, not ending in active benevolence.
7. Keep good blazing fires.
8. Be firm and constant in the exercise of rational religion.

This illustrates well enough both the virtues of his mind and its limitations. Such a man will always have an excellent grasp of the concrete and the immediately possible, but one must not expect from him profound speculative insights. Sydney Smith was perfectly sincere in his religious faith, but one is not surprised to find that, as a young man, his ambition was to read for the Bar and that it was only lack of money which compelled him instead to take Holy Orders. In his admirable attacks on religious intolerance the reader cannot but be conscious of a distrust of all theological dogma until

he wonders whether Sydney Smith could have explained just why
he was an Anglican and not, say, a Unitarian. His criticisms of the
Methodists and the Puseyites are acute enough but one cannot help
feeling that it was religious "enthusiasm" as such, not merely the
follies to which it is liable, which aroused his scorn and distrust.

II

The finances of the Church Visible are always a fascinating subject.
As a State Church, the revenues of the Church of England are derived, partly from property which it owns, partly from taxation
but comparatively little from the alms of the faithful. Patronage
is not solely in the hands of the Crown; some livings are bestowed
by bishops, some by cathedral chapters and many by private
patrons. With its money it has to pay for the upkeep of churches
and parsonages and to secure for every parish, if it can, a vicar of
good manners and education. Moreover, since most Anglican
clergymen are married men, they will need enough money to support and educate their families.

In Sydney Smith's time, by his own calculations, the total revenues of the Church would, if equally divided, have been sufficient
to give every minister, excluding curates, an annual income of £250
—"about the same as that enjoyed by the upper domestic of a
nobleman." Needless to say, its revenues were not so divided, but
ranged from rich sees like Canterbury, worth £25,000, to country
livings worth no more than £150. In the competition for preferment, those who had sufficient private means to endure the rigors
of their early clerical years and those with good social connections
who could gain the ears of the disposers of patronage had, naturally, a great advantage. It was not, however, impossible for a
person of humble birth to succeed. Sydney Smith paints the following picture of the ecclesiastical career of a baker's son:

> Young Crumpet is sent to school—takes to his books—
> spends the best years of his life, as all eminent Englishmen
> do, in making Latin verses—knows that the *crum* in crum-
> pet is long, and the *pet* short—goes to the University—gets
> a prize for an Essay on the Dispersion of the Jews—takes
> orders—becomes a Bishop's chaplain—has a young noble-

man for his pupil—publishes an useless classic, and a serious call to the unconverted—and then goes through the Elysian transitions of Prebendary, Dean, Prelate, and the long train of purple, profit and power.

It is not hard to deduce from this description the personal qualities best fitted for a rise from obscurity to a mitre: an unoriginal brightness of intellect which is good at passing exams but not at thinking for itself, a proper respect for titles, a talent for flattery, a solemn mien and, above all, Tory political opinions.

Sydney Smith possessed none of these; intellectual ability he had in abundance but a dangerously lively kind; though he came to number many titled and rich people among his friends, he was utterly without snobbery and incapable of flattery; he was continually making jokes and, worst of all, he was a convinced Whig. Yet, starting from the bottom—with an income of £100 a year and no influential friends—he rose, if not to a bishopric, to a residential canon of St. Paul's at a salary of £2000 a year. It may be not without interest to consider how he did it. His career began with a stroke of good luck: the local squire of the Wiltshire village where he was a young curate took a shine to him and asked him to accompany his son as a tutor on the Grand Tour. Sydney Smith recommended Weimar but the outbreak of war made it impossible and they went to Edinburgh instead. There he met Jeffrey, Brougham, and Francis Horner and started with them *The Edinburgh Review,* devoted to the criticism of contemporary literature and the furthering of Whig policies. The review was an instantaneous success and Smith began to be talked about. In 1800 he married for love and the marriage seems to have remained a singularly happy one. The only gift he had for his bride was six worn silver teaspoons and she, though she possessed some small means of her own, had presently to sell her mother's jewelry to meet expenses. In 1803 the couple moved to London, where he managed to live by preaching at the Foundling Hospital and lecturing on Moral Philosophy at The Royal Institution. Through his elder brother he was introduced into the Holland House circle, the center of Whig society, of which he quickly became a popular and admired member. He was still, however, too poor to afford an umbrella, far less a carriage; moreover, his new friends, while cultivated and rich, belonged to the party which was out of power and likely to remain so. Again, he had a stroke of luck for, after Pitt's death, the Whigs came into power for a few months, just long enough to appoint him to the living of Foston in Yorkshire, worth £500 a year. Foston had not had a resident vicar since the reign of Charles II and Smith had no intention of leaving the social amenities of London which he loved for the country which he regarded as "a healthy grave" and where it seemed to him as if "the whole creation were going to expire at tea-time." In 1808, however, a Tory government passed the Clergy Residence Bill and he was banished, at the age of thirty-eight, to a village "twelve miles from a lemon," its existing parsonage a brick-floored kitchen with one room above it, there to do duty for the next twenty years.

Any man might have quailed at the prospect but for an intellectual and man-about-town like Smith, anonymous author of *The Peter Plymley Letters* which had electrified the public and enraged the government, accustomed to the best tables, the best conversation, the most elegant ladies and gentlemen, it must have seemed the end, and a stranger might well have expected him to lapse into despondency and drink. He did nothing of the kind. He kept up his reading, his reviewing, and his large correspondence; he designed a new parsonage for himself and got the local carpenter to furnish it; he devised all sorts of ingenious gadgets—devices for adding draft to the fires, devices to prevent smoky chimneys, lamps burning mutton-fat to save the expense of candles, a special scratcher pole for all his animals etc., and, far from neglecting his parish duties, became one of the best county vicars of whom there is record, and the idol of his parishioners. Church services were only a small part of his ministrations: he started small vegetable gardens, let out to the laborers at very low rents, to help them augment their food supply; he experimented with diets to discover which were both cheap and nourishing; he acted as their doctor and, as a local magistrate, saved many of them from going unjustly to jail.

During the first half of his residence at Foston, he was never free from financial anxiety—during the bad harvest year of 1816, for instance, he could no more afford to buy white flour than could his parishioners—but in 1820 an unexpected legacy from an aunt lightened his burden and in 1828, as in 1808, a brief Coalition Ministry including Whigs remembered him and procured him a canonry at Bristol and the living of Combe Florey in Somerset which, though it did not increase his income, was a step up in the Ecclesiastical Hierarchy.

From then on his life was smooth sailing: two causes in which he was a leader triumphed—the Catholic Emancipation Act was passed in 1829 and the Reform Bill in 1832; his services were rewarded in his sixty-first year by a canonry at St. Paul's; and then his unmarried younger brother died, leaving him a third of his very large fortune. He was now rich, popular, and famous. A letter he wrote shortly before his death aptly describes the last fourteen years of his life:

> Being Canon of St. Paul's in London, and a rector of a parish in the country, my time is divided equally between town and country. I am living among the best society in the Metropolis, and at ease in my circumstances; in tolerable health, a mild Whig, a tolerating Churchman, and much given to talking, laughing and noise. I dine with the rich in London, and physic the poor in the country; passing from the sauces of Dives to the sores of Lazarus. I am, upon the whole, a happy man, have found the world an entertaining place, and am thankful to Providence for the part alloted to me in it.

III

Many of Sydney Smith's wisecracks are widely known. Nowell Smith's definitive edition of his letters (Oxford Press, 1953) must already have convinced many readers that he is among the supreme masters of the epistolary art, but his published writings still seem to be little known. This is understandable because Smith was not a poet or a novelist but from first to last a writer of polemics, as pure an example as we have in English of *l'écrivain engagé*.

As a general rule it is the fate of the polemical writer to be forgotten when the cause for which he fought has been won or is no longer a live issue, and it will always be difficult to persuade a later generation that there can be exceptions, polemical writers, journalists if you will, of such brilliance and charm that they can be read with delight and admiration by those to whom their subject matter is in itself of little interest.

Literary criticism, too, is apt to avoid the polemical writer because there is little to say about him. Unlike the creator of "pure" literature, the poet, the novelist, the dramatist etc., he rarely shows "development," stylistic or ideological. His cast of mind, his way of expressing himself are generally established early and any variety that his work may show will come mostly from a variety in the topics upon which he writes.

Nevertheless there are a few such authors who must be ranked very high by any literary standard and first among such I would place Hooker, Swift, Sydney Smith and Bernard Shaw. Milton in his polemical works is too bad-mannered and abusive, and Junius, for all his brilliance, too biased.

Of them all, Sydney Smith has, perhaps, the most exact sense of the particular audience he is addressing on any given occasion, and the widest variation of tone. He can equally well speak to the average educated man—

> It is necessary that the Archbishop of Canterbury should give feasts to Aristocratic London; and that the domestics of the Prelacy should stand with swords and bag-wigs round pig and turkey, and venison, to defend, as it were, the Orthodox gastronome from the fierce Unitarian, the fell Baptist, and all the famished children of Dissent.
> *(Letters to Archdeacon Singleton)*

to the unlettered rustic—

> I don't like that red nose, and those blear eyes, and that stupid, downcast look. You are a drunkard. Another pint, and one pint more; a glass of gin and water, rum and milk, cider and pepper, a glass of peppermint, and all the beastly fluids which drunkards pour down their throats. . . . It is all nonsense about not being able to work without ale, and gin, and cider, and fermented liquors. Do lions and cart-horses drink ale? It is mere habit. . . . I have no objection, you will observe, to a moderate use of ale, or any other liquor you can *afford* to purchase. My objection is, that you cannot afford it; that every penny you spend at the ale-

house comes out of the stomachs of the poor children, and strips off the clothes of the wife—

(Advice to Parishioners)

and a child—

Lucy, dear child, mind your arithmetic. You know, in the first sum of yours I ever saw, there was a mistake. You had carried two (as a cab is licensed to do) and you ought, dear Lucy, to have carried but one. Is this a trifle? What would life be without arithmetic but a scene of horrors? . . . I now give you my parting advice. Don't marry any body who has not a tolerable understanding and a thousand a year, and God bless you, dear child.

Always lucid, well-informed and fair to his opponents, he is equally at home with the long period and the short, the ornate vocabulary and the plain, and is a master of every rhetorical effect, the satirical inversion—

Their object is to preserve game; they have no objection to preserve the lives of their fellow creatures also, if both can exist at the same time; if not, the least worthy of God's creatures must fall—the rustic without a soul—not the Christian partridge—not the immortal pheasant—not the rational woodcock, or the accountable hare.

the ironic description of shocking facts in tea-table terms—

One summer's whipping, only one: the thumb-screw for a short season; a little light easy torturing between Lady-day and Michaelmas.

the homely simile—

You may not be aware of it yourself, most reverend Abraham, but you deny their freedom to the Catholics upon the same principle that Sarah your wife refuses to give the receipt for a ham or a gooseberry dumpling: she refuses her receipts, not because they secure to her a certain flavour, but because they remind her that her neighbours want it: a feeling laughable in a priestess, shameful in a priest; venial when it withholds the blessings of him, tyrannical and execrable when it narrows the boon of religious freedom.

and the ringing peroration of righteous anger—

> If I lived at Hampstead upon stewed meats and claret; if I
> walked to church every Sunday before eleven young gentle-
> men of my own begetting with their faces washed, and their
> hair pleasingly combed; if the Almighty had blessed me
> with every earthly comfort—how awfully would I pause
> before I sent forth the flame and the sword over the cabins
> of the poor, brave, generous, open-hearted peasants of
> Ireland. . . . The vigour I love consists in finding out
> wherein subjects are aggrieved, in relieving them, in study-
> ing the temper and genius of a people, in consulting their
> prejudices, in selecting proper persons to lead and manage
> them, in the laborious, watchful, and difficult task of in-
> creasing happiness by allaying each particular discontent.
> . . . But this, in the eyes of Mr. Percival, is imbecility and
> meanness: houses are not broken open—women are not
> insulted—the people seem all to be happy; they are not rode
> over by horses, and cut by whips. Do you call this vigour?
> Is this government?

His command of comic effects is equally extensive and masterly.
Many of his impromptu puns are still remembered, such as his
remarks on hearing two women screaming insults at each other
from upper stories on opposite sides of a narrow street in Edinburgh:

> Those two women will never agree: they are arguing from
> different premises.

His particular forte, perhaps, is the treatment of analogical
situations as identical; during the period of the Luddite riots he
wrote to a friend:

> What do you think of all these burnings? and have you
> heard of the new sort of burnings? Ladies' maids have taken
> to setting their mistresses on fire. Two dowagers were
> burned last week, and large rewards are offered! They are
> inventing little fire-engines for the toilet table, worked with
> lavender water!

Lastly, he can create pictures in what might be called the
ludicrous baroque style, as surely as Pope:

Frequently did Lord John meet the destroying Bishops; much did he commend their daily heap of ruins; sweetly did they smile on each other, and much charming talk was there of meteorology and catarrh, and the particular cathedral they were pulling down at the time; till one fine morning the Home Secretary, with a voice more bland, and a look more ardently affectionate, than that which the masculine mouse bestows on his nibbling female, informed them that the Government meant to take all the Church property into their own hands, to pay the rates out of it, and deliver the residue to the rightful possessors. Such an effect, they say, was never before produced by a *coup de théâtre*. The Commission was separated in an instant: London clenched his fist; Canterbury was hurried out by his chaplains, and put into a warm bed; a solemn vacancy spread itself over the face of Gloucester; Lincoln was taken out in strong hysterics.

IV

Sydney Smith is a perfect expression of the Whig mentality, of that English form of Liberalism which has always perplexed and sometimes enraged Continental observers both on the political Right and on the political Left. European liberalism, which has normally been anti-clerical, republican, and materialist, finds it bewildering that social reform in England should owe so much to religion—that the British Labour Party, for example, should be so closely associated with the Evangelical movement, and the increasing concern over juvenile delinquency and other cultural problems of urbanization with Anglo-Catholicism—and that the English Liberal who desires the abolition of the Crown or the House of Lords should be so rare a bird. Liberals like Godwin and H. G. Wells are atypical, and much closer to the European mind.

For the European who knows a little history, it is all the more puzzling, since he is aware that Voltaire and the French Encyclopaedists of the Enlightenment who were the founders of continental Liberalism were inspired by and took many of their ideas from Locke, the Deists, and the Whig authors of the Glorious

Revolution of 1688. If he is a pro-clerical monarchist, he is apt to conclude that the English Liberal is a materialist at heart who is only using religious sentiments as a smoke-screen, and to point to the ambiguities of the Thirty-Nine Articles as proof that an Anglican does not know what he believes; if he is an anti-clerical rationalist, he is apt to come to similar doubts about the Englishman's Liberal convictions, citing in evidence his devotion to irrational political institutions.

The clue to the difference is to be found in the difference in meaning of the word *Revolution* as applied to the events which took place in France in 1789 and as applied to the events which took place in England in 1688. In the former case it means a radical transformation, the birth of a new kind of society, in the latter it is an astronomical metaphor, meaning a restoration of balance.

The radical transformation of English society which corresponds to the French Revolution was the work of the Tudors. The execution of Charles I was not, like the execution of Louis XVI, a revolutionary breach with the past but the restoration of a conservative, even medieval, idea, namely, that the ruler is not above but subject to Natural Law. Then, from their experiences under the Protectorate, Englishmen learned that the dangers of arbitrary power were not necessarily removed simply by the abolition of the Crown, for the claims of self-appointed saints to know by divine inspiration what the good life should be and to have the right to impose their notions on the ungodly could be as great a threat as the divine right of kings. The historical experience with which the Whigs of 1688 and their successors had to cope was a century and a half of bitter quarrels and drastic changes imposed upon the public by individuals or minorities. The most fundamental notion in English Liberalism, therefore, is the notion of limited sovereignty and its characteristic way of thinking goes something like this:

1. All people differ from each other in character and temperament so that any attempt to impose an absolute uniformity is a tyranny. On the other hand there can be no social life unless the members of a society hold certain beliefs in common, and behave in certain commonly accepted ways.

2. The beliefs which it is necessary to hold in common must therefore be so defined that differences of emphasis are possible and the laws which regulate social conduct must be such that they command common consent. Insofar as conformity has to be enforced, this should be in matters of outward behavior not of private belief, firstly because there can be no doubt whether an individual does or does not conform, and secondly because men find behaving in a way with which they are not in complete sympathy more tolerable than being told to believe something they consider false. Thus, in the English Prayer Book the rules for conducting the Liturgy are precise, while the meaning of the Thirty-Nine Articles is purposely left vague.

3. The way in which a reform is effected is just as important as the reform itself. Violent change is as injurious to freedom as inertia.

4. Utopians are a public menace. Reformers must concern themselves with the concrete and the possible.

The authors of the French Enlightenment were confronted with a very different situation, a static society in which nothing had changed. To the French Liberal, therefore, nothing could seem to matter except that a radical change should occur and the threat to freedom was not absolute sovereignty as such but the imprisonment of the majority in an arbitrary social status. A Jacobin like St. Just could accept the notion of absolute sovereignty without question so long as it was taken from the Crown and given to the people. Materialism was a natural philosophy for French Liberalism to adopt since its enemy was the aristocrat who claimed privilege on biological grounds (few of the English peerages in the eighteenth century were more than two hundred years old), and it was no less natural that this materialism should be militantly dogmatic since the philosophy European Liberalism associated with the *ancien régime,* the theology of the Roman Catholic Church, was itself rigid and uncompromising.

Sydney Smith is an example of English Liberalism at its best. He is never utopian or given to large generalizations but always attacks a specific abuse, and the reform he proposes is equally specific and always possible to realize. Further, he assumes that, though most people are selfish and many people are stupid, few are either lunatics or deliberate scoundrels impervious to rational argument.

Thus, in attacking the Game Laws, he avoids raising ultimate questions about the justice or injustice of private property and its unequal distribution, and sticks to the immediate issue of man-traps, spring-guns and the like. Assuming that no sane man will deny that they are cruel, he points out that they are unnecessary for the purpose for which they are intended; the prevention of poaching can be achieved by humane means, namely by giving every landlord, great or small, the right to kill game, by making game private property like geese or ducks and by allowing the owner to sell game to whom he chooses since, as long as the sale of game is forbidden and there are rich men who want it, a black market supplied by poachers is inevitable.

Knowing both the world of the rich and the world of the poor and an enemy of neither, he is aware that many injustices to the poor exist, not because the rich are intentionally unjust but because their own world has never felt them. In attacking the law which denied defense counsel to prisoners accused of a felony, a leftover from feudal times when a defense of prisoners accused by the Crown was felt to imply disloyalty, he explains very simply why, though this feeling no longer existed, the law still remained on the statute books.

> To ask why there are not petitions—why the evil is not more noticed, is mere parliamentary froth and ministerial juggling. Gentlemen are rarely hung. If they were so, there would be petitions without end for counsel.

There is a certain type of professional Liberal who assumes that in every issue the liberal position must be on the Left. Sydney Smith was never fooled in this way as a comparison of his two principal set of pamphlets, the *Peter Plymley Letters* and the *Letters to Archdeacon Singleton,* clearly demonstrates. In the former his opponent is the conservative. Laws prohibiting Roman Catholics from voting or holding public offices which, when they were originally passed may have had some justification—an attempt to bring back the Stuarts might have met with their support

—were still in effect, long after any such danger had passed. Sydney Smith assumes that the vast majority of those who opposed their repeal were capable of seeing that they were unjust, if he can demonstrate that there was no danger incurred by removing them. With the inveterately stupid or demogogic minority, his argument is different; he warns them of the unpleasant material consequences to themselves which will follow if they refuse to listen to their conscience.

In the case of the Singleton letters, his enemies are not those who refuse to make a needed reform but those who would impose a necessary reform from above in a hasty and unjust manner. What right, he asks, have the bishops to make changes without considering the lower clergy who will be most affected by them and whose experience of parochial life make them better equipped to make concrete judgments about abuses instead of generalizations. Further he complains that much of the plan for reform was utopian, since to do what it was intended to do would require a sum of money which the Church did not possess.

In his opposition to secret ballot, later experience has shown us that he was mistaken, because he did not foresee—neither, for that matter, did his opponents—a day when there would arise one-party governments prepared to use all the instruments of coercion at their disposal to ensure an overwhelming vote in their favor. Even so, he makes two points in his pamphlet which no liberal democracy should forget; firstly, that the free voter must hold himself responsible for the consequence of his vote:

> Who brought that mischievous profligate villain into Parliament? Let us see the names of his real supporters. Who stood out against the strong and uplifted arm of power? Who discovered this excellent and hitherto unknown person? . . . Is it not a dark and demoralising system to draw this veil over human actions, to say to the mass, be base, and you will not be despised; be victorious and you will not be honored—

and secondly that the free voter is the voter whose choice is determined by what he believes to be in the best interest of his country and by nothing else.

] 165 [

The Radicals are quite satisfied if a rich man of popular manners gains the votes and affections of his dependents; but why is not this as bad as intimidation? The real object is to vote for the good politician, not for the kind-hearted or agreeable man: the mischief is just the same to the country whether I am smiled into a corrupt choice, or frowned into a corrupt choice.

V

Today the Whig tradition which Sydney Smith represented is under a cloud. It is under attack for being aesthetically unappealing and psychologically or metaphysically shallow.

> . . . what is Whiggery?
> A levelling, rancorous, rational sort of mind
> That never looked out of the eye of a saint
> Or out of a drunkard's eye.

Yet, unattractive and shallow as one may feel so many liberals to be, how rarely on any concrete social issue does one find the liberal position the wrong one. Again, how often, alas, do those very philosophers and writers who have most astounded us by their profound insights into the human heart and human existence, dismay us by the folly and worse of their judgments on the issues of everyday life.

Liberalism is also under criticism for being ineffective and insofar as we have to combat enemies with whom rational discussion is impossible because the absolute presuppositions on both sides are radically different, the criticism has some justification. Some of us, however, seem in danger of forgetting that rational discussion is desirable and that liberty is not just a value of which one approves in the abstract but, to be real must be embodied in one's own person and daily acts. Indeed, the more critical a situation, the less the opinions a man expresses matter in comparison with his behavior. On this, if nothing else, the sober Whig and the wild Existentialist will agree. What a challenge to a second Landor it would be to compose an Imaginary Conversation between the shades of the author of the *Letters to Archdeacon Singleton* and the author of *Attack on Christendom*.

I should not be surprised if they understood each other much better than one would naturally expect. They both disliked abstract systems, they were both strikingly original personalities and they could both be very funny. Kierkegaard, whose chief complaint against the bourgeois was that they were a parody of the Knight of Faith, would have appreciated, I think, Sydney Smith's use of bourgeois terms to define *A Nice Person:*

> A nice person is neither too tall nor too short, looks clean and cheerful, has no prominent features, makes no difficulties, is never displaced, sits bodkin, is never foolishly affronted, and is void of affectations. . . . A nice person is clear of trumpery little passions, acknowledges superiority, delights in talent, shelters humility, pardons adversity, forgives deficiency, respects all men's rights, never stops the bottle, is never long and never wrong, always knows the day of the month, the name of everybody at table, and never gives pain to any human being. . . . A nice person never knocks over wine or melted butter, does not tread upon the dog's foot, or molest the family cat, eats soup without noise, laughs in the right place, and has a watchful and attentive eye.

SØREN KIERKEGAARD

I am not Christian severity contrasted with Christian leniency. I am . . . mere human honesty.

—Kierkegaard.

Though his writings are often brilliantly poetic and often deeply philosophic, Kierkegaard was neither a poet nor a philosopher, but a preacher, an expounder and defender of Christian doctrine and Christian conduct. The near contemporary with whom he may properly be compared is not someone like Dostoevsky or Hegel, but that other great preacher of the nineteenth century, John Henry, later Cardinal, Newman: both men were faced with the problem of preaching to a secularized society which was still officially Christian, and neither was a naïve believer, so that in each case one is conscious when reading their work that they are preaching to two congregations, one outside and one inside the pulpit. Both were tempted by intellectual ambition. Perhaps Newman resisted the temptation more successfully (occasionally, it must be confessed, Kierkegaard carried on like a spiritual prima donna), but then Newman was spared the exceptional situation in which Kierkegaard found himself, the situation of unique tribulation.

Every circumstance combined to make Kierkegaard suffer. His father was obsessed by guilt at the memory of having as a young boy cursed God; his mother was a servant girl whom his father had seduced before marriage; the frail and nervously labile constitution he inherited was further damaged by a fall from a tree. His intellectual precociousness combined with his father's intense religious instruction gave him in childhood the consciousness of an adult. Finally he was fated to live, not in the stimulating surroundings of Oxford or Paris, but in the intellectual province of Copenhagen, without competition or understanding. Like Pascal, whom in more ways than one he resembles, or like Richard III, whom he frequently thought of, he was fated to be an exception and a sufferer, whatever he did. An easygoing or prudent bourgeois he could never become, any more than Pascal could have become Montaigne.

The sufferer by fate is tempted in peculiar ways; if he concentrates on himself, he is tempted to believe that God is not good but malignantly enjoys making the innocent suffer, i.e., he is tempted into demonic defiance; if he starts from the premise that God is good, then he is tempted to believe that he is guilty without knowing what he is guilty of, i.e., he is tempted into demonic despair; if he be a Christian, he can be tempted in yet a third way, because of the paradoxical position of suffering in the Christian faith. This paradox is well expressed by the penitent shade of Forese when he says to Dante:

> "And not once only, while circling this
> road, is our pain renewed:
> I say pain and ought to say solace."

For, while ultimately the Christian message is the good news: "Glory to God in the highest and on earth peace, good-will towards men—" "Come unto me all that travail and are heavy laden and I will refresh you"; it is proximately to man's self-love the worst possible news—"Take up thy cross and follow me."

Thus to be relieved of suffering in one sense is voluntarily to accept suffering in another. As Kafka says: "The joys of this life are not its own but our dread of ascending to a higher life: the torments of this life are not its own but our self-torment because of that dread."

If the two senses of suffering are confused, then the Christian who suffers is tempted to think this a proof that he is nearer to God than those who suffer less.

Kierkegaard's polemic, and all his writings are polemical, moves simultaneously in two directions: outwardly against the bourgeois Protestantism of the Denmark of his time, and inwardly against his suffering. To the former he says, "You imagine that you are all Christians and contented because you have forgotten that each of you is an existing individual. When you remember that, you will be forced to realize that you are pagans and in despair." To himself he says, "As long as your suffering makes you defiant or despairing, as long as you identify your suffering with yourself as an existing individual, and are defiantly or despairingly the exception, you are not a Christian."

Kierkegaard and the Existential

However complicated and obscure in its developments it has become, Existentialism starts out from some quite simple observations.

a) All propositions presuppose the existence of their terms as a ground, i.e., one cannot ask, "Does X exist?" but only, "Has this existing X the character A or the character B?"

b) The subjective presupposition "I exist" is unique. It is certainly not a proposition to be proven true or false by experiment, yet unlike all other presuppositions it is indubitable and no rival belief is possible. It also appears compulsive to believe that other selves like mine exist: at least the contrary presupposition has never been historically made. To believe that a world of nature exists, i.e., of things which happen of themselves, is not however invariably made. Magicians do not make it. (The Christian expression for this presupposition is the dogma, "In the beginning God created the Heaven and the Earth.")

c) The absolute certainty with which I hold the belief that I exist is not its only unique characteristic. The awareness of existing is also absolutely private and incommunicable. My feelings, desires, etc., can be objects of my knowledge and hence I can imagine what other people feel. My existence cannot become an object of knowledge; hence while, if I have the necessary histrionic imagination and talent I can act the part of another in such a way that I deceive his best friends, I can never imagine what it would be like to *be* that other person but must always remain myself pretending to be him.

d) If I take away from my sense of existence all that can become an object of my consciousness, what is left?

    (1) An awareness that my existence is not self-derived. I can legitimately speak of *my* feelings. I cannot properly speak of *my* existence.

    (2) An awareness that I am free to make choices. I cannot observe the act of choice objectively. If I try, I shall not choose. Doctor Johnson's refutation of determinism, to kick the stone and say, "We know we are free and there's an end of it" is correct, because the awareness of freedom is subjective, i.e., objectively undemonstrable.

    (3) An awareness of being *with* time, i.e., experiencing time as an eternal present to which past and future refer, instead of my knowledge of my feelings and of the outer world as moving or changing *in* time.

    (4) A state of anxiety (or dread), pride (in the theological sense), despair or faith. These are not emotions in the way that fear or lust or anger are, for I cannot know them objectively; I can only know them when they have aroused such feelings as the above which are observable. For these states of anxiety or pride, etc., are anxiety about existing, pride in existing, etc., and I cannot stand outside them to observe them. Nor can I observe them in others. A gluttonous man may succeed when he is in my presence in concealing his gluttony, but if I could watch him all the time, I should catch him out. But I could watch a man all his life, and I should never know for certain whether or not he was proud, for the actions which we call proud or humble may have quite other causes. Pride is rightly called the root of all sin, because it is invisible to the one

who is guilty of it and he can only infer it from results.

These facts of existence are expressed in the Christian doctrines of Man's creation and his fall. Man is created in the image of God; an image because his existence is not self-derived, and a divine image because like God each man is aware of his existence as unique. Man fell through pride, a wish to become God, to derive his existence from himself, and not through sensuality or any of the desires of his "nature."

Kierkegaard's Three Categories

Every man, says Kierkegaard, lives either aesthetically, ethically, or religiously. As he is concerned, for the most part, with describing the way in which these categories apply in Christian or post-Christian society, one can perhaps make his meaning clearer by approaching these categories historically, i.e., by considering the Aesthetic and the Ethical at stages when each was a religion, and then comparing them with the Christian faith in order to see the difference, first, between two rival and incompatible Natural Religions and, secondly, between them and a Revealed Religion in which neither is destroyed or ignored, but the Aesthetic is dethroned and the Ethical fulfilled.

The Aesthetic Religion
(e.g., The Greek Gods)

The experience from which the aesthetic religion starts, the facts which it sets out to overcome, is the experience of the physical weakness of the self in the face of an overwhelmingly powerful not-self. To survive I must act strongly and decisively. What gives me the power to do so? Passion. The aesthetic religion regards the passions not as belonging to the self, but as divine visitations, powers which it must find the means to attract or repel if the self is to survive.

So, in the aesthetic cosmology, the gods are created by nature, ascend to heaven, are human in form, finite in number (like the passions) and interrelated by blood. Being images of passions, they themselves are not *in* their passion—Aphrodite is not in love; Mars is not angry—or, if they do make an appearance of passionate behavior, it is frivolous; like actors, they do not suffer or change. They bestow, withhold or withdraw power from men as and when they choose. They are not interested in the majority of men, but only in a few exceptional individuals whom they specially favor and sometimes even beget on mortal mothers. These exceptional individuals with whom the gods enter into relation are heroes. How does one know that a man is a hero? By his acts of power, by his good fortune. The hero is glorious but not responsible for his successes or his failures. When Odysseus, for instance, succeeds, he has his friend Pallas Athene to thank; when he fails, he has his enemy Poseidon to blame. The aesthetic either/or is not good or bad but strong or weak, fortunate or unfortunate. The temporal succession of events has no meaning, for what happens is simply what the gods choose arbitrarily to will. The Greeks and the Trojans must fight because "hateful Ares bids." To the aesthetic religion all art is ritual, acts designed to attract the divine favors which will make the self strong, and ritual is the only form of activity in which man has the freedom to act or refrain from acting and for which, therefore, he is responsible.

The facts on which the aesthetic religion is shattered and despairs, producing in its death agony Tragic Drama, are two: man's knowledge of good and evil, and his certainty that death comes to all men, i.e., that ultimately there is no either/or of strength or weakness, but even for the exceptional individual the doom of absolute weakness. Both facts it tries to explain in its own terms and fails. It tries to relate good and evil to fortune and misfortune, strength and weakness, and concludes that if a man is unfortunate, he must be guilty. Oedipus' parricide and incest are not really his sins but his punishment for his sin of *hubris*. The Homeric hero cannot sin, the tragic hero must sin, but neither is tempted. Presently the observation that some evil men are fortunate and some good men unfortunate brings forth a doubt as to whether the gods are really good, till in the *Prometheus* of Aeschylus it is openly stated that power and goodness are not identical. Again, the aesthetic religion tries to express the consciousness of universal death aesthetically, that is, individually, as the Fates to which even the gods must bow, and betrays its failure to imagine the universal by having to have three of them.

The Ethical Religion
(The God of Greek Philosophy)

To solve the problem of human death and weakness, the ethical religion begins by asking, "Is there anything man knows which does not come and go like his passions?" Yes, the concepts of his reason which are both certain and independent of time or space or individual, for the certainty is the same whether a man be sick or well, a king or a slave.

In place of the magnified passions of the aesthetic religion, the ethical sets up as God, the Ideas, the First Cause, the Universal. While to the former, the world begot the gods who then ruled over it because they were stronger than any other creature, in the latter God and the world are coeternal. God did not create the world of matter; he is only the cause of the order in it, and this not by any act of his—the neuter gender would be more fitting to him—for to be divine means to be self-sufficient, "to have no need of friends." Rather it is matter which, wishing to escape from the innate disorder of its temporal flux, "falls in love" with God and imitates his unchangeableness in such ways as it can, namely by adopting regular movements. (Plato's introduction of a mysterious third party, the Demiurge who loves the Ideas and then imposes them on matter, complicates but does not essentially alter the cosmology.) Man, however, being endowed with reason, can apprehend God directly as Idea and Law, transcend his finite bodily passions, and become like God.

For the aesthetic either/or of strength or weakness, fortune or misfortune, the ethical religion substitutes the either/or of Knowledge of the Good or Ignorance of the Good. To the aesthetic, evil was lack of power over the finite world, for all finiteness, all passion is weakness, as goodness is gained by transcending the finite world, by a knowledge of the eternal and universal truths of reason which cannot be known without being obeyed. To the aesthetic, time was unmeaning and overwhelming; to the ethical, it is an appearance which can be seen through. The aesthetic worshipper was dependent on his gods who entered into relationship with him if and when he chose; the ethical worshipper enters into relationship with his god through his own efforts and, once he has done so, the relationship is eternal, neither can break it. The ethical hero is not the man of power, the man who does, but the philosopher, the man who knows.

Like his predecessor, however, he is not tempted and does not choose, for so long as he is ignorant he is at the mercy of his passions, i.e., he *must* yield to the passion of the moment, but so soon as he knows the good, he must will it; he can no more refuse assent to the good than he can to the truths of geometry.

As in the case of the aesthetic religion, there are facts with which the ethical religion cannot deal and on which it founders. Its premise "Sin is ignorance; to know the good is to will it" is faced with the fact that all men are born ignorant and hence each individual requires a will to know the universal good in order to will it. This will cannot be explained ethically, first because it is not a rational idea so that the ethical has to fall back on the aesthetic idea of a heavenly Eros to account for it. Secondly, it is not a universal; it is present or appeals to some individuals and not to others, so that the ethical has to call in the aesthetic hero whom it instructs in the good, and who then imposes justice by force. Art to the elect is no longer a religious ritual, but an immoral sham, useful only as a fraudulent but pragmatically effective method of making the ignorant masses conform to the law of virtue which they do not understand.

Lastly, there comes the discovery that knowledge of the good does not automatically cause the knower to will it. He may know the law and yet not only be tempted to disobey but yield to the temptation. He may even disobey deliberately out of spite, just to show that he is free.

Revealed Religion (Judaism and Christianity)

A revealed religion is one in which God is not present as an object of consciousness, either as a feeling or a proposition. He is not begotten by the world, nor does he impose order on its coeternal flux but creates it out of nothing, so that while God and the world are at every moment related, God is not knowable as an object. While in the aesthetic religion the feelings, and in the ethical religion, the ideas *were* the presence of God, they are now only *my* feelings, *my* ideas and if I believe that what I feel (e.g., God is present) or think (e.g., God is righteous) is caused by my relation to God, this belief is a revelation, for the cause is outside my consciousness. As one term of a relation, the other term of which is God, I cannot overlook the whole relation objectively and can only describe it analogically in terms of the human relation most like it, e.g., if the feeling of which I have immediate certainty is one which I would approximately describe as sonship, I may speak of God as Father.

There is no longer a question of establishing a relation between God and myself for as my creator he is necessarily related to his creature and the relation is presupposed by my existence; there is only a question of the right relation. The uniqueness of the relation is that it is a relation to an Other yet at the same time as continuous and inescapable as my relation to myself. The relation of the aesthetic worshipper to his gods is intermittent and depends on their pleasure—they do not have to get in touch with him at all. The relation of the ethical worshipper to the Ideas is intermittent or not depending on his pleasure. They are always there to be contemplated if he choose, as a river is always there to be drunk from if one is thirsty, but if he doesn't choose to contemplate them, there is no relation. But the relation to the creator God of revealed religion is unbreakable: I, his creature, can forget it as I can forget my relation to myself when I am thinking of other things, but it is permanently there, and, if I try to banish it permanently from consciousness, I shall not get rid of it, but experience it negatively as guilt and despair. The wrath of God is not a description of God in a certain state of feeling, but of the way in which I experience God if I distort or deny my relation to him. So Dante inscribed on the portals of Hell: "Divine Power made me, Wisdom supreme and Primal Love"—and Landor justly remarked about the Inferno that its inhabitants do not want to get out. To both the aesthetic and the ethical religion, evil was a lack of relation to God, due in the one case to God's will, in the other to man's ignorance; to the revealed religion, evil is sin, that is to say, the rebellion of man's will against the relation.

The aesthetic commands cannot be codified because they are arbitrary commands of the gods and always novel. The ethical commands ought to be able to be completely codified as a set of universal moral laws. Revealed religion shows why this is impossible. A law is either a law *of* or a law *for*. Laws *of*, like the laws of science, are patterns of regular behavior as observed by a disinterested observer. Conformity is necessary for the law to exist, for if an exception is found, the law has to be rewritten in such a way that the exception becomes part of the pattern, for it is a presupposition of science that events in nature conform to law, i.e., a physical event is always related to some law, even if it be one of which scientists are at present ignorant. Laws *for*, like human legislation, are patterns of behavior imposed on behavior which was previously lacking in pattern. In order for the laws to come into existence, there must be at least some people who do not conform to them. Unlike laws *of* which must completely explain how events occur, laws *for* are only concerned with commanding or prohibiting the class of actions to which they refer, and a man is only related to the law when it is a question of doing or not doing one act of such a class; when his actions are covered by no law, e.g., when he is sitting alone in his room, he is related to no law at all.

If the commands of God were laws *of* man, then disobedience would be impossible; if they were laws *for* man, then his relation to God would not be permanent but intermittent. The commands of God are neither the aesthetic fiat, "Do what you must" nor the ethical instruction, "These are the things which you may or must not do," but the call of duty, "Choose to do what at this moment in this context I am telling you to do."

Christ the Offense

To one who believes that Jesus was what he claimed to be, the incarnation as an existing individual of the Son of God begotten of his Father before all worlds, by whom all things were made, his birth, life and death are, first, a simultaneous revelation of the infinite love of God—to be righteous means to love—and of the almost infinite sinfulness of man—without the gift of the Holy Spirit it is impossible for him to accept the truth; secondly, a revelation that God is related to all men, but to each of them uniquely as an existing individual, i.e., God is the father of all men, not of a chosen people alone, and all men are exceptions, not aesthetically, but as existing individuals—it is their existence not their natures which makes each of them unique; thirdly, a revelation that the Life is not an object for aesthetic admiration nor the Truth an object for ethical appropriation, but a Way to be followed, an inclination of the heart, a spirit in which all actions are done. Insofar as collectively they considered their relation to God to be aesthetically unique, and individually an ethical relation to his Law, this revelation is an offense to the Jews; insofar as it proclaims that God the Father is not *a* God but *the* God, that Christ is not a teacher of truths but the Truth, it is an offense to the Gentiles.

The Jews would have welcomed a Messiah for them alone, but not one who demanded that they give up their claim to be the unique people of God or their belief that the Law covers the whole duty of the individual; the Gentile imagination could have accepted another culture-hero to add to its old ones, the Gentile reason, another teacher to add new stores to its knowledge, but could not accept one who was a passive sufferer, put faith before reason, and claimed exclusive attention. The Jews crucified Jesus on the serious charge that he was a blasphemer, the Gentiles, on the frivolous charge that he was a public nuisance.

Preaching to the Non-Believer

"It is," Newman observed, "as absurd to argue men, as to torture them, into believing." However convincing the argument, however holy the arguer, the act of faith remains an act of choice which no one can do for another. Pascal's "wager" and Kierkegaard's "leap" are neither of them quite adequate descriptions, for the one suggests prudent calculation and the other perverse arbitrariness. Both, however, have some value: the first calls men's attention to the fact that in all other spheres of life they are constantly acting on faith and quite willingly, so that they have no right to expect religion to be an exception; the second reminds them that they cannot live without faith in something, and that when the faith which they have breaks down, when the ground crumbles under their feet, they *have to* leap even into uncertainty if they are to avoid certain destruction.

There are only two Christian propositions about which it is therefore possible to argue with a non-believer:

(1) That Jesus existed; (2) That a man who does not believe that Jesus is the Christ is in despair.

It is probably true that nobody was ever genuinely converted to Christianity who had not lost his "nerve," either because he was aesthetically unfortunate or because he was ethically powerless, i.e., unable to do what he knew to be his duty. A great deal of Kierkegaard's work is addressed to the man who has already become uneasy about himself, and by encouraging him to look more closely at himself, shows him that his condition is more serious than he thought. The points that Kierkegaard stresses most are, firstly, that no one, believer or not, who has once been exposed to Christianity can return to either the aesthetic or the ethical religion as if nothing had happened. Return he will, if he lose his Christian faith, for he cannot exist without some faith, but he will no longer be a naïve believer, but a *rusé* one compelled to excess by the need to hide from himself the fact that he does not really believe in the idols he sets up.

Thus the aesthetic individual is no longer content with the passive moderation of paganism; he will no longer simply obey the passions of his nature, but will have by will power to arouse his passions constantly in order to have something to obey. The fickle lover of paganism who fell in and out of love turns into Don Giovanni, the seducer who keeps a list so as not to forget. Similarly, the ethical philosopher will no longer be content to remain a simple scientist content to understand as much and no more than he can discover; he must turn into the systematic philosopher who has an explanation for everything in existence except, of course, his own existence which defeats him. Nothing must occur except what he can explain. The multitude of ordinary men and women cannot return to the contented community of the Greek chorus for they cannot lose the sense that they are individuals; they can only try to drown that sense by merging themselves into an abstraction, the crowd, the public ruled by fashion. As Rudolf Kassner says in his fascinating book, *Zahl und Gesicht*:

"The pre-Christian man with his Mean (*Mitte*) bore a charmed life against mediocrity. The Christian stands in greater danger of becoming mediocre. If we bear in mind the idea, the absolute to which the Christian claims to be related, a mediocre Christian becomes comic. The pre-Christian man could still be mediocre without becoming comic because for him his mediocrity was the Mean. The Christian cannot."

To show the non-believer that he is in despair because he cannot believe in *his* gods and then show him that Christ cannot be a man-made God because in every respect he is offensive to the natural man is for Kierkegaard the only true kind of Christian apologetics. The false kind of apologetics of which he accuses his contemporary Christians is the attempt to soft-pedal the distinction between Christianity and the Natural Religions, either by trying to show that what Christians believe is really just what everybody believes, or by suggesting that Christianity pays in a worldly sense, that it makes men healthy, wealthy, and wise, keeps society stable, and the young in order, etc. Apart from its falsehood, Kierkegaard says, this method will not work because those who are satisfied with this world will not be interested and those who are not satisfied are looking for a faith whose values are not those of this world.

Preaching to Believers

The danger for the Christian in an officially Christian society is that he may think he is a Christian. But nobody except Christ and, at the end of their lives perhaps, the saints *are* Christian. To say "I am a Christian" really means "I who am a sinner am required to become like Christ." He may think he believes as an individual when all he is doing is believing what his parents said, so that he would be a Mohammedan if they had been. The task of the Christian preacher is therefore first to affirm the Christian commands and arouse the consciousness of sin, and secondly to make the individual's relationship with Christ real, that is, contemporary.

The world has changed greatly since Kierkegaard's time and all too many of his prophetic insights have come to pass. The smug bourgeois Christendom he denounced has crumbled and what is left is an amorphous, despairing mass of displaced persons and paralyzed Hamlets. The ubiquitous violence of the present age is not truly passionate, but a desperate attempt to regress from reflection into passion instead of leaping forward into faith. The worst feature, for example, of the massacre of the Jews by the Nazis is not its cruelty but its frivolity; they did not seriously believe that the Jews were a menace as the Inquisition believed about heretics; no, it was rather a matter of "We must do something. Why not kill all the Jews?"

It is almost bound to be the fate of Kierkegaard, as of so many polemical writers, to be read in the wrong way or by the wrong people. The contented will not read him or read him only scientifically as an interesting case history. The unhappy and, for the most part, agnostic intellectuals who will read him, will confine themselves to his psychological analyses like *The Sickness unto Death* or his philosophical polemics like *Concluding Unscientific Postscript,* which they will read poetically as sympathetic and stimulating reflections of their feelings and thoughts, but they will fight shy of books like *Training in Christianity* or *The Works of Love,* either because they are not as unhappy as they pretend or because they really despair of comfort and cling in defiance to their suffering.

Kierkegaard is particularly vulnerable to such misunderstanding because the only force which can compel us to read an author as he intends is some action of his which becomes inexplicable if we read him any other way, e.g., Newman's conversion to Roman Catholicism. In Kierkegaard's case there is indeed such an action, but the action is another book, *The Attack upon "Christendom."* The whole of his writings up to this one, written in the last year of his life, even the sermons, are really "poetical," i.e., Kierkegaard speaks in them as a genius not as an apostle, so that they all might have been published, as many of them were, anonymously. *The Attack upon "Christendom,"* on the other hand, is that contradiction in terms, an "existential" book. What for the author was the most important book of his life is for us, as readers, the least, for to us the important point is not what it contains, but the fact that Kierkegaard wrote it. For this reason, no selection from it appears here.

A KNIGHT OF DOLEFUL COUNTENANCE
(Second Thoughts on Kierkegaard)

Sooner or later it was bound to happen, though for an "Existentialist" writer it is a slightly comic fate: Kierkegaard has become a Classic, to be published in a definitive edition with full scholarly apparatus. The English translation of his *Papirer* (*Journals and Papers*) is to be issued in five volumes, of which the first has now been published by the Indiana University Press. The translators and editors, Howard and Edna Hong—their translation, by the way, reads very well indeed—have decided to group the entries by subject matter instead of printing them in their chronological order. This decision seems to me wise for two reasons. In the first place, the journal is a chronicle of ideas, not of events; in the second, it is of enormous length and frequently repetitive. For this we have no right to blame Kierkegaard, since he did not write it for publication, but I cannot imagine any human being reading straight through it without skipping. Classification by subject matter is a question of editorial judgment, which must to some extent be arbitrary. For example, this volume begins with "Abstract" and ends with "The Exception." Under the "C" entries I expected to find some devoted to what Kierkegaard himself always calls "Catholicism," but found none; I presume they will appear in a later volume, under "R."

Like Pascal, Nietzsche, and Simone Weil, Kierkegaard is one

of those writers whom it is very difficult to estimate justly. When one reads them for the first time, one is bowled over by their originality (they speak in a voice one has never heard before) and by the sharpness of their insights (they say things which no one before them has said, and which, henceforward, no reader will ever forget). But with successive readings one's doubts grow, one begins to react against their overemphasis on one aspect of the truth at the expense of all the others, and one's first enthusiasm may all too easily turn into an equally exaggerated aversion. Of all such writers, one might say that one cannot imagine them as children. The more we read them, the more we become aware that something has gone badly wrong with their affective life—a derangement which, though it may, and probably does, include some kind of sexual neurosis, extends far beyond the bounds of the sexual; it is not only impossible to imagine one of them as a happy husband or wife, it is impossible to imagine their having a single intimate friend to whom they could open their hearts. It is significant, surely, and sad, that though Kierkegaard was the most brilliant Dane of his time and a famous, even notorious, figure, there are, to the best of my knowledge, no references to him in the memoirs of his contemporaries, no descriptions, friendly or hostile, of what he seemed like to others. All we know about Kierkegaard is what he tells us himself.

I hope that someone will soon write a fully documented history of the *Corsair* affair. All I know about it is that Kierkegaard challenged its proprietor, Meyer Goldschmidt, who had hitherto praised his writings, to attack him, which Goldschmidt thereupon proceeded to do, and my only information about the nature of the attack comes from the account given by David Swenson in his *Something About Kierkegaard:*

> For several months thereafter, there appeared little articles in the *Corsair* satirizing one or another feature of the pseudonymous writings. The articles were illustrated with pictures of Kierkegaard walking through the streets, his umbrella under his arm, and one trouser leg depicted as considerably longer than the other. The result of this campaign was that Kierkegaard could not show himself on the streets without being followed by a gaping and howling mob of boys and young men. So deeply did the attack sink into

the popular consciousness of Copenhagen that we have
from Brandes a narrative of how his nurse used to bring
him back from the error of his ways, whenever his clothes
were not properly put on, by pointing at him a warning
finger and saying reprovingly, "*Søren, Søren!*"

This must have been very disagreeable, but can it really be
considered, as Kierkegaard himself considered it, an example of a
righteous man's being martyred for the sake of the truth? As a
scandal sheet, the *Corsair* was clearly a social evil, and Kierkegaard was not alone in thinking so. For a writer, the normal way
of trying to abolish a social evil is to write attacks on it, demonstrating by quotations and facts the kind of evil it represents and
does. Such attacks are likely to be the more effective the less the
writer draws attention to himself and the more he seems to speak
as the voice of public conscience. But instead of attacking, Kierkegaard demanded to be attacked, and this, I must confess, I find
distastefully egotistic. Goldschmidt, incidentally, must have been
a stupid man: a moment's thought should have told him that if he
really wished to torment Kierkegaard he should ignore the challenge and go on praising his work to the skies.

If I, suffering, were to have become an object of attack
by mob-vulgarity, admiration for me would have increased.
But the fact that I myself demanded it shocked men. They
felt alienated by anything that went over their heads.

Thus Kierkegaard in his *Journals*. But was it so unnatural that
they should be shocked? Further, is there any evidence, outside his
own testimony, that *nobody* sympathized with him in the persecution to which he was subjected?

Then there is the question of the persecution itself. When a
newspaper proprietor has it in for somebody, his usual procedure
is to publish innuendos (or facts, if he can get them) about the
private or public morality of his victim: it is suggested that he has
a taste for young girls or has been involved in some shady financial
or political deal. All that Goldschmidt was able to do was to make
fun of Kierkegaard's writings—one would be curious to know if
these criticisms were at all funny—and to make fun of his physical
appearance. Caricature exaggerates, but it is only possible if there

is some peculiarity to exaggerate. If the *Corsair* caricatures showed one of Kierkegaard's trouser legs considerably longer than the other, then it seems certain to me that he must have been somebody, like myself, who was careless about the way he dressed. One would have expected him to laugh and say, "Yes, I am a careless dresser, but I don't care." On the other hand, if his feelings were seriously hurt, as it seems they were, he had only to dress more carefully in the future for the caricatures to lose their sting. If the vulgar laughed at him on the streets, it was because they could recognize him as the original of the caricatures. His second attempt to get himself persecuted for the Truth's sake—his polemic against Bishops Mynster and Martensen—was even less successful. The public may have been shocked and thought his articles in bad taste, but they read them. Nobody tried to silence him. For all his contempt for the press, he made use of it, and the editors of *Fædrelandet* were perfectly willing to publish what he wrote. Far from getting stoned or imprisoned, he made the headlines. One has to draw attention to this failure to get martyred not as a personal reproach, which would be cheap and unjust, but because Kierkegaard was continually attacking the Danish clergy of his time for failing to achieve something which, under the circumstances of his time, he was unable to achieve himself.

Of what he calls the "wilting" of Christianity, Kierkegaard says:

> It will appear most easily in a Protestant country that does not have the counterweight of Catholicism in the same country. Furthermore, it will appear most readily in a small country, which by being small is only too close to pettiness, mediocrity, spiritlessness; and, again, it will appear most readily in this little land if it has its own language entirely by itself and does not even through its language participate in possible movements elsewhere. It will most readily appear in such a small country if the people are prosperous, have no great differences in life, and have a common and regularized abundance, which is related all too easily to secular security. It will most readily appear in or show itself as the fruits of good days of peace.

Leaving aside the first sentence for later consideration, let us examine the rest of this passage. To condemn a society for being small and provincial is to condemn it not for being worldly, but for not being worldly enough: a provincial society lacks the worldly virtues of broad-mindedness and cynical tolerance exhibited by more cosmopolitan societies. As someone who had to write in Danish, Kierkegaard could reasonably complain that this severely limited the size of his potential audience, but this is a worldly objection. Further, I cannot believe that the cultural situation in Denmark in Kierkegaard's day was radically different from what it is today there or in any other country, like Holland or Sweden or Hungary, where few strangers can be expected to understand its mother tongue: in such countries both intellectuals and businessmen are obliged, like Kierkegaard himself, to learn the more cosmopolitan languages. I should be extremely surprised, for example, to hear that Bishop Martensen or any other members of the Danish Ecclesiastical Establishment could only read and speak Danish. Kierkegaard then goes on to reproach Denmark for qualities which common sense surely would regard as blessings—the absence of serious poverty, the freedom from sharp class distinctions, the lack of involvement in war; for being, in other words, a society without gross and obvious social evils. Whether this was really the case I do not know, but it must certainly have been Kierkegaard's opinion, for never, when he is attacking the Danish clergy for worldly prudence and cowardice, does he specify a concrete issue about which he thinks it their Christian duty to protest. In England during the first half of the nineteenth century, there were a number of issues one can think of—the slave trade, the treatment of the industrial poor in mines and cotton mills, the criminal law, the unjust treatment of Catholics—about which, to their shame, most of the Anglican clergy remained silent, though a few did have the courage to protest, at the cost of losing preferment. Were there really no comparable issues in Denmark? I have the uneasy feeling that if there were, Kierkegaard would have considered them unimportant.

About Roman Catholicism as a "counterweight" Kierkegaard was acute. In Catholic countries one may find, as in all countries, worldly, even immoral, prelates, but one also finds monastic orders of men and women vowed to chastity, poverty, and obedience: a parish priest may be more stupid and tiresome than many of his congregation, but he is a celibate, who has made a sacrifice which they know they would not or could not make themselves. By doing away with the monasteries and fasting, by not only permitting but encouraging the clergy to marry, by abolishing all visible "works" of self-sacrifice, Luther and Calvin made piety a matter of internal conscience. As C. S. Lewis has said of Calvin:

> The moral severity of his rule . . . did not mean that his theology was, in the last resort, more ascetic than that of Rome. It sprang from his refusal to allow the Roman distinction between the life of "religion" and the life of the world, between the Counsels and the Commandments. Calvin's picture of the fully Christian life was less hostile to pleasure and to the body than Fisher's, but then Calvin demanded that every man should be made to live the fully Christian life. In academic jargon, he lowered the honours standard and abolished the pass degree.

Similarly, Kierkegaard says of Luther:

> Luther set up the highest spiritual principle: pure inwardness. . . . And so in Protestantism a point may be reached at which worldliness is honoured and highly valued as—piety. And this—as I maintain—cannot happen in Catholicism. . . . Because Catholicism has the universal premise that we men are pretty well rascals. And why can it happen in Protestantism? Because the Protestant principle is related to a particular premise: a man who sits in the anguish of death, in fear and trembling and much tribulation—and of those there are not many in any one generation.

There is another aspect of Protestantism which Kierkegaard seems to have overlooked—one which makes the position of a Protestant minister more ambiguous and vulnerable than that of a Catholic priest; namely, that in the Lutheran and Calvinist churches, and increasingly so as time went on, the sermon, the ministry of the Word, took precedence over the Sacraments, the ritual acts of worship. The Catholic priest, of course, also preaches, but his primary function is to celebrate Mass, hear confessions, and give absolution. His right to perform such actions depends not on his moral character or even his faith but on the fact that he has been ordained by a bishop. But when a man preaches, all kinds of questions begin to arise. While it is meaningless to ask of a priest "Does he celebrate Mass well or badly?" the question "Does he preach well or badly?" is a real one, with a real answer. Preaching, like lecturing, demands an aesthetic gift: a preacher may himself be a hypocrite but still have the power to stir the hearts of his congregation; conversely, he may be personally a holy man but because he lacks a gift for verbal expression he leaves them cold. Also, the preacher must necessarily address his congregation not as individuals but as a group. As long as his sermon is confined to doctrinal instruction, to telling them what the Church believes and what her credal formulas mean, this presents no problem, but the moment he turns to moral exhortation, to telling them what they should or should not do here and now, he is in difficulties, for each member of his congregation has his or her unique spiritual problems. At confession, a priest may give a confessand stupid, even harmful, advice, but at least this is given to a particular sinner, not to sinners in general. But the preacher in the pulpit is confronted by sinners in general. If he is to avoid generalities which will leave most of them exactly as they were before, he must speak of some concrete situation in which he knows they are all equally guilty, and this, in practice, usually means one about which they not only feel no guilt but are convinced that they are righteous. As Bonhoeffer said:

> The preacher must be concerned so to incorporate the contemporary situation in his shaping of the commandment itself relevant to the real situation. It cannot be "War is evil" but, rather, "Fight this war," or "Don't fight this war."

He will have small occasion to say either, unless he knows his congregation are going to be shocked; that, in the first case, they are willing, out of cowardice, to appease a tyrant, or, in the second, that they are jingoist patriots who say, "My country, right or wrong." In doing so, he risks martyrdom. Attacking sinfulness in general is always perfectly safe, for each listener will assume that it is not he personally but people in general who are being attacked. It is only when a preacher attacks a concrete case of worldliness that he is likely to get into trouble. A clergyman in Mississippi can scold his congregation for not loving God and their neighbor, and they will sit there in smiling agreement, but if he tells them that God demands that they love Negroes as themselves the atmosphere will soon change.

Of the Danish clergy in his day, Kierkegaard complains:

> Like children playing war games (in the security of the living room), so all of Christendom (or the preachers insofar as they are the actors) plays at Christianity; in the security of worldliness they play the game that the Christian is persecuted (but no one persecutes him, the speaker), that the truth is crucified (but the speaker himself already ranks with the court justices).

This complaint seems to suggest either that they only preached on such texts as "Sell all thou hast and give to the poor" and "Marvel not if the world hate you," which cannot have been the case, or that such texts are the only ones on which a true Christian may preach, which is heretical. Secondly, it lacks effectiveness, because Kierkegaard does not or cannot specify any concrete issue for which it was their duty to invite persecution and crucifixion.

It is curious that the author of "Repetition," who could analyze so subtly the difficulty for human beings in their daily life of having to live in and with time, should have failed to see that any church, as a visible organization on earth, has the same problem. Ideally, of course, everyone who calls himself a Christian, whether a clergyman or a layman, should be an apostle, but to imagine that at any time in history this has been, or could be, the case is a sheer Donatist fantasy. It is true, as Kierkegaard says, that "Christianity cannot be 'introduced' into a country as one introduces improved sheep breeding," but if an individual is ever to become a Christian he must be introduced to the Christian faith, and this is one of the church's functions. The Danish Lutheran Church may have been as worldly as Kierkegaard thought it was, but if it had not existed he would never have heard of the Gospels, in which he found the standards by which he condemned it. Actually, it was his father rather than the Lutheran Church who "introduced" Kierkegaard, as a child, to Christianity, and no introduction, as he himself half realized, could have been more unfortunate:

> The greatest danger for a child, where religion is concerned.
>
> The greatest danger is not that his father or tutor should be a freethinker, not even his being a hypocrite. No, the danger lies in his being a pious, Godfearing man, and in the child being convinced thereof, but that he should nevertheless notice that deep in his soul there lies hidden an unrest which, consequently, not even the fear of God and piety could calm. The danger is that the child in that situation is almost provoked to draw a conclusion about God, that God is not infinite love.

He did not realize, however, exactly how peculiar and unlucky he had been, for in discussing the difficulty of bringing up children in the Christian faith he attributes to the average child thoughts which would never occur to one brought up in a normal Christian home:

> Christianity presupposes the actuality of a conviction of sin; it is the glad news that God in Christ accepts sinners. . . . But now the child: he has no actual consciousness of sin. What then? Well, all that talk about how good God and Christ are—the child must have his own thoughts about that—he notices that an *aber* is included: if one has sinned. Take an analogy. Describe the family physician to a child as a very rare and lovable man, etc. What happens? The child thinks something like this: yes, it is very possible that there is such a rare man. I would gladly believe it, but I would also rather steer clear of him, for the fact that I become the object of his special love means that I am sick— and to be sick is no fun; and therefore I am far from being happy at the thought that he has been called.

But what Christian parents in their senses ever spoke to a child about God in Christ accepting sinners? If they are intelligent, they will see that a child's first encounter with the religious life should be aesthetic, not reflective, with exciting rituals, not with sermons. As far as possible, they will avoid talking to the child *about* God, for they know that, as Ferdinand Ebner said, "This is on a par with telling him he was brought to his mother by a stork," but if they must speak of Him they will speak of Him as the Creator who loves all the creatures He has made, never of His actions as Redeemer or Judge. The church has always believed that though we are all born in sin, no child under seven can become guilty of a personal sin. Consequently, it is wicked to talk to a child about sin or guilt. One can only speak of the difference between a good little boy and a bad little boy. Good little boys do what is expected of them when put on the potty and do not pull their sisters' hair. Good little boys get candy; bad little boys get none.

Given his extraordinary upbringing, it is hardly surprising that Kierkegaard should have become—not intellectually but in his sensibility—a Manichee. That is to say, though he would never have denied the orthodox doctrine that God created the world, and asserted that matter was created by an Evil Spirit, one does not feel in his writings the sense that, whatever sorrows and sufferings a man may have to endure, it is nevertheless a miraculous blessing to be alive. Like all heretics, conscious or unconscious, he is a monodist, who can hear with peculiar acuteness one theme in the New Testament—in his case, the theme of suffering and self-sacrifice—but is deaf to its rich polyphony. By anthologizing the New Testament, selecting the passages that appeal to him but ignoring their concrete context, and omitting those passages which do not appeal to him, a man can produce a Pelagian, a Calvinist, a Montanist, a Gnostic Gospel as he pleases, and claim that he has Scriptural authority: what he says is true enough in itself, but it is falsified by what he omits. The Passion of Christ, for example, was to Kierkegaard's taste, the Nativity and Epiphany were not. It is quite true that, as he complained, an overemphasis on the joy of Christmas at the expense of the sorrow of Good Friday can produce an all too cozy version of Christianity, but to reject Christmas altogether is to say that the importance given it in the Gospel narratives was un-Christian. One's suspicions about Kierkegaard's antipathy to Christmas are confirmed when one reads his description of ordinary human birth:

> . . . the entrance to this room [life on earth] is a nasty, muddy, humble stairway and it is impossible to pass with-

out getting disgustingly soiled, and admission is paid by prostituting oneself.

To this, Bonhoeffer, who speaks with the authority of someone who, unlike Kierkegaard, was actually martyred, has the proper corrective:

> We should love God eternally with our whole hearts, yet not so as to compromise or diminish our earthly affections, but as a kind of cantus fermus to which the other melodies of life provide the counterpoint. Earthly affection is one of these contrapuntal themes, a theme which enjoys autonomy of its own.

It is certainly at least partially true that, as Kierkegaard says, "Erotic love is self-love, friendship is self-love," but according to the Gospels Christ never condemns erotic love and friendship as sinful; He merely says that since they come "naturally" to human beings, men and women must not take moral credit for them.

Again Bonhoeffer:

> To long for the transcendent when you are in your wife's arms is, to put it mildly, a lack of taste and it is certainly not what God expects of us. . . . If He pleases to grant us some overwhelming earthly bliss, we ought not to try and be more religious than God Himself.

Kierkegaard could not honestly have said this about himself, but in his extraordinary portrait of the Knight of Faith one discovers to one's amazement that he knew—bless him!—that it was a defect, not a virtue, in him that he could not say it. The ideal Christian he describes is happily married, looks like a cheerful grocer, and is respected by his neighbors. "That," Kierkegaard says, "is what one should be, but, alas, to me he is incomprehensible: I only understand the Knight of the Doleful Countenance."

Even reading him in an English translation, one can tell that Kierkegaard is a master of his mother tongue, who can manage with equal effectiveness every style—the high, the homely, the abstract, the concrete—but he suffers from one great literary defect, which is often found in lonely geniuses: he never knows when to stop. Lonely people are apt to fall in love with the sound of their own voice, as Narcissus fell in love with his reflection, not out of conceit but out of despair of finding another who will listen and respond. As Hammarskjöld wrote:

> Narcissus leaned over the spring, enthralled by the only man in whose eyes he had ever dared—or been given the chance—to forget himself.

The writer who believes that he has, or will have, an audience always shows a sense of proportion in what he writes; he knows when to pause so that his readers may have the chance to respond. But the writer who despairs of an audience dares not stop for fear of the blank silence which might follow if he did. Further, he will tend to believe that no genuine writer can communicate with his fellow-men, that when a writer seems to have an audience who understand him, this must be an illusion:

> Imagine a poet. I do not deny that he is truly great as a poet: but it is probably not for this reason that he becomes so highly regarded and admired by his contemporaries. No, he is also a weak character, cowardly: he maintains good public relations with the voices of envy, bolstering himself up with good connections, etc.—therefore he lives honored and esteemed.

There is some truth in this, but only some. Any poet who has had a measure of public success has encountered admirers who did not seem to have the slightest comprehension of what he was about, but he has also met others who have read his work as he would wish it to be read. Then, while, as we all know, some poets are cunning literary politicians, many, including the best, are not.

Or, again:

> There lived in a market town a small group of dancers; only one of them could leap two feet in the air, the others only a half-foot. Yet there was one among the others who could leap a half-foot plus two inches. He was greatly admired and praised. The one who could leap two feet high was ridiculed, regarded as demented and eccentric.

This parable seems to me simply untrue. Kierkegaard might have said that the citizens of the town could not see any difference between the many who jumped a half foot, the one who jumped eight inches, and the one who jumped two feet—that all the audience could see was that they were all dancers. But the dancers themselves would not ridicule the two-footer; they might envy him and intrigue maliciously against him, but they would be envious precisely because they recognized his superiority.

Kierkegaard once said that if Luther had lived in the nineteenth century he would have said the opposite of what he said in the sixteenth, and one cannot help speculating upon what Kierkegaard might be saying were he living today, in what Harvey Cox has called the Secular City. The religious and cultural situation with which he was familiar lasted more or less until 1914. Till then, Official Christendom existed; that is to say, large areas of the earth where the majority of the population, with various degrees of understanding but nearly all of them sincerely, professed the Christian faith, and on Sundays and feast days attended some place of public worship. This meant that, as a matter of social fact, it was a worldly advantage to be a Christian and a churchgoer, a worldly disadvantage to be a confessed atheist, or freethinker. It did not mean, of course, that people went to church *because* it was a worldly advantage. Secondly, it meant that to enter the Catholic priesthood or the Protestant ministry was one out of various possible worldly careers. In Catholic countries, the bright son of poor peasants might rise to be a cardinal, and even if he got no further than becoming a parish priest, as such he enjoyed a power and a prestige which his parents lacked. In Protestant countries, it was predominantly sons of the middle classes who entered the ministry; when I was a boy, children still used to play at divining their future careers by counting the plum or cherry stones on their plates and reciting "Army, Navy, Law, Church." Again, it would be false and unjust to call those who become clergymen in this way hypocrites; nearly all were devout and most of them very hard-working and conscientious.

Today, in our part of the world, society could not care less what one believes; to be a Christian is regarded by the majority as a rather silly but quite harmless eccentricity, like being a Baconian or a flat-earth man. But there are large areas elsewhere where Christianity is taken seriously, where a Christian is debarred from all but the lowliest jobs and may even lose his life. What would Kierkegaard say to all this? Maybe he would think the situation behind the Iron Curtain a healthier one than that of his Denmark. But what would he think of the present state of the churches in the West? The worldly prestige of the priest and the minister has declined, and what is the result? Those who teach in seminaries, whether Catholic or Protestant, are disturbed not only by the dwindling number of would-be ordinands but by the low intellectual level of those who do apply. Among them there are a few, as there always have been, with a real sense of an apostolic calling, but the majority are persons who are too dumb to stand a chance of success in one of the more remunerative and high-status worldly professions. Holy Orders is their last resort; they cannot dig, and to beg they are ashamed.

There is a parlor game I sometimes play with friends called Purgatory Mates. Each player has to name two persons of such different temperaments that on meeting they would dislike each other intensely, and they are condemned to live together in Purgatory until they come to understand and love each other. The other players have to be convinced that a reconciliation between the pair is ultimately possible. For example, T. S. Eliot and Walt Whitman, Tolstoy and Oscar Wilde. My choice of a Purgatory Mate for Kierkegaard would be the Anglican clergyman who ended up as a canon of St. Paul's—Sydney Smith. I can imagine the look of horror on Kierkegaard's face as he listens to this portly member of the Establishment stating his views on the finances of the Church Visible:

> Could not all the duties of religion be performed as well by poor clergymen as by men of good substance? My great and serious apprehension is that such would not be the case. . . . A picture is drawn of a clergyman with a hundred and thirty pounds per annum, who combines all moral, physical, and intellectual advantages, dedicating himself intensely to the care of his parish—of charming manners and dignified deportment—six feet two inches high, beautifully proportioned, with a magnificent countenance, expressive of all the cardinal virtues and the Ten Commandments—and it is asked with an air of triumph if such a man would fall into

contempt on account of his poverty? But substitute for him an average, ordinary, uninteresting Minister; obese, dumpy, neither ill-natured or good-natured, striding over the styles, with a second-rate wife—dusty and deliquescent —and four parochial children, full of catechism and bread-and-butter; or let him be seen in one of those Shem-Ham-and Japhet buggies driving among his pecuniary, saponaceous, oleaginous parishioners. Can any man of common sense say that all these outward circumstances of the Ministers of Religion have no bearing on religion itself?

And I can picture Sydney Smith's initial dismay of the prospect of being confined to the company of a fanatical dissenter with no sense for the conventions of polite conversation. But after a frigid century or two, both, I believe, would begin to thaw. Each would discover that his companion was, like himself, a wit and, like most funny men, liable to melancholia. Presently they would be able to make each other laugh and to exchange recipes for dealing with low spirits. Then, in time, Kierkegaard would discover that his worldly, society-loving colleague had been banished, at the age of thirty-eight, to a rural parish in Yorkshire; where, instead of taking to drink, he served his rustic flock devotedly for the next twenty years. He would discover, too, that Sydney Smith had unsparingly and effectively attacked both the Established Church and the government for such specific evils as their treatment of Catholics and the game laws, for which attacks he had paid a price: though everyone knew him to be the ablest man in the Anglican Church of his day, not even a Whig government dared make him a bishop. On his side, Sydney Smith would discover that Kierkegaard was not a fanatic but a serious thinker, and under his influence would come to see that he had been wrong when he said, "There is no enthusiasm in the Gospels."

Kierkegaard had, and always will have, an audience for whom it is imperative that they listen to him. His essential warning is directed not to the man-in-the-street, not to the bourgeois man, not even to the clergyman, but to the gifted man, the individual endowed with an exceptional talent for art or science or philosophy. The fact that such a gift is granted to one and not to all means that it is ethically neutral, for only those demands are ethical which apply to all human beings. It is meaningless to say that it is the duty of an artist or a scientist to exercise his talent, for there is nothing he wants to exercise more. The question of duty can arise only in circumstances in which it might be his duty not to exercise it: if his country is invaded it might be required of a painter that he stop painting and become a soldier. And because talent is, humanly speaking, a matter of accident, the relation between a man's talent and his character is accidental. The question "Is X a good or a bad poet?" and the question "Is X a good or a bad husband?" have nothing to do with each other.

The spiritual dangers for the man of great talent are two. He is tempted to take personal credit for a gift which he has done nothing to deserve, and so to conclude that since he is superior to most others at art or science he is a superior human being to whom ethical and religious norms do not apply. And he is tempted to imagine that the particular activity for which he has a talent is of supreme importance, that the world and all its inhabitants are of value only insofar as they provide material for art or science or philosophical speculation.

At exposing such pretensions, Kierkegaard is better than anybody else; here, indeed, he is a prophet, calling the talented to repentance. No person of talent who has read him can fail to realize that the talented man, even more than the millionaire, is the rich man for whom it is so difficult to enter the Kingdom of Heaven.

On this subject, Kierkegaard speaks with absolute authority; one may doubt his theological orthodoxy, one may question his right to demand of others a martyr's death which he did not suffer himself, but one can have no doubt whatsoever that he was a genius.

GRIMM AND ANDERSEN

*

Many deplorable features of modern life, irrationalism, nationalism, idolization of mass-feeling and mass-opinion, may be traced back to the Romantic reaction against the Enlightenment and its Polite Learning; but that same reaction is also responsible for the work of Jacob and Wilhelm Grimm who, with their successors, made the fairy story a part of general education, a deed which few will regret. Much, too, can be said against middle-class family life in the nineteenth century, but in the midst of its heavy moral discipline, its horsehair sofas and stodgy meals, the average child was permitted and even encouraged to lead an exciting life in its imagination. There are more Gradgrinds now than there were then, and the twentieth century has yet to produce books for children equal to Hans Andersen's *Tales,* Edward Lear's *Books of Nonsense,* the two *Alices, Struwelpeter,* or even Jules Verne.

Houses are smaller, servants are fewer, mothers have less time, or think they have, to read to their children, and neither the comic strip nor the radio has succeeded so far in providing a real substitute for the personally told tale which permits of interruptions and repeats.

Anyone who has to do with professional education today is aware that the schools are more and more being expected to replace

] 198 [

the parents and take over the whole of the child's development, a task which is not only impossible but highly dangerous.

If people are sincere when they say that the great contemporary menace in every country is the encroachment of the power of the State over the individual citizen, they must not invite it to mold the thinking of their children in their most impressionable years by refusing to help with their education themselves.

It is to be hoped that the publication of the tales of Grimm and Andersen in one inexpensive volume will be a step in the campaign to restore to parents the right and the duty to educate their children, which, partly through their own fault, and partly through extraneous circumstances, they are in danger of losing for good.

II

There are quite a number of people who disapprove of fairy tales for children, and on various grounds. Let us take the most reasonable first: those who claim that the fairy tale as we know it from Grimm and Andersen is not viable in modern culture. Such tales, they argue, developed in a feudally organized society which believed in magic, and are irrelevant to an industrialized democracy like our own. Luckily the test of viability is a simple one. If a tale is enjoyed by the reader, or audience, it is viable; if he finds it boring or incomprehensible, it is not. It is unlikely, for instance, that a culture without natural science and its methodology would make head or tail of Sherlock Holmes, or that a society which believed the future to be completely determined would find much sense in a story which turned on wishing, and it is very possible that certain details in European fairy stories cannot be transplanted to America. Miss Margaret Mead tells me that the traditional stepmother, which in Europe is a psychological euphemism for the mother in a malevolent aspect, is here a source of misunderstanding because there are too many actual stepmothers; one suspects, too, that in a society where the father plays as minor a role as he plays in America, the fairy tale giant is a less frighteningly important figure than he was to those of us who grew up under the shadow of a paternal discipline. However, one has only to tell the stories and observe the reaction to find out what, if anything, needs changing.

A child who has once been pleased with a tale likes, as a rule, to have it retold in identically the same words, but this should not lead parents to treat printed fairy stories as sacred texts. It is always much better to tell a story than read it out of a book, and, if a parent can produce what, in the actual circumstances of the time and the individual child, is an improvement on the printed text, so much the better.

The second charge against fairy tales is that they harm the child by frightening him or arousing his sadistic impulses. To prove the latter, one would have to show in a controlled experiment that children who have read fairy stories were more often guilty of cruelty than those who had not. Aggressive, destructive, sadistic impulses every child has and, on the whole, their symbolic verbal discharge seems to be rather a safety valve than an incitement to overt action. As to fears, there are, I think, well-authenticated cases of children being dangerously terrified by some fairy story. Often, however, this arises from the child having only heard the story once. Familiarity with the story by repetition turns the pain of fear into the pleasure of a fear faced and mastered.

Lastly there are the people who object to fairy stories on the grounds that they are not objectively true, that giants, witches, two-headed dragons, magic carpets, etc., do not exist; and that, instead of indulging his fantasies in fairy tales, the child should be taught how to adopt to reality by studying history and mechanics. I find such people, I must confess, so unsympathetic and peculiar that I do not know how to argue with them. If their case were sound, the world should be full of Don Quixote-like madmen attempting to fly from New York to Philadelphia on a broomstick or covering a telephone with kisses in the belief that it was their enchanted girl friend.

No fairy story ever claimed to be a description of the external world and no sane child has ever believed that it was. There are children (and adults), certainly, who believe in magic, i.e., who expect their wishes to be granted without any effort on their part, but that is because their parents have spoiled them to despair by loving them too little, and their behavior would be the same if they had never heard the word "magic." An introverted child, as I know from personal experience, can as easily withdraw from the outer world with a water turbine as with a flying horse.

The only danger to healthy development that I can see in the fairy tale is the danger inherent in all works of art, namely, that the reader is tempted to identify himself with the hero in his triumphs and withdraw from him during his sufferings. Knowing, as the reader of the story, that it ends happily, he ignores the fact that the hero *in* the story does not know it is going to end, and so fails to feel the hero's trials as real. Imagination, like reason, is a human faculty and therefore not foolproof.

III

A fairy story, as distinct from a merry tale, or an animal story, is a serious tale with a human hero and a happy ending. The progression of its hero is the reverse of the tragic hero's: at the beginning he is either socially obscure or despised as being stupid or untalented, lacking in the heroic virtues, but at the end, he has surprised everyone by demonstrating his heroism and winning fame, riches, and love. Though ultimately he succeeds, he does not do so without a struggle in which his success is in doubt, for opposed to him are not only natural difficulties like glass mountains, or barriers of flame, but also hostile wicked powers, stepmothers, jealous brothers and witches. In many cases, indeed, he would fail were he not assisted by friendly powers who give him instructions or perform tasks for him which he cannot do himself; that is, in addition to his own powers, he needs luck, but this luck is not fortuitous but dependent upon his character and his actions. The tale ends with the establishment of justice; not only are the good rewarded but also the evil are punished.

Take, for example, "The Water of Life." Three brothers set out in turn on a difficult quest to find the water of life to restore the King, their sick father, to health. Each one meets a dwarf who asks him where he is going. The two elder give rude answers and are punished by being imprisoned in ravines. The third brother gives a courteous answer and is rewarded by being told where the water of life is and how to appease the lions who guard it, but is warned to leave before the clock strikes twelve. He reaches the enchanted castle, where he finds a princess who tells him to return in a year and marry her. At this point he almost fails because he falls asleep and only just manages to escape as the clock strikes twelve and the iron door shuts, carrying away a piece of his heel. On the way home he again meets the dwarf and begs him to release his brothers, which he does with a warning that they have bad hearts. The brothers steal the water of life from him and substitute salt water so that his father condemns him to be secretly shot. The huntsman entrusted with the task has not the heart to do it, and lets the young prince go away into the forest. Now begins a second quest for the Princess. She has built a golden road to test her suitors. Whoever rides straight up it is to be admitted, whoever rides to the side is not. When the two elder brothers come to it, they think "it would be a sin and a shame to ride over that" and so fail the test. At the end of the year, the exiled brother rides thither but is so preoccupied with thinking of the Princess that he never notices the golden road and rides straight up. They are married, the King learns how the elder brothers had betrayed the Prince, and they, to escape punishment, put to sea and never come back.

The hero is in the third or inferior position. (The youngest son inherits least.)* There are two quests, each involving a test which the hero passes and his brothers fail.

The first test is the encounter with the dwarf. The elder brothers disregard him a) because he looks like the last person on earth who could help them; b) they are impatient and thinking only of their success; and c) what is wrong with their concentration on their task is, firstly, over-self-confidence in their own powers and, secondly, the selfishness of their motive. They do not really love their father but want him to reward them.

The hero, on the other hand, is a) humble enough; b) cares enough for his father's recovery; and c) has a loving disposition toward all men, so that he asks the dwarf for assistance and gets it.

The second test of the golden road is a reversal of the first: the right thing to do this time is to take no notice of it. The brothers who dismissed the dwarf notice the road because of its worldly value, which is more to them than any Princess, while the hero, who paid attention to the dwarf, ignores the road because he is truly in love.

---

* I now think I was mistaken. In many peasant communities, where early marriages are the rule, it is the youngest son who inherits the farm.

The Water of Life and the Princess are guarded by lions; these, in this tale, are not malevolent but ensure that no one shall succeed who has not learned the true way. The hero almost fails here by forgetting the dwarf's warning and falling asleep; further it is through falling asleep and not watching his brothers that they almost succeed in destroying him. The readiness to fall asleep is a sign of the trustfulness and lack of fear which are the qualities which bring about his success; at the same time it is pointed out that, carried too far, they are a danger to him.

IV

If such a tale is not history, what is it about? Broadly speaking, and in most cases, the fairy tale is a dramatic projection in symbolic images of the life of the psyche, and it can travel from one country to another, one culture to another culture, whenever what it has to say holds good for human nature in both, despite their differences. Insofar as the myth is valid, the events of the story and its basic images will appeal irrespective of the artistic value of their narration; a genuine myth, like the Chaplin clown, can always be recognized by the fact that its appeal cuts across all differences between highbrow and lowbrow tastes. Further, no one conscious analysis can exhaust its meaning. There is no harm, however, if this is realized, in trying to give one.

Thus reading "The Water of Life," it occurs to me that the two quests, for the water which heals the old sick King and the Princess through marriage with whom the new life will come into being are one and the same, though it is only by first trying to restore the past that one comes to discover one's future path. One's true strength rarely lies in the capacities and faculties of which one is proud, but frequently in those one regards as unimportant or even as weaknesses. Success can never be achieved by an act of conscious will alone; it always requires the co-operation of grace or luck. But grace is not arbitrary; it is always there to assist anyone who is humble enough to ask for it and those who reject it convert it by their own act of rejection into a negative force; they get what they demand. There is no joy or success without risk and suffering, and those who try to avoid suffering fail to obtain the joy, but get the suffering anyway. Finally, and above all, one must not be anxious about ultimate success or failure but think only about what it is necessary to do at the present moment. What seems a story stretched out in time takes place in fact at every instant; the proud and the envious are even now dancing in red-hot shoes or rolling downhill in barrels full of nails; the trustful and loving are already married to princesses.

V

The Grimm brothers were the first men to attempt to record folk tales exactly as they were told by the folk themselves without concessions to bourgeois prudery or cultured literary canon, an example which, in the case of prudery, at least, has not been followed, I am sorry to say, by their translators.

Hans Andersen, so far as I know, was the first man to take the fairy tale as a literary form and invent new ones deliberately. Some of his stories are, like those of Perrault, a reworking of folk material—"The Wild Swans," for example, is based on two stories in the Grimm collection, "The Six Swans," and "The Twelve Brothers"—but his best tales, like "The Snow Queen," or "The Hardy Tin Soldier," or "The Ice Maiden" are not only new in material but as unmistakably Andersen's as if they were modern novels.

Compared with the Grimm tales, they have the virtues and the defects of a conscious literary art. To begin with, they tend to be parables rather than myths.

> "Little Kay was blue with cold—nay almost black— but he did not know it, for the Snow Queen had kissed away the icy shiverings, and his heart was little better than a lump of ice. He went about dragging some sharp flat pieces of ice which he placed in all sorts of patterns, trying to make something out of them, just as when we at home have little tablets of wood, with which we make patterns and call them a 'Chinese puzzle.'
>
> "Kay's patterns were most ingenious, because they were the 'Ice Puzzles of Reason.' In his eyes they were excellent and of the greatest importance: this was because of the

grain of glass still in his eye. He made many patterns forming words, but he never could find the right way to place
them for one particular word, a word he was most anxious
to make. It was 'Eternity.' The Snow Queen had said to
him that if he could find out this word he should be his own
master, and she would give him the whole world and a new
pair of skates. But he could not discover it."

Such a passage could never occur in a folk tale. Firstly, because
the human situation with which it is concerned is an historical one
created by Descartes, Newton, and their successors, and, secondly,
because no folk tale would analyze its own symbols and explain
that the game with the ice-splinters was the game of reason.
Further, the promised reward, "the whole world and a new pair
of skates" has not only a surprise and a subtlety of which the folk
tale is incapable, but, also a uniqueness by which one can identify
its author.

It is rarely possible, therefore, to retell an Andersen story in
other words than his; after the tough and cheerful adventurers of
the folk tales, one may be irritated with the Sensitive-Plantishness
and rather namby-pamby Christianity of some of Andersen's
heroes, but one puts up with them for the sake of the wit and
sharpness of his social observation and the interest of his minor
characters. One remembers the old lady with the painted flowers
in her hat and the robber's daughter in "The Snow Queen" as
individuals in a way that one fails to remember any of the hundreds
of witches and young girls in the folk tales. The difference may
be most clearly seen by a comparison of stories about inanimate
objects.

"Soon . . . they came to a little brook, and, as there
was no bridge or foot-plank, they did not know how they
were to get over it. The straw hit on a good idea, and said:
'I will lay myself straight across, and then you can walk
over on me as a bridge.' The straw therefore stretched itself
from one bank to the other, and the coal, who was of an
impetuous disposition, tripped quite boldly onto the newly
built bridge. But when she had reached the middle, and
heard the water rushing beneath her, she was, after all,
afraid, and stood still, and ventured no further. The straw,

however, began to burn, broke in two pieces, and fell into the stream. The coal slipped after her, hissed when she got into the water, and breathed her last. The bean, who had prudently stayed behind on the shore, could not but laugh at the event, was unable to stop, and laughed so heartily that she burst. It would have been all over with her, likewise, if, by good fortune, a tailor who was traveling in search of work, had not sat down to rest by the brook. As he had a compassionate heart, he pulled out his needle and thread and sewed her together. The bean thanked him most prettily, but, as the tailor used black thread, all beans since then have a black seam."

So Grimm. The fantasy is built upon a factual question. "Why do beans have a black seam?" The characterization of the straw, the coal, and the bean does not extend beyond the minimum required by their respective physical qualities. The whole interest lies in the incidents.

Andersen's story, "The Darning Needle," on the other hand, presupposes no question about its protagonist.

"The darning needle kept her proud behavior and did not lose her good humor. And things of many kinds swam over her, chips and straws and pieces of old newspapers.

" 'Only look how they sail!' said the darning needle. 'They don't know what is under them! . . . See, there goes a chip thinking of nothing in the world but of himself—of a chip! There's a straw going by now. How he turns! how he twirls about! Don't think only of yourself, you might easily run up against a stone. There swims a bit of newspaper. What's written upon it has long been forgotten, and yet it gives itself airs. I sit quietly and patiently here. I know who I am and I shall remain what I am.'

"One day something lay close beside her that glittered splendidly; then the darning needle believed that it was a diamond; but it was a bit of broken bottle; and because it shone, the darning needle spoke to it, introducing herself as a breastpin.

" 'I suppose you are a diamond?' she observed.

" 'Why, yes, something of that kind.'

"And then each believed the other to be a very valuable thing; and they began speaking about the world, and how very conceited it was.

" 'I have been in a lady's box,' said the darning needle, 'and this lady was a cook. She had five fingers on each hand, and I never saw anything so conceited as those five fingers. And yet they were only there that they might take me out of the box and put me back into it.'

" 'Were they of good birth?' asked the bit of bottle.

" 'No, indeed, but very haughty. . . . There was nothing but bragging among them, and therefore I went away.'

" 'And now we sit here and glitter!' said the bit of bottle."

Here the action is subordinate to the actors, providing them with a suitable occasion to display their characters which are individual, i.e., one can easily imagine another Darning Needle and another Bit of Bottle who would say quite different things. Inanimate objects are not being treated anthropomorphically, as in Grimm; on the contrary, human beings have been transmuted into inanimate objects in order that they may be judged without prejudice, with the same objective vision that Swift tries for through changes of size. The difference is one that distinguishes all primitive literature, primitive, that is, in attitude, not in technique, from modern.

In the folk tale, as in the Greek epic and tragedy, situation and character are hardly separable; a man reveals what he is in what he does, or what happens to him is a revelation of what he is. In modern literature, what a man is includes all the possibilities of what he may become, so that what he actually does is never a complete revelation. The defect of primitive literature is the defect of primitive man, a fatalistic lack of hope which is akin to a lack of imagination. The danger for modern literature and modern man is paralysis of action through excess of imagination, an imprisonment in the void of infinite possibilities. That is why, maybe, contemporary novelists seem to have their greatest difficulties with their plots, for we, their characters, find it so much easier to stop to think than to go into action with the consequence, all too often, that, more apathetic than any primitive hero, we wait helplessly for something, usually terrible, to be done to us.

VI

There'll Always Be a Teachers' College.

"How is it possible that human sense should conceive there ever were in the World such multitudes of famous Knights-Errant, so many Emperors . . . palfreys, rambling damsels, serpents, monsters, giants, unheard-of adventures, so many sorts of enchantments. . . . As for my own particular, I confess, that, while I read them, and do not reflect that they are nothing but Falsehood and Folly, they give me some satisfaction, but I no sooner remember what they are, but I cast the best of them from me and would deliver them up to the flames if I had a fire near me. . . . If, led away by your natural inclination, you will read books of heroism and great exploits, read in the Holy Scriptures the Book of Judges, where you will find wonderful truths and glorious actions not to be questioned, the reading of which diverts, instructs, pleases, and surprises the most judicious readers."

"Very well," cried Don Quixote, "then all those books must be fabulous, though licensed by kings, approved by the Examiners, read with general satisfaction, and applauded by the Better Sort and the Meaner, rich and poor, learned and unlearned. . . ."

"For shame, Sir, forbear uttering such blasphemies. And do you, good Sir, believe me, and, as I said to you before, read these books, which you may find will banish all melancholy, if you are troubled with it, and sweeten your disposition if it be harsh."

＊

EDGAR ALLAN POE

＊

What every author hopes to receive from posterity—a hope usually disappointed—is justice. Next to oblivion, the two fates which he most fears are becoming the name attached to two or three famous pieces while the rest of his work is unread and becoming the idol of a small circle which reads every word he wrote with the same uncritical reverence. The first fate is unjust because, even if the pieces known are indeed his best work, the reader has not earned the right to say so; the second fate is embarrassing and ridiculous, for no author believes he is that good.

Poe's shade must be more disappointed than most. Certain pieces—how he must hate these old war horses—are probably more familiar to non-Americans than are any pieces by any other American author. I myself cannot remember hearing any poetry before hearing "The Raven" and "The Bells"; and *The Pit and the Pendulum* was one of the first short stories I ever read. At the same time, the known works of no other author of comparable rank and productivity are so few and so invariably the same. In preparing to make this selection, for example, I asked a number of persons whom I knew to be widely read, but not specialists in American letters, if they had read *Gordon Pym* and *Eureka,* which seem to me to rank among Poe's most important works; not one of them had. On the other hand, I was informed by everyone that to omit *The Cask of Amontillado,* which for my taste is an inferior story, would be commercial suicide. Poor Poe! At first so forgotten that his grave went without a tombstone twenty-six years—when one was finally erected the only American author to attend the ceremony was Whitman; and today in danger of becoming the life study of a few professors. The professors are, of course, very necessary, for it is through their devoted labors that Poe may finally reach the kind of reader every author hopes for, who will read him all, good-humoredly willing to wade through much which is dull or inferior for the delight of discovering something new and admirable.

The Tales: Varied in subject, treatment, style as Poe's stories are, they have one negative characteristic in common. There is no place in any of them for the human individual as he actually exists in space and time, that is, as simultaneously a natural creature subject in his feelings to the influences and limitations of the natural order, and an historical person, creating novelty and relations by his free choice and modified in unforeseen ways by the choices of others.

Poe's major stories fall roughly into two groups. The first group is concerned with states of willful being, the destructive passion of the lonely ego to merge with the ego of another (*Ligeia*), the passion of the conscious ego to be objective, to discover by pure reason the true relationships which sensory appearances and emotions would conceal (*The Purloined Letter*), self-destructive states in which the ego and the self are passionately hostile (*The Imp of the Perverse*), even the state of chimerical passion, that is, the passionate unrest of a self that lacks all passion (*The Man of the Crowd*). The horror tales and the tales of ratiocination belong together, for the heroes of both exist as unitary states—Roderick Usher reasons as little as Auguste Dupin feels. Personages who are the embodiment of such states cannot, of course, change or vary in intensity either through changes in themselves or their environment. The problem in writing stories of this kind is to prevent the reader from ever being reminded of historical existence, for, if he once thinks of real people whose passions are interrupted by a need for lunch or whose beauty can be temporarily and mildly impaired by the common cold, the intensity and timelessness become immediately comic. Poe is sometimes attacked for the operatic quality of the prose and *décor* in his tales, but they are essential to preserving the illusion. His heroes cannot exist except operatically. Take, for example, the following sentence from *William Wilson:*

> Let it suffice, that among spendthrifts I out-heroded Herod, and that, giving name to a multitude of novel follies, I added no brief appendix to the long catalogue of vices then usual in the most dissolute university of Europe.

In isolation, as a prose sentence, it is terrible, vague, verbose, the sense at the mercy of a conventional rhetorical rhythm. But dramatically, how right; how well it reveals the William Wilson who narrates the story in his real colors, as the fantastic self who hates and refuses contact with reality. Some of Poe's successors in stories about states of being, D. H. Lawrence for example, have tried to be realistic with fatal results.

In the second group, which includes such tales as *A Descent into the Maelstrom* and *Gordon Pym,* the relation of will to environment is reversed. While in the first group everything that happens is the consequence of a volition upon the freedom of which there are no natural limits, in these stories of pure adventure the hero is as purely passive as the I in dreams; nothing that happens is the result of his personal choice, everything happens *to* him. What the subject feels—interest, excitement, terror—are caused by events over which he has no control whatsoever. The first kind of hero has no history because he refuses to change with time; this kind has none because he cannot change, he can only experience.

The problem for the writer of adventure stories is to invent a succession of events which are both interesting and varied and to make the order of succession plausible. To secure variety without sacrificing coherence or vice versa is more difficult than it looks, and *Gordon Pym,* one of the finest adventure stories ever written, is an object lesson in the art. Every kind of adventure occurs—adventures of natural origin like shipwreck; adventures like mutiny, caused by familiar human beings, or, like the adventures on the island, by strange natives; and, finally, supernatural nightmare events—yet each leads credibly into the next. While in the stories of passionate states a certain vagueness of description is essential to the illusion, in the adventure story credibility is secured by the minutest details, figures, diagrams, and various other devices, as in Poe's description of the mysterious ravines.

> The total length of this chasm, commencing at the opening *a* and proceeding round the corner *b* to the extremity *d,* is five hundred and fifty yards.

Both these types of Poe story have had an extraordinary influence. His portraits of abnormal or self-destructive states contributed much to Dostoevsky, his ratiocinating hero is the ancestor of Sherlock Holmes and his many successors, his tales of the future lead to H. G. Wells, his adventure stories to Jules Verne and Stevenson. It is not without interest that the development of such fiction in which the historical individual is missing should have coincided with the development of history as a science, with its own laws, and the appearance of the great nineteenth-century historians; further, that both these developments should accompany the industrialization and urbanization of social life in which the individual seems more and more the creation of historical forces while he himself feels less and less capable of directing his life by any historical choice of his own.

Poe's minor fiction also falls into two groups. The first is composed, not of narratives, but physical descriptions of Eden, of the Great Good Place *The Domain of Arnheim.* Such descriptions, whoever they may be written by, are bound to be more interesting as revelations of their authors than in themselves, for no one can imagine the ideal place, the ideal home, except in terms of his private fantasies and the good taste of his day. In Poe's case, in particular, his notions of the stylish and luxurious, if they are not to seem slightly vulgar and comic, must be read in the light of his history and the America of the first half of the nineteenth century. And, lastly there is the group of humorous-satiric pieces unrepresented in this selection. Though Poe is not so funny in them as in some of his criticism, at least one story, *A Predicament,* is of interest. A parody of the kind of popular horror story appearing in *Blackwood's,* it is, in a sense, a parody of Poe's serious work in this vein; and it actually uses the same notion of the swinging descending knife which he was later to employ in *The Pit and the Pendulum.*

The Poems: Poe's best poems are not his most typical or original. "To Helen," which could have been written by Landor, and "The City in the Sea," which could have been written by Hood, are more successfully realized than a poem like "Ulalume," which could have been written by none but Poe.

His difficulty as a poet was that he was interested in too many poetic problems and experiments at once for the time he had to give to them. To make the result conform to the intention—and the more experimental the intention, the more this is true—a writer has to keep his hand in by continual practice. The prose writer who must earn his living has this advantage, that even the purest hack work is practice in his craft; for the penniless poet there is no corresponding exercise. Without the leisure to write and rewrite he cannot develop to his full stature. When we find fault with Poe's poems we must never forget his own sad preface to them.

> In defence of my own taste, it is incumbent upon me to say that I think nothing in this volume of much value to the public, or very creditable to myself. Events not to be controlled have prevented me from making, at any time, any serious effort in what, under happier circumstances, would have been the field of my choice.

For faulty they must be admitted to be. The trouble with "The Raven," for example, is that the thematic interest and the prosodic interest, both of which are considerable, do not combine and are even often at odds.

In *The Philosophy of Composition* Poe discusses his difficulties in preventing the poem from becoming absurd and artificial. The artificiality of the lover asking the proper series of questions to which the refrain would be appropriate could be solved by making him a self-torturer. The difficulty of the speaker of the refrain, however, remained insoluble until the poet hit on the notion of something nonhuman. But the effect could still be ruined unless the narration of the story, as distinct from the questions and answers, flowed naturally; and the meter Poe chose, with its frequent feminine rhymes, so rare in English, works against this and at times defeats him.

Not the least obeisance made he; not a minute stopped or stayed he;
But with mien of lord or lady, perched above my chamber door.

Here it is the meter alone and nothing in the speaker or the situation which is responsible for the redundant alternatives of "stopped or stayed he" and "lord or lady."

Similarly, "Ulalume" is an interesting experiment in diction but only an experiment, for the poem is about something which never quite gets said because the sense is sacrificed to the vowel sounds. It is an accident if the sound of a place name corresponds to the emotion the place invokes, and the accidental is a comic quality. Edward Lear, the only poet, apparently, to be directly influenced by Poe, succeeds with such names as "The Hills of the Chankly Bore" because he is frankly writing "nonsense" poetry, but "Ulalume" has a serious subject and the comic is out of place. "The Bells," though much less interesting a conception than "Ulalume," is more successful because the subject is nothing but an excuse for onomatopoeic effects.

There remains, however, *Eureka*. The man who had flatly asserted that no poem should much exceed a hundred lines in length —"that music (in its modifications of rhythm and rhyme) is of so vast a moment to Poesy as never to be neglected by him who is truly poetical," that neither Truth, the satisfaction of the Intellect, nor Passion, the excitement of the Heart, are the province of Poetry but only Beauty, and that the most poetical topic in the world is the death of a beautiful woman—this man produces at the end of his life a work which he insists is a poem and commends to posterity as his crowning achievement, though it violates every article in his critical creed. It is many pages in length, it is written in prose, it handles scientific ideas in the truth of which the poet is passionately convinced, and the general subject is the origin and destiny of the universe.

Outside France the poem has been neglected, but I do not think Poe was wrong in the importance he attached to it. In the first place, it was a very daring and original notion to take the oldest of the poetic themes—older even than the story of the epic hero—namely, cosmology, the story of how things came to exist as they do, and treat it in a completely contemporary way, to do in English in the nineteenth century what Hesiod and Lucretius had done in Greek and Latin centuries before. Secondly, it is full of remarkable intuitive guesses that subsequent scientific discoveries have confirmed. As Paul Valéry says:

> It would not be exaggerating its importance to recognize, in his theory of consistency, a fairly definite attempt to describe the universe by its *intrinsic properties*. The following proposition can be found toward the end of *Eureka:* "Each law of nature depends at all points on all the other laws." This might easily be considered, if not as a formula, at least as the expression of a tendency toward generalized relativity.
>
> That its tendency approaches recent conceptions becomes evident when one discovers, in the poem under discussion, an affirmation of the *symmetrical* and reciprocal relationship of matter, time, space, gravity, and light.

Lastly, it combines in one work nearly all of Poe's characteristic obsessions: the passion for merging in union with the one which is at the root of tales like *Ligeia,* the passion for logic which dominates the detective and cryptographic studies, the passion for a final explanation and reconciliation which informs the melancholy of much of his verse—all are brought together in this poem of which the prose is as lucid, as untheatrical, as the best of his critical prose.

The Critical Writings: Poe's critical work, like that of any significant critic, must be considered in the literary content which provoked it. No critic, however pontifical his tone, is really attempting to lay down eternal truths about art; he is always polemical, fighting a battle against the characteristic misconceptions, stupidities, and weaknesses of his contemporaries. He is always having, on the one hand, to defend tradition against the amateur who is ignorant of it and the crank who thinks it should be scrapped so that real art may begin anew with him and, on the other, to assert the real novelty of the present and to demonstrate, against the academic who imagines that carrying on the tradition means imitation, what modern tasks and achievements are truly analogues to those of the past.

Poe's condemnation of the long poem and of the didactic or true poem is essentially a demand that the poets of his time be themselves and admit that epic themes and intellectual or moral ideas did not in fact excite their poetic faculties and that what really interested them were emotions of melancholy, nostalgia, puzzled yearning, and the like that could find their proper expression in neither epic nor epigram but in lyrics of moderate length. Poe was forced to attack all long poems on principle, to be unfair, for example, to *Paradise Lost* or *An Essay on Criticism,* in order to shake the preconceived notions of poets and public that to be important a poet must write long poems and give bardic advice.

His rejection of passion is really a variation of Wordsworth's observation that, to be capable of embodiment in a poem, emotion must be recollected in tranquillity; immediate passion is too obsessive, too attached to the self. Poe's attack is further directed against the popular and amateur notion of poetic inspiration which gives the poet himself no work to do, a reminder that the most inspired poem is also a contraption, a made thing.

> We do not hesitate to say that a man highly endowed with the powers of Causality—that is to say a man of metaphysical acumen—will, even with a very deficient share of Ideality, compose a finer poem than one who without such metaphysical acumen, shall be gifted, in the most extraordinary degree, with the faculty of Ideality. For a poem is not the Poetic faculty, but the *means* of exciting it in mankind.

Through its influence on the French, Poe's general aesthetic is well known. The bulk of his critical writing, and perhaps that which was of the greatest service, is concerned with poetic technique and practical criticism of details. No one in his time put so much energy and insight into trying to make his contemporary poets take their craft seriously, know what they were doing prosodically, and avoid the faults of slovenly diction and inappropriate imagery that can be avoided by vigilance and hard work.

If Poe never developed to his potential full stature as a critic, this was entirely his misfortune, not his fault. Much of his best criticism will never be read widely because it lies buried in reviews of totally uninteresting authors. If he sometimes overpraised the

second-rate like Mrs. Osgood or wasted time and energy in de-
molishing nonentities like Mr. English, such were inevitable consequences when a critical mind, equipped by nature for digesting
the toughest of foods, is condemned by circumstances to feed on
literary gruel. The first-rate critic needs critical issues of the first
importance, and these were denied him. Think of the subjects that
Baudelaire was granted—Delacroix, Constantin Guys, Wagner—
and then of the kind of books Poe was assigned to review:

Mephistopheles in England, or the Confessions of a Prime Minister
The Christian Florist
Noble Deeds of Women
Ups and Downs in the Life of a Distressed Gentleman
The History of Texas
Sacred Philosophy of the Seasons
Sketches of Conspicuous Living Characters in France
Dashes at Life with a Free Pencil
Alice Day; A Romance in Rhyme
Wakondah; The Master of Life
Poetical Remains of the Late Lucretia Maria Davidson

One is astounded that he managed to remain a rational critic at all,
let alone such a good one.

The Man: If the Muses could lobby for their interest, all
biographical research into the lives of artists would probably be
prohibited by law, and historians of the individual would have to
confine themselves to those who act but do not make—generals,
criminals, eccentrics, courtesans, and the like, about whom information is not only more interesting but less misleading. Good
artists—the artist *manqué* is another matter—never make satisfactory heroes for novelists, because their life stories, even when
interesting in themselves, are peripheral and less significant than
their productions.

As a person, for example, Poe is a much less interesting figure
than is Griswold. Since Professor Quinn published side by side the
original versions of Poe's letters and Griswold's doctored versions,
one is left panting with curiosity to know more about the latter.
That one man should dislike another and speak maliciously of him
after his death would be natural enough, but to take so much

trouble, to blacken a reputation so subtly, presupposes a sustained hatred which is always fascinating because the capacity for sustained emotion of any kind is rare, and, in this instance, particularly so since no reasonable cause for it has yet been found.

In his personal reputation, as in so much else, Poe has been singularly unfortunate. Before the true facts were known, he was dismissed by respectable men of letters as a dissolute rake and hailed by the antirespectable as a romantically doomed figure, the Flying Dutchman of Whitman's dream.

> In a dream I once had, I saw a vessel on the sea, at midnight in a storm . . . flying uncontrolled with torn sails and broken spars through the wild sleet and winds and waves of the night. On the deck was a slender, slight, beautiful figure, a dim man, apparently enjoying all the terror, the murk, and the dislocation of which he was the centre and the victim.

Today this portrait has been shown to be false, but the moral climate has changed, and Poe would be more respected if it had been true. Had he been a really bad lot like Villon or Marlowe or Verlaine, someone who drank like a fish and was guilty of spectacular crimes and vices, we should rather admire him; but it turns out that he was only the kind of fellow whom one hesitates to invite to a party because after two drinks he is apt to become tiresome, an unmanly sort of man whose love-life seems to have been largely confined to crying in laps and playing house, that his weaknesses were of that unromantic kind for which our age has least tolerance, perhaps because they are typical of ourselves.

If our present conception of Poe as a person is correct, however, it makes Poe the artist a much odder figure. Nobody has a good word to say for his foster father, John Allan, who certainly does not seem to have been a very attractive gentleman; but if we imagine ourselves in his place in the year 1831, what sort of view would we have taken of Poe's future?

Remembering his behavior at the university, his pointless enlistment in the army, his behavior at West Point, his behavior to ourselves, would he not have seemed to us an obvious case of a certain kind of neurotic with which we are quite familiar—the talented youngster who never comes to anything because he will not or cannot work, whose masterpieces never get beyond the third page, who loses job after job because he cannot get to work on time or meet a date line? We might find psychological excuses for him in his heredity and early childhood—the incompetent, irresponsible father, the death of his mother when he was two—but our prognosis for his future not only as a man but also as a writer would hardly have been sanguine. At the very best we might have hoped that in the course of a lifetime he would produce one or two exquisitely polished lyrics.

But what in fact did happen? While remaining in his personal life just as difficult and self-destructive as we foresaw, he quickly became a very hard-working and conscientious professional writer. None of his colleagues on magazines seems to have had any professional difficulty with him. Indeed, when one compares the quality of most of the books he had to review with the quality of his reviews, one is inclined to wish that, for the sake of his own work, he had been less conscientious. The defects we find in his work are so often just the defects we should have least expected—the errors of a professional who is overtaxed and working against the clock.

As to his private life and personality, had it been more romantically wicked, his work would not have the importance it has as being, in some senses, the first modern work. He was one of the first to suffer *consciously* the impact of the destruction of the traditional community and its values, and he paid the heaviest price for this consciousness. As D. H. Lawrence says in an essay conspicuous for its insights:

> Poe had a pretty bitter doom. Doomed to seethe down his soul in a great continuous convulsion of disintegration, and doomed to register the process. And then doomed to be abused for it, when he had performed some of the bitterest tasks of human experience, that can be asked of a man. Necessary tasks too. For the human soul must suffer its own disintegration, consciously, if ever it is to survive.

To which one might add: "Abused?" No, a worse doom than that. Doomed to be used in school textbooks as a bait to interest the young in good literature, to be a respectable rival to the pulps.

Still, he has had some rewards. Not many authors have been invoked as intercessors with God in an hour of need, as Poe was named by Baudelaire when he felt himself going mad; not many have been celebrated in poems as beautiful as Mallarmé's Sonnet, of which this is Roger Fry's translation.

THE TOMB OF EDGAR POE

Such as to himself eternity's changed him,
The Poet arouses with his naked sword
His age fright-stricken for not having known
That Death was triumphing in that strange voice!

They, with a Hydra's vile spasm at hearing the angel
Giving a sense more pure to the words of their tribe
Proclaimed aloud the sortilege drunk
In the dishonored flow of some black brew.

Oh, Grief! From soil and from the hostile cloud,
If thence our idea cannot carve a relief
Wherewith to adorn Poe's shining tomb

Calm block fallen down here from some dark disaster
May this granite at least show forever their bourn
To the black flights of Blasphemy sparse in the future.

TENNYSON

✳

During the latter half of the eighteenth century there lived in Grimsby, Lincolnshire, a successful solicitor and businessman called George Tennyson. Robust, cheerful, interested in genealogy, he made and married money, became a member of Parliament, bought a country estate, and begat two sons, George and Charles. For reasons unknown he disinherited the elder and sent him, against his will, into the Church, making him Rector of Somersby. In 1805 the Reverend George Tennyson married Elizabeth Fytch, a clergyman's daughter with a taste for Felicia Hemans, begat eight sons and four daughters, and died in 1831. His sixth child and fourth son, born at midnight of August 6, 1809, was the poet.

Alfred Tennyson was sent to Louth Grammar School, where he was unusually unhappy; he was taken away and educated at home until 1828, when he went up to Trinity College, Cambridge. There he met Arthur Henry Hallam, belonged to a group of earnest young intellectuals who called themselves The Apostles, won the Chancellor's medal for a poem on Timbuctoo, and went down in 1831 without taking his degree. He had, however, already published two books. *Poems by Two Brothers,* written in collaboration with his brother Frederick, had been published by a Louth bookseller in 1827, and his *Poems, Chiefly Lyrical,* by Moxon, a London publisher, in 1830.

In the summer of 1831 he made a curious journey with Hallam to the Pyrenees to take money from English sympathizers to a Spanish revolutionary general, his first and last excursion into practical politics, and his first and apparently fatal contact with France.

In December 1832 Moxon published *Poems*, which contained an epigram attacking Christopher North for his review of the 1830 volume. Partly on this account, and partly, perhaps, out of irritation at the uncritical admiration of Tennyson's friends, Lockhart wrote a review in the *Edinburgh Quarterly* of such effective virulence that for some years people were ashamed to be caught reading Tennyson. In the same year, on October 1, he received news of Hallam's sudden death in Vienna. For the next ten years he published no book, had no regular occupation, drank port, smoked strong tobacco, and was poor and unhappy. He became engaged to his future wife; the engagement was broken off. Somersby Rectory was sold; he moved to the neighborhood of London. He invested his capital and his mother's in the project of a certain Dr. Allen for making woodcarving by machinery; the doctor absconded. But all this time he was writing, and in 1842 *Poems* appeared which established his reputation with the intelligentsia and the critics. In 1846 the grant of a pension from the Civil List made him financially secure, and in 1850 he published his masterpiece *In Memoriam,* married, and succeeded Wordsworth as Poet Laureate.

From then on he led the life of a famous author. He bought a house in the Isle of Wight, he wrote, he grew a beard, he visited Queen Victoria at Osborne, he built another house in Surrey, he went on writing, he visited the Queen at Windsor, he was gazetted to the Peerage, he still wrote. On October 8, 1892, he died, and was buried in Westminster Abbey.

He had a large, loose-limbed body, a swarthy complexion, a high, narrow forehead, and huge bricklayer's hands; in youth he looked like a gypsy; in age like a dirty old monk; he had the finest ear, perhaps, of any English poet; he was also undoubtedly the stupidest;* there was little about melancholia that he didn't know; there was little else that he did.

* T. S. Eliot pointed out to me that he could think of two or three English poets who were stupider, and I had to agree.

In his excellent study of the poet,* Mr. Harold Nicholson divides his literary development into four phases.

The first, which extends from the *Poems by Two Brothers* in 1827 to the publication of the 1842 volume, represents his luxuriant period—the period in which, whatever people may say, he was under the influence of Keats and, in a lesser degree, of Coleridge. He sings throughout to "one clear harp in Diverse tones," but beautiful as the poems are, there is little impression of any central or directing purpose or inspiration. The second phase, which the first slightly overlaps, begins with the death of Hallam in 1833 and concludes with *Maud* in 1855. To this period, which is clearly the most important of the four, belong *The Two Voices,* and *Break, Break, Break,* which were actually published in the 1842 volume, *The Princess* in 1847, and *In Memoriam* in 1850. The magnificent *Ode to the Duke of Wellington,* which appeared in 1852, falls also within this period. With 1857 we come to the third, the unfortunate mid-Victorian phase of Tennyson's development, and we enter upon the series of the *Idylls,* the *Enoch Arden* poems of 1866, *The Holy Grail* of 1870, and the final *Idylls* of 1872. From 1873 onward there is an interval in which the Laureate was occupied, with amazing obstinacy, in writing plays, but in 1880, the fourth and last period, the splendid *Aldworth* period, opens with *Ballads and Other Poems,* with *Rizpah,* and *Lucknow* and *De Profundis.* In 1885 we find *Tiresias* and the *Ancient Sage* and the lines to Fitzgerald, and the period closes only with the posthumous publication of *The Death of Oenone* in 1892.

It is important, I think, clearly to mark the difference between these four periods. For whereas the early period has given us things like *Mariana* and *The Lady of Shalott;* whereas the second period has revealed to us the essential lyrical inspiration of Tennyson, and convinced us of his greatness and permanence as a poet; whereas the last period is a magnificent monument to his vitality and his mastery of language; the third period, the mid-Victorian period,

---

* *Tennyson, Aspects of His Life, Character, and Poetry.* (Houghton Mifflin, 1934.) See also the introduction to the Tennyson volume in the Nelson Classics, by T. S. Eliot. Reprinted under the title of *In Memoriam* in *Essays Ancient and Modern.* (Harcourt, Brace, 1936.)

can make no appeal whatsoever to the modern mind. And, unfortunately, it is by this third period, the Farringford period, by the *Idylls* and *Enoch Arden,* that he is condemned. And that this should be so is both unfair and unintelligent.

We must not, however, make the mistake of concluding from this that the Victorians had exceptionally bad taste and did not appreciate these poems of Tennyson which we think good, or that we are any better judges of our own contemporaries. A poet may write bad poetry in three ways. He may be bored or in a hurry and write work which is technically slipshod or carelessly expressed. From this fault, of which Shakespeare is not infrequently guilty, Tennyson is quite free. Secondly, by overlooking verbal and visual associations he may be unintentionally funny at a serious moment; e.g., in describing the martyrdom of St. Stephen, Tennyson writes:

> But looking upward, full of grace,
> He pray'd, and from a happy place
> God's glory smote him on the face.

And in his dedicatory poem to Lord Dufferin, on whose yacht his own son had died:

> But ere he left your fatal shore,
> And lay on that funereal boat,
> Dying, "Unspeakable" he wrote
> "Their kindness," and he wrote no more;

Thirdly, he may suffer from a corruption of his own consciousness and produce work, the badness of which strikes the reader as intentional; i.e., in the case of carelessness or accidental bathos, one feels it would only have to be pointed out to the poet for the latter to recognize it instantly, but in the case of this kind of badness, one feels certain that the poet is very pleased with it. The faults, for instance, of the following extracts, could not be cured by literary criticism alone; they involve Tennyson's personality.

Love for the maiden, crown'd with marriage, no regrets for aught
    that has been,
Household happiness, gracious children, debtless competence,
    golden mean;

> For think not, tho' thou would'st not love thy lord,
> Thy lord has wholly lost his love for thee.
> I am not made of so slight elements.
> Yet must I leave thee, woman, to thy shame. . . .
> I did not come to curse thee, Guinevere,
> I, whose vast pity almost makes me die . . .
> Lo, I forgive thee, as Eternal God
> Forgives: do thou for thine own soul the rest.

> > Kiss in the bower,
> > Tit on the tree!
> > Bird mustn't tell,
> > Whoop! he can see.

For poetry which is bad in this essential sense, there are different
specific causes in each case, but they may all, perhaps, be included
in one basic error; trash is the inevitable result whenever a person
tries to do for himself or for others by the writing of poetry what
can only be done in some other way, by action, or study, or
prayer. That is why so many adolescents write poetry. Those who
have no poetic gift quickly give it up, but those who have talent,
and hence discover that *something* can be achieved by artistic
creation, namely a consciousness of what one really feels, remain
subject to the temptation to think that everything can be achieved
in this way; the elimination, for example, of unpleasant or disgrace-
ful feelings, particularly if they are talented enough to acquire a
professional status and rich enough to need no other occupation.
This temptation was, in Tennyson's case, particularly acute. In the
first place, his genius was lyrical, and the lyric poet is perpetually
confronted with the problem of what to do with his time between
the few hours when he is visited by his muse. If Tennyson, like
others before and after him, occupied himself from his fiftieth to
his seventieth year with epic and dramatic forms for which he had

no talent whatsoever,* it would be unjust to attribute this wholly
or even mainly to a conceited ambition to rival Milton and Shakespeare; one, by no means the least important factor, was certainly
the laudable wish not to be as idle in the second half of his life
as he had been in the first. As we know from the lives of other lyric
poets, the alternative to writing long, unreadable poems is apt to be
the less innocent and not necessarily more fruitful pastime of
debauchery.

And in the second place, the feelings which his gift revealed
to Tennyson were almost entirely those of lonely terror and desire
for death. From the *Song* written when he was still an undergraduate

> The air is damp, and hush'd, and close,
> As a sick man's room when he taketh repose
>   An hour before death;
> My very heart faints and my whole soul grieves
> At the moist rich smell of the rotting leaves,
>   And the breath
>   Of the fading edges of box beneath.
> And the year's last rose.

to *Demeter* written when he was nearly eighty.

> . . . . and see no more,
> The Stone, the Wheel, the dimly-glimmering lawns,
> Of that Elysium, all the hateful fires
> Of torment, and the shadowy warrior glide
> Along the silent field of Asphodel.

The note successfully struck is consistently that of numb elegaic
sadness. Nietzsche's description of Wagner applies in a lesser degree to Tennyson too.

---

* If England had only possessed in the nineteenth century an operatic composer of the rank of Verdi or Wagner, Tennyson might have found in the
libretto a medium at once lyrical and dramatic. *Maud*, a libretto *manqué*, is
an indication of what gifts he had in that direction. He is one of the few
poets who has been able to write poetry which is meaningful in itself and
at the same time settable to music.

Nobody can approach him in the colours of late Autumn, in the indescribably touching joy of a last, a very last, and all too short gladness; he knows of a chord which expresses those secret and weird midnight hours of the soul when cause and effect seem to have fallen asunder and at every moment something may spring out of nonentity. . . . He knows that weary shuffling along of the soul which is no longer able either to spring or to fly, nay which is no longer able to walk . . . his spirit prefers to squat peacefully in the corners of broken-down houses: concealed in this way, and hidden even from himself, he paints his really great masterpieces, all of which are very short, often only one bar in length—there only does he become quite good, great and perfect, perhaps there alone. . . .

When one begins to make a selection from Tennyson's work, one is startled by the similarity of the symbolic situations his best poems present. One can almost construct an archetypal pattern and say that the Tennysonian subject must contain one or more of the following elements:

1. An act of desertion, whether by marriage or by death; e.g., *Mariana and Oenone* (desertion of a man by a woman), *In Memoriam* (desertion of a man by a man), *Rizpah* (desertion of a mother by a son), *Demeter* (desertion of a mother by a daughter), *Despair* (desertion by God).
2. An insensitive, cruel other; e.g., *Oenone* (Aphrodite), *Locksley Hall* (husband), *Maud* (brother), *Rizpah* (The Law).
3. An accidental crime committed by the hero; e.g., *Oriana, Maud, Tiresias*.
4. A thief; e.g., *Maud* (grandfather), *Despair* (son).
5. A contrast of landscape. The barren landscape of loneliness and passion (rocks and sea) versus the fertile landscape of coziness and calm (village and river plain).

In no other English poet of comparable rank does the bulk of his work seem so clearly to be inspired by some single and probably very early experience.

Tennyson's own description of himself as

An infant crying in the night;
An infant crying for the light.
And with no language but a cry

is extraordinarily acute. If Wordsworth is the great English poet
of Nature, then Tennyson is the great English poet of the Nursery,
of

das ungewisse Licht von Nachmittagen
in denen man sich fürchtete als Kind.

i.e., his poems deal with human emotions in their most primitive
states, uncomplicated by conscious sexuality or intellectual ration-
alization. (No other poetry is easier, and less illuminating, to
psychoanalyze.)

Two admissions of Tennyson's, that the first poetry which excited him was his own, and that at the age of five he used to walk
about saying "Alfred, Alfred" are significant, as are his lines on
science.

Let Science prove we are, and then
What matters Science unto men.

Two questions: Who am I? Why do I exist? and the panic fear
of their remaining unanswered—doubt is much too intellectual and
tame a term for such a vertigo of anxiety—seem to have obsessed
him all his life. Why he should have felt them so strongly and at
such an early age we cannot, of course, know, but it seems not
unlikely that his experience was similar to one described by Kierkegaard in his journals.

The greatest danger is not that his father or tutor should
be a free-thinker, not even his being a hypocrite. No, the
danger lies in his being a pious, God-fearing man, and in
the child being convinced thereof, but that he should nevertheless notice that deep in his soul there lies hidden an unrest which, consequently, not even the fear of God and
piety could calm. The danger is that the child in that situation is almost provoked to draw a conclusion about God,
that God is not infinite love.

But whatever the initiating cause, Tennyson became conscious in childhood of Hamlet's problem, the religious significance of his own experience. Emotions of early childhood are hard to express except accidentally because the original events associated with them are not remembered. Hallam's death, a repetition of the abandonment experience, gave Tennyson the symbolic event which mobilized what he had already suffered and gave his fear a focus and a *raison d'être*. St. Augustine gives an illuminating account of a similar experience.

> Thus I was wretched, and my wretched life was dearer to me than my friend had been. Gladly as I would have changed it, I would rather have been deprived of my friend than of my grief. . . . I was sick of living, yet afraid to die. I suppose that the intensity of my love made death, which has robbed me of him, seem hateful and dreadful, like some horrid enemy; and I thought that it must soon destroy all men because it had slain him. . . . I marvelled that other men should be alive since he was dead whom I had loved as if he could never die, and I marvelled still more that I, his other self, should be alive when he was dead. Well did the poet say of his friend: "O thou half of my soul." For I felt that my soul and his had been but one in two bodies; and life seemed horrible to me, because I was cut in two. And perhaps, that is why I feared to die, lest the other half of him whom I had loved so dearly, should perish.
>
> *Confessions, Book IV, Chap. 6*

In this basic anxiety about his existence Tennyson is the brother of another and greater nineteenth-century poet, Baudelaire, and it may not be unrewarding to compare these two figures, superficially so dissimilar yet fundamentally so alike, the provincial Englishman with his terror of political and domestic disorder and the cosmopolitan satanic dandy of Paris.

> And crowds that stream from yawning doors,
>   And shoals of puckered faces drive;
>   Dark hulks that tumble half alive,
> And lazy lengths on boundless shores;

Bitter barmaid, waning fast!
See that sheets are on my bed.

He seems as one whose footsteps halt,
Toiling in immeasurable sand,
And o'er a weary sultry land,
Far beneath a blazing vault,
Sown in a wrinkle of the monstrous hill,
The city sparkles like a grain of salt.

Ask me no more: thy fate and mine are seal'd;
   I strove against the stream and all in vain;
   Let the great river take me to the main.
No more, dear love, for at a touch I yield;
                 Ask me no more.

are closer in spirit to

Un damné descendant sans lampe,
Au bord d'un gouffre dont l'odeur
Trahit l'humide profondeur,
D'éternels escaliers sans rampe,

Le beau valet de cœur et la dame de pique
Causent sinistrement de leurs amours défunts.

Et mon esprit, toujours du vertige hanté,
Jalouse du néant l'insensibilité.
—Ah! ne jamais sortir des Nombres et des Êtres!

than to any other English poetry.

In their verse technique, both display the same musical ear and love of "line."* (Pope is to Tennyson what Racine is to Baude-

---

* It is interesting to speculate on the relation between the strictness and musicality of a poet's form and his own anxiety. It may well be, I think, that the more he is conscious of an inner disorder and dread, the more value he will place on tidiness in the work as a *defense,* as if he hoped that through his control of the means of expressing his emotions, the emotions themselves, which he cannot master directly, might be brought to order.

laire.) Both felt themselves to be exiles from a lost paradise, desert dwellers (the barren rocks and desolate fens of Tennyson correspond to the gas-lit Paris of Baudelaire); both shared the same nostalgia for the Happy Isles, *le vert paradis des amours enfantines,* to be reached only after long voyages over water; both imagine Eden in the same Rousseauistic terms; i.e., as a place of natural innocence rather than supernatural illumination.

But in their conceptions of how to endure this present life, in which direction to sail, they part company.

Baudelaire wrote:

> *Je plains les poêtes que guide le seul instinct; je les crois incompletes . . . l'homme de génie a les nerfs solides; l'enfant les a faibles. Chez un le raison a pris une place considerable; chez l'autre, la sensibilité occupe presque tout l'être.*

If Baudelaire became the greater poet, it was not because his initial sensibility was any keener than Tennyson's, but because in addition he developed a first-rate critical intelligence which prevented him from writing an epic about Roland or a tragedy about Joan of Arc to escape from his vision of the abyss. On the other hand, it led him into an error which Tennyson escaped—the error of making a religion of the aesthetic.

Baudelaire was right in seeing that art is beyond good and evil, and Tennyson was a fool to try to write a poetry which would teach the Ideal; but Tennyson was right in seeing that an art which is beyond good and evil is a game of secondary importance, and Baudelaire was the victim of his own pride in persuading himself that a mere game was

> *le meilleur témoignage*
> *que nous puissions donner de notre dignité.*

Thus if Tennyson embarrasses us by picturing Paradise as an exact replica of Somersby Rectory or Torquay, he has at least a conception, however naïve, of a *good* place, and does not, like Baudelaire, insist that its goodness and badness are unimportant, for all that matters is its novelty, to be attained at whatever cost by a cultivation of hysteria with delight and terror.

The same difference shows itself in their respective attitudes to society and personal relations. Both were profoundly lonely men who viewed the loud, gregarious extrovert with fear and distaste. The Tennyson who wrote

> . . . and in one month
> They wedded her to sixty thousand pounds
> To lands in Kent and messuages in York,
> And slight Sir Robert with his watery smile
> And educated whisker.

O, I see thee old and formal, fitted to thy petty part,
With a little hoard of maxims preaching down a daughter's heart.

is close to the Baudelaire who hated *l'esprit belge*. And what is *Ulysses* but a covert—the weakness of the poem is its indirection—refusal to be a responsible and useful person, a glorification of the heroic dandy?

Rejecting the bourgeois parody of marriage and home, both sought impossible extremes, but in opposite directions. Tennyson dreamed of an affectionate circle without conflict, the coziness of childhood (in all his praise of marriage there is no sense of a historical relation between individuals); Baudelaire, judging a relation by its intensity alone, thought only of a childless sexual relation from which cruelty was inseparable.

The aspects of Tennyson that are now so distasteful to us, the "schoolmistress Alfred" of *The Miller's Daughter* and *Guinevere*, the schoolboy Froggie-hater of *Riflemen, Form,* are the counterpart of the "shocking" Baudelaire to whom the sole pleasure in love was the knowledge of doing evil and who hoped to conquer solitude by inspiring universal horror and disgust. If the latter's pose still appeals to us, it is because it flatters our modern forms of egoism in the same way that the former's flattered the Victorians, for both are attempts to evade the need for a religious faith by finding some form of magical certainty, and both lead to disaster, the one, as Baudelaire himself realized too late, to hearing the "wind of the wing of madness," the other to an infantile torpor, a "glory without history, the poetic character more worn than paid for, or at least more saved than spent."

A VERY INQUISITIVE OLD PARTY

*

Such was the description of Henry Mayhew given by a prostitute he was interviewing. His own description of his activities does not deny it:

> When I first went among you, it was not very easy for me to make you comprehend the purpose I had in view. You at first fancied that I was a Government spy, or a person in some way connected with the police. I am none of these, nor am I a clergyman wishing to convert you to his particular creed, nor a teetotaler anxious to prove the source of all evil to be overindulgence in intoxicating drink; but I am simply a literary man, desirous of letting the rich know something more about the poor. Some persons study the stars, others study the animal kingdom, others again direct their researches into the properties of stones, devoting their whole lives to these particular vocations. I am the first who has endeavored to study a class of my fellow-creatures whom Providence has not placed in so fortunate a position as myself, my desire being to bring the extremes of society together—the poor to the rich, and the rich to the poor.

After a random sampling of *London Labour and the London Poor,* I am inclined to think that, if I had to write down the names of the ten greatest Victorian Englishmen, Henry Mayhew would head the list. I say "random sampling" because I can no more imagine a man reading straight through it from beginning to end than I can imagine him so reading the Encyclopædia Britannica. The new reprint appears to be a photo-offset of the 1865 edition. The four volumes contain nearly two thousand pages in double columns and a print so small that even a myopic like myself finds it a strain on the eyes.

The son of a London solicitor, Henry Mayhew was born in 1812 and died in 1887. He was one of the original proprietors and editors of *Punch,* which first appeared in 1841. In collaboration with a brother, Augustus, he wrote a number of comic novels which enjoyed considerable success in their day, and one cannot help wondering if they have been undeservedly forgotten. His magnum opus began as a series of articles in the *Morning Chronicle* in 1849 and 1850. Volume I and parts of Volumes II and III were published in 1851, and the complete work in 1862.

Mayhew was a compulsive classifier. Grouped under four main headings—"Those Who Will Work," "Those Who Cannot Work," "Those Who Will Not Work," "Those Who Need Not Work"— his list of human occupations takes up sixteen pages. "Authors" are classed not as "Benefactors," like teachers and clergy, but appear under Sub-Group D, "Makers or Artificers," sub-sub-group 3:

> Workers connected with the Superlative Arts, that is to say, with those arts which have no products of their own, and are engaged either in adding to the beauty or usefulness of the products of other arts, or in inventing or designing the work appertaining to them.

Among those with whom he ranks us are "Desiccators, Anti-dry-rot Preservers, Scourers, Calenderers and French Polishers."

On the function of "Employers," Mayhew disagrees violently with J. S. Mill:

> Mr. Mill's mistake in ranking the Employers and Distributors among the Enrichers, or those who increase the exchangeable commodities of the country, arose from a desire to place the dealers and capitalists among the productive labourers, than which nothing could be more idle, for surely they do not add, *directly,* one brass farthing, as the

saying is, to the national stock of wealth. A little reflection would have shown that gentleman that the true function of employers and dealers was that of the *indirect aiders* of production rather than the direct producers.

A metropolis like London is seldom, if ever, the center of a heavy industry like mining or steelworking or cottonspinning. In Mayhew's London, the largest class of employed worker was the domestic servant. Consequently, unlike Engels, Mayhew is not concerned with the lot of factory hands. He does deal with the problems of small craft industry, but devotes most of his attention to those who earned their living, honestly or dishonestly, on the streets—a class which in his day, he reckoned, comprised one in forty of the population of London. His first two volumes are concerned with street sellers, street collectors, and street cleaners; his third with vermin exterminators, street entertainers, small artisans, and casual laborers like dockhands; his fourth with prostitutes, thieves, swindlers, and beggars.

Among social anthropologists Mayhew is unique, so far as I know, in his combination of a Fabian Society passion for statistics, a Ripley passion for believe-it-or-not facts as sheer oddities, and a passion for the idiosyncrasies of character and speech such as only the very greatest novelists have exhibited. Lovers of statistics can learn from him, for example, that the rate of alcoholics among button-molders was 1 in 7.2, among clergymen 1 in 417, and among domestic servants 1 in 585.7, and that a horse excretes 38 lbs. 2 oz. of dung every twenty-four hours. Lovers of odd facts will learn that the first modern water closet was patented by Bramah in 1808, that the poets who sold best in the street were Shakespeare, Pope, Thomson, Goldsmith, Burns, Byron, and Scott, but there was little demand for Milton, Dryden, Shelley, or Wordsworth, that rape was commonest in Monmouthshire, bigamy in Cheshire, and that Herefordshire came second only to London in the number of its female criminals. I myself was particularly enchanted by the results of his enquiry among a group of boys as to the first article they ever stole. His list runs thus:

> Six rabbits, silk shawl from home, a pair of shoes, a Dutch cheese, a few shillings from home, a coat and trousers, a bullock's heart, four "tiles" of copper, fifteen and

sixpence from master, two handkerchiefs, half a quartern loaf, a set of tools worth 3 £, clothes from a warehouse, worth 22 £, a Cheshire cheese, a pair of carriage lamps, some handkerchiefs, five shillings, some turnips, watchchain and seals, a sheep, three and sixpence, and an invalid's chair.

As for his powers as a reporter, I can only quote a few short extracts, which is unfair to him, as they should be read *in toto*. I would recommend the reader to sample his interviews with Jack Black, Rat-Killer to Her Majesty (III, 11–20), with Billy the whistling and dancing boy (III, 199–204), and with a young pickpocket (IV, 316–324). These have led me to revise my critical notions of Dickens, whom I had always thought of as a fantastic creator of over-life-size characters; it is evident that he was much more of a "realist" than he is generally taken for.

The following extracts will, I hope, give some idea of Mayhew's amazing ear for speech:

A Fourteen-Year-Old Boy.

Yes, he had heer'd of God who made the world. Couldn't exactly recollec' when he'd heer'd on him, but he had, most sartenly. . . . Knew there was a book called the Bible; didn't know what it was about; didn't mind to know; knew of such a book to a sartinty, because a young 'oman took one to pop (pawn) for an old 'oman what was on the spree—a brand new 'un—but the cove wouldn't have it, and the old 'oman said he might be d-d. . . . Didn't know what happened to people after death, only that they was buried. Had seen a dead body laid out; was a little afeared at first; poor Dick looked so different, and when you touched his face, he was so cold! oh, so cold! Had heer'd on another world; wouldn't mind if he was there hisself, if he could do better, for things was often queer here. . . .

Was never in a church; had heer'd they worshipped God there; didn't know how it was done; had heer'd singing and playing inside when he'd passed; never was there, for he hadn't no togs to go in, and wouldn't be let in among such swells as he had seen coming out. . . . Had heer'd of the Duke of Wellington; he was Old Nosey; didn't think he ever seed him, but he had seed his statty. Hadn't heer'd of the battle of Waterloo, nor who it was atween. . . . Thought he had heer'd speak of Buonaparte; didn't know what he was; thought he had heer'd of Shakespeare, but didn't know whether he was alive or dead, and didn't care. . . . Had seen the Queen, but didn't recollec' her name just at the minute; oh! yes, Wictoria and Albert.

A Middle-Aged Sewer-Scavenger.

Bless your heart the smell's nothink; it's a roughish smell at first, but nothink near so bad as you thinks, 'cause, you see, there's sich lots o' water always a coming down the sewer, and the air gits in from the gratings, and that helps sweeten it a bit. . . . The rats is wery dangerous, that's sartain, but we always goes three or four on us together, and the varmint's too wide awake to tackle us then, for they know they'd git off second best. . . . I've found sovereigns and half sovereigns over and over ag'in, and three on us has often cleared a couple of pound apiece in one day out of the sewers. But we no sooner got the money than the publican had it. I only wish I'd back all the money I've guv to the publican, and I wouldn't care how the wind blew for the rest of my life. . . . The reason I likes this sort of life is, 'cause I can sit down when I likes, and nobody can't order me about. When I'm hard up, I knows as how I must work, and then I goes at it like sticks a breaking; and tho' the times isn't as they was, I can go now and pick up my four or five bob a day, where another wouldn't know how to get a brass farden.

A Kept Woman.

I am not tired of what I am doing, I rather like it. I have all I want, and my friend loves me to excess. I am the daughter of a tradesman at Yarmouth. I learned to play the piano a little, and I have naturally a good voice. Yes, I find these accomplishments of great use to me; they are, perhaps, as you say, the only ones that could be of use to a girl like myself. I am three and twenty. I was seduced four years ago. I tell you candidly I was as much to blame as my seducer; I wished to escape from the drudgery of my father's shop. . . . We then went to London, and I have since that time lived with four different men. . . . Well,

my father and mother don't exactly know where I am or
what I am doing, although if they had any penetration they
might very well guess. O yes! they know I am alive, for
I keep them pleasantly aware of my existence by occasionally sending them money. What do I think will become of
me? What an absurd question. I could marry tomorrow
if I liked.

A Street Prostitute.

You folks as has honour, and character, and feelings,
and such, can't understand how all that's been beaten out
of people like me. I don't feel. I'm used to it. I did once,
more especial when Mother died. . . . I did cry and go on
then ever so, but, Lor', where's the good of fretting? I
arn't happy either. It isn't happiness, but I get enough
money to keep me in victuals and drink, and it's the drink
mostly that keeps me going. You've no idea how I look
forward to my drop of gin. It's everything to me. I don't
suppose I'll live much longer, and that's another thing that
pleases me. I don't want to live. And yet I don't care
enough about dying to make away with myself.

Among the city poor, then as now, the police were universally
hated and feared. For most of these poor, religion was a concern
of the rich and of unpleasant busybodies who thrust unintelligible
tracts into the hands. One of Mayhew's informants, however,
makes an interesting observation about coster-mongers:

I'm satisfied that if the costers had to profess themselves
of some religion tomorrow, they would all become Roman
Catholics, every one of them. This is the reason:—London
costers live very often in the same courts and streets as the
poor Irish, and if the Irish are sick, be sure there comes to
them the priest, the Sisters of Charity—they *are* good
women—and some other ladies. . . . The costers reckon
that religion's the best that gives the most in charity, and
they think the Catholics do this.

In their political opinions, as one might expect, there was a
marked difference between the artisans and the more intelligent
workers on the one hand and casual laborers and vagrants on the
other. The former were mostly Chartists, the latter "as unpolitical

as footmen." For the comfortably off, Chartism was a bogey word like Communism, and trade societies, the prototypes of trades unions, were regarded as criminally subversive. It must have taken considerable courage on his part for Mayhew to speak up for both:

> If property has its duties as well as its rights; labour, on the other hand, they say, has its rights as well as its duties. The artisans of London seem to be generally well-informed upon these subjects. That they express their opinions violently, and often savagely, it is my duty to acknowledge; but that they are the unenlightened and un-thinking body of people that they are generally considered by those who never go among them, and who see them only as "the dangerous classes," it is my duty also to deny. So far as my experience has gone, I am bound to confess, that I have found the skilled labourers of the metropolis the very reverse, both morally and intellectually, of what the popular prejudice imagines them.
>
> The public, generally, are deplorably misinformed as to the character and purpose of trade societies. The common impression is that they are combinations of working-men, instituted and maintained solely with the view of exacting an exorbitant rate of wages from their employers. . . . The maintenance of the standard rate of wages is not the sole object of such societies—the majority of them being organised as much for the support of the sick and aged as for the regulation of the price of labour; and even in those societies whose efforts are confined to the latter purpose alone, a considerable sum is devoted annually for the subsistence of their members when out of work.

Since Mayhew's primary purpose is to present the objective facts about the life of the poor and let the reader draw his own conclusions, he is generally as reticent about his political opinions as he is about his religious convictions, but now and again he has an outburst of rage:

> The only effectual mode of preventing this system of jobbing being persevered in, *at the expense of the work-men,* is by the insertion of a clause in each parish contract similar to that introduced by the Commissioners of Sewers —that at least a fair living rate of wages shall be paid by

each contractor to the men employed by him. This may be an interference with the freedom of labour, according to the economists' "cant" language, but at least it is a restriction of the tyranny of capital, for free labour means, when literally translated, *the unrestricted use of capital,* which is (especially when the moral standard of trade is not of the highest character) perhaps the greatest evil with which a State can be afflicted.

Of the average Victorian equivalent of a welfare worker he takes a dim view. If, he is never tired of insisting, you wish to do anything to raise the cultural and moral level of the poor, then you must stop thinking in terms of your own middle-class experiences and values, and learn to think in terms of theirs. Employment, to someone of the middle classes, means a regular job with a regular salary, however modest, paid at regular and foreseeable intervals; to him, therefore, thrift is an obvious virtue and its practice possible. But to a casual laborer who lives from one day to the next, the idea of saving is unimaginable. The discipline of regular hours, natural to the middle class, becomes a tyranny when, as in model lodging houses, it is imposed on the poor:

> It is thought by the managers of these establishments, and with some share of propriety, that persons who get their living by any honest means may get home and go to bed, according to strict rule, at a certain prescribed hour —in one house it is ten o'clock, in the others eleven. But many of the best conducted of these poor people, if they be street-folk, are at those very hours in the height of their business, and have therefore to pack up their goods, and carry homeward their cumbersome and perhaps heavy load a distance usually varying from two or three to six or seven miles. If they are a minute beyond time, they are shut out, and have to seek lodgings in a strange place. On their return next morning, they are charged for the bed they were prevented from occupying, and if they demur they are at once expelled!

Again, it is very difficult for the average middle-class person to believe that some people are by temperament rovers. (Reading Mayhew, I have been astonished at the number of young persons in nineteenth-century England who ran away from home, many of them from good homes.) Addressing a group of ticket-of-leave men, Mayhew told them:

> I know that as a class you are distinguished mainly by your love of a roving life, and that at the bottom of all your criminal practices lies your indisposition to follow any settled occupation. Continuous employment of a monotonous nature is so irksome to you that immediately you engage in it you long to break away from it. . . . Society, however, expects that, if you wish to better yourselves, you will at once settle down as steadily as it does, and immediately conform to all its notions; but I am satisfied that if anything effectual is to be done in the way of reforming you, Society must work in consonance and not in antagonism with your nature. In this connection it appears to me that the great outlet for you is street-trading, where you are allowed to roam at will unchafed by restraints not congenial to your habits and feelings.

Social-history textbooks taught me in my youth that the living conditions of the poor in 1850, though still grim, were an improvement upon the horrors they had suffered at the beginning of the century. So far as conditions in mills and mines are concerned, this may have been true, but Mayhew demonstrates beyond all possible doubt that the position of craft artisans, like carpenters and tailors, and of casual laborers was much worse than it had been twenty years before. The wages of cabinetmakers, for example, had been no less than three hundred per cent greater in 1830 than they were in 1850. Between 1840 and 1848, although the increase in production and the national wealth had been much greater than the increase in population, the annual increase in paupers on relief had been seven per cent. Mayhew attributes this deterioration to a change in the methods of hiring labor and of distributing work to be done. In agriculture and, it would seem, in some trades as well, the traditional method had been to hire laborers by the year, during which time the employer was bound to pay them an agreed wage, whether he had work for them or not. Increasingly, this method had been replaced by hiring them by the day and turning them off whenever work was slack. The change in working methods had been the adoption of piecework and the contract system. In 1830, for example, the cabinet trade had been mainly in the hands of "trade-working masters."

> They worked not on speculation, but to order, and were themselves employers. Some employed, at a busy time, from twenty to forty hands, all working on their premises, to whom they supplied the materials.

By 1850, the trade-working master had been largely replaced by the "garret-master":

> [The garret-masters] are in manufacture what the peasant-proprietors are in agriculture, their own employers and their own workmen. There is, however, this one marked distinction between the two classes—the garret-master cannot, like the peasant proprietor, eat what he produces: the consequence is, that he is obliged to convert each article into food immediately he manufactures it, no matter what the state of the market may be. . . . If the market is at all slack, he has to force a sale by offering his goods at the lowest possible price. What wonder, then, that the necessities of such a class of individuals should have created a special race of employers, known by the significant name of "slaughter-house men;" or that these, being aware of the inability of the garret-masters to hold out against any offer, no matter how slight a remuneration it affords for their labour, should continually lower and lower their prices until the entire body of the competitive portion of the cabinet trade is sunk in utter destitution and misery?

Yet, for all its harrowing descriptions of squalor, crime, injustice, and suffering, the final impression of Mayhew's great book is not depressing. From his many transcripts of conversations it is clear that Mayhew was that rare creature, a natural democrat; his first thought, that is to say, was never "This is an unfortunate wretch whom it is my duty, if possible, to help" but always "This is a fellow-human being whom it is fun to talk to." The reader's final impression of the London poor is not of their misery but of their self-respect, courage, and gaiety in conditions under which it seems incredible that such virtues could survive.

Today, urban poverty is very much on all our minds. The percentage of the population that is really poor is, I suppose, less than it was in Mayhew's time. I am not at all sure, however, that for those today who are really poor the situation is any better; I suspect that it may be worse—at least psychologically. It is astonishing, reading Mayhew, to learn how many of the poor were self-employed and the extraordinary diversity of the ways by which they managed to earn a living, however meager. Even when I was a child, the streets were still full of venders, musicians, Punch-and-Judy men, and such. Today they have vanished. In all modern societies, the public authorities, however at odds politically, are at one in their fear and hatred of private enterprise in the strict sense; that is to say, self-employment. The fiscal authorities hate the self-employed man because he keeps no books to audit, the health authorities hate him because it is easy for him to avoid their inspectors, etc. Aside from crime and prostitution, the only contemporary alternative for the poor is either to be the employee of a firm, a factory, or the municipality, or to be on relief. Perhaps this is inevitable, perhaps it is better, but I have yet to be convinced that it is.

*

THE GREATEST OF THE MONSTERS

*

In sitting down to write another full-length book on Wagner after Ernest Newman's magnum opus, Mr. Robert Gutman was taking a risk, but I am happy to say that *Richard Wagner, The Man, His Mind, and His Music* is an admirable and indispensable addition to Wagnerian criticism. Among its many virtues I must mention one because it is not as common as it should be: the index is excellent. I have two very minor criticisms. I do not understand why Mr. Gutman has anglicized the titles of the operas. Both at the Met and at Covent Garden they are always given in German; I have never myself seen *Die Walküre* billed as *The Valkyrie*. Secondly, when he makes a joke, he ends his sentence with an exclamation mark; such superfluous punctuation should be left to Queen Victoria.

On principle, I object to biographies of artists, since I do not believe that knowledge of their private lives sheds any significant light upon their works. For example, the scene between Wotan and Fricka in *Die Walküre* is no doubt based upon Wagner's reminiscences of marital rows with Minna, but this does not explain why it is, musically, one of the greatest scenes in all opera. However, the story of Wagner's life is absolutely fascinating, and it would be so if he had never written a note. It is sad, but a fact, that while the lives of decent folk usually make dull reading, the lives of bad hats are nearly always interesting, and Wagner, aside from being one of the greatest musical geniuses who ever lived, was a very bad hat indeed.

In financial matters, from early youth till the day of his death he was a common or garden-variety, though highly successful, crook:

> He pleaded with Breitkopf and Härtel and with Liszt to purchase his publishing venture from Meser and secure the copyrights of *Rienzi, Dutchman,* and *Tannhäuser.* Typically, it escaped Wagner's memory that he had already conveyed to Pusinelli ownership in his published works as collateral for loans. He was even to ask the doctor to purchase a second time this very security that was becoming his by default! That the rights to *Tristan and Isolde* were later given him as general compensation did not stop Wagner from subsequently negotiating their sale to Breitkopf and Härtel. Nor was Pusinelli to be the only victim of such chicanery. Otto Wesendonk, who bought the publishing rights to *Rhinegold* and *Valkyrie* in 1859, had wide experience with Wagner's character and was perhaps not too startled to learn that *Rhinegold* was soon sold again to Schott of Mainz without any intention on Wagner's part of repaying the original advances. As requital Otto was granted the rights to *The Twilight of the Gods*—an unwritten work! But in 1865 Wagner demanded that Otto without reimbursement give up all claims to the Ring (he had also paid for the incomplete *Siegfried*) and even surrender—"amiably and generously"—the autographed orchestral score of *Rhinegold,* his only remaining asset of these transactions, to the Ring's newest proprietor, the Bavarian king. The climax of double dealing came after the first Bayreuth festival, when King Ludwig's ownership rights, for which he had paid untold thousands of marks, were ignored by Wagner, who proceeded to sell the Ring to individual theatres for his own profit.

Socially, he was a spoiled brat:

> On one famous occasion he became so upset to discover himself not leading the discussion and in fact to observe his guests quietly chatting with one another that, to regain their attention, he simply opened his mouth and screamed.

Many artists are jealous of their colleagues and say nasty things about them, but as a rule they reserve their malice for those who are on a rival artistic track and they are willing to give credit to those by whom they have themselves been influenced. But it was precisely about those composers from whom he had learned most that Wagner was nastiest. It is obvious, for instance, that he was influenced by two works of Mendelssohn's, "The Scottish Symphony" and "Lobgesang"; the latter he called "purblind ingenuousness," the former "effeminately depressed," which, coming from Wagner, of all people, is a bit steep.

In his sexual life, he indulged in one affair after another. Again, many artists have done the same, but they have not, as Wagner did in opera after opera, extolled the virtues of renunciation and chastity, just as, in his prose pamphlets, he preached vegetarianism while continuing himself to enjoy a French cuisine.

His tastes in clothes and interior decoration were those of a drag queen:

> That his skin was extremely sensitive may explain his silk chokers and underwear but hardly those quilted, shirred, bowed, laced, flowered, fringed, and furred gowns he dragged through his private rooms. In a famous letter to Bertha, his seamstress, he once poetically described and sketched a sash five yards in length to be made for a fantastic pink satin robe of his own design. Considering his height of little over five feet, one must wonder how he managed to walk in these costumes without tripping. Coincidentally with his work on the first act of *Parsifal* he wrote frankly to his "douce amie," Judith [asking her] to ship limitless amounts of amber, Milk of Iris (he poured half a bottle of it into his daily bath), and Rose de Bengale, and he called for powdered scents to sprinkle over fabrics. . . . His study in Wahnfried was directly over the bath, which he would inundate with rare odors. Seated at his desk and attired in incredible silk and fur outfits douched with sachet, he breathed in the aromatic fumes rising from below and with them memories of Judith's glowing embraces. Amid scenes worthy of Huysmans' Des Esseintes, the first act of the "religious" drama, *Parsifal,* came into being.

Such weaknesses and eccentricities make amusing reading, but there is nothing funny about Wagner's hatred of the French and the Jews. He was furious at Bismarck for not razing Paris to the ground, and when the Parisians were starving during the siege he wrote a farce about it, *A Capitulation,* in which the chorus were to sing, "Rats with sauce! Sauce with rats!" Most nineteenth-century anti-Semites would have been genuinely horrified by Auschwitz, but one has the uncomfortable suspicion that Wagner would have wholeheartedly approved. His vocabulary in *Know Thyself,* written in 1881, is hair-raisingly prophetic.

> Only when his [Wagner's] countrymen awakened and ceased party bickering would there be no more Jews. A "great solution" (*gross Lösung*) he foresaw as uniquely within the reach of the Germans if they could conquer false shame and not shrink from ultimate knowledge (*nach der Überwindung aller falschen Scham die letzte Erkenntnis nicht zu scheuen*).

Before leaving this unpleasant topic, let us recall with admiration that King Ludwig, though he idolized Wagner, refused to pay the slightest attention to his anti-Semitic ravings.

I said earlier that I do not believe an artist's life throws much light upon his works. I do believe, however, that, more often than most people realize, his works may throw light upon his life. An artist with certain imaginative ideas in his head may then involve himself in relationships which are congenial to them. In Wagner's case, this is unusually clear. For example, his affair with Mathilde Wesendonk was, as Mr. Gutman says, the "result" rather than the "cause" of *Tristan,* and when, in order to write the last act, he found it necessary for them to part, it cost him little grief. More mysteriously, a situation already treated in his work may turn up later in an artist's life. Anyone who pays close attention to the text and the music in that same opera is aware of the homosexual triangle Mark-Melot-Tristan. In his long monologue after the lovers are surprised, Mark ignores Isolde completely and addresses himself to Tristan alone, causing a problem for the stage director:

> For all practical purposes Isolde might well vanish from the garden with Mark's entry. . . . How many Isoldes

have desperately rearranged their veils a thousand times
while awaiting those few lines near the end of the act!

(Flagstad solved this problem by sitting down with her back to
the audience.) And at the end of the third act, Melot dies with
the name Tristan on his lips. In the first act, also, Isolde has four
lines which seem to indicate that she is aware of the situation:

> *Ich pflag des Wunden,*
> *dass den Heilgesunden*
> *rächend schlüge der Mann,*
> *der Isolden ihn abgewann.*

(I nursed the wounded man so that, when recovered,
he might be slain in vengeance by the man who won him
from Isolde.)

Ernest Newman tried to explain these lines away as a grammatical
error: Wagner, he suggested, had written the accusative *ihn* when
he should have written the ablative *ihm,* and what he meant the
fourth line to say was

by the man who won Isolde from him

thus expressing Isolde's hope that Tristan would meet his death
at the hands of one of her future lovers. Not only does this
emendation make no emotional sense in the context but, as Mr.
Gutman says:

> Though Wagner's grammar was at times weak, he did
> know the difference between *ihn* and *ihm,* and, as New-
> man himself admitted, the passage appears in Wagner's
> manuscript and was printed in poem and score for all the
> world to see.

(I am shocked to discover that in the Böhm recording the
emendation has been quietly adopted.)

A biographer who did not know when *Tristan* was composed would naturally suspect that the Mark-Melot-Tristan triangle
was an artistic metamorphosis of the real-life triangle Ludwig-
Prince Paul-Wagner, especially when he discovered that Prince

Paul was known in the Ludwig-Wagner circle by the nickname Melot.

Before we consider his compositions, a few words should be said about Wagner as a professional musician and man of the theater. In these spheres he deserves almost unqualified praise. However "bohemian" his life, however chaotic and absurd his verbal ideas, when it came to music and its performance Wagner exhibited all the "bourgeois" virtues—bee-like industry, patient attention to detail, tidiness (his scores are beautiful to look at), and even common sense. However justly one may complain about prima-donna conductors and the sort of public that is more interested in a conductor with a "name" than in the music he conducts, one must admit that the recognition that conducting is in itself an art has enormously raised the standard of orchestral and operatic performances, and for this recognition Wagner is very largely responsible. I have always felt that Wagner's own works should be taken at a clip. (My favorite Wagner conductor, though I never heard him in the flesh, was Albert Coates. On the other hand, I once sat through a *Götterdämmerung* conducted by Knappertsbusch as if it were the "Siegfried Idyll," and thought I should go out of my mind.) I am happy to learn that Wagner felt the same. In *Aspects of Wagner,* Mr. Bryan Magee gives some interesting facts:

> I once timed all the available recordings of the prelude to *Die Meistersinger:* the longest lasted ten and a half minutes and the shortest eight and three-quarters; yet when Wagner himself conducted it in Mannheim in 1871 it lasted only a few seconds over eight minutes." On one occasion we find him complaining of a performance of the overture to *Tannhäuser* that it had lasted over twenty minutes, pointing out that under his own baton in Dresden it had lasted twelve. He also complained of a performance of *Das Rheingold* in Augsburg that it had taken three hours and reminded everyone that under a conductor coached by himself it had lasted two and a half. Liszt, after conducting the première of *Lohengrin* at Weimar in 1850, received a letter of complaint from Wagner that the performance had taken a full hour too long.

With his singers Wagner took endless pains, and he was always willing to make cuts or changes to suit their voices:

> To accommodate Tichatschek and Niemann he consented to alterations in the second act of *Tannhäuser,* and, for his niece, Johanna Wagner, he shortened the prayer in the third. . . . In 1861 by cuts, transpositions, and text changes he recast the part of Tristan to meet the limitations of the panic-stricken Viennese tenor, Ander. Unhappy with his Wotan after the first Bayreuth festival, he wished the role to be assumed by the bass Siehr, whose anxieties over its great range he allayed by assurances that high notes might always be lowered.

Indeed, as Bernard Shaw pointed out, Wagner's vocal writing is more considerate to tenors and sopranos than Verdi's; his roles may demand more lung power, but they are less taxing on the vocal cords. I am glad to learn from Mr. Gutman that the Wagnerian "bark" with which we are all too familiar was not Wagner's handiwork but was developed only after Cosima took over Bayreuth. Wagner himself wanted a *bel-canto* style.

It has become a commonplace to say that Wagner had no sense of stage direction, but after seeing what some of our "famous" modern stage directors can do with his operas I only wish he could come back to earth and take charge. Technical advances in stage lighting have made certain effects possible of which Wagner would no doubt approve, but stage directors today seem to imagine that everything can be done with light, or, rather, with darkness. Ever since someone made the happy discovery that the love scene in the second act of *Tristan* is more effective if the scrim is lowered and only the faces of the lovers are spotlighted, we have had to sit through performances of entire operas which seem to have been designed for an audience of owls. Take the opening scene of *Die Walküre.* The whole dramatic tension depends upon *Gastrecht:* once Siegmund has got inside Hunding's home, the latter is obliged to give his enemy food, fire, and shelter. In all the recent performances I have attended, there was no food, no fire, and not even a hut.

Of course, in Wagner's Bayreuth, as in every opera house, comic mishaps occurred. The first papier-mâché Fafner arrived with its neck missing (it had been addressed by mistake to Beirut); at the first performance of *Parsifal*:

> Carl Brandt had miscalculated the rate at which the painted landscape was to unfold across the stage during the two orchestral interludes depicting Parsifal's progress along the almost inaccessible paths to Monsalvat. There were yards and yards of excess canvas. The error was discovered at rehearsals, but too late to change the complicated roller mechanism especially constructed for this *Wandeldekoration*. In order to bring pit and stage together, Wagner was obliged to order the first-act interlude played twice and with liberal retards.

The mere fact, however, that some of Wagner's demands are difficult to meet does not excuse modern stage directors from ignoring them completely. About Grane, they are probably right: the kind of horse which can stand the footlights is too elderly and docile for a daughter of Wotan to ride. Fafner and Lohengrin's swan are another matter; the sooner they are restored the better.

The best-known of Wagner's theoretical writings about opera as an art form is *Opera and Drama,* published in 1851. The theory he then put forward may be summarized as follows:

1. In opera, the words are at least as important as, perhaps more important than, the music. The poet presents the conceptual elements which beget the musician's vocal line. The latter interprets the text emotionally through artfully calculated juxtapositions of rhythm, accents, pitch, and key relationships.

2. There must be no duets or ensembles because these make the words difficult to hear. There must be no repetition of words. Strict metrical forms, even rhyme, are to be avoided.

3. The orchestra takes over the operatic role of the chorus.

4. The traditional formal arias linked by recitative are to be replaced by a free, continuous melody, unified by a series of motifs. Certain musical phrases are to be repeated by voice or orchestra whenever the ideas associated with the original words have particular relevance.

5. Historical subjects are unsuited to opera. The proper subjects are myths.

Essentially, this theory is a polemic directed against the "singers' " opera, in which words, plot, and orchestra have only one function—to provide opportunities for vocal display. To this negative tenet Wagner remained faithful, but the only works of his which conform to the positive dogmas are *Das Rheingold* and the first two acts of *Die Walküre*. When he started composing *Siegfried,* the conflict between the dogmas and the kind of music he wanted to write had become so acute that he had to stop, and he did not resume work on it until after he had written *Tristan* and *Die Meistersinger.* In *Tristan,* the duet reappears, the words are swamped by the flood of orchestral sound, and, though he does not literally repeat words, Wagner does not hesitate to string together a series of appositives and synonyms whenever they suit his musical needs. In *Die Meistersinger* and all his subsequent operas, the *Gesamtkunstwerk* theory is thrown out of the window, and what Wagner gives us is post-Meyerbeer nineteenth-century grand opera. As Mr. Gutman says:

> *Meistersinger* boasted a libretto obviously modelled on the practice of Wagner's detested French foeman, Eugène Scribe; and there were distinct arias, marches, choruses, a rousing crescendo finale, a ballet, and elaborate ensembles capped by—*horrible dictu*—a quintet! All the closed Italian forms on the Wagnerian Index were shamelessly exhibited.

And of *Götterdämmerung,* with its "poisoned drinks, conspirators' ensemble, massed chorus, and Scribe-inspired *coups de théâtre,*" Bernard Shaw quite rightly remarked that it has much in common with *Un Ballo in Maschera.*

Though Wagner continued to use leitmotivs, these become less and less like what Debussy called "visiting cards"; that is to say, it became harder and harder to identify them with a specific character, emotion, or dramatic situation. He used them freely, and sometimes recklessly:

> Not far from the absurd is that *locus classicus* in the final act of *Siegfried* where Brynhild's sudden wild passion, burning glance, and enfolding embrace are painted by the Dragon motif . . . and those two bars in the prelude to *The*

Twilight of the Gods where Siegmund's and Sieglinde's love theme underlines Brynhild's devotion to her horse.

The principal difference between Wagnerian and Italian grand opera is that in the former the vocal line is subordinate to, sometimes even dictated by, what the orchestra is doing. Hanslick was only slightly exaggerating when he wrote:

> Given the text and the orchestral accompaniment, a good musician, well versed in Wagner's music, would be able to insert suitable vocal parts in the empty spaces, just as a sculptor can restore the missing hand of a statue. But one could as little restore the lost orchestral accompaniment to Hans Sachs' or Eva's vocal parts as create the whole statue with only the single hand to go on.

Could Wagner revisit the earth, he would, I think, view the contemporary operatic scene with mixed feelings. On the one hand, he would be gratified to find that all over the world his operas have become part of the standard repertory, and savagely exultant to discover that the archfiend Meyerbeer has disappeared from it. On the other hand, he would be dismayed to learn that the race of Wagnerites has died out (Hitler was probably the last of them), that the opera public listens one night to Wagner and the next, with equal pleasure and admiration, to Verdi, whom he had dismissed as a composer of no account. He would be right, I believe, in feeling dismay, though not for the reasons he would himself give. Wagner's operas are freaks, and if we are to appreciate them correctly we must listen in a way unlike that in which we listen to most operas.

Of all guides to Wagner, Nietzsche is by far the best. (Mr. Gutman, incidentally, demonstrates convincingly that in his discussion of the break between Nietzsche and Wagner Newman was inaccurate and unfair to the former.) Nietzsche perceived the one-track obsessiveness of Wagner's imagination; in opera after opera, the same theme turns up in a new disguise:

> Someone always wants to be saved in his operas—now it is a youth; anon it is a maid—this is *his problem*—and how lavishly he varies his leitmotif! What rare and melancholy modulations! If it were not for Wagner, who would

teach us that innocence has a preference for saving interesting sinners (the case in *Tannhäuser*)? Or that even the
Wandering Jew gets saved and *settled down* when he marries (the case in *Der Fliegende Holländer*)? Or that corrupt
females prefer to be saved by chaste young men (the case
of Kundry)? Or that young hysterics like to be saved by
their doctor (the case in *Lohengrin*)? Or that beautiful girls
love to be saved by a knight who also happens to be a
Wagnerite (the case in *Die Meistersinger*)? Or that even
married women also like to be saved by a knight (the case
of Isolde)? . . .

That it is possible to draw yet another lesson from the
works above mentioned, I am much more ready to prove
than dispute. That one may be driven by a Wagner ballet
to desperation *and* to virtue! (Once again the case in *Tannhäuser.*) That not going to bed at the right time may be
followed by the worst consequences. (Once again the case
of *Lohengrin.*) That one can never be too sure of the
spouse one actually marries. (For the third time, the case
of *Lohengrin.*)

And he perceived the true nature of the Wagnerian hero and
heroine:

Wagner's heroines one and all, once they have been di-
vested of their heroic husks, are almost indistinguishable
from *Madame Bovary*. Just as one can conceive conversely
of Flaubert being *well able* to transform all his heroines
into Scandinavian or Carthaginian women, and then offer
them to Wagner in this mythologized form as a libretto.
Indeed, generally speaking, Wagner does not seem to have
become interested in any other problems than those which
engross the little Parisian decadents of today. Always five
paces away from the hospital! All very modern problems,
all problems which are at home in big cities. Have you
noticed (it is in keeping with this association of ideas) that
Wagner's heroines never have any children? They *cannot*
have them. The despair with which Wagner tackled the
problem of arranging in some way for Siegfried's birth betrays how modern his feelings on this point actually were.
Siegfried "emancipated" woman, but not with any hope of
offspring. And now here is a fact which leaves us speechless: Parsifal is Lohengrin's father! How ever did he do it?

Ought one at this juncture to remember that "chastity works miracles"?

Nietzsche also—and this was the most important of his insights—grasped the true nature of Wagner's musical genius:

> Here is a musician who is a greater master than anyone else in the discovery of tones peculiar to suffering, oppressed, and tormented souls, who can endow even dumb misery with speech. Nobody can approach him in the colors of late autumn, in the indescribably touching joy of a last, a very last, and all too short gladness; he knows of a chord which expresses those secret and weird midnight hours of the soul, when cause and effect seem to have fallen asunder.

Wagner, like Milton, another monster, whom he resembles in more ways than one, is a striking example of an artist whose actual achievement is quite other than his conscious intention. Just as Milton expected the reader to take his God the Father and God the Son as the Christian God, when in fact they are Homeric deities employing a pseudo-Christian vocabulary, so Wagner expected his audience to admire his heroes and heroines when in fact he presents a succession of underbred neurotics, portrayed with consummate skill. As no one else can, he paints all that is irrational, morbid, cranky, self-destructive, "Wagnerite" in human nature as it really is; that is to say, in all its formidable enchantment. Had he been conscious of this he could not have done it, for he would then inevitably have portrayed such weaknesses satirically, without the enchantment which makes us succumb to them. When he is consciously satirical, as in his portrait of Beckmesser, the result is unsatisfactory; according to the libretto, Beckmesser is a serious rival to Walther, both as a wooer and as a musician, but the music Wagner gives Beckmesser to sing makes it impossible to take him seriously as either.

If we are to get the full benefit from Wagner's operas, we have simultaneously to identify ourselves with what we hear and see on stage—"Yes, all that is in me"—and to "distance" ourselves from it—"But all that is precisely what I must overcome." If we can do this, then we shall find that, just as Milton was "of the Devil's Party without knowing it," so Wagner, equally unknowingly, was on the side of Reason, Order, and Civilization.

*

A GENIUS AND A GENTLEMAN

*

A few years before his death Verdi wrote: "Never, never shall I write my memoirs! It's good enough that the musical world has put up with my notes for so long a time. I shall never condemn it to read my prose." I don't think, however, that he would have any objection to our reading this selection of his letters, admirably translated and edited by Charles Osborne. It contains no embarrassing "human" documents, no love letters, for instance. Whether this is because Verdi never wrote any or because Mr. Osborne has had the good taste to omit them, I don't know. Anyway, I am very glad. There is only one letter that could possibly be called "private and confidential," Verdi's reply to his old benefactor, Antonio Barezzi, who had taken him to task for not regularizing his relationship with Giuseppina Strepponi by marrying her.

> I have nothing to hide. In my house there lives a lady, free and independent, who, like myself, prefers a solitary life, and who has a fortune capable of satisfying all her needs. Neither I nor she is obliged to account to anyone for our actions. But who knows what our relations are? What affairs? What ties? What rights I have over her or she over me? . . . I will say this to you, however: in my house she is entitled to as much respect as myself, more even.

As we know, they did finally get married in 1859. All that is puzzling, in view of how obviously well suited to each other they were, is why they did not do so earlier. My guess would be that it was she rather than Verdi who kept putting it off. There is one other piece of information in the letters that leaves me curious. In 1844–45 Verdi came near to a nervous breakdown, suffering severely from psychosomatic headaches and stomach cramps. What can the psychological trouble have been?

As we all recognize, the nineteenth century was the Golden Age of Opera, but I doubt if any of us, whether composers or opera-goers, would have liked to live in it. So far as composers were concerned, they were terribly overworked. It was a common clause in a contract that the finished score of a full-length opera was to be delivered within four months after the composer received the libretto. (Of all the great opera composers of the age, the only one who was not prolific was Bellini, and I have always wondered how this was financially possible for him.)

Then there were problems of copyright. In 1855 the House of Lords decreed that no foreign opera in England would have copyright unless the composer conducted the first performance himself. Then there was censorship. The setting of *Ballo in Maschera* had to be transferred from Sweden to Boston, and changes had to be made in the text of *Rigoletto*. Prima donnas were even more difficult to handle than they are now. (Today, the real pests are the stage directors.) When Sophie Loewe was to sing in *Ernani,* she objected to the opera ending in a trio. She wanted a brilliant cabaletta for herself alone and made the librettist, Piave, write one for her. Luckily, Verdi was adamant. The singer who was to sing Banquo in *Macbetto* objected to also taking the role of Banquo's ghost.

Opera-goers, too, had much to put up with. There were boxes on the stage so that the curtain could not be brought up to the footlights, and there does not seem to have been an orchestral pit as we know it. (I was interested to learn that Verdi, like Wagner, wanted an invisible orchestra.) Then, as now, standards varied, of course, from opera house to opera house. After the premiere of *Giovanna d'Arco* at La Scala, Milan, Verdi was so disgusted that he refused to let them have another for forty-three years, when he gave them the first performance of *Otello*. The worst of all, he thought, was the Paris Opéra.

Everyone wants to pass judgment according to his own ideas, his own taste, and, which is worst of all, according to a system, without taking into account the character and individuality of the composer. . . . if a composer lives for too long in this atmosphere of doubt, he cannot escape having his convictions shaken a little, and begins to correct and adjust, or, to put it better, to look askance at his own work. Thus, in the end, you will have not a work in one piece, but a mosaic. . . . No one, surely, will deny the genius of Rossini. All right, but, despite all his genius, his *Guillaume Tell* has about it this fatal atmosphere of the Opéra; and sometimes, though more rarely than in the work of other composers, you feel there's too much here, not enough there, and that it doesn't move with the honesty and security of *Il barbiere*.

In one respect the musical scene has greatly improved since Verdi's time. There are still many lovers of Wagner but no "Wagnerites." We listen to Wagner one evening and to Verdi the next with equal pleasure and admiration. When one remembers the contempt in which the Wagnerites held Verdi as a composer, one is astounded by Verdi's good temper and common sense. He believed that each country should be loyal to its own musical traditions. Thus, for Germans, whose musical founder was Bach, the Wagnerian development was right, but not for Italians, whose music stemmed from Palestrina. Though Verdi wrote a string quartet, a charming if not very important work, he did not approve of Italian string quartet societies: they were right for the Germans, but the Italians should found vocal quartet societies. The chief danger for contemporary composers, he thought, was a lack of simplicity.

Art which lacks naturalness is simply not art. Inspiration is necessarily born of simplicity. . . . We create big works rather than great works. And from the big are born the small and the baroque.

By simplicity, though, he did not mean *verismo*.

To copy truth may be a good thing, but to invent truth is much better.

His ideas about musical education are most interesting.

Practice the fugue constantly, tenaciously, to satiety, until
your hands are strong enough to bend the notes to your
will. Thus you will learn to compose with confidence, will
dispose the parts well, and will modulate without affectation.
Study Palestrina, and a few of his contemporaries. Then
skip until you come to Marcello, and direct your attention
especially to his recitatives. . . . don't let yourself be fascinated by beauties of harmony and instrumentation, or the
chord of the diminished seventh, that rock and refuge of all
of us who don't know how to compose four bars without a
half-dozen of these sevenths.

. . . *No study of the moderns!* That will seem strange
to many. But when I hear and see so many works today,
constructed the way bad tailors make clothes based on a
model, I cannot change my opinion. . . . When a young
man has undergone strict training, when he has found his
own style and has confidence in his own powers, he can
then, if he thinks it useful, study these works somewhat,
and there will be no danger of his turning into an imitator.

It is clear from his own productions that he practiced what he
preached. As a young man he did study very hard until he could
make the notes go where he wanted and felt secure enough to obtain the effects he had in mind. But, on his own admission, he was
one of the least *erudite* of musicians. He tells us, for instance, that
he could not "get" a piece of music by reading the score, and he
complained that many people went into ecstasies over much
"classical" music when, if they had been honest, they would have
admitted they found it boring. Nor did he ever try to ingratiate
himself either with critics or the public. He was willing, he said, to
accept their hisses on condition that he didn't have to beg for their
applause.

Though, unlike Wagner, he did not write his own librettos, he
always knew exactly what he wanted and, if he was dissatisfied,
could tell his librettist in detail why. Thus he writes to Piave, who
was revising *La Forza del destino:*

You talk to me about 100 syllables!! And it's obvious that
100 syllables aren't enough when you take 25 to say the

] 259 [

sun is setting!!! The line "Duopo e sia L'opra truce compita" is too hard and even worse is "Un Requiem, un Pater . . . e tutto ha fin." First of all, this "tutto ha fin" rhymes with "Eh via prendila Morolin." It neither sounds well nor makes sense. . . .

Then, the seven-syllabled lines!!! For the love of God, don't end lines with "che," "piu" and "ancor."

And here are his instructions to Ghizlanzoni about the finale of *Aida.*

Duet

> *O life farewell, earthly love*
> *Farewell, sorrows and joys. . . .*
> *In infinity already I see the dawn,*
> *We shall be united for ever in heaven.*

(Four beautiful twelve-syllabled lines. But to make them suitable for singing the accent must be on the fourth and eighth syllables.)

And he was equally clear in his mind about details of stage direction. He gave Morelli, who was to direct *Otello,* a precise description of what he wanted Iago to look like, and when he himself directed *Macbetto,* he had Banquo's ghost emerge from a trap door immediately in front of Macbeth's chair, whereas in most other productions he had merely entered from the wings.

Though there was one great tragedy in Verdi's life when, in his middle twenties, he lost both his children and his first wife, one must say that, on the whole, his life was singularly fortunate. The son of an illiterate innkeeper's family, he would never have gotten anywhere had not Barezzi made it financially possible for him to study in Milan. His life with Giuseppina Strepponi was obviously very happy. By the age of forty he was famous, and he might well have never written two of his most beautiful operas had he not, when old, found in Boito the ideal librettist for what he had in mind. (Incidentally, I am astounded to learn from an editorial note by Mr. Osborne that, as late as 1863, Boito, in praising Faccio, a composer of whom I have never heard, likened Verdi's music to a "stained brothel wall.") One feels that both as a composer and as a human being Verdi richly deserved his good fortune. In the case of most great men, I am content to enjoy their works. There are very few who make me also wish that I could have known them personally. Verdi is one of them.

*

A POET OF THE ACTUAL

*

Every reviewer, I'm sure, must be conscious of having to read more quickly than one should. If the book is bad, little harm is done, but if, as in this case—*Anthony Trollope,* by James Pope Hennessy —it is both good and long, he knows that he cannot do proper justice to it. If Trollope's biography was to be written at all, Mr. Pope Hennessy, who has already displayed his remarkable gift for the genre in his Life of Queen Mary, was the obvious man, for his grandfather was almost certainly the model for Phineas Finn. As a rule, I am opposed to biographies of writers, but in Trollope's case, for a number of reasons, I approve. To begin with, Trollope wrote an autobiography, published posthumously, which, though probably accurate so far as it goes, leaves out a great deal. What puzzles me is why he wrote one at all, for he himself asserted that no man has ever written a truthful record of his inner life:

> Who could endure to own to a mean thing? Who is there that has done none?

Then, he was not simply a novelist. As an employee of the Post Office, he was also a man of action, and a most successful one. Then, he was an addicted traveler, forever "banging about" the world. More important, he happened to be what one would never suspect from his writings—a very eccentric character who might well, though he would have hated to admit it, have come straight out of a novel by Dickens. James Russell Lowell thus describes their meeting:

> Dined the other day with Anthony Trollope; a big, red-faced, rather underbred Englishman of the bald-with-spectacles type. A good roaring positive fellow who deafened me (sitting on his right) till I thought of Dante's Cerberus. . . . He and Dr. Holmes were very entertaining. The Autocrat started one or two hobbies, and charged, paradox in rest—but it was pelting a rhinoceros with seed-pearl—
>
> Dr. You don't know what Madeira is in England?
> T. I'm not so sure it's worth knowing.
> Dr. Connoisseurship with us is a fine art. There are men who will tell a dozen kinds, as Dr. Waagen would know a Carlo Dolci from a Guido.
> T. They might be better employed!
> Dr. Whatever is worth doing is worth doing well.
> T. Ay, but that's begging the whole question. I don't admit it's worse doing at all. If they earn their bread by it, it may be worse doing (roaring).
> Dr. But you may be assured—
> T. No, but I mayn't be asshorred. I don't intend to be asshorred (roaring louder).

As he grew older, he got even louder. A friend described him as "crusty, quarrelsome, wrong-headed, prejudiced, obstinate, kind-hearted and thoroughly honest old Tony Trollope."

In view of which it seems only fitting that his fatal stroke should have been brought on, as it appears, firstly by a fit of rage at a noisy German band and then by a fit of laughter as one of the assembled company read aloud from Anstey's *Vice Versa*.

Trollope has told us himself about his exceptionally wretched childhood and early manhood. His father was clearly a little crazy. Suffering acutely from migraines, he became a calomel addict who ruined his law practice by an ungovernable temper. Anthony's elder brother, Tom, said of him:

> I do not think it would be an exaggeration to say that for many years no person came into my father's presence

who did not forthwith desire to escape from it. . . . Happiness, mirth, contentment, pleasant conversation seemed to fly before him as if a malevolent spirit emanated from him.

Their mother, the famous authoress, seems to have had great charm, but Tom was so obviously her favorite child that Anthony felt neglected.

To any observer who met him during the first twenty-six years of his life, his future must have looked grim, for, as a schoolboy and as a clerk in the Post Office, he was unsociable, dirty, slovenly, and lazy both in his person and in his work. The transformation effected by his move to Ireland, where, within two or three years, he became a compulsive writer, an efficient civil servant, a passionate fox hunter, and a happily married man, would be incredible in a novel. Yet it happened. Why? My own guess is that for the first time in his life he found himself a member of the ruling class; there were, Mr. Pope Hennessy tells us, more British soldiers in Ireland at that time than there were in the whole of India, and he was in a position to give orders and see that they were obeyed. From then on, his life pattern was fixed, and in due course it led to fame and wealth.

Mr. Pope Hennessy is probably the only person now living who has read all of Trollope's sixty-five books, the majority of which are in two or three volumes, and he devotes a good many pages to describing and assessing the little-known ones. For this I am most grateful to him. Like everybody who reads Trollope at all, I have read the Barchester novels and several others, but I had never even heard of *He Knew He Was Right,* which Mr. Pope Hennessy thinks one of the best, and what he says about it makes me eager to read it at the first opportunity.

At this point, a personal digression. I was born a member of the upper professional middle class—clergymen, lawyers, doctors, etc.—and the world I knew as a child was still in most respects the world of Barchester. There were rich and poor clerical livings, often in the gift of laymen, and there were endless squabbles between High, Broad, and Low churchmen. The Married Women's Property Acts had made things more difficult for fortune-hunting young males, but the snobberies were still the same. Persons in business or industry, however rich, were "in trade"—i.e., not quite gentle-men—and Dissenters came in through the back door, not the front.

I find Trollope's insistence that writing novels is a craft like making shoes, and his pride in the money he got by writing them, sympathetic. He was aware, of course, that craft and art are not the same: a craftsman knows in advance what the finished result will be, while the artist knows only what it will be when he has finished it. But it is unbecoming in an artist to talk about inspiration; that is the reader's business. Again, Trollope would never have denied that his primary reason for writing was that he loved the activity. He once said that as soon as he could no longer write books he would wish to die. He believed that he wrote best when he wrote fastest, and in his case this may well have been true: a good idea for a novel stimulated his pen. Though large sales are not necessarily a proof of aesthetic value, they are evidence that a book has given pleasure to many readers, and every author, however difficult, would like to give pleasure.

To preach, as Trollope did, the Protestant work ethic is fine, provided one is aware, as he was not, of the difference between a worker—i.e., someone who is paid to do what he enjoys doing—and a laborer whose job has no interest in itself: he does it only because he must, in order to feed himself and his family. Trollope's failure to make this distinction is responsible for his unfeeling, even cruel attitude toward the Irish peasants, the West Indian slaves, and the Australian aborigines.

Of Trollope's virtues as a novelist, Henry James said, very rightly:

> His first, his inestimable merit was a complete appreciation of the usual. . . . Trollope will remain one of the most trustworthy, though not one of the most eloquent, of the writers who have helped the heart of man to know itself.

For "usual" one might substitute "actual," and the most actual of actualities in the modern world is surely money. Important as they are to us, our emotions are less actual, for we are frequently deceived about what we feel, whereas we always know exactly how much money we have. Money is a medium of exchange which af-fects all our relations with others. As Walter Sickert said, "Nothing knits man to man like the frequent passage from hand to hand of cash." Money is the necessity that frees us from necessity. Of all novelists in any country, Trollope best understands the role of money. Compared with him, even Balzac is too romantic. It is odd that Dickens, who, like Trollope, had known poverty in early life, should have shown so little insight into the problem. Mr. Pope Hennessy says:

> In *David Copperfield* and in *Oliver Twist* the little heroes' penury is turned off like a tap at the appearance on the scene of a fairy godmother and a fairy godfather. These transformation scenes are pantomimic, delightful, and illogical, but they have little or nothing to do with reality. . . . Trollope's attitude to money was neither romantic nor . . . cynical. . . . In Trollope's very earliest novels—the Irish ones—money is already a predominant theme, money in the ugly shape of unpaid land rents, of contested wills or of the unhappiness of Trollope's first heiress-orphan, Miss Fanny Wyndham. When he turned to England for the source-material for his novels, his increasing pessimism about the British upper and middle class began to show itself. . . . In Trollope's accounts of all this there is no cynicism, but only humor and sadness. . . . His simmering distaste for what he saw is reflected in successive novels until, in the year 1873, it boiled over and goaded him into writing that bitter satire on London society *The Way We Live Now*.

About the relation between money and love, Trollope knew that (if I may be excused for quoting myself)

> Money cannot buy
> the fuel of Love,
> but is excellent kindling.

To Trollope himself, making money was a proof of his manhood, of doing better than Papa. In this he was more American than European, for in Europe, till recently, most wealth had been inherited.

Trollope believed that

> the object of a novel should be to instruct in morals while it amuses. . . . The novelist creeps in closer than the school-

master, closer than the father, closer almost than the mother. He is the chosen guide, the tutor whom the young pupil chooses for herself.

I wish more modern novelists shared his belief, though today one would probably speak of "values" rather than "morals." If the Victorians were sometimes a little too reticent about sex, at least they knew that sex is a private, not a public, activity. If I have to choose, I prefer veils to nudity. (Actually, when they are read carefully, Trollope's novels turn out to be much less prudish than one thought at first.) The task of teaching morality is not easy; the Victorians and, indeed, most novelists have tried to solve it by making their bad characters come to a bad and unhappy end, their good characters to a good and happy one. Of course, both they and their readers knew perfectly well that in real life the righteous often have to beg their bread while the ungodly flourish like a green bay tree. But they were in a real dilemma. It seems to be a law of the imagination that bad characters are more fun to write and read about than good ones. As Simone Weil wrote:

> Imaginary evil is romantic and varied; real evil is gloomy, monotonous, barren, boring. Imaginary good is boring, real good is always new, marvellous, intoxicating. "Imaginative literature," therefore, is either boring or immoral or a mixture of both.

GEORGE MACDONALD

＊

For the writing of what may comprehensively be called Dream
Literature, though it includes many works, like detective stories and
opera libretti which are, formally, "feigned histories," the primary
requirement is the gift of mythopoeic imagination. This gift is one
with which criticism finds it hard to deal for it seems to have no
necessary connection with the gift of verbal expression or the
power to structure experience. There have been very great writers,
Tolstoy, for example, who appear to have been without it; on the
other hand, because they possessed it, writers like Conan Doyle
and Rider Haggard, whom nobody would call "great," continue to
be read.

A genuine "mythical" character like Sherlock Holmes can
always be recognized by two characteristics: his appeal, at least
within a given culture, transcends all highbrow-lowbrow, child-
adult differences of taste, and his nature is independent of his
history; one cannot imagine Anna Karenina apart from what we
are told happened to her, but no adventure can change Mr. Pick-
wick—if he changes he ceases to exist—the number of adventures
which might happen to him are potentially infinite, and every
reader can imagine some which Dickens, as it were, forgot.

George Macdonald is pre-eminently a mythopoeic writer.

Though he has very considerable literary gifts in the usual sense, his style sometimes lapses into Ossian Gothic and Victorian sentimentality (the baby talk of The Little Ones in *Lilith* is, frankly, shy-making, though partly redeemed by the fact that they represent not real children but people who, afraid of the risks and suffering involved in becoming adult, refuse to grow up) and, in reissuing *Phantastes,* the editors have been wise, I think, in their decision to omit most of the hero's songs, for George Macdonald was not endowed with that particular verbal gift which the writing of verse requires. In his power, however, to project his inner life into images, events, beings, landscapes which are valid for all, he is one of the most remarkable writers of the nineteenth century. *The Princess and The Goblins* is, in my opinion, the only English children's book in the same class as the Alice books, and *Lilith* is equal if not superior to the best of Poe.

The Scylla and Charybdis of Dream Literature are incoherence and mechanical allegory. Without some allegorical scheme of meaning—it is not always necessary that the reader know what it is—the writer has no principle by which to select and organize his material and no defense against his private obsessions; on the other hand, if he allows the allegory to take control so that symbol and thing symbolized have a mere one-to-one correspondence, he becomes boring. In the supreme master of the dream, Dante, we find simultaneously an inexhaustible flow of images of the profoundest resonance and a meticulous logical and mathematical structure which even dictates the number of verses. If *Lilith* is a more satisfactory book than *Phantastes,* one reason is that its allegorical structure is much tighter: there seems no particular reason, one feels, why Anodos should have just the number of adventures which he does have—they could equally be more or less —but Mr. Vane's experiences and his spiritual education exactly coincide. The danger of the chain adventure story is that perpetual novelty gives excitement at the cost of understanding; the landscape of *Lilith* becomes all the more vivid and credible to the reader because he is made to repeat the journey Adam's-Cottage to Bad-Burrow to Dry-River to Evil-Wood to Orchard-Valley to Rocky-Scaur to Hot-Stream to Bulika-City several times.

In comparison with his colleague, the novelist of our social waking life, the novelist of dream life is freer in his choice of events but most restricted in his choice of characters, for the latter must all be variations on a few "archetypes," the Wise Old Man, the Wise Old Woman, the Harlot-Witch, the Child-Bride, the Shadow-Self, etc., and it is no easy matter to present these types in unique and personal figures. George Macdonald, however, almost invariably manages to do so: there is a clear affinity between Lilith and the Alder Witch, between Eve and the old woman in the cottage with four doors, yet each is herself, and not a mere repetition.

But his greatest gift is what one might call his dream realism, his exact and profound knowledge of dream causality, dream logic, dream change, dream morality: when one reads him, the illusion of participating in a real dream is perfect; one never feels that it is an allegorical presentation of wakeful conscious processes. Nobody can describe better that curious experience of dreaming that one is awake:

> . . . looking out of bed, I saw that a large green marble basin, in which I was wont to wash, and which stood on a low pedestal of the same material in a corner of my room, was overflowing like a stream; and that a stream of clear water was running over the carpet, all the length of the room, finding its outlet I knew not where. . . . Hearing next a slight motion above me, I looked up, and saw that the branches and leaves designed upon the curtains of my bed were slightly in motion. Not knowing what change might follow next, I thought it high time to get up; and, springing from the bed, my bare feet alighted on a cool green sward; and, although I dressed in all haste, I found myself completing my toilet under the boughs of a great tree.

To describe how a dreamer reasons without making him sound either too arbitrary or too logical is not easy, but Macdonald's characters always argue like real dreamers:

> I saw, therefore, that there was no plan of operation offering any probability of success but this: to allow my mind to be occupied with other thoughts, as I wandered around the great center-hall; and so wait till the impulse to enter one of the others should happen to arise in me just at the moment when I was close to one of the crimson curtains.

Like real dreamers, too, their consciences are aware of ambiguities of feeling and motive before and during their actions in a way that, when we are awake, we can only become aware, if at all, after we have acted.

> But a false sense of power, a sense which had no root and was merely vibrated into me from the strength of the horse, had, alas, rendered me too stupid to listen to anything he said.

In waking life, it would be psychologically false to make the rider so aware of his self-deception at the moment of choice; in a dream it is true.

As for his power of exact dream description, one can open his books at random and find passage after passage like this:

> We rushed up the hills, we shot down their further slopes; from the rocky chasms of the river-bed he did not swerve; he held on over them in his fierce terrible gallop. The moon, half way up the heaven, gazed with a solemn trouble in her pale countenance. Rejoicing in the power of my steed and in the pride of my life, I sat like a king and rode.
>
> We were near the middle of the many channels, my horse every other moment clearing one, sometimes two in his stride, and now and then gathering himself for a great bounding leap, when the moon reached the key-stone of her arch. Then came a wonder and a terror: she began to descend rolling like the nave of Fortune's wheel bowled by the gods, and went faster and faster. Like our own moon, this one had a human face, and now the broad forehead now the chin was uppermost as she rolled. I gazed aghast.
>
> Across the ravines came the howling of wolves. An ugly fear began to invade the hollow places of my heart; my confidence was on the wane. The horse maintained his headlong swiftness, with ears pricked forward, and thirsty nostrils exulting in the wind his career created. But there was the moon jolting like an old chariot-wheel down the hill of heaven, with awful boding. She rolled at last over the horizon-edge and disappeared, carrying all her light with her.
>
> The mighty steed was in the act of clearing a wide shallow channel when we were caught in the net of the

darkness. His head dropped; its impetus carried his helpless bulk across, but he fell in a heap on the margin, and where he fell he lay. I got up, kneeled beside him, and felt him all over. Not a bone could I find broken, but he was a horse no more. I sat down on the body, and buried my face in my hands.

Descended from one of the survivors of the Massacre of Glencoe, George Macdonald was born in 1824, took a degree in Chemistry and Natural Philosophy and entered the Congregational Ministry in which he soon acquired a considerable reputation as a preacher.

Presently, however, like many of his contemporaries, he was suspected, with reason, of holding unorthodox theological opinions —in his case the orthodoxy was Calvinist—and in 1850 he abandoned pastoral work in order to devote himself to literature. His first book was a long poem *Within and Without* which aroused the admiration of Tennyson and Lady Byron. In addition to the dream stories for which he is best known, he wrote a number of realistic stories about Scotch peasant life some of which, like *Alec Forbes* and *Robert Falconer,* deserve to be better known. By all accounts a saintly and lovable man, he was a friend of most of the famous mid-Victorian writers, among them Lewis Carroll. In 1872 he made a successful lecture tour through the United States. Delicate health obliged him to spend much of his later years in Bordighera. He died in 1905.

If unorthodox on certain points—for example, he believed, like Origen, in the ultimate salvation of the Devil—he never, like many "liberals" of his day, abandoned the Christian doctrines of God, Sin and Grace for some vague emergent "force making for righteousness" or a Pelagian and secular belief in "Progress." *Lilith* is a surprisingly tough book. Bulika, its *civitas terrenae,* where all human beings are born, is a nightmare of suspicion, greed, sterility, and cruelty, and, if in Mr. Vane's dream it is captured by the innocent, it is, one feels, only in his dream; the reader is not left with the impression that Bulika has ceased to exist for others. The life-giving waters are restored to the Waste Land, but evil is not thereby abolished:

We came to the fearful hollow where once had wallowed the monsters of the earth: it was indeed, as I had beheld it in my dream, a lovely lake. I gazed into its pellucid depths. A whirlpool had swept out the soil in which the abortions burrowed, and at the bottom lay visible the whole horrid brood: a dim greenish light pervaded the crystalline water, and revealed every hideous form beneath it. . . . Not one of them moved as we passed. But they were not dead.

When Mr. Vane comes to in his library, his life is only just beginning; he has now to start obeying the advice which the raven gave him when they first met:

"The only way to come to know where you are is to begin to make yourself at home."

"How am I to begin that when everything is so strange?"

"By doing something."

"What?"

"Anything; and the sooner you begin the better! for until you are at home, you will find it as difficult to get out as it is to get in. . . . Home, as you may or may not know, is the only place where you can go out and in. There are places you can go into, and places you can go out of; but the one place, if you do but find it, where you may go out and in both, is home."

A RUSSIAN AESTHETE

Since I know no Russian, all I can say about Mr. George Reavey's translation of *Against the Current,* a selection from the writings of Konstantin Leontiev, is that it reads easily and well. In making his selection, Mr. George Ivask has clearly tried, in the limited space at his disposal (two hundred and seventy-three pages), to do justice to all of Leontiev's concerns—as a writer of memoirs and fictionalized autobiography, as an observer of life in the Middle East, as a political theorist, and as a literary critic. Nearly all the extracts are interesting, but, speaking for myself, I wish he had devoted more pages to the literary critic, even if this meant a sacrifice of range. Leontiev's views on most topics were, to put it mildly, extravagant, but in literary criticism he was completely sane and one of the best critics I have read. *Essays in Russian Literature: The Conservative View,* edited and translated by Spencer E. Roberts, prints the whole of his hundred-and-twenty-five-page essay on Tolstoy's novels, which I would recommend to readers who are beguiled by the twenty-four pages of it in this new selection.

Leontiev was born in 1831, the child of minor gentry. He studied medicine at Moscow University, served as a surgeon in the Crimean War and then as a household physician on a country estate. After his marriage, he gave up medicine, entered the Russian Consular Service, and spent ten years in the Middle East, during which time, after being "miraculously" cured of dysentery or cholera while praying to the Virgin, he became devoutly Orthodox. In 1874, he returned to Russia, and from 1880 to 1887 he served on the Censorship Committee. Then he entered the Optina Monastery and, just before his death, in 1891, was consecrated as a monk. In 1851, he met Turgenev, who was impressed by his talent, but they quarreled later over politics. Leontiev's books, it seems, received little attention, but in the last year of his life he found an admirer in the writer Vasily Rozanov, twenty-five years his junior.

For some mysterious reason, Leontiev's mother, instead of marrying the man she loved, married his brother, whom she did not, and her son evidently shared her distaste:

> My father was one of those frivolous and easily distracted Russians (and gentry, especially) who reject nothing and uphold nothing rigorously. In general, it may be said that my father was neither very clever nor very serious.

His mother, on the other hand, he adored and admired. The reasons he gives for this are revealing:

> She was incomparably more elegant than my father, and because of an inborn instinct, that was very important to me.

From her, he said he learned

> the lessons of patriotism and feeling for monarchy, the examples of a strict order, constant work, and refined taste in everyday life.

Leontiev, that is, was both by nature and by choice an aesthete and a narcissist. Aesthetes and narcissists can be found in every country, but Leontiev was also a Russian, and to me, at least, who was born and bred a British Pharisee, Russians are not quite like other folk. If their respective literatures in the nineteenth century are a guide, no two sensibilities could be more poles apart than the Russian and the British. (The American sensibility seems closer to the Russian. I can imagine a Russian equivalent of *Moby Dick* but not of *Sense and Sensibility*.) Time and time again, when reading even the greatest Russian writers, like Tolstoy and Dostoevsky, I find myself exclaiming, "My God, this man is bonkers!" In his introduction, Mr. Ivask quotes a remark by Alexander Blok: "It is worth living if only to make absolute demands on life." What a contrast to the advice given by the Red Queen to Alice—"Speak in French when you can't think of the English for a thing, turn out your toes as you walk, and remember who you are!"—or this definition by an Anglican bishop: "Orthodoxy is reticence." In British English, even today, the word *enthusiastic* is a pejorative. For this reason, the Russian writers we feel most at home with are Turgenev and Chekhov, though I suspect that if there were any decent translations we should find Pushkin even more to our taste.

Leontiev may extol the virtues of order and constant work, but he does not seem to have practiced them:

> The conflict of ideas in my mind was so violent in 1862 that I lost weight and not infrequently spent whole winter nights in Petersburg without any sleep, with my head and arms resting on a table in a state of exhaustion as a consequence of my martyrlike reflections.

No Englishman could possibly do such a thing. Reading accounts of Russian life, whether in the past or in the present, one gets the impression that the Protestant ethic of self-discipline, prudence, and regular hours has had no influence. Is this the cause or the effect of the despotism under which Russians have always lived? In Russia, says Leontiev,

> only that becomes established which, I repeat, is created somewhat arbitrarily and artificially by the government.

This seems as true of the New Russia of Lenin and Stalin as of the Old Russia of Peter and Catherine.

Western aesthetes have as a rule subscribed to the doctrine of Art for Art's Sake and deliberately averted their eyes from the realms of the political and social. This, to his credit, a Russian aesthete like Leontiev would never do. "The devil," he says, "take art without life!" The socially concerned aesthete, however, who judges society by the standards which apply to works of art, though his negative criticisms may be cogent, is, when it comes to making positive suggestions as to how to correct its defects, almost certain to talk nonsense, often pernicious nonsense. The aesthetic imagination is excited by the extraordinary person, deed, or event; the ethical question "Are these good or evil, just or unjust?" is not its concern. I myself do not believe an artist can entirely ignore the claims of the ethical, but in a work of art goodness and truth are subordinate to beauty. In the political and social realms it is just the other way round; a government, a society that ignores the aesthetic does so at its peril, but the ethical demand for justice must take precedence. Good looks and bearing are always to be admired. Says Leontiev:

> Dzheffer Dem was still young and extremely handsome. His face was pleasantly round, very swarthy and fresh-complexioned. About his whole person, in his huge black eyes, in his small black mustache that was twirled up, in his graceful carriage, in his smooth unhurried gait, in his white hands peacefully held behind his back, there was so much that was inexplicable, of good breeding, calm pride, secret self-assurance, that I cannot put it all into words!

But when, as in this case, their owner is a ruthless killer, one must admit that even the drabbest conformist bank clerk in a frock coat is preferable as a citizen. Or, again:

> "Would you like to have a world in which all people everywhere live in identical small, clean, and comfortable little houses—the way people of middle income live in our Novorossiisky towns?"
> "Of course. What could be better than that?" Piotrovsky replied.
> "Well, then I am no longer your man," I retorted. "If democratic movements must lead to such terrible prose, I shall lose the last vestige of my feeling for democracy. Henceforth I shall be its enemy!"

Piotrovsky was, of course, wrong in thinking of Suburbia as a utopia, but he was right in thinking that Suburbia was preferable to slums, however picturesque. Leontiev, incidentally, had to live in neither.

In judging social and political life, what the aesthete overlooks is the fact that while every human being is a unique person, a member of a class of one, very few human beings are extraordinary, whether in looks or talents or character; for the average man to seek to become extraordinary and therefore aesthetically interesting would be unauthentic, and as a rule he knows this. A playwright is free to select his heroes and heroines and ignore the mass of mankind; the politician can ignore no one, and, since they comprise the majority, ordinary men and women are his primary concern, for in politics to ignore usually means to oppress or to kill.

Leontiev's recommendations—at least for Russia, though I do not think he had any hope they would be listened to—were as follows:

> The State should be diversified, complex, strong, class-structured, and cautiously mobile. In general, strict, sometimes to the point of ferocity.
> The Church should be more independent than the present one. . . . The Church should have a mitigating influence on the State, and not vice versa. . . .
> The laws and principles of authority should be stricter; people should try to be personally kinder; the one will balance the other.

In coming to such conclusions he did not, as one might have expected, draw analogies from the process of artistic fabrication; he drew them from biology. Unfortunately, biological analogies are equally misleading. An organism lives under the necessity of being itself—an oak tree cannot turn into a butterfly—but it is false to call this necessity "despotism," since it is unconscious, whereas political despotism is consciously imposed. It would seem that all specific social structures are, like individual organisms, mortal, so one can speak of the rise, flowering, and decay of a particular society like the Roman Empire, but only with great caution. Like every species, the human race is potentially immortal, but, unlike all the others, man is a history-making creature whose "nature" is not identical with his social habits. A social animal like the bee could not change its hive-ways without ceasing to be a bee; man can and does continually change his ways. When a particular society disappears, human beings do not disappear but, by choice or necessity, become members of some new kind of society. One may prefer *this* society to *that,* but both are equally *human.*

Living, as we do, in an age when *liberal* has become a dirty word, it may be easier for us than for Leontiev's contemporaries to listen to his objections to the liberal philosophy. Everyone today will agree that the world we have fabricated during the last two hundred years is hideous compared with any fabricated in earlier times. And no one, I think, believes anymore in the liberal dogma of Progress; namely, that all change must be for the better. On the contrary, most of us, both old and young, are terrified of what the future may bring. The nineteenth-century "reactionaries" like Kierkegaard, Nietzsche, and Leontiev prophesied that liberalism, if successful, would produce a drably uniform society, Ortega y Gasset's mass man, and, as we all know, their prophecies have come true, but this, surely, was not what the original liberals intended. On the contrary, they must have hoped that political liberty would encourage diversity, that, granted equality before the law, equality of opportunity, and greater affluence, each individual, freed from the despotism of birth and poverty, would be able to develop into the kind of person he wished. That their hopes were disappointed may, I think, be mainly attributed to two factors, neither of them political in the strict sense. Firstly, to the development of technology. Starting with Locke, the creators of philosophical liberalism were eighteenth-century figures who lived before the Industrial Revolution, so they thought in terms of a society composed mostly of farmers and craftsmen. Machines have no political opinions, but they have profound political effects. They demand a strict regimentation of time, and, by abolishing the need for manual skill, have transformed the majority of the population from workers into laborers. There are, that is to say, fewer and fewer jobs which a man can find a pride and satisfaction in doing well, more and more which have no interest in themselves and can be valued only for the money they provide. Leontiev, like Herzen, was shocked by the materialism and philistine ambitions of the European working class, but what can men who have never known what it is to take pleasure in one's work hope for except more money and more consumer goods? Secondly, the liberals underestimated the desire of most human beings for conformity—

their fear of being unlike their neighbors and of standing alone in their opinions and tastes. It is true, as the critics of liberalism said, that the class-stratified societies of earlier times present a picture of much greater variety and aesthetic interest than the egalitarian society we know, but this was only because the class structure compelled the classes to live, dress, and think differently; within each class, whether that of the aristocrats or the peasants, the urge for conformity was probably no less strong than it is today, when, as we know, tight pants and long hair are just as de rigueur for a rebel hippie as a Brooks Brothers suit and a crew cut are for a junior executive.

Before considering Leontiev as a literary critic, I suppose I must say a word about his attitude toward the Christian faith and the Church, though I am loath to do so because I find it repellent. He seems to have been one of those persons who alternate between leading a dissolute life and weeping over their sins, not out of genuine repentance but out of fear of going to Hell. Faugh!

By vocation, Leontiev was a writer, not a political theorist, and when he discusses literature he speaks not as an amateur but with professional authority. Because he believed that Life was more important than Art, his literary preference was for "realism"— novels and poems, that is to say, which try to depict as truthfully as possible the Primary World in which we all live. Thus, comparing *War and Peace* with *Anna Karenina,* he says:

> Is the general trend of *War and Peace* as true in spirit and style to the life of the year 1812 as the trend of *Anna Karenina* is faithful to the spirit and style of our time? It seems to me not so true.

To explain what he means, he tries to imagine what *War and Peace* would be like if Pushkin had written it. He admits at once that it would not be anywhere near as great a novel, but he thinks it would have been more "realistic":

> Pushkin would not have (probably) even called the French marshals and generals, who were running away from themselves in carriages and fur coats, "wicked and insignificant men who have done a great deal of evil," just as the Russian heroes, who were chasing them from Moscow,

probably did not call them that in their soul in the year 1812, but chided them in passion rather than according to the precepts of a tediously moral philosophy.

What Leontiev hated—and I heartily agree with him—was "naturalism" which identifies the "real" with the ignoble and the ugly. As with Karl Kraus, his criticism is never generalized but always specific and concrete: he picks out phrases, verbal habits, even single words which seem to him symptomatic of a literary disease:

> When Tolstoy's Ivan Ilyich uses the "bed-pan," that is all right. Ivan Ilyich is a sick, dying man. I like it here. But when Gogol's Tentetnikov, awakening in the morning, still lies in bed and "rubs his eyes," and his eyes are "small," this is very nasty and unnecessary. . . .
>
> When, at the end of *War and Peace,* the already married Natasha brings out the childbed linen to show it in the drawing room, the green stain on the linen has turned yellow; although this is unattractive and crude, yet it is appropriate here; it has great significance. . . . But when Pierre "dandles" ("dandles," indeed! why not simply "nurses"?) on the palm of his large hand (those hands) that same infant and the infant suddenly soils his hands, this is completely unnecessary and proves nothing. . . . It is ugliness for the sake of ugliness. . . .
>
> These constant repetitions—"hurriedly," "involuntarily," "involuntary," "alien," "alien," "nervously," "pudgy," "pudgy," and so on; "juicy mouth," "toothless mouth"—these frequent psychological scrutinies and unnecessary corporeal observations when we read aloud not only Tolstoy but the majority of our best authors—Turgenev, Pisemsky, Dostoevsky—are sometimes simply intolerable!

Leontiev, with what justice I do not know, thought that Russian writers and readers were more addicted to this vice of "nose-picking" than those of other countries:

> Suppose, for example, it is necessary to say that one of the male characters was frightened. An Englishman would more than likely say, without exaggerating one way or the

other, either positively or negatively: "Intensely frightened, James stood motionless, etc." A Frenchman: "Alfred began to tremble. A deathly pallor covered his handsome face. He withdrew, but with dignity." The Russian writer would prefer to express himself thus: "My hero, like a blackguard, got cold feet and trudged off home." Perhaps even better: "dashed off home."

A first-rate critic, as distinct from a run-of-the-mill one, always shows respect for the author he is considering, even in attack. When his author does something he disapproves of, he tries to put himself in the author's place and asks, "What were his reasons for doing this?" So, after objecting to Tolstoy's tendency to "nose-pick," Leontiev is willing to concede that, much as he dislikes it, Tolstoy, given the nature of his readers, was probably justified:

> The Russian reader of our time (especially the reader who occupies a middle position in society) . . . [has been] educated . . . in such a way that a wart will make him believe more strongly in nobility, a snort will make him feel love more intensely, and so on; and if someone "with a nervous gesture pours out a glass of vodka" and then, instead of smiling, "smirks," his confidence will be complete! . . .
> Tolstoy . . . has rendered his readers a patriotic service by all this slight, external humiliation of life.

I hope very much that someone will soon publish an English translation of Leontiev's collected critical essays.

*

LEWIS CARROLL

*

In the evening of Friday, July 4, 1862, the Reverend Charles Lutwidge Dodgson, lecturer and tutor in mathematics at Christ Church, Oxford, wrote in his diary:

> Atkinson brought over to my rooms some friends of his, a Mrs. and Miss Peters, of whom I took photographs, and who afterward looked over my album and stayed to lunch. They then went off to the Museum and Duckworth and I made an expedition *up* the river to Godstow with the three Liddells: we had tea on the bank there, and did not reach Christ Church again till quarter past 8, when we took them on to my rooms to see my collection of micro-photographs, and restored them to the Deanery just before 9.

"The three Liddells" were the daughters of the Dean of Christ Church, one of the authors of the famous Liddell & Scott Greek lexicon. Their names were Lorina Charlotte, Alice, and Edith—nicknamed Matilda. Alice was ten years old.

This was by no means their first expedition together. For some years they had been seeing a lot of one another. In the winter, they would go to Dodgson's rooms and sit on the sofa beside him while he told them stories, which he illustrated by pencil or ink drawings as he went along. Four or five times in the summer term

] 283 [

he would take them out on the river, bringing with him a large basket of cakes and a kettle. On such occasions, Dodgson exchanged his clerical suit for white flannel trousers and his black top hat for a hard white straw hat. He always carried himself upright "as if he had swallowed a poker."

Outwardly there was nothing to distinguish the Godstow expedition from any other. And nobody today would remember that it ever took place but for what seems almost a pure accident. He had told the children many stories before, to which they had listened with delight, and they begged him to tell them another. This time, perhaps, he was in better storytelling form than usual, for his friend Mr. Duckworth was evidently impressed:

> I rowed *stroke* and he rowed *bow* . . . the story was actually composed and spoken *over my shoulder* for the benefit of Alice Liddell, who was acting as "cox" of our gig. I remember turning round and saying "Dodgson, is this an extempore romance of yours?" And he replied: "Yes, I'm inventing as we go along."

Anyway, this time Alice did what she had never done before—she asked him to write the story down. At first he said he would think about it, but she continued to pester him until, eventually, he gave his promise to do so. In his diary for November 13, he notes: "Began writing the fairy-tale for Alice—I hope to finish it by Christmas."

In fact, the text was finished on February 10, 1863. Tenniel's illustrations were not completed until September, 1864, and *Alice in Wonderland* was published by Macmillan in 1865 (which is also, incidentally, the year of the first performance of another masterpiece, Wagner's *Tristan und Isolde*).

These events are memorable because they reveal a kind of human being who is, I believe, extremely rare—a man of genius who, in regard to his genius, is without egoism. In other respects, Dodgson was neither selfless nor without vanity. As a member of Senior Common Room, he was a difficult colleague, forever complaining about some minor negligence or inconvenience. He held strong and conservative views upon almost every question affecting the College or the University, and the savagery of his polemical pamphlets, like "The New Belfry of Christ Church" or "Twelve Months in a Curatorship," cannot have endeared him to his opponents.

He was proud of his photography, and justly so, for he was one of the best portrait photographers of the century. He had great hopes for his theory of Symbolic Logic, which is, I understand, more highly regarded today than it was at the time. As his diaries show, he also thought well of his little inventions—and he was always inventing something: a *memoria technica* for the logarithms of all primes under 100; a game of arithmetical croquet; a rule for finding the day of the week for any date of the month, a substitute for glue; a system of proportional representation; a method of controlling the carriage traffic at Covent Garden; an apparatus for making notes in the dark; an improved steering gear for a tricycle; and he always sought publication for his light verse. But when it came to the one thing which he did superbly well, where he was without any rival—namely, telling stories to children—the thought of himself, of publication and immortal fame, never seems to have entered his head.

The two *Alice* books were no freak achievements. There are passages in letters to children where the writing is just as good. For example:

It's so frightfully hot here that I've been almost too weak to hold a pen, and even if I had been able, there was no ink—it had all evaporated into a cloud of black steam, and in that state it has been floating about the room, inking the walls and ceiling till they're hardly fit to be seen: today, it is cooler, and a little has come back into the ink bottle in the form of black snow.

He went on telling impromptu stories to children all his life, which were never written down and, for all we know, may have surpassed the ones that were.

Though no human character can be explained away in terms of his upbringing or environment, it is legitimate to look for influencing factors. In Dodgson's case, one such factor may have been his position as the oldest boy—the son of a clergyman—in a large family: he had seven sisters and three brothers. By the time he was eleven he had made himself the family entertainer. He constructed a train, built out of a wheelbarrow, a barrel, and a small truck, which conveyed passengers from one station in the rectory garden to another, and in the rules he drew up for this game, the Lewis Carroll imagination is already evident:

> All passengers when upset are requested to lie still until picked up—as it is requisite that at least three trains should go over them, to entitle them to the attention of the doctor and assistants.
> When a passenger has no money and still wants to go by train, he must stop at whatever station he happens to be at, and earn money—making tea for the stationmaster (who drinks it at all hours of the day and night) and grinding sand for the company (what use they make of it they are not bound to explain).

Two years later, he became the editor and chief contributor for a succession of family magazines, the last of which, *The Rectory Umbrella,* was still appearing after he had become an Oxford don and first printed the opening quatrain of "Jabberwocky."

Thus, at the beginning of his career as a writer, he was writing directly for an audience with which he was intimate and in which he had no literary rival. The average writer, at least today, has a very different experience. When he begins writing, he has no audience except himself; his first audience is likely to be one of rival, as yet unpublished, authors, and his only chance of acquiring an audience of his own is to get published, in little magazines or popular ones; and this audience consists of readers whom he does not know personally.

It seems clear that what, as an imaginative creator, Dodgson valued most was the immediate and intimate response of his audience, and its undivided attention (hence, perhaps, his passion for the theater). His writings for adults, no less than his children's stories, are for the "family"—Oxford to him was another and larger rectory. Even in the only company with whom he felt so completely at home that his stammer disappeared, the company of little girls, he preferred to see them singly. As he wrote to one mother:

Would you kindly tell me if I may reckon your girls as invitable to tea, or dinner, singly. I know of cases where they are invitable in sets only (like the circulating-library novels), and such friendships I don't think worth going on with. I don't think anyone knows what girl-nature *is,* who has only seen them in the presence of their mothers or sisters.

Many guesses, plausible and implausible, have been made as to the historical origins of the characters and events in the *Alice* books, but one may be sure that many allusions which were apparent to the Liddell children are now irrecoverable. When he told a story, it was always for a particular child. One of them, not Alice, records:

One thing that made his stories particularly charming to a child was that he often took his cue from her remarks— a question would set him off on quite a new trail of ideas, so that one felt one had somehow helped to make the story, and it seemed a personal possession.

Very few writers, I believe, however much they desire fame for their books, enjoy being a public figure who is recognized on the street by strangers, but Dodgson hated publicity more than most. He refused to allow any picture of himself to appear—"Nothing would be more unpleasant for me than to have my face known to strangers"—and he gave orders that any letters addressed to L. Carroll, Christ Church, Oxford, were to be returned to the sender with the endorsement "not known."

But thanks to Alice Liddell's importunity, and luckily for us, the intimate narrator became a world-famous author. As usually happens with a masterpiece, the initial critical reception of *Alice in Wonderland* was mixed. The *Illustrated London News* and the *Pall Mall Gazette* liked it; the *Spectator,* though generally approving, condemned the Mad Hatter's tea-party; the *Athenaeum* thought it a "stiff, overwrought story," and the *Illustrated Times,* while conceding that the author possessed a fertile imagination, declared that Alice's adventures "are too extravagantly absurd to produce more diversion than disappointment and irritation."

When, seven years later, *Through the Looking-Glass* appeared, the critics knew, from the enormous public success of its predecessor, that it must be good—though I can think of no more unlikely literary comparison than that of Henry Kingsley, who wrote: "This is the finest thing we have had since *Martin Chuzzlewit*."

And the book's fame has continued to grow. I have always thought one might learn much about the cultural history of a country by going through the speeches made by its public men over a certain period, in legislatures, in law courts, and at official banquets, and making a list of the books quoted from without attribution. So far as Great Britain is concerned, I strongly suspect that, for the past fifty years, the two *Alice* books and *The Hunting of the Snark* have headed it.

How do American readers react? Though nearly all the Americans I know personally loved Lewis Carroll as children, they may not be representative of American taste in general. Certainly, in every American book read by children—from *Huckleberry Finn* to the *Oz* books—which I have come across, nothing could be more remote from their worlds than the world of Alice.

The American child-hero—are there any American child-heroines?—is a Noble Savage, an anarchist, and, even when he reflects, predominantly concerned with movement and action. He may do almost anything except sit still. His heroic virtue—that is to say, his superiority to adults—lies in his freedom from conventional ways of thinking and acting: *all* social habits, from manners to creeds, are regarded as false or hypocritical or both. All emperors are really naked. Alice, surely, must come to the average American as a shock.

To begin with, she is a "lady." When, puzzled by the novelty of Wonderland, she asks herself if she could have changed into some other child, she is quite certain what sort of child she does *not* want to be:

> "I'm sure I can't be Mabel, for I know all sorts of things, and she, oh, she knows such a very little . . . . I must be Mabel after all, and I shall have to go and live in that poky little house, and have next to no toys to play with . . . . No, I've made up my mind about it: if I'm Mabel, I'll stay down here."

Among grownups, she knows the difference between servants and mistresses:

"He took me for his house-maid," she said to herself as she ran. "How surprised he'll be when he finds out who I am." . . .

"The governess would never think of excusing my lessons for that. If she couldn't remember my name, she'd call me 'Miss' as the servants do."

And when the Red Queen advises her: "Speak in French when you can't think of the English for a thing—turn out your toes as you walk—and remember who you are!"—she knows that the answer to the question, "Who am I?" is really: "I am Alice Liddell, daughter of the Dean of Christ Church."

What is most likely to bewilder an American child, however, is not Alice's class-consciousness, which is easy to miss, but the peculiar relation of children and grownups to law and social manners. It is the child-heroine Alice who is invariably reasonable, self-controlled, and polite, while all the other inhabitants, human or animal, of Wonderland and the Looking-Glass are unsocial eccentrics—at the mercy of their passions and extremely bad-mannered, like the Queen of Hearts, the Duchess, the Hatter, and Humpty Dumpty, or grotesquely incompetent, like the White Queen and the White Knight.

What Alice finds so extraordinary about the people and events in these worlds is the anarchy which she is forever trying to make sense and order out of. In both books, games play an important role. The whole structure of *Through the Looking-Glass* is based on chess, and the Queen of Hearts' favorite pastime is croquet—both of them games which Alice knows how to play. To play a game, it is essential that the players know and obey its rules, and are skillful enough to do the right or reasonable thing at least half the time. Anarchy and incompetence are incompatible with play.

Croquet played with hedgehogs, flamingos, and soldiers instead of the conventional balls, mallets, and hoops is conceivable, provided that they are willing to imitate the behavior of these inanimate objects, but, in Wonderland, they behave as they choose and the game is impossible to play.

In the Looking-Glass world, the problem is different. It is not, like Wonderland, a place of complete anarchy where everybody says and does whatever comes into his head, but a completely determined world without choice. Tweedledum and Tweedledee, the Lion and the Unicorn, the Red Knight and the White, must fight at regular intervals, irrespective of their feelings. In Wonderland, Alice has to adjust herself to a life without laws; in Looking-Glass Land, to one governed by laws to which she is unaccustomed. She has to learn, for example, to walk away from a place in order to reach it, or to run fast in order to remain where she is. In Wonderland, she is the only person with self-control; in Looking-Glass Land, the only competent one. But for the way she plays a pawn, one feels that the game of chess would never be completed.

In both worlds, one of the most important and powerful characters is not a person but the English language. Alice, who had hitherto supposed that words were passive objects, discovers that they have a life and will of their own. When she tries to remember poems she has learned, new lines come into her head unbidden, and, when she thinks she knows what a word means, it turns out to mean something else.

> "And so these three little sisters—they were learning to draw, you know—"
> "What did they draw?" . . .
> "Treacle—*from a treacle well. . . .*"
> "But they were in the well."
> "Of course they were: well in." . . .
>
> "How old did you say you were?"
> "Seven years and six months."
> "Wrong! You never said a word like it!" . . .
>
> "You take some flour."
> "Where do you pick the flower? In a garden or in the hedges?"
> "Well, it isn't *picked* at all: it's *ground*."
> "How many acres of ground?"

Nothing, surely, could be more remote from the American image of the pioneering, hunting, prepolitical hero than this preoccupation with language. It is the concern of the solitary thinker, for language is the mother of thought, and of the politician—in the Greek sense—for speech is the medium by which we disclose ourselves to others. The American hero is neither.

Both of Alice's "dreams" end in a state of developing chaos from which she wakes just in time before they can become nightmares:

> At this the whole pack rose up in the air, and came flying down upon her; she gave a little scream, half of fright and half of anger, and tried to beat them off, and found herself lying on the bank with her head in the lap of her sister. . . .

> Already several of the guests were lying down in the dishes, and the soup ladle was walking up the table towards Alice's chair, and beckoning to her impatiently to get out of its way.
> "I can't stand this any longer!" she cried, as she jumped up and seized the table-cloth with both hands: one good pull, and plates, dishes, guests and candles came crashing down together in a heap on the floor.

Wonderland and Looking-Glass Land are fun to visit but no places to live in. Even when she is there, Alice can ask herself with some nostalgia "if anything would ever happen in a natural way again," and by "natural" she means the opposite of what Rousseau would mean. She means peaceful, civilized society.

There are good books which are only for adults, because their comprehension presupposes adult experiences, but there are no good books which are only for children. A child who enjoys the *Alice* books will continue to enjoy them when he or she is grown up, though his "reading" of what they mean will probably change. In assessing their value, there are two questions one can ask: first, what insight do they provide as to how the world appears to a child?; and, second, to what extent is the world really like that?

According to Lewis Carroll, what a child desires before anything else is that the world in which he finds himself should make sense. It is not the commands and prohibitions, as such, which adults impose that the child resents, but rather that he cannot perceive any law linking one command to another in a consistent pattern.

The child is told, for example, that he must not do such-and-such, and then sees adults doing precisely that. This occurs especially often in the realm of social manners. In well-bred society, people treat each other with courtesy but, in trying to teach their children to be polite, their method of instruction is often that of a drill sergeant. Without realizing it, adults can be rude to children in ways which, if they were dealing with one of their own kind, would get them knocked down. How many children, when they are silenced with the command, "Speak when you're spoken to!" must have longed to retort as Alice does:

> "But if everybody obeyed that rule, and if you only spoke when you were spoken to, and the other person always waited for *you* to begin, you see that nobody would ever say anything."

It would be an exaggeration to say that children see adults as they really are, but, like servants, they see them at moments when they are not concerned with making a favorable impression.

As everybody knows, Dodgson's Muse was incarnated in a succession of girls between the ages of eight and eleven. Little boys he feared and disliked: they were grubby and noisy and broke things. Most adults he found insensitive. At the age of twenty-four, he wrote in his diary:

> I think that the character of most that I meet is merely refined animal. How few seem to care for the only subjects of real interest in life!

Naturally, most of his "child-friends" came from middle- or upper-middle class English homes. He mentions having met one American child and the encounter was not a success:

> Lily Alice Godfrey, from New York: aged 8; but talked like a girl of 15 or 16, and declined to be kissed on wishing good-by, on the ground that she 'never kissed gentlemen'. . . . I fear it is true that there are no children in America.

And the children he understood best were the quiet and imaginative ones. Thus Irene Vanbrugh, who must have been going through a tomboy phase when she met him, says:

> He had a deep love for children, though I am inclined to think not such a great understanding of them. . . . His

great delight was to teach me his Game of Logic. Dare I say this made the evening rather long, when the band was playing outside on the parade, and the moon shining on the sea?

The question for an adult reader of Lewis Carroll, however, is not the author's psychological peculiarities, but the validity of his heroine. Is Alice, that is to say, an adequate symbol for what every human being should try to be like?

I am inclined to answer yes. A girl of eleven (or a boy of twelve) who comes from a good home—a home, that is, where she has known both love and discipline and where the life of the mind is taken seriously but not solemnly—can be a most remarkable creature. No longer a baby, she has learned self-control, acquired a sense of her identity, and can think logically without ceasing to be imaginative. She does not know, of course, that her sense of identity has been too easily won—the gift of her parents rather than her own doing—and that she is soon going to lose it, first in the *Sturm und Drang* of adolescence and then, when she enters the adult social world, in anxieties over money and status.

But one cannot meet a girl or a boy of this kind without feeling that what she or he is—by luck and momentarily—is what, after many years and countless follies and errors, one would like, in the end, to become.

CALM EVEN IN THE CATASTROPHE

✳

The great masters of letter-writing as an art have probably been more concerned with entertaining their friends than disclosing their innermost thoughts and feelings; their epistolary style is characterized by speed, high spirits, wit, and fantasy. Van Gogh's letters are not art in this sense, but human documents; what makes them great letters is the absolute self-honesty and nobility of the writer.

The nineteenth century created the myth of the Artist as Hero, the man who sacrifices his health and happiness to his art and in compensation claims exemption from all social responsibilities and norms of behavior.

At first sight Van Gogh seems to fit the myth exactly. He dresses and lives like a tramp, he expects to be supported by others, he works at his painting like a fiend, he goes mad. Yet the more one reads these letters, the less like the myth he becomes.

He knows he is neurotic and difficult but he does not regard this as a sign of superiority, but as an illness like heart disease, and hopes that the great painters of the future will be as healthy as the Old Masters.

> But this painter who is to come—I can't imagine him living in little cafés, working away with a lot of false teeth, and going to the Zouaves' brothels, as I do.

He sees the age in which he is living as one of transition rather than fulfillment, and is extremely modest about his own achievements.

> Giotto and Cimabue, as well as Holbein and Van Dyck, lived in an obeliscal solidly-framed society, architecturally constructed, in which each individual was a stone and all the stones clung together, forming a monumental society. . . . But, you know, we are in the midst of downright *laisser-aller* and anarchy. We artists who love order and symmetry isolate ourselves and are working to define *only one thing*. . . . We *can* paint an atom of the chaos, a horse, a portrait, your grandmother, apples, a landscape. . . .
>
> We do not feel that we are dying, but we do feel the truth that we are of small account, and that we are paying a hard price to be a link in the chain of artists, in health, in youth, in liberty, none of which we enjoy, any more than the cab-horse that hauls a coachful of people out to enjoy the spring.

Furthermore, though he never wavers in his belief that painting is his vocation, he does not claim that painters are superior to other folk.

It was Richepin who said somewhere,

> *L'amour de l'art fait perdre l'amour vrai.*

> I think that is terribly true, but on the other hand real love makes you disgusted with art. . . .
>
> The rather superstitious ideas they have here about painting sometimes depress me more than I can tell you, because basically it is really fairly true that a painter as a man is too absorbed in what his eyes see, and is not sufficiently master of the rest of his life.

It is true that Van Gogh did not earn his living but was supported all his life by his brother who was by no means a rich man. But when one compares his attitude towards money with that of say, Wagner, or Baudelaire, how immeasurably more decent and self-respecting Van Gogh appears.

No artist ever asked less of a patron—a laborer's standard of living and enough over to buy paints and canvases. He even wor-

ries about his right to the paints and wonders whether he ought
not to stick to the cheaper medium of drawing. When, occasionally, he gets angry with his brother, his complaint is not that Theo
is stingy but that he is cold; it is more intimacy he craves for, not
more cash.

> . . . against my person, my manners, clothes, world,
> you, like so many others, seem to think it necessary to raise
> so many objections—weighty enough and at the same time
> obviously without redress—that they have caused our per-
> sonal brotherly intercourse to wither and die off gradually
> in the course of the years.
>
> This is the dark side of your character—I think you are
> mean in this respect—but the bright side is your reliability
> in money matters.
>
> Ergo conclusion—I acknowledge being under an obli-
> gation to you with the greatest pleasure. Only—lacking re-
> lations with you, with Teersteg, and with whomever I knew
> in the past—I want *something else*. . . .
>
> There are people, as you know, who support painters
> during the time when they do not yet earn anything. But
> how often doesn't it happen that it ends miserably, wretch-
> edly for both parties, partly because the protector is an-
> noyed about the money, which is or at least seems quite
> thrown away, whereas, on the other hand, the painter feels
> entitled to more confidence, more patience and interest than
> is given him? But in most cases the misunderstandings arise
> from carelessness on both sides.

Few painters read books and fewer can express in words what
they are up to. Van Gogh is a notable exception: he read vora-
ciously and with understanding, he had considerable literary talent
of his own, and he loved to talk about what he was doing and
why. If I understood the meaning of the word *literary* as a prejorative
adjective when applied to painting, those who use it are asserting
that the world of pictures and the world of phenomenal nature are
totally distinct so that one must never be judged by reference to
the other. To ask if a picture is "like" any natural object—it makes
no difference whether one means a "photographic" or a platoni-
cally "real" likeness—or to ask if one "subject" for a picture is
humanly more important than another, is irrelevant. The painter

creates his own pictorial world and the value of a painting can only be assessed by comparison with other paintings. If that is indeed what critics mean, then Van Gogh must be classified as a literary painter. Like Millet, whom all his life he acknowledged as his master, and like some of his contemporary French novelists, Flaubert, the Goncourts, Zola, he believed that the truly human subject for art in his day was the life of the poor. Hence his quarrel with the art-schools.

As far as I know there isn't a single academy where one learns to draw and paint a digger, a sower, a woman putting the kettle over the fire or a seamstress. But in every city of some importance there is an academy with a choice of models for historical, Arabic, Louis XV, in short, *all really* non-existent figures. . . . All academic figures are put together in the same way and, let's say, *on ne peut mieux.* Irreproachable, *faultless.* You will guess what I am driving at, they do not reveal anything new. I think that, however correctly academic a figure may be, it will be superfluous, though it were by Ingres himself, when it lacks the essential modern note, the intimate character, the real *action.* Perhaps you will ask: When will a figure not be superfluous? . . . When the digger digs, when the peasant is a peasant and the peasant woman a peasant woman. . . . I ask you, do you know a single digger, a single sower in the old Dutch school? Did they ever try to paint "a labourer"? Did Velasquez try it in his water-carrier or types from the people? No. The figures in the pictures of the old master do not *work.*

It was this same moral preference for the naturally real to the ideally beautiful which led him, during his brief stay at an art-school in Antwerp, when he was set to copy a cast of the Venus de Milo, to make alterations in her figure and roar at the shocked professor: "So you don't know what a young woman is like, God damn you! A woman must have hips and buttocks and a pelvis in which she can hold a child."

Where he differs from most of his French contemporaries is that he never shared their belief that the artist should suppress his own emotions and view his material with clinical detachment. On the contrary, he writes:

> . . . whoever wants to do figures must first have what is printed on the Christmas number of *Punch:* "Good Will to all"—and this to a high degree. One must have a warm sympathy with human beings, and go on having it, or the drawings will remain cold and insipid. I consider it very necessary for us to watch ourselves and to take care that we do not become disenchanted in this respect.

and how opposed to any doctrine of "pure" art is this remark written only two months before his death.

> Instead of grandiose exhibitions, it would have been better to address oneself to the people and work so that each could have in his home some pictures or reproductions which would be lessons, like the work of Millet.

Here he sounds like Tolstoy, just as he sounds like Dostoevsky when he says:

> It always strikes me, and it is very peculiar, that whenever we see the image of indescribable and unutterable desolation—of loneliness, poverty and misery, the end and extreme of all things, the thought of God comes into one's mind.

When he talks of the poor, indeed, Van Gogh sounds more honest and natural than either Tolstoy or Dostoevsky. As a physical and intellectual human being Tolstoy was a king, a superior person; in addition he was a count, a socially superior person. However hard he tried, he could never think of a peasant as an equal; he could only, partly out of a sense of guilt at his own moral shortcomings, admire him as his superior. Dostoevsky was not an aristocrat and he was ugly, but it was with the criminal poor rather than the poor as such that he felt in sympathy. But Van Gogh preferred the life and company of the poor, not in theory but in fact. Tolstoy and Dostoevsky were, as writers, successful in their lifetime with the educated; what the peasants thought of them as men we do not know. Van Gogh was not recognized as an artist in his lifetime; on the other hand, we have records of the personal impression he made upon the coal-miners of the Borinage.

People still talk of the miner whom he went to see after the accident in the Marcasse mine. The man was a habitual drinker, "an unbeliever and blasphemer," according to the people who told me the story. When Vincent entered his house to help and comfort him, he was received with a volley of abuse. He was called especially a *mâcheux d'capelots* (rosary chewer) as if he had been a Roman Catholic priest. But Van Gogh's evangelical tenderness converted the man. . . . People still tell how, at the time of the *tirage au sort,* the drawing of lots for conscription, women begged the holy man to show them a passage in the Holy Scripture which would serve as a talisman for their sons and ensure their drawing a good number and being exempted from service in the barracks. . . . A strike broke out; the mutinous miners would no longer listen to anyone except *"l'pasteur Vincent"* whom they trusted.

Both as a man and as a painter Van Gogh was passionately Christian in feeling though, no doubt, a bit heterodox in doctrine. "Resignation," he declared, "is only for those who *can* be resigned, and religious belief is for those who *can* believe. My friends, let us love what we love. The man who damn well refuses to love what he loves dooms himself." Perhaps the best label for him as a painter would be Religious Realist. A realist because he attached supreme importance to the incessant study of nature and never composed pictures "out of his head"; religious because he regarded nature as the sacramental visible sign of a spiritual grace which it was his aim as a painter to reveal to others. "I want," he said once, "to paint men and women with that something of the eternal which the halo used to symbolise, and which we seek to convey by the actual radiance and vibration of our colouring." He is the first painter, so far as I know, to have consciously attempted to produce a painting which should be religious and yet contain no traditional religious iconography, something which one might call "A Parable for the Eye."

Here is a description of a canvas which is in front of me at the moment. A view of the park of the asylum where I am staying; on the right a grey terrace and a side wall of a house. Some deflowered rose bushes, on the left a stretch of the park—red ochre—the soil scorched by the sun, covered with fallen pine needles. This edge of the park is planted with large pine trees, whose trunks and branches are red-ochre, the foliage green gloomed over by an admixture of black. These high trees stand out against the evening sky with violet stripes on a yellow ground, which higher up turns into pink, into green. A wall—also red-ochre—shuts off the view, and is topped only by a violet and yellow-ochre hill. Now the nearest tree is an enormous trunk, struck by lightning and sawed off. But one side branch shoots up very high and lets fall an avalanche of dark green pine needles. This sombre giant—like a defeated proud man—contrasts, when considered in the nature of a living creature, with the pale smile of a last rose on the fading bush in front of him. Underneath the trees, empty stone benches, sullen box trees; the sky is mirrored—yellow —in a puddle left by the rain. A sunbeam, the last ray of daylight, raises the sombre ochre almost to orange. Here and there small black figures wander among the tree trunks.

You will realise that this combination of red-ochre, of green gloomed over by grey, the black streaks surrounding the contours, produces something of the sensation of anguish, called "rouge-noir," from which certain of my companions in misfortune frequently suffer. Moreover, the motif of the great tree struck by lightning, the sickly green-pink smile of the last flower of autumn serve to confirm this impression.

I am telling you (about this canvas) to remind you that one can try to give an impression of anguish without aiming straight at the historic Garden of Gethsemane.

Evidently, what Van Gogh is trying to do is to substitute for a historic iconography, which has to be learned before it can be recognized, an iconography of color and form relations which reveals itself instantaneously to the senses, and is therefore impossible to misinterpret. The possibility of such an iconography depends upon whether or not color-form relations and their impact upon the human mind are governed by universal laws. Van Gogh certainly believed that they were and that, by study, any painter could discover these laws.

The *laws* of the colours are unutterably beautiful, just because they are not *accidental*. In the same way that people nowadays no longer believe in a God who capriciously and despotically flies from one thing to another, but begin to feel more respect and admiration for faith in nature—in the same way, and for the same reasons, I think that in art, the old-fashioned idea of innate genius, inspiration, etc., I do not say must be put aside, but thoroughly reconsidered, verified—and greatly modified.

In another letter he gives Fatality as another name for God, and defines Him by the image—"Who is the White Ray of Light, He in Whose eyes even the Black Ray will have no plausible meaning."

Van Gogh had very little fun, he never knew the satisfaction of good food, glory, or the love of women, and he ended in the bin, but, after reading his correspondence, it is impossible to think of him as the romantic *artiste maudit,* or even as tragic hero; in spite of everything, the final impression is one of triumph. In his last letter to Theo, found on him after his death, he says, with a grateful satisfaction in which there is no trace of vanity:

I tell you again that I shall always consider you to be something more than a simple dealer in Corots, that through my mediation you have your part in the actual production of some canvases, which will retain their calm even in the catastrophe.

What we mean when we speak of a work of art as "great" has, surely, never been better defined than by the concluding relative clause.

AN IMPROBABLE LIFE

When we were young, most of us were taught that it is dishonorable to read other people's letters without their consent, and I do not think we should ever, even if we grow up to be literary scholars, forget this early lesson. The mere fact that a man is famous and dead does not entitle us to read, still less to publish, his private correspondence. We have to ask ourselves two questions—firstly, "Would he mind?" and, secondly, "Are the contents of such historical importance as to justify publication even if he would?" In the case of the born letter writer, like Horace Walpole, to whom letter writing is as natural and "impersonal" a form of literary composition as poetry or fiction, one generally feels that he would be pleased to have his letters read by the public, and in the case of men of action—statesmen, generals, and the like, whose decisions have affected the history of the society in which they lived—we are entitled to know anything about their lives that sheds light upon their public acts. Writers and artists, however, are another matter. Some of them have been born letter writers as well, but the average productive poet or novelist or dramatist is too busy, too self-centered, to spend much time and trouble over his correspondence; if and when he does, the letters are probably love letters and, since knowledge of an artist's private life never throws any significant light upon his work, there is no justification for intruding upon his privacy. Keats' letters to Fanny Brawne, and Beethoven's to his nephew, should either not have been published at all or, like psychological case histories, have been published anonymously.

What, then, about the letters of Oscar Wilde? Is their publication justified? Somewhat to my surprise, I find myself saying yes. Yeats said of Wilde that he seemed to be a man of action rather than a writer. What Yeats should have said, I think, is that Wilde was, both by genius and by fate, primarily an "actor," a performer. Even those of his contemporaries who most admired his writings admitted that they were inferior to his conversation; what inspired his imagination most was a physically present audience and its immediate response. From the beginning Wilde performed his life and continued to do so even after fate had taken the plot out of his hands. Drama is essentially revelation; on the stage no secrets are kept. I feel therefore, that there is nothing Wilde would desire more than that we should know everything about him. There remains the question of the recipients of his letters. They could not have been published until many of his most intimate friends— Alfred Douglas, Robbie Ross, Reggie Turner, More Adey, and others—were dead, because of the allusions to their homosexuality that they contain. With one exception, the revelation of what was in any case an open secret would not embarrass them in the least, and it is a trivial matter compared with what these letters reveal of their loyalty, compassion, and generosity toward Wilde at a time when to be his friend required great moral courage. The exception is, of course, Lord Alfred Douglas, who emerges from these letters as a vicious, gold-digging, snobbish, anti-Semitic, untalented little horror for whom no good word can be said. One might feel sorry for him if, after the catastrophe, he had kept his mouth shut, but he did not. He not only wrote an account of their relationship that is full of lies but also dared to put on virtuous airs, and it is only just that he should be exposed for what he was.

As all the reviewers have rightly pointed out, Mr. Rupert Hart-Davis, who has put together *The Letters of Oscar Wilde,* has done a masterly editorial job and one that must have been fiendishly difficult. Wilde's handwriting became very hard to read, he seldom dated his letters, few of his early biographers are to be trusted on matters of fact, some of the letters have been mutilated, and a number of forged ones exist. Out of the twelve hundred and ninety-eight letters Mr. Hart-Davis succeeded in collecting, he has printed all but two hundred unimportant brief notes. His own footnotes and index provide all the background information one could desire, and I have never read a work of this kind in which it was so easy to refind a note or make a cross-reference.

Wilde's life was a drama, and in reading his letters chronologically there is an excitement similar to that of watching a Greek tragedy in which the audience knows what is going to happen while the hero does not. The play begins, idyllically, in Oxford during the eighteen-seventies. Onstage are Wilde and two nice-looking fellow-undergraduates, Reginald Harding and William Ward, one destined to become a stockbroker, the other a solicitor in Bristol. Remembering my own years at Oxford, I would have expected Wilde's letters to them to be full of references to literary discoveries, of extravagant praise of this author and violent denunciations of that, or of philosophical arguments. But they are neither literary nor intellectual. There is scarcely a word in them about the "modern" poets of the time, like Swinburne, Morris, Rossetti, James Thomson, Coventry Patmore. Indeed, the only poem he speaks of with enthusiasm is, of all things, Mrs. Browning's *Aurora Leigh,* which he ranks with *Hamlet* and *In Memoriam,* and if his comment on the poem were to be quoted anonymously, I do not think anybody would guess the author:

> It is one of those books that, written straight from the heart—and such a large heart too—never weary one: because they are sincere. We tire of art but not of nature after all our aesthetic training.

This lack of interest in what others are writing and, on the rare occasion when interest is taken, the lack of perceptive critical judgment are characteristic of Wilde's letters up to the end. Of the poets who were beginning to publish between 1880 and 1899, only four—Bridges, Kipling, Yeats, and Housman—have really survived. (Myself, I would add Canon Dixon and Alice Meynell, but they are not widely read nor likely to be.) Wilde never mentions Bridges' nor Kipling's poetry, Yeats he knew personally and presumably read, Housman sent him a copy of "A Shropshire Lad," the manner and matter of which one would have expected to be exceptionally congenial to him, but he never seems to have realized that their poetry was in a completely different class from that of, say, Dowson or Le Gallienne. Nor was it, I think, personal infatuation that made him so absurdly overestimate Douglas's versified drivel; he quite honestly thought it was good. As a critic of drama he was a little better. He recognized the genius of Ibsen and—even more surprisingly, considering the difference in their views of art—that of Shaw. At a time when he was the most successful playwright in England and *Widowers' Houses* had just been hooted off the stage, Wilde had the insight and generosity to rank it with his own plays and say:

> I have read it twice with the keenest interest. I like your superb confidence in the dramatic value of the mere facts of life. I admire the horrible flesh and blood of your creatures, and your preface is a masterpiece—a real masterpiece of trenchant writing and caustic wit and dramatic instinct.

To return to his early letters. Their contents are for the most part affectionate personal chat, and almost the only impersonal topic is the aesthetic beauty of Roman Catholicism; flirtation with Rome seems to have been fashionable in Oxford at the time:

> If I *could hope* that the Church would wake in me some earnestness and purity I would go over *as a luxury,* if for no better reason. But I can hardly hope it would, and to go over to Rome would be to sacrifice and give up my two great gods "Money and Ambition."

The Oxford scene closes with Wilde's attainment of his immediate ambition, a First in Mods and Greats—a feat nobody, however brilliant, can bring off without much hard work. Now he goes up to London, takes rooms with a painter, Frank Miles, and within three years has become a friend of famous beauties like Lily Langtry, published a volume of poems (he sent a complimentary copy to Gladstone), and made himself one of the most talked-of persons in town. In April of 1881, Gilbert and Sullivan's *Patience* had its première; according to Mr. Hart-Davis, Gilbert may originally have had Rossetti in mind as the model for Bunthorne, but the public certainly took him to be a caricature of Wilde.

Except for those written from America, one cannot say that, taken as a whole, the letters Wilde wrote up till the time of his imprisonment are particularly interesting in their subject matter, or, knowing his extraordinary conversational powers, particularly funny. Wilde, that is to say, was a born talker, not a born letter writer—a master of the improvised word in response to the spur of the moment. Compared with speech, even the most casual letter is contrived, and its writer cannot be present to witness the response of the audience for whom he is writing. During the years of his social and literary triumphs, Wilde always had an audience for his conversation, and therefore most of his letters were written not for the sake of writing one but because a letter was called for; somebody else's letter had to be answered, an editor had to be consulted, a contribution to a magazine had to be solicited, etc. Nevertheless, they make a very agreeable impression: they convince one that the writer was a gracious, affectionate, generous, and, above all, kindhearted man, without the least malice or literary envy, and when one considers how malicious most witty people are and how ungenerous and envious most writers are, one is filled with admiration.

In 1881, *Patience* opened in New York, and D'Oyly Carte's American manager, Colonel Morse, thinking that Wilde's presence would provide useful publicity, booked him for a lecture tour through the United States. How big a name he already was at the age of twenty-eight may be gauged from the fees he could command: in Boston and Chicago he got a thousand dollars for a lecture, and he never got less than two hundred. (When I think what the dollar was worth then, it makes *me* green with envy.) Almost immediately he became involved in a highly publicized and comic quarrel with a rival British lecturer, Archibald Forbes. Wilde, wearing knee breeches, a tight velvet doublet, and hair almost down to his shoulders, was lecturing on Decorative Art in America and the English Renaissance; Forbes, with closely cropped hair and his chest covered with military medals, was lecturing on his adventures as a war correspondent in the Balkans. It seems that the more manly prima donna was the lesser draw; at any rate, it was Forbes who picked the quarrel—Wilde did everything he could to placate him—and the press had a field day. Many of the papers were hostile to Wilde, but he could always win over an audience, even so unlikely a one as the miners of Leadville, Colorado, to whom he talked about Benvenuto Cellini. Afterward there was a banquet underground:

> The amazement of the miners when they saw that art and appetite could go hand in hand knew no bounds; when I lit a long cigar they cheered till the silver fell in dust from the roof on our plates; and when I quaffed a cocktail without flinching, they unanimously pronounced me in their grand simple way "a bully boy with no glass eye." . . . Then I had to open a new vein, or lode, which with a silver drill I brilliantly performed, amidst unanimous applause. The silver drill was presented to me and the lode named "The Oscar."

It is interesting for the reader today to learn that Wilde stayed with Jefferson Davis in the South, and that he was in St. Joseph, Missouri, the week after Jesse James was shot; the reader also feels his first shivers of pity and fear. In Lincoln, Nebraska, his hosts

> drove me out to see the great prison afterwards! Poor odd types of humanity in hideous striped dresses making bricks in the sun, and all mean-looking, which consoled me, for I should hate to see a criminal with a noble face.

and in Chicago he talks to the journalists about three of his heroes —Whistler, Labouchère, and Irving. The second of these was responsible for the amendment to the criminal laws under which Wilde was to be convicted, and after the sentence he publicly expressed his regret that the maximum sentence had not been made seven years instead of only two.

On his return, in 1883, Wilde spent three months in Paris, where he met one of his future biographers, Robert Sherard. In November he became engaged to Constance Lloyd and in the following May he married her. This was certainly the most immoral and perhaps the only really heartless act of Wilde's life. It can happen that a homosexual does not recognize his condition for a number of years and marries in good faith, but one cannot believe that Wilde was such an innocent. Most homosexuals enjoy the company of women and, since they are not tempted to treat them as sexual objects, can be most sympathetic and understanding friends to them; like normal men, many of them long for the comfort and security of a home and the joy of having children, but to marry for such reasons is heartless. I have never seen a marriage of this kind—at least if the partners were under fifty—in which the wife, even when she knew all about her husband's tastes, did not suffer acutely. Even if there had been no scandal to bring public humiliation upon her and disgrace on their children, Constance Wilde would have been very unhappy, because she must have felt that her husband was, as he himself admitted later, "bored to death with married life." With a wife and, presently, two children to support, Wilde was now faced with the problem of securing a steady income. His first idea, oddly, was to become, like Matthew Arnold, a school inspector. When this failed to materialize, he took on the editorship of *Woman's World*. His letters from this period show him to have been a conscientious and hard-working editor. He even wrote to Queen Victoria to ask if she had any poems written in her youth that he might have the honor of publishing, and her minute concerning this request still exists:

> Really what will people not say and invent. Never did the Queen in her whole life write *one line* of *poetry* serious or comic or make a *Rhyme* even. This is therefore all *invention* & a *myth*.

As a writer he turned, fortunately for all concerned, from poetry to prose, and by 1889 was doing sufficiently well to give up being an editor and live by his pen. *The Picture of Dorian Gray* caused a scandal but sold well. *Salomé* was banned, but the four plays he wrote between 1891 and 1894 were all of them stage triumphs and made him the most admired and richest dramatist of his day. During these years of mounting success, the names of the principal characters in his drama make their entrance—Ross, Leonard Smithers, Turner, Adey, Frank Harris, Ada Leverson (whose novels, incidentally, are now shamefully neglected), and, of course, Bosie Douglas. The first warning note of doom is heard in 1894, when Alfred Taylor, who ran a male whorehouse that Wilde frequented, is arrested. This time the charge is dismissed, but less than a year later they will be standing in the dock together. Whatever his vices, Taylor will be remembered forever as a man of honor, for he went to prison rather than turn Queen's Evidence.

Thanks to the movies, everyone is familiar with the details of the three trials. Whether a law which makes homosexual acts between consenting adults a crime be just or unjust is debatable. What is unarguable fact is, firstly, that such a law encourages the crime of blackmail and, secondly, that it is unenforceable; that is to say, to ninety-nine per cent of practicing homosexuals, it makes no difference, so far as their personal liberty is concerned, whether such a law be on the statute book or not. Of the one per cent or less who get into trouble, nearly all are either persons with a taste for very young boys, one of whom sooner or later tells his parents, or compulsive cruisers of public conveniences who sooner or later run into an *agent provocateur*. But for his incredible folly in suing Queensberry, Wilde would have been perfectly safe. As he himself wrote later to Douglas:

> Do you think I am here on account of my relations with the witnesses on my trial? My relations, real or supposed, with people of that kind were matters of no interest to either the Government or Society. They knew nothing of them, and cared less. I am here for having tried to put your father into prison.

Even then he might have escaped had not that eternally infamous pair of actors, Hawtrey and Brookfield, told Queensberry's lawyers where to look for evidence. And in order to secure a conviction the Crown had to promise immunity from prosecution to a series of blackmailers and male prostitutes.

After his release, Wilde described what English prisons were like at the time in two letters to the *Daily Chronicle* which cannot be read without tears and indignation; it is nice to learn that some of the reforms he proposed were presently adopted. In the latter part of his term he was fortunate to have a humane prison governor, Major Nelson, who allowed him writing materials, and he composed his epistle to Lord Alfred Douglas, which takes up eighty-seven pages in this volume. When, in 1905, Ross published less than half of it under the title *De Profundis,* his intentions no doubt were good, but in fact he did Wilde a disservice, for the passages he selected are precisely those that are stylistically weakest and of dubious emotional honesty. When I read the book as a boy, I was revolted; it seemed awful to me that, under such terrible circumstances, a man could still write so stagily. Now, thanks to Mr. Hart-Davis, we have the whole definitive text, and it turns out to be a very different kind of document. (It appears that even the version based on a typescript which Wilde's son, Mr. Vyvyan Holland, published in 1949 was full of errors and omissions.)

Wilde on Jesus or redemption through suffering is as childish and boring as Gide on the same subjects, but Wilde on Bosie Douglas displays the insight, honesty, and unself-conscious style of a great writer. Their relationship is of the greatest psychological interest. It is clear that Wilde's infatuation for Bosie was not primarily a sexual one; one surmises that any sexual relations they may have had were infrequent and probably not very satisfactory. Bosie was leading a promiscuous life when they first met, he continued to lead it, and Wilde shows no signs of having been jealous. So far as sex was concerned, the main importance of Bosie in Wilde's life was that it was he who introduced Wilde, whose affairs had hitherto been confined to persons of his own class, to the world of male prostitution. When they met, Bosie, who was only just twenty-two, was already being blackmailed.

> Your defect was not that you knew so little about life, but that you knew too much. . . . The gutter and the things that live in it had begun to fascinate you. . . . terribly fascinating though the one topic round which your talk invariably centred was, still at the end it became quite monotonous to me.

Their mutual attraction—incapable of love as Bosie was, Wilde's existence was more important to him than the existence of anybody else except his father—was an affair of their egos rather than of their senses; one might say that the Overloved met the Underloved, and such an encounter is always extremely dangerous. Any child who discovers, as Bosie had, that he is hated and rejected by his father is bound to suffer from a feeling, however deeply he represses it, of profound unworthiness. If, when such a child grows up, he meets someone who appears to love him, particularly if this someone be older, his subconscious finds it impossible to believe that such a love is genuine, and he is driven, therefore, continually to test it by behaving badly. If the other rejects him, his suspicion is confirmed, but however often the other forgives, his suspicion can never be laid to rest for good and all. Further, if the feeling of unworthiness is strong enough, he may feel, again subconsciously, a contempt for anyone who offers him affection: if his father was right to reject him, then anyone who accepts him is a fool and deserves to be tormented. Wilde was a famous and successful author; the first test, therefore, was to find out whether his love for Bosie was stronger than his love of writing. Wilde's time had to be wasted:

> At twelve o'clock you drove up, and stayed smoking cigarettes and chattering till 1.30, when I had to take you out to luncheon at the Café Royal or the Berkeley. Luncheon with its *liqueurs* lasted usually till 3.30. For an hour you retired to White's. At tea-time you appeared again and stayed till it was time to dress for dinner. You dined with me either at the Savoy or at Tite Street. We did not separate as a rule till after midnight, as supper at Willis's had to wind up the entrancing day. That was my life for those three months, every single day, except during the four days when you went abroad.

Then, since the giving of money, particularly the giving of money for the primal childish pleasure of eating, is in our culture the symbol of all-giving love, Bosie had to see how much money he could get Wilde to spend on him:

> My ordinary expenses with you for an ordinary day in London—for luncheon, dinner, supper, amusements, hansoms and the rest of it—ranged from £12 to £20. . . . For our three months at Goring my expenses (rent of course included) were £1340. . . . My expenses for eight days in Paris for myself, you, and your Italian servant were nearly £150: Paillard alone absorbing £85.

Significantly, Bosie, on the ground that he would not give up their friendship, renounced his allowance from his father, and, on the ground that his mother's allowance was insufficient, refused to take money from her, but this did not mean that he was prepared to deny himself any luxuries; Wilde was to take the place of both of his parents as provider.

On the other hand, a child who, like Wilde, has been overloved and indulged by his mother, and who has discovered that he has the power to charm even those who are initially hostile, may consciously be vain but unconsciously feels insecure, for he cannot believe he is as lovable as his mother seems to think, and his power to charm others seems a trick that is no indication of his real value. When such a child grows up, his emotional involvements with others, especially if there is a sexual element present, are apt to be short-lived if the other succumbs to his charm without any resistance, but he can be fascinated by someone who, without rejecting him completely, treats him badly. If he is confronted with this novel experience, his very vanity is excited by the challenge of seeing how much he can endure, until enduring and forgiving become a habit.

> In every relation of life with others one has to find some *moyen de vivre*. In your case, one had either to give up to you or to give you up. . . . I gave up to you always. As a natural result, your claims, your efforts at domination, your exactions grew more and more unreasonable. . . . Knowing that by making a scene you could always have your way, it was but natural that you should proceed, almost unconsciously I have no doubt, to every excess of vulgar violence. . . . I had always thought that my giving up to you in small things meant nothing: that when a great moment arrived I could reassert my will-power in its natural superiority. It was not so. . . . My habit—due to indifference chiefly at first—of giving up to you in everything had become insensibly a real part of my nature. Without my knowing it, it had stereotyped my temperament to one permanent and fatal mood.

One cannot help speculating about what would have happened to their relationship if Queensberry had died; perhaps Bosie would simply have lost interest. As it was, his hatred of his father was the guiding passion of his life, so that Wilde as a person was less important to him than Wilde as a weapon, and subconsciously, maybe, Wilde and his father were symbolically interchangeable; it hardly mattered which went to prison so long as one of them did.

> When your father first began to attack me it was as your private friend, and in a private letter to you. . . . You insisted that the quarrel had nothing to do with me: that you would not allow your father to dictate to you in your private friendships: that it would be most unfair of me to interfere. You had already, before you saw me on the subject, sent your father a foolish and vulgar telegram. . . . That telegram conditioned the whole of your subsequent relations with your father, and consequently the whole of my life. . . . From pert telegrams to priggish lawyers' letters was a natural progress, and the result of your lawyer's letters to your father was, of course, to urge him on still further. You left him no option but to go on. . . . If his interest had flagged for a moment your letters and postcards would soon have quickened it to its ancient flame. They did so.

On one point only, I think, Wilde shows a lack of self-knowledge. He did, of course, realize exactly enough the folly he had committed in suing Queensberry:

> The one disgraceful, unpardonable, and to all time contemptible action of my life was my allowing myself to be forced into appealing to Society for help and protection against your father. . . . Once I had put into motion the forces of Society, Society turned on me and said, "Have you been living all this time in defiance of my laws, and do you now appeal to those laws for protection? . . . You shall abide by what you have appealed to."
>
> People thought it dreadful of me to have entertained at dinner the evil things of life, and to have found pleasure in their company. But they . . . were delightfully suggestive and stimulating. It was like feasting with panthers. . . . I don't feel at all ashamed of having known them. . . . Clibborn and Atkins were wonderful in their infamous war against life. To entertain them was an astounding adven-

ture. . . . What is loathsome to me is the memory of interminable visits paid by me to the solicitor Humphreys in your company, when in the ghastly glare of a bleak room you and I would sit with serious faces telling serious lies to a bald man.

What Wilde failed to realize, however, was that, given the circumstances and his own character, he would sooner or later have had to take the action he did even if Bosie had not egged him on. If his card had been ignored, Queensberry would certainly have gone on to make louder accusations in even more public places, and a refusal by Wilde to answer them would have been taken by Society to mean that they were true; he would have escaped prison but not social ostracism. Some artists are indifferent to their social reputation; immersed in their work, they do not care which side of the tracks they are on. Had Verlaine received Queensberry's card, he would probably have written on it, *"Mais oui, je suix pédéraste,"* and sent it back. But for Wilde the approval of Society was essential to his self-esteem.

Bosie was a horror and responsible for Wilde's ruin, but if at the end of his life Wilde had been asked whether he regretted ever having met him, he would probably have answered no, and it would be presumptuous of us to regret it either. We cannot know what Wilde might have written if he had never met Bosie or had fallen in love with someone else; we can only note that during the four years between his meeting with Bosie and his downfall Wilde wrote the greater part of his literary work, including his one masterpiece. Perhaps Bosie had nothing to do with this, but perhaps he did, if only by forcing Wilde to earn money to support him.

The fact that, in spite of all he knew about him and everything which had happened. Wilde could write to Bosie, a few months after his release from prison:

> I feel that my only hope of again doing beautiful work in art is being with you. It was not so in the old days, but now it is different, and you can really recreate in me that energy and sense of joyous power on which art depends

and to Ross:

> Do let people know that my only hope of life or literary
> activity was in going back to the young man whom I loved

suggests that, despite the endless rows, the time-wasting and the
expense, or even because of them. Bosie had served him as a
Muse. Their reunion was unfruitful, to be sure, but by that time
Wilde had lost the will to be inspired.

The post-prison letters are more interesting than the pre-prison.
To begin with, Wilde is now a lonely man, without an audience of
his social and intellectual equals, so he puts into his letters what
in happier times he would have expressed in talk, and the reader
gets glimpses of what his conversation must have been like:

> I assure you that the type-writing machine, when
> played with expression, is not more annoying than the piano
> when played by a sister or a near relation. Indeed many,
> among those most devoted to domesticity, prefer it.

> The sea and sky one opal, no horrid drawing-master's
> line between them, just one fishing boat, going slowly, and
> drawing the wind after it.

> Cows are very fond of being photographed, and, unlike
> architecture, don't move.

> The automobile was delightful, but, of course, it broke
> down: they, like all machines, are more wilful than animals
> —nervous, irritable, strange things: I am going to write an
> article on "nerves in the inorganic world."

> . . . the Blessed St. Robert of Phillimore, Lover and
> Martyr—a saint known in *Hagiographia* for his extraordi-
> nary power, not in resisting, but in supplying temptations to
> others. This he did in the solitude of great cities, to which
> he retired at the comparatively early age of eight.

> I believe they [the British public] would like me to edit
> prayers for those at sea, or to recant the gospel of the joy of
> life in a penny tract.

Wilde has some comic adventures. On the Riviera he meets a
rich admirer, Harold Mellor, who treats him to champagne and
invites him to Switzerland. Wilde accepts with joy and looks forward to living in the lap of luxury. But Switzerland is cold and

damp, the boys are ugly, and Mellor turns out, like so many rich men, to be stingy; he serves only cheap Swiss wine and keeps his cigarettes locked up. In Paris, Wilde meets Morton Fullerton, an American journalist who had become bewitched by Henry James's prose style, and tries to borrow money from him. Fullerton refuses his request in the following words:

> The maker of those masterpieces has too much delicacy and *esprit* not to sympathize sincerely with the regret of a man obliged to reply thus to an appeal which certainly he could not have expected, and for which it was impossible for him to prepare but which is none the less precious for that. I grope at the hope that meanwhile the stress has passed, and that you will not have occasion to put, *malgré vous,* either me or anyone else again into such a position of positive literal chagrin.

But as a whole these letters are, naturally, very sad reading—the record of a desperately unhappy man, who is going downhill and knows it. Other writers—Villon, Cervantes, Verlaine, for example—have suffered imprisonment (Villon even suffered torture), or, like Dante, suffered exile, without their creative powers being affected; indeed, they often wrote their best work after disaster. It was not his experiences in Reading Gaol, dreadful as these were, that put an end to Wilde's literary career, but the loss of social position. Another kind of writer might have found the disreputable bohemian existence to which, as an ex-convict, he was limited a relief—at least there was no need to keep up pretenses—but for Wilde the Bunburying, the double life, at one and the same time a bohemian in secret and in public the lion of respectable drawing rooms, had been the exciting thing, and when the drawing rooms withdrew their invitations he lost the will to live and write.

An artist by vocation may, like most men, be vain, desire immediate fame and fortune and suffer if they are withheld, but his vanity is always subordinate to his pride, which has no doubt whatever that what he writes is of unique importance. If, like Stendhal, he tells himself that he is writing for posterity, this is not, strictly speaking, true, since it is impossible to imagine what posterity will be like; it is his way of saying he is so convinced of the permanent value of his work that he is certain the world sooner or later will recognize it. He does not write to live, he lives to write, and what he enjoys or suffers outside the act of creation—his social and personal life—is to him of minor importance; no failure in either can diminish his confidence in his powers. Though he wrote one imperishable masterpiece, Wilde was not an artist by vocation but a performer. In all performers, vanity is stronger than pride, for a performer is truly himself only when he is in a sympathetic relation to an audience; alone, he does not know who he is. As Wilde said of himself:

> It is curious how vanity helps the successful man, and wrecks the failure. In old days half of my strength was my vanity.

So long as he was in prison and permitted to receive only a few letters, his knowledge of the outside world was confined to what his friends would tell him, and they, naturally, were anxious to cheer him up and refrained from dwelling on disagreeable facts. He did not realize either how poor he was going to be or how irrevocable was his loss of social position. Thus he can write hopefully, "I must live in England, if I am to be a dramatist again." The day after his release he visits his old friends the Leversons, and behaves, Mrs. Leverson records, as if nothing serious had happened:

> He came in with the dignity of a king returning from exile. He came in talking, laughing, smoking a cigarette, with waved hair and a flower in his button hole.

Ross adds:

> During that day and for many days afterwards he talked of nothing but Reading Prison and it had already become for him a sort of enchanted castle of which Major Nelson was the presiding fairy. The hideous machicolated turrets were already turned into minarets, the very warders into benevolent Mamelukes and we ourselves into Paladins welcoming Coeur de Lion after his captivity.

According to Ross, it took him five months before he fully realized that the Leversons' drawing room was not typical and that Society had neither forgotten nor forgiven and never would. For a vain man, his situation was appalling. Not only was he penniless and wholly dependent upon the charity of others but there was small possibility of his ever being able to earn his living again. Even if he had continued to write books and plays, no respectable publisher or producer would have dared print one or put one on the stage. He does manage to write one piece, *The Ballad of Reading Gaol,* and hopes to get three hundred pounds for it from an American newspaper, but the highest offer made is one hundred, though he is offered a thousand for an interview. The only publisher he can find is Leonard Smithers, who has an ill name in the trade as a publisher of pornography, and when Smithers publishes *The Importance of Being Earnest,* not one of the major English papers reviews it. Wilde's name is still "news" and where he goes and whom he sees is written up or invented by reporters, but in a very different way:

> I am in the Public Press sometimes "the ex-convict," which is too obvious: sometimes "*le poète-forçat,*" which I like, as it puts me in good company: sometimes I am "Mr. Oscar Wilde," a phrase I remember: sometimes "the man Wilde," a phrase I don't.

Social humiliation and insult are something he has to learn to expect:

> The middle-class English who are at the hotel have objected to my presence, and this morning I was presented with my bill and requested to leave by twelve o'clock. I declined to do this, and said I could not pay the bill today. They have given me till tomorrow at noon, and have asked me not to have my meals in the hotel.

> Yesterday I was by the sea and suddenly George Alexander appeared on a bicycle. He gave me a crooked, sickly smile, and hurried on without stopping.

> Cossie [Lennox] and Harry Melvill both cut me! I felt as if I had been cut by two Piccadilly renters. For people whom one has had to give themselves moral or social airs is childish. I was very much hurt.

A man who suffers an exceptional misfortune usually has another trial to bear. In addition to those who avoid him, since they fear that misfortune, like influenza, may be infectious, there are the professional pitiers who seek him out precisely *because* he is unfortunate, and for a vain man the latter are probably the harder to endure. Wilde does not mention meeting such persons himself, but there is a remark in one of Ross's letters which suggests that he did not escape their kind of attention.

To be financially dependent upon the charity of a wife whom he had treated very badly would have been humiliating enough, but the legal strings attached to his allowance were outrageous. Payment was to be withheld if, in the opinion of the solicitor, Wilde was keeping disreputable company. Since nobody respectable would speak to him, a literal obedience would have condemned him not to speak to anybody. Ross courageously offered to come and live with him but, with his characteristic decency, Wilde refused to let Ross risk his reputation for his sake. He saw his friends whenever they came to Paris, but most of the time he had nobody to talk to. It is hardly surprising, therefore, that he turned to the only consolations readily available—drink and boys:

> I cannot bear being alone, and while the literary people are charming when they meet me, we meet rarely. My companions are such as I can get, and I of course have to pay for such friendships. . . . To suggest I should have visitors of high social position is obvious, and the reason why I cannot have them is obvious also.

> How evil it is to buy Love, and how evil to sell it! And yet what purple hours one can snatch from that grey slowly-moving thing we call Time! . . . The Cloister or the Café—there is my future. I tried the Hearth, but it was a failure.

In France during the nineties, a single man could easily lead a life of modest comfort on a hundred and fifty pounds a year, but Wilde was incapable of living modestly. Besides social position, an essential thing for him was, as Ross wrote, "contact with comely things," meaning a certain standard of living—good food, drink, tobacco, clothes. Any deprivation of comfort threw him into a depression:

> A hole in the trousers may make one as melancholy as Hamlet, and out of bad boots a Timon may be made.
> Like dear St. Francis of Assisi I am wedded to Poverty:

but in my case the marriage is not a success; I hate the
bride that has been given me.

Not the least of the many merits of Mr. Hart-Davis's editing is
that it finally disposes of a legend in which many, including myself,
have believed—namely, that Wilde's last years were spent in abject
poverty. From his own letters one might think so, for money—the
lack of it, appeals for it, thanks for it, complaints that what is
justly his has not been sent him, paranoid suspicions that he is
being swindled—is an ever-recurring topic. There were certainly
occasions when he found himself unable to pay essential bills—to
hotels, for example—but nobody can be blamed for this except
himself. The four months during which his wife stopped his allowance may have been difficult; otherwise, it was paid and continued
to be paid after her death, and it was by no means his only source
of income. Lady Queensberry sent him money regularly, his
friends sent him checks whenever they could, and there were
assuredly givers whose names we do not know. Where money was
concerned, he became sly and untruthful, like an alcoholic; he
sold the option on an idea for a play, finally written by Frank
Harris under the title *Mr. and Mrs. Daventry,* to six different
people. Ross, who had known him in the old days, and knew,
therefore, what Wilde meant by "a certain standard of living," says
categorically, "This, since his release, he *was able to have* except
for a few weeks at a time, or perhaps months." Of Wilde's income
during the last eleven months of his life, Ross states:

> To *my* knowledge since January last he had £400 over
> and above the annuity of £150 paid from his wife's trust-
> ees through me—£300 came from the Queensberry family
> and £100 from a theatrical manager, while his expenses
> in Italy were all paid by a Mr. Mellor who was travelling
> with him and has always been most kind to him. There are
> so many grievous circumstances in his later career, that
> there is no necessity for those who were interested in him
> to be harrowed by imaginary pictures of his poverty.

How did he get through what was, in those days, quite a considerable sum? It is not hard to guess that little of it was spent on
necessities like food and lodging, and a good deal on drink, on
boys who "bayed for boots," and, most likely, too, on over-

generous gifts to beggars and excessive tips, for a person who, like Wilde, has loved playing the role of a king distributing largess finds it impossible to abandon even when he has lost his throne and the purse is no longer his.

The tape recorder is not my favorite instrument. In the old days only God heard every idle word; today it is not only broadcast to thousands of the living but also preserved to gratify the idle curiosity of the unborn. But this invention does allow full justice to be done to the great performer; Malibran is merely a name in operatic history, yet our great-grandchildren will be able to pass their personal judgment upon Flagstad and Callas. Malibran, at least, did nothing but sing; we easily believe that she was a great singer because all her contemporaries thought so and we have no evidence that might lead us to doubt their taste. But suppose she had also been a second-rate composer whose music had been greatly overestimated by her contemporaries; we should then inevitably wonder whether their taste in singing was any more reliable than their taste in music. It is impossible for us to be just to Wilde because, although his contemporaries all agreed that his improvised conversation was superior to his writings, they also thought the latter much better than we do. Of his poems not one has survived, for he was totally lacking in a poetic voice of his own; what he wrote was an imitation of poetry-in-general. His prose letters to the *Daily Chronicle* about prison life are authentic, *The Ballad of Reading Gaol* is not; reading such stanzas as the following, the reader would never guess that their author had been in prison himself, only that he had read "The Ancient Mariner":

> They glided past, they glided fast,
>   Like travellers through a mist:
> They mocked the moon in a rigadoon
>   Of delicate turn and twist,
> And with formal pace and loathsome grace
>   The phantoms kept their tryst.
>
> With mop and mow, we saw them go,
>   Slim shadows hand in hand:
> About, about, in ghostly rout
>   They trod a saraband:

> And the damned grotesques made arabesques,
> Like the wind upon the sand!

Of his nondramatic prose, we can still read *The Happy Prince and Other Tales* with great pleasure, and *The Soul of Man Under Socialism* and *Intentions,* for all their affectation, contain valuable criticism, but "The Portrait of Mr. W. H." is shy-making and *The Picture of Dorian Gray* a bore.

His development as a dramatist is interesting. Both in England and in France, even the most talented playwrights of the day were bewitched by a conception of drama that was sterile and self-frustrating—one that Shaw correctly diagnosed as an attempt to produce a genus of opera without music:

> The drama can do little to delight the senses: all the apparent instances to the contrary are instances of the personal fascination of the performers. The drama of pure feeling is no longer in the hands of the playwright; it has been conquered by the musician.

The typical fashionable play of the period was a melodramatic libretto *manqué;* indeed, a number of plays, including *Salomé,* which have long since vanished from the theater, are flourishing to this day in the opera house. Shaw's conclusion, which was valid for himself, was that the future of drama without music lay in the drama of thought. Wilde could not have taken the Shavian path because he was not a thinker; he was, however, a verbal musician of the first order. While *Salomé* could become a successful libretto, *Lady Windermere's Fan, A Woman of No Importance,* and *An Ideal Husband* could not, because their best and most original elements—the epigrams and comic nonsense—are not settable; at the same time, their melodramatic operatic plots spoil them as spoken drama. But in *The Importance of Being Earnest,* Wilde succeeded—almost, it would seem, by accident, for he never realized its infinite superiority to all his other plays—in writing what is perhaps the only pure verbal opera in English. The solution that, deliberately or accidentally, he found was to subordinate every other dramatic element to dialogue for its own sake and create a verbal universe in which the characters are determined by the kinds of things they say, and the plot is nothing but a succession of opportunities to say them. Like all works of art, it drew its sustenance from life, and, speaking for myself, whenever I see or read the play I always wish I did not know what I do about Wilde's life at the time he was writing it—that when, for instance, John Worthing talks of going Bunburying, I did not immediately visualize Alfred Taylor's establishment. On rereading it after his release, Wilde said, "It was extraordinary reading the play over. How I used to toy with that Tiger Life." At its conclusion, I find myself imagining a sort of nightmare Pantomime Transformation Scene in which, at the touch of the magician's wand, instead of the workaday world's turning into fairyland, the country house in a never-never Hertfordshire turns into the Old Bailey, the features of Lady Bracknell into those of Mr. Justice Wills. Still, it is a masterpiece, and on account of it Wilde will always enjoy the impersonal fame of an artist as well as the notoriety of his personal legend.

For many years, both in England and in America, the Wilde scandal had a disastrous influence, not upon writers and artists themselves but upon the attitude of the general public toward the arts, since it allowed the philistine man to identify himself with the decent man. Though the feeling that it is sissy for a boy to take an interest in the arts has probably always existed among the middle class and is not yet extinct, for many years after Wilde's trial it was enormously intensified. In fairness to the middle class, however, one must admit that such a feeling is not totally without justification. The artist and the homosexual are both characterized by a greater-than-normal element of narcissism, though neither has as much as the performing *artiste;* it is only likely that among artists and *artistes* as a class a higher-than-average per cent will also be homosexual, compared with many other professions. Again, while the prudery and self-righteousness of the middle class in the nineteenth century were repellent traits, we must not romanticize either the working class or the aristocracy of the period because of their relative tolerance; the working-class husband beat up his wife when drunk, the aristocrat regarded sexual exploitation of the poor as his natural right. Had Wilde been an aristocrat, his class brothers would have seen to it that there was no public scandal; since he was a person of middle-class origin who had pushed his way into high society, they left him to his fate with, perhaps, a certain feeling of satisfaction at the downfall of someone who had risen above his proper station.

In the long run, I think one may say that the effect of what in itself was a horrid business has been beneficial. Today, nearly seventy years later, both the working class and the aristocracy in the nineteenth-century sense have disappeared and we live in a middle-class society, but one which has learned that the problem not of homosexuality only but of sexual life in general cannot be solved by pretending it does not exist. If we have learned to listen to what Freud and others tell us about the complicated role which sexuality plays in our lives and the dubious character of violent moral indignation at the sexual behavior of our neighbor, if, indeed, we are now able to read these letters without prurient interest as we would read the letters of anybody else who wrote entertaining ones, Wilde has certainly helped us to do so.

A WORCESTERSHIRE LAD

*

Mr. Henry Maas informs us that Arthur Platt's widow destroyed all Housman's "Rabelaisian" letters to him. I am delighted to hear it. His letters to Moses Jackson have also not yet been made available. I hope they never will be. If the reader of *The Letters of A. E. Housman,* edited by Mr. Maas, occasionally finds himself yawning or skipping, at least he never feels like a Peeping Tom, and if he hopes to find something titillating he will be disappointed. All he will learn is that Housman took an interest in "naughty" books like *The Whippingham Papers, My Life and Loves,* and Corvo's letters, and that he published in a scholarly journal, under the title "Praefanda," an article on obscene phrases in the Latin poets. This is, surely, as Housman himself would have wished. Apropos of somebody who wished to interview him, he wrote:

> Tell him that the wish to include a glimpse of my personality in a literary article is low, unworthy, and American. Tell him that some men are more interesting than their books but my book is more interesting than its man. Tell him that Frank Harris found me rude and Wilfrid Blunt found me dull. Tell him anything else that you think will put him off.

To the letters on everyday and literary topics Mr. Maas has added a forty-two-page supplement of letters on technical classical matters. These will be fully intelligible only to classical scholars, but I think he was quite right to include them. To Housman himself, his scholarship came first, his poetry second: he believed he had been put on earth not to write *A Shropshire Lad* (I never knew before that this title was proposed by A. W. Pollard; Housman's own title had been *Poems by Terence Hearsay*) but to produce a definitive edition of Manilius. His choice of this particular Latin poet may have been influenced by his own interest in astronomy, which is Manilius's subject, but the decisive factor was probably that the text presented an exceptional challenge to an editor. He was certainly under no illusions as to Manilius's literary merits. Thus he says, in a letter to Robert Bridges:

> I adjure you not to waste your time on Manilius. He writes on astronomy and astrology without knowing either. My interest in him is purely technical.

Most of the letters in the supplement are concerned with textual minutiae. The only general statement I have found is a judgment on Virgil:

> Virgil's besetting sin is the use of words too forcible for his thoughts.

However, speaking for myself, though I cannot understand much of them, I am fascinated by the glimpses one gets of how the mind of a textual scholar works:

> With *optandum* you require something like *quicquam,* which Estaço obtained by writing *dicere quid.* With *optandum* of course you can supply *uitam* from *uita;* but yet the MS reading is *optandus.* Because Catullus once elides *que* at the end of a verse it cannot safely be inferred that he would elide anything else. I have seen nothing better than Munro's *magis aeuom optandum hac uita,* though it is not all the heart could desire.

Incidentally, I had occasion not so long ago to compare three translations of the last stanza of the Horace Ode, Book IV, 7— one by Dr. Johnson, one by James Michie, and one by Housman.

To my surprise, the one which departed most widely from the Latin was Housman's. Indeed, had I not known the source, I would have thought that it was a verse from a Housman poem.

About his emotional life little needs to be said. It is now no secret that at Oxford he fell deeply in love with a fellow-under-graduate, Moses Jackson, an experience which, on his own testi-mony, he was never to repeat. Since Jackson was perfectly "straight," there could be no question of reciprocation. About this, Mr. Maas writes:

> Too clear-headed and honest to deceive himself about the nature of this absorption, he was also too well trained in conventional morality to accept it with resignation. The evidence of his poetry suggests that he was overwhelmed with shame.

If by "conventional morality" Mr. Maas means Housman's Chris-tian upbringing, I think he is mistaken. If Housman did feel shame and guilt, this was caused not by the Bible but by classical litera-ture. I am pretty sure that in his sexual tastes he was an anal passive. Ancient Greece and Rome were both pederastic cultures in which the adult passive homosexual was regarded as comic and contemptible.

As to his attitude to life in general, though often labeled a Stoic, he denied this:

> In philosophy I am a Cyrenaic or egoistic hedonist, and regard the pleasure of the moment as the only possible mo-tive of action. As for pessimism, I think it almost as silly, though not as wicked, as optimism. George Eliot said she was a meliorist: I am a pejorist [i.e., someone who believes the world is steadily getting worse].

In his relation to others, he remained all his life a shy and essentially solitary man. His generation was more formal than mine, but even in those days it must have been unusual for a sixteen-year-old boy to sign a letter to his stepmother "A. E. Housman," and it was only in writing to members of his family that he ever used Christian names. Even such intimate friends as A. S. F. Gow and his publisher, Grant Richards, continued to the end to be "Dear Gow," "Dear Richards."

This reserve and distance from others was probably due, I think, to his experiences in early childhood. His mother, after suffering for years from cancer, died when he was twelve, while his father took to the bottle. It is significant, surely, that out of a family of seven—five boys and two girls—only one son and one daughter married and only the latter had children.

"Vanity, not avarice," Housman once wrote, "is my ruling passion," but I don't think he ever realized just how vain he was. A man who refuses honors like honorary degrees from universities or the O.M. from the State declines them not because he feels unworthy but because he feels that no honor can possibly do justice to his merits, and a poet who refuses to be included in anthologies of contemporary verse reveals that he considers himself superior to all of his colleagues. But vanity did not distort Housman's judgment. He was always aware of what he could and could not do:

> I do regard myself as a connoisseur; I think I can tell good from bad in literature. But literary criticism, referring opinions to principles and setting them forth so as to command assent, is a high and rare accomplishment and quite beyond me.

He was also a good judge of his own work. Most of the posthumously published poems are inferior. Of "Hell Gate," which happens to be my favorite poem of his, he says, acutely:

> . . . the whole thing is on the edge of the absurd: if it does not topple over, that is well so far.

As a letter writer, he could when he tried—which, it must be admitted, was not very often—be most entertaining, both vivid and witty:

> This afternoon Ruskin gave us a great outburst against modern times. He had got a picture of Turner's, framed and glassed, representing Leicester and the Abbey in the distance at sunset, over a river. . . . Then he said, "You, if you like, may go to Leicester to see what it is like now. I never shall. But I can make a pretty good guess." Then he caught up a paintbrush. "These stepping-stones of course have been done away with, and are replaced by a be-au-ti-ful iron bridge." Then he dashed in the iron bridge on the

glass of the picture. "The colour of the stream is supplied on one side by the indigo factory." Forthwith one side of the stream became indigo. "On the other side by the soap factory." Soap dashed in. "They mix in the middle—like curds," he said, working them together with a sort of malicious deliberation. "This field, over which you see the sun setting behind the Abbey, is now occupied in a *proper* manner." Then there went a flame of scarlet across the picture, which developed itself into windows and roofs and red brick, and rushed up into a chimney. "The atmosphere is supplied—thus!" A puff and cloud of smoke all over Turner's sky: and then the brush thrown down, and Ruskin confronting modern civilisation amidst a tempest of applause.

Housman was one of the very first civilians to travel by air, and the jumbo-jet tourist of the seventies will be interested to learn what it was like to fly in the early twenties:

> It was rather windy, and the machine sometimes imitated a ship at sea . . . but not in a very lifelike manner. . . . The noise is great, and I alighted rather deaf, not having stuffed my ears with the cotton-wool provided. Nor did I put on the life-belt which they oblige one to take. . . . On the return journey we were two hours late in starting because the machine required repairs, having been damaged on the previous day by a passenger who butted his head through the window to be sick.

I knew he had written parodies and comic verse, but I had never seen any. From the few examples quoted in this book, I should like to see more. His parody of Frances Cornford's "Why do you walk through the fields in gloves," though not quite as good as Chesterton's, is amusing enough, and, for a sixteen-year-old, this pastiche of Milton is a remarkable feat:

> Or where, high rising over all,
> Stands the Cathedral of St. Paul
> And in its shadow you may scan
> Our late lamented ruler, Anne;
> Or where the clouds of legend lower

Around the mediaeval Tower,
And ghosts of every shape and size
With throttled throats and staring eyes
Come walking from their earthy beds
With pillow cases on their heads
And various ornaments beside
Denoting why or how they died.

In these letters he mentions surprisingly few English authors. Among the poets he approved of were Coventry Patmore, Robert Bridges for his early poems (not the later). Masefield, Blunden, and Edna St. Vincent Millay. Among prose writers he admired Wilkie Collins (his only two letters to T. S. Eliot are about him), Arthur Machen, and Aldous Huxley. One suspects that he found the work of most of his contemporaries and juniors antipathetic.

What has fascinated me most is the descriptions these letters contain of the minor headaches which plague an author's life. Anyone who publishes a book these days must expect it to contain misprints and errors in punctuation. (One British reviewer has listed a series of those that occur in this volume.) I had thought that careless printing and proofreading was a recent phenomenon. Apparently it is not so:

> When the next edition of the Shropshire Lad is being prepared, it would save trouble to the compositor as well as to me if he were told that the third edition is almost exactly correct, and that he had better not put in commas and notes of exclamation for me to strike out of the proof, as was the case last time.

> On former occasions the proofs have come to me full of the usual blunders,—numerals wrong, letters upside-down, stops missing, and so on. I have then, at the cost of much labour, removed all these errors. Then, when the last proof has left my hands, the corrector for the press has been turned on to it, and has found nothing to correct; whereupon, for fear his employers should think he is not earning his pay, he has set to work meddling with what I have written.

And every poet will sympathize with Housman over the following:

> I have marked for correction, if possible, certain ugly over-running of words from one line to another. Since these over-runnings existed in neither the 1896 nor the 1900 edition, it seems absurd that they should be necessary in this, which has smaller print than the former and a larger page than the latter.

Then, if, like Housman, an author achieves popular success, there are other nuisances: Requests for autographs from total strangers who hardly ever enclose postage stamps. Requests for a handwritten copy of a poem. Visits by professed admirers who then betray their ignorance of his work:

> I had a visit not long ago from Clarence Darrow, the great American barrister for defending murderers. He had only a few days in England, but he could not return home without seeing me, because he had so often used my poems to rescue his clients from the electric chair. Loeb and Leopold owe their life sentence partly to me; and he gave me a copy of his speech, in which, sure enough, two of my pieces are misquoted.

As regards Mr. Maas's editing of these letters, his footnoting seems for the most part excellent. I have only two complaints. I think I know Housman's poems pretty well, but when a poem is identified only as "A Shropshire Lad LXIII," I am flummoxed. Why not quote the first line? Then, in one letter, Housman writes:

> My feelings are much the same as [Aldous] Huxley's; but in my case school is not the cause, for I was quite uninfluenced by my school, which was a small one. I think the cause is in the home.

Surely we ought to be informed as to what Huxley had said.

Naturally, one cannot read Housman's letters without thinking again about his status and achievement as a poet. A minor poet, certainly, which, of course, does not mean that his poems are inferior in artistic merit to those of a major poet, only that the range of theme and emotion is narrow, and that the poems show no development over the years. On the evidence of the text alone, it would be very difficult to say whether a poem appeared in *A Shrop-shire Lad,* published when he was thirty-seven, or in *Last Poems,* published when he was sixty-three. I don't know how it is with the young today, but to my generation no other English poet seemed so perfectly to express the sensibility of a male adolescent. If I do not now turn to him very often, I am eternally grateful to him for the joy he gave me in my youth.

C. P. CAVAFY

Ever since I was first introduced to his poetry by the late Professor R. M. Dawkins over thirty years ago, C. P. Cavafy has remained an influence on my own writing; that is to say, I can think of poems which, if Cavafy were unknown to me, I should have written quite differently or perhaps not written at all. Yet I do not know a word of Modern Greek, so that my only access to Cavafy's poetry has been through English and French translations.

This perplexes and a little disturbs me. Like everybody else, I think, who writes poetry, I have always believed the essential difference between prose and poetry to be that prose can be translated into another tongue but poetry cannot.

But if it is possible to be poetically influenced by work which one can read only in translation, this belief must be qualified.

There must be some elements in poetry which are separable from their original verbal expression and some which are inseparable. It is obvious, for example, that any association of ideas created by homophones is restricted to the language in which these homophones occur. Only in German does *Welt* rhyme with *Geld,* and only in English is Hilaire Belloc's pun possible.

> When I am dead, I hope it may be said:
> "His sins were scarlet, but his books were read."

When, as in pure lyric, a poet "sings" rather than "speaks," he is rarely, if ever, translatable. The "meaning" of a song by Campion is inseparable from the sound and the rhythmical values of the actual words he employs. It is conceivable that a genuine bilingual poet might write what, to him, was the same lyric in two languages, but if someone else were then to make a literal translation of each version into the language of the other, no reader would be able to recognize their connection.

On the other hand, the technical conventions and devices of verse can be grasped in abstraction from the verse itself. I do not have to know Welsh to become excited about the possibility of applying to English verse the internal rhymes and alliterations in which Welsh verse is so rich. I may very well find that they cannot be copied exactly in English, yet discover by modifying them new and interesting effects.

Another element in poetry which often survives translation is the imagery of similes and metaphors, for these are derived, not from local verbal habits, but from sensory experiences common to all men.

I do not have to read Pindar in Greek in order to appreciate the beauty and aptness with which he praises the island of Delos.

> . . . motionless miracle of the
> wide earth, which mortals call Delos, but the
> blessed on Olympus, the far-shining star of
> dark-blue earth.

When difficulties in translating images do arise, this is usually because the verbal resources of the new language cannot make the meaning clear without using so many words that the force of the original is lost. Thus Shakespeare's line

> The hearts that spanielled me at heels

cannot be translated into French without turning the metaphor into a less effective simile.

None of the translatable elements in poetry which I have mentioned so far applies, however, to Cavafy. With the free relaxed iambic verse he generally uses, we are already familiar. The most original aspect of his style, the mixture, both in his vocabulary and his syntax, of demotic and purist Greek, is untranslatable. In English there is nothing comparable to the rivalry between demotic and purist, a rivalry that has excited high passions, both literary and political. We have only Standard English on the one side and regional dialects on the other, and it is impossible for a translator to reproduce this stylistic effect or for an English poet to profit from it.

Nor can one speak of Cavafy's imagery, for simile and metaphor are devices he never uses; whether he is speaking of a scene, an event, or an emotion, every line of his is plain factual description without any ornamentation whatsoever.

What, then, is it in Cavafy's poems that survives translation and excites? Something I can only call, most inadequately, a tone of voice, a personal speech. I have read translations of Cavafy made by many different hands, but every one of them was immediately recognizable as a poem by Cavafy; nobody else could possibly have written it. Reading any poem of his, I feel: "This reveals a person with a unique perspective on the world." That the speech of self-disclosure should be translatable seems to me very odd, but I am convinced that it is. The conclusion I draw is that the only quality which all human beings without exception possess is uniqueness: any characteristic, on the other hand, which one individual can be recognized as having in common with another, like red hair or the English language, implies the existence of other individual qualities which this classification excludes. To the degree, therefore, that a poem is the product of a certain culture, it is difficult to translate it into the terms of another culture, but to the degree that it is the expression of a unique human being, it is as easy, or as difficult, for a person from an alien culture to appreciate as for one of the cultural group to which the poet happens to belong.

But if the importance of Cavafy's poetry is his unique tone of voice, there is nothing for a critic to say, for criticism can only make comparisons. A unique tone of voice cannot be described; it can only be imitated, that is to say, either parodied or quoted.

To be writing an introduction to Cavafy's poetry, therefore, is to be in the embarrassing position of knowing that what one writes can only be of interest to people who have not yet read him; once they have, they will forget it as completely as, when one makes a new friend at a party, one forgets the person who made the introduction.

Cavafy has three principal concerns: love, art, and politics in the original Greek sense.

Cavafy was a homosexual, and his erotic poems make no attempt to conceal the fact. Poems made by human beings are no more exempt from moral judgment than acts done by human beings, but the moral criterion is not the same. One duty of a poem, among others, is to bear witness to the truth. A moral witness is one who gives true testimony to the best of his ability in order that the court (or the reader) shall be in a better position to judge the case justly; an immoral witness is one who tells half-truths or downright lies: but it is not a witness's business to pass verdict. (In the arts, one must distinguish, of course, between the lie and the tall story that the audience is not expected to believe. The tall-story teller gives himself away, either by a wink or by an exaggerated poker face: the born liar always looks absolutely natural.)

As a witness, Cavafy is exceptionally honest. He neither bowdlerizes nor glamorizes nor giggles. The erotic world he depicts is one of casual pickups and short-lived affairs. Love, there, is rarely more than physical passion, and when tenderer emotions do exist, they are almost always one-sided. At the same time, he refuses to pretend that his memories of moments of sensual pleasure are unhappy or spoiled by feelings of guilt. One can feel guilty about one's relation to other persons—one has treated them badly or made them unhappy—but nobody, whatever his moral convictions, can honestly regret a moment of physical pleasure as such. The only criticism that might be made is one that applies to all poets, namely, that Cavafy does not, perhaps, fully appreciate his exceptional good fortune in being someone who can transmute into valuable poetry experiences which, for those who lack this power, may be trivial or even harmful. The sources of poetry lie, as Yeats said, "in the foul rag-and-boneshop of the heart," and Cavafy illustrates this by an anecdote:

> The fulfillment of their deviate, sensual delight
> is done. They rose from the mattress,

and they dress hurriedly without speaking.
They leave the house separately, furtively; and as
they walk somewhat uneasily on the street, it seems
as if they suspect that something about them betrays
into what kind of bed they fell a little while back.
But how the life of the artist has gained.
Tomorrow, the next day, years later, the vigorous verses
will be composed that had their beginning here.

("Their Beginning")

But what, one cannot help wondering, will be the future of the artist's companion?

Cavafy's attitude toward the poetic vocation is an aristocratic one. His poets do not think of themselves as persons of great public importance and entitled to universal homage, but, rather, as citizens of a small republic in which one is judged by one's peers and the standard of judgment is strict. The young poet Eumenes is depressed because, after struggling for two years, he has only managed to write one idyll. Theocritus comforts him thus:

> And if you are on the first step,
> you ought to be proud and pleased.
> Coming as far as this is not little;
> what you have achieved is great glory. . . .
> To set your foot upon this step
> you must rightfully be a citizen
> of the city of ideas.
> And in that city it is hard
> and rare to be naturalized.
> In her market place you find Lawmakers
> whom no adventurer can dupe. . . .

("The First Step")

His poets write because they enjoy writing and in order to give aesthetic satisfaction, but they never exaggerate the importance of aesthetic satisfaction.

Let the flippant call me flippant.
In serious matters I have always been

most diligent. And I will insist that
no one is more familiar than I
with Fathers or Scriptures, or the Synodical Canons.
In each of his doubts,
in each difficulty concerning church matters,
Botaneiatis consulted me, me first of all.
But exiled here (may the malevolent Irene Doukaina
suffer for it), and dreadfully bored,
it is not at all peculiar that I amuse myself
composing sestets and octets—
that I amuse myself with mythological tales
of Hermes, Apollo, and Dionysus,
or the heroes of Thessaly and the Peloponnese;
and that I compose impeccable iambics,
such as—permit me to say—Constantinople's men of
    letters cannot compose.
This very accuracy, probably, is the cause of their censure.
               (*"A Byzantine Noble in Exile Writing Verses"*)

Cavafy is intrigued by the comic possibilities created by the indirect relation of poets to the world. While the man of action requires the presence of others here and now, for without a public he cannot act, the poet fabricates his poem in solitude. He desires, it is true, a public for his poem, but he himself need not be personally related to it and, indeed, the public he most hopes for is composed of future generations which will only come into being after he is dead. While he is writing, therefore, he must banish from his mind all thoughts of himself and of others and concentrate on his work. However, he is not a machine for producing verses, but a human being like other human beings, living in a historical society and subject to its cares and vicissitudes. The Cappadocian poet Phernazis is composing an epic on Darius and is trying to imagine the feelings and motives which led Darius to act as he did. Suddenly his servant interrupts him to say that Rome and Cappadocia are at war.

Phernazis is impatient. How unfortunate!
At a time when he was positive that with his "Darius"

he would distinguish himself, and shut forever
the mouths of his critics, the envious ones.
What a delay, what a delay to his plans.

But if it were only a delay, it would still be all right.
But let us see if we have any security at all
in Amisus. It is not a very well-fortified city.
The Romans are the most horrible enemies.
Can we get the best of them, we
Cappadocians? Is that ever possible?
Can we measure ourselves in a time like this against legions?
Mighty Gods, protectors of Asia, help us.—

Yet amid all his agitation and the trouble,
the poetic idea persistently comes and goes.—
The most probable, surely, is arrogance and drunkenness;
Darius must have felt arrogance and drunkenness.

("Darius")

Aside from those dealing with his personal experiences, the
settings of Cavafy's poems are seldom contemporary. Some are concerned with the history of Ancient Greece, one or two with the fall of
Rome, but his favorite historical periods are two: the age of the
Greek satellite kingdoms set up by Rome after the Alexandrian
Empire had fallen to pieces, and the period of Constantine and his
successors when Christianity had just triumphed over paganism
and become the official religion.

Of these periods he gives us a number of anecdotes and character vignettes. His Panhellenic world is politically powerless, and
in it, therefore, politics are regarded with cynical amusement.
Officially, the satellite kingdoms are self-governing, but everyone
knows that the rulers are puppets of Rome. Political events that are
immensely important to the Romans, like the Battle of Actium,
mean nothing to them. Since they must obey in any case, why
should they care what name their master bears?

The news of the outcome of the naval battle, at Actium,
was most certainly unexpected.
But there is no need to compose a new address.

Only the name needs to be changed. There, in the last
lines, instead of "Having liberated the Romans
from the ruinous Octavius,
that parody, as it were, of Caesar,"
now we will put, "Having liberated the Romans
from the ruinous Antony."
The whole text fits in beautifully.

                        (*"In a Township of Asia Minor"*)

    There are some, like the Syrian Demetrius Sôtêr, who dream
of restoring their country to its former greatness, but they are
forced to realize that their dream is vain.

He suffered, he felt much bitterness in Rome
as he sensed in the talk of his friends,
young people of prominent houses,
amid all the delicacy and politeness
that they kept showing to him, the son
of the King Seleucus Philopator—
as he sensed however that there was always
a covert indifference to the hellenized dynasties;
that had declined, that are not for serious works . . .

If only he could find a way to get to the East,
to succeed in escaping from Italy— . . .

Ah, if only he could find himself in Syria!
He was so young when he left his country,
that he can barely remember its face.
But in his thought he always studied it
as something sacred you approach with adoration,
as a vision of a lovely land, as a spectacle
of Greek cities and harbors.—

And now?
        Now despair and grief.
The young men in Rome were right.
It is not possible for dynasties to survive
that the Macedonian Conquest gave rise to.

No matter: He himself had tried,
he had struggled as much as he could.
And in his dark discouragement,
one thing alone he reckons
with pride, that, even in his failure,
to the world he shows the same indomitable manliness.

The rest—were dreams and vain efforts.
This Syria—scarcely looks like his own country,
it is the land of Heracleides and Balas.

("Of Demetrius Sôtêr, 162–150 B.C.")

As this poem illustrates, Cavafy is one of the very few poets who can write a patriotic poem that is not embarrassing. In most poetic expressions of patriotism, it is impossible to distinguish what is one of the greatest human virtues from the worst human vice, collective egoism.

The virtue of patriotism has generally been extolled most loudly and publicly by nations that are in the process of conquering others, by the Romans, for example, in the first century B.C., the French in the 1790's, the English in the nineteenth century, and the Germans in the first half of the twentieth. To such people, love of one's country involves denying the right of others, of the Gauls, the Italians, the Indians, the Poles, to love theirs. Moreover, even when a nation is not actively aggressive, the genuineness of its patriotic feelings remains in doubt so long as it is rich, powerful, and respected. Will the feeling survive if that nation should become poor and of no political account and aware, also, that its decline is final, that there is no hope for the return of its former glory? In this age, no matter to which country we belong, the future is uncertain enough to make this a real question for us all, and Cavafy's poems more topical than, at first reading, they seem.

In Cavafy's Panhellenic world, there is one great object of love and loyalty of which defeat has not deprived them, the Greek language. Even peoples to whom it had not originally been their native tongue have adopted it, and the language has become all the richer for having had to accommodate itself to sensibilities other than Attic.

The inscription, as usual, in Greek;
not exaggerated, not pompous—
lest the proconsul who is always poking about
and reporting to Rome misconstrue it— . . .
Above all I charge you to see to it
(Sithaspes, in God's name, let this not be forgotten)
that after the words King and Savior,
there be engraved in elegant letters, Philhellene.
Now don't try your clever sallies on me,
your "Where are the Greeks?" and "Where is anything Greek
behind Zagros here, beyond Phraata?"
Since so many others more barbarous than we
write it, we too shall write it.
And finally do not forget that at times
sophists from Syria visit us,
and versifiers, and other wiseacres.
So we are not un-Greek, I reckon.

("Philhellene")

In his poems about the relations between Christians and Pagans in the age of Constantine, Cavafy takes no sides. Roman paganism was worldly in the sense that the aim of its ritual practices was to secure prosperity and peace for the state and its citizens. Christianity, while not necessarily despising this world, has always insisted that its principal concern was elsewhere: it has never claimed to guarantee worldly prosperity to believers, and it has always condemned excessive preoccupation with success as a sin.

So long as worship of the Emperor as a god was required by law of all citizens, to become a Christian meant to become a criminal. In consequence, the Christians of the first four centuries A.D., though subject like everybody else to the temptations of the Flesh and the Devil, had been spared the temptation of the World. One could become converted and remain a thorough rascal, but one could not be converted and remain a gentleman.

But after Constantine, it was the Christian who had a better chance than the Pagan of getting on in the world, and the Pagan, even if not persecuted, who became the object of social ridicule.

In one of Cavafy's poems the son of a pagan priest has become a Christian convert.

> O Jesus Christ, my daily effort
> is to observe the precepts
> of Thy most holy church in every act of mine,
> in every word, in every single thought.
> And all those who renounce Thee,
> I shun them.—But now I bewail;
> I lament, O Christ, for my father
> even though he was—a horrible thing to say—
> a priest at the accursed Serapeum.
> ("*Priest at the Serapeum*")

In another, the Emperor Julian comes to Antioch and preaches his self-invented neopagan religion. But to the citizens of Antioch, Christianity has become the conventional religion which they hold without letting it interfere in any way with their amusements, and they merely laugh at him as a puritanical old fuddy-duddy.

> Was it ever possible that they should renounce
> their lovely way of life; the variety of their
> daily amusement; their magnificent theater . . .
>
> To renounce all these, to turn to what after all?
>
> To his airy chatter about false gods;
> to his tiresome self-centered chatter;
> to his childish fear of the theater;
> his graceless prudery; his ridiculous beard?
>
> Ah most surely they preferred the CHI,
> ah most certainly they preferred the KAPPA; a hundred times.
> ("*Julian and the People of Antioch*")

I hope these quotations have given some idea of Cavafy's tone of voice and his perspective on life. If a reader find them unsympathetic, I do not know how one can argue against him. Since language is the creation of a social group, not of an individual, the standards by which it can be judged are relatively objective. Thus, when reading a poem in one's native tongue, one can find the sensibility personally antipathetic and yet be compelled to admire its verbal manifestation. But when one is reading a translation, all one gets is the sensibility, and either one likes it or one does not. I happen to like Cavafy's very much indeed.

A MARRIAGE OF TRUE MINDS

The mating of minds is, surely, quite as fascinating a relationship as the mating of the sexes, yet how little attention novelists have paid to it. Most of us owe our intellectual initiation to an older person as, in *Rosenkavalier,* Octavian owes his initiation into love to the Marschallin, and, like her, our master has to endure being left for minds of our own generation. The mind is naturally and, probably, rightly promiscuous, so that its typical affair (which may be with one of the dead) is short-lived, ending "with the necessity for it as it ought" and with no hard feelings. Sometimes, however, it ends unhappily. One thinks of Fliess and Freud, the one a talented eccentric, the other a genius. It is fortunate for the world that they met, but one has to pity poor Fliess, his brains picked and then deserted. The normal intellectual marriage produces one child, e.g., Liddell and Scott, Russell and Whitehead for example, but occasionally (more commonly, I suspect among scientists than among artists) a union is formed which begets a succession of works; the collaboration of Hofmannsthal and Strauss is a striking example and the only one of which, thanks to their correspondence, we possess a detailed record. One rather suspects that we should not have been so fortunate if they had liked each other more as persons or, at least, if Hofmannsthal had liked Strauss more. It seems evident that Hofmannsthal did not care to see Strauss more often than was absolutely necessary, and he made it quite clear on what plane their relationship was to be.

> I am always, and each time anew, pleased to see you. But we are spoilt: we have shared the best men can share: being united in creative effort. Every hour we have spent together was connected with our joint work; the transition to ordinary social "intercourse" would now be almost impossible.

Even after collaborating for twenty-three years, they were still not on first-names terms—Strauss will write *Lieber Freund* but Hofmannsthal sticks to *Leiber Doktor Strauss.*

The distance they kept between each other as persons is of great benefit to their letters, for, in consequence, they contain no irrelevant chat. Aside from conventional seasonal greetings and conventional condolences on sickness or bereavement, they write of nothing but the work in hand or matters, like their health, which affect it. The outbreak of World War I is just mentioned (Strauss was certain of a quick German victory): otherwise the world outside the opera house might not exist.

The first tentative courtship was made by Hofmannsthal in 1900 when he was twenty-six. He sent Strauss, who was ten years older and already internationally famous, the scenario of a ballet *Der Triumph der Zeit.* Strauss replied, in a very friendly letter, that he could not set it. Six years passed during which Hofmannsthal wrote a play *Elektra* (1903) and Strauss his first successful opera *Salome* (1905). In 1906 Strauss approached Hofmannsthal with the request that they make an opera together out of *Elektra,* though he thought they might do something else first.

> I would ask you urgently to give me first refusal with anything composable that you write. Your manner has so much in common with mine; we were born for one another and are certain to do fine things if you remain faithful to me. . . . Have you got an entertaining renaissance subject for me? A really wild Borgia or Savanarola would be the answer to my prayers.

This was almost fatal. Back, in acid tones of displeasure which Strauss was to hear quite often in the future, came Hofmannsthal's answer.

Allow me, my dear sir, to make you a frank reply. I do not believe there is any epoch in history which I and, like me, every creative poet among our contemporaries would bar from his work with feelings of such definite disinclination, indeed such unavoidable distaste, as this particular one.

Fortunately, Strauss set to work immediately on *Elektra,* the collaboration went well and a few months later Hofmannsthal was writing:

I know we are destined to create together one, or several truly beautiful and memorable works: I should like at the same time to explain to you my notions (fairly liberal as they are) of what I consider possible opera subjects and what, on the other hand, I consider absolutely out of the question nowadays.

In their collaboration, that is to say, the choice of dramatic subject and its style of treatment was to be the librettist's business, not the composer's who must wait patiently till the librettist finds a subject which excites his imagination. As in a marriage, for a collaboration to endure and be successful, each partner must have something valuable to give and to receive. Strauss received from Hofmannsthal a succession of libretti which, while being admirably settable, are a pleasure to read by themselves. The poetry is often beautiful, the characters and situations are interesting. Furthermore, each is unique and sets the composer a new musical and stylistic challenge.

Hofmannsthal also did a great deal, not only for Strauss, but also for the general cause of opera by insisting that, in the production of their works, as much attention be paid to their visual aspects as to their musical. At the time when they began collaborating, the decor, costumes and stage direction of most productions in most opera houses were appallingly bad—heavy, crude, huggermugger. Strauss, who was not very visually minded, was used to this and expected no better, but Hofmannsthal belonged to a group, led by Reinhardt, who were determined to revolutionize stage production and succeeded. (Only too well, alas: today most operas suffer from being over-produced.) Strauss had the good sense to realize that in such matters Hofmannsthal had better taste than himself and gave him complete authority. If Hofmannsthal was sometimes excessive in his demands and unnecessarily rude when they were not met—he could not understand why a composer should prefer a plain singer with a great voice to a beautiful singer with a second-rate one—it was probably necessary to bully Strauss a bit or he would have let things slide.

In return, Strauss gave Hofmannsthal much. In the first place, he gave him the opportunity to write libretti at all, which had always fascinated him.

> There pre-existed within me something which enabled me to fulfill—within the limits of my gifts—your wishes and made this fulfillment in turn satisfy a most profound need of my own. Much of what I produced in all the loneliness of youth, entirely for myself, hardly thinking of readers, were phantastic little operas and *Singspiele*—without music. Your wishes, subsequently, supplied a purpose without restricting my freedom.

And in the second place he taught him a lot about how to write a good one. As Hofmannsthal himself admitted, Strauss had the better theatrical sense, at least for opera in which the action must be much more immediately intelligible than it need be in a spoken play. If the alterations which Strauss suggested sometimes offended Hofmannsthal's artistic conscience and sent him into fits, there was always some flaw which prompted them, and often, as in the second acts of *Rosenkavalier* and *Arabella,* they were brilliantly right.

Again like marriage, any artistic collaboration must have its ups and downs: there are factors, some personal, some external, which cause friction and even a threat of divorce. If most of the irritation was on Hofmannsthal's part, there were more reasons for this than his touchy temperament. Before Berlioz, Wagner, and Verdi in his middle years, no composer worried much about the libretto; he took what he was given and did the best he could with it. This was possible because a satisfactory convention had been established as to how libretti should be written, the forms for arias and ensembles, the style for *opera buffa,* the style for *opera seria,* etc., which any competent versifier could master. This meant, however, that while a composer could be assured of getting a settable text, one libretto was remarkably like another, all originality and interest had to come from the music. Some librettists might be better than others and enjoy a reputation among composers, but to the public all were anonymous and content to remain so. Aside from Goethe, who never found a good enough composer, Hofmannsthal was the first poet with an established public literary reputation to write libretti, and in his day this was a daring thing to do. In the literary circle to which he belonged, opera was not highly regarded as an art form and it may well have been that Strauss' music was not much admired either. Certainly, most of his friends thought that he was wasting his time and talents writing libretti of which few words would be heard in performance, and, of course, the managers of opera houses and his musical friends, accustomed to the conventional libretto, thought Strauss was wasting *his* time and talents trying to set such dense and incomprehensible texts.

A librettist is always at a disadvantage because operas are reviewed, not by literary or dramatic critics, but by music critics whose taste and understanding of poetry may be very limited. What is worse, a music critic who wishes to attack the music but is afraid to do so directly, can always attack it indirectly by condemning the libretto. A librettist is at a further disadvantage because music is an international language and poetry a local one. Wherever an opera is performed, audiences hear the same music but, outside the country of its origin, either they hear alien words which are meaningless to them or a translation which, however good—and most translations are very bad—are not what the librettist wrote. To know that however valuable your contribution, your public fame will always be less than that of your collaborator is not an easy position for anyone, and for Hofmannsthal, to whom fame mattered a great deal, it must often have been a torture.

> You have every reason to be grateful to me for bringing you
> that element which is sure to bewilder people and provoke
> a certain amount of antagonism, for you already have too
> many followers, you are already all too obviously the hero
> of the day, all too universally accepted.

This may be just: it is certainly envious.

While following this correspondence, the reader must bear in mind the difficulty of Hofmannsthal's position if he is not to do an injustice. Strauss has the reputation of not having been a very nice man but, in his relation to Hofmannsthal as revealed in these letters, he appears much the more sympathetic of the two.

In the first German edition of this correspondence some passages were omitted, most of them at Hofmannsthal's request. He was afraid that the jocular tone in which Strauss would sometimes speak of "Art" would be misunderstood by the public.

> As soon as the German Philistines light, as *ipsissima verba magistri,* upon the following amusing sentence: "Flourishes a la Rückert must do the trick where the action leaves me cold," you yourself, the creator of this incomparable opera (*Ariadne*), become the veritable spokesman of this chorus of the Philistines . . . I must, above all, still ask you for the following: you use repeatedly the metaphor that I ought to spur, or urge on, my Pegasus, etc. Taken out of the context of this intimate, quite unrestrained exchange of letters and printed, I would not care very much for this description of my methods of "poetizing."

If Philistia is to be taken into account, he was right; it is always the unbeliever who is most shocked by blasphemy. But should one care what Philistia thinks?

THE POET OF THE ENCIRCLEMENT

Art, as the late Professor R. G. Collingwood pointed out, is not Magic, i.e., a means by which the artist communicates or arouses his feelings in others, but a mirror in which they may become conscious of what their own feelings really are: its proper effect, in fact, is disenchanting.

By significant details it shows us that our present state is neither as virtuous nor as secure as we thought, and by the lucid pattern into which it unifies these details, its assertion that order is *possible,* it faces us with the command to make it *actual.* Insofar as he is an artist, no one, not even Kipling, is intentionally a magician. On the other hand, no artist, not even Eliot, can prevent his work being used as magic, for that is what all of us, highbrow and lowbrow alike, secretly want Art to be. Between the schoolmaster who quoted "If," and the undergraduate who quoted "The Waste Land," there was not so much difference. Had the former really read his poem, he would have had to say, "Yes, *if.* Unfortunately, I do not keep my head . . . etc. I realize now that I am not a man." Instead, of course, he said, "Admirably put. That's exactly what the boys need to realize." Similarly, had the undergraduate really read his poem, he would have had to say: "Now I realize I am not the clever young man I thought, but a senile hermaphrodite.

Either I must recover or put my head in the gas-stove." Instead, of course, he said, "That's wonderful. If only they would read this, Mother would understand why I can't stay home nights, and Father would understand why I can't hold a job."

If today the war makes people discover that Kipling is good, it will be an excellent thing, but if at the same time they start saying that Eliot is "defeatist," it will prove that they have not discovered a poet, but only changed their drug to suit the new climate.

In his essay, Mr. Eliot draws a distinction between poetry and verse:

> For other poets—at least, for some other poets—the poem may begin to shape itself in fragments of musical rhythm, and its structure will first appear in terms of some-thing analogous to musical form. . . . What fundamentally distinguishes his (Kipling's) "verse" from "poetry" is the subordination of musical interest. . . . There is a harmonics of poetry which is not merely beyond the range of the poems—it would interfere with the intention.

This distinction is real and neatly describes the difference be-tween the kind of poetry written by Eliot and the kind written by Kipling, but, so defined, there are more verse or ballad writers and fewer poets, I think, than Mr. Eliot seems to imply. Ben Jonson, for instance, who wrote out a prose draft which he then versified, Dunbar, Butler's *Hudibras,* most of Burns, Byron's *Don Juan,* etc.

I mention this only because I agree with Mr. Eliot that Kipling is an odd fish, but doubt if his capacity to write great verse is a sign of this.

What is it then, that makes Kipling so extraordinary? Is it not that while virtually every other European writer since the fall of the Roman empire has felt that the dangers threatening civilization came from *inside* that civilization (or from inside the individual consciousness), Kipling is obsessed by a sense of dangers threaten-ing from *outside?*

Others have been concerned with the corruptions of the big city, the *ennui* of the cultured mind; some sought a remedy in a return to Nature, to childhood, to Classical Antiquity; others looked forward to a brighter future of liberty, equality and fraternity: they called on the powers of the subconscious, or prayed for the grace of God to inrupt and save their souls; they called on the oppressed to arise and save the world. In Kipling there is none of this, no nostalgia for a Golden Age, no belief in Progress. For him civilization (and consciousness) is a little citadel of light surrounded by a great darkness full of malignant forces and only maintained through the centuries by everlasting vigilance, willpower and self-sacrifice. The philosophers of the Enlightenment shared his civilization-barbarism antithesis, but their weapon was reason, i.e., coming to consciousness, whereas for Kipling too much thinking is highly dangerous, an opening of the gates to the barbarians of melancholia and doubt. For him the gates are guarded by the conscious Will (not unlike the Inner Check of Irving Babbitt).

Poem after poem, under different symbolic disguises, presents this same situation of the danger without, the anxiety of encirclement—by inanimate forces, the Picts beyond the Roman Wall:

> No indeed! We are not strong
>   But we know Peoples that are.
> Yes, and we'll guide them along
>   To smash and destroy you in War.
> *We* shall be slaves just the same?
>   Yes, we have always been slaves,
> But you—you will die of the shame,
>   And then we shall dance on your graves.

The Danes, the Dutch, the Huns, the "new-caught sullen peoples, half devil and half child," even the Female of the Species—by inanimate forces, Karela, the club-footed vine, the sea:

> Coming, like stallions they paw with their hooves,
>   going, they snatch with their teeth,

the ice

> Once and again as the Ice came South
> The glaciers ground over Lossiemouth

and by Spiritual Powers:

> They builded a tower to shiver the sky and wrench
>   the stars apart,
> Till the Devil grunted behind the bricks: "It's
>   striking, but is it Art?"

> Very softly down the glade runs a waiting watching shade
>   And the whisper spreads and widens far and near,
> And the sweat is on thy brow, for he passes even now—
>   He is Fear, O little Hunter, he is Fear.

It is noteworthy that the *interested* spirits are all demonic; the Divine Law is aloof.

Given such a situation, the important figure in society is, of course, the man on guard, and it is he who, in one form or another, from the sentry on the Afghanistan frontier to the gardener

> Grubbing weeds from gravel paths with broken dinner knives

is the Kipling hero. Unlike the epic hero, he is always on the *defensive*. Thus Kipling is interested in engineering, in the weapons which protect man against the chaotic violence of nature, but not in physics, in the intellectual *discovery* that made the weapons possible.

His ethics and his politics are those of a critical emergency, which is why it is impossible to classify them under conventional party labels, for they presuppose a state where differences of opinion are as irrelevant as they are to a soldier in a foxhole, and, insofar as they apply at all, apply to everyone, Democrat, Nazi or Communist.

Of the guardians, Kipling has profound understanding. He knows that most of them are prodigal sons, given to drink and fornication, acquainted with post-dated checks, now cruel, now sentimental, and he does not try to present them as nice people. But when he turns from them to the Sons of Mary whom they are paid to guard (the shift from social to religious meaning is significant), his vision becomes dim and his touch uncertain, for his interest is not really in them, but only in their relation to the sons of Martha, so that what he sees is either too soft, the exile's nostalgic daydream of Mom and the roses round the door, or too hard, the sentry's resentful nightmare of the sleek and slack stay-at-homes dining and wining while he and his sufferings are forgotten.

Kipling has been rightly praised for his historical imagination, but it is questionable if historical is the right word. If by history we mean *irreversible* temporal changes as contrasted with the cyclical and reversible changes of Nature, then Kipling's imaginative treatment of the past is an affirmation of Nature and a denial of History, for his whole concern is to show that the moment of special emergency is everlasting:

As it will be in the future, it was at the birth of Man—
There are only four things certain since Social Progress began.
That the Dog returns to his Vomit and the Sow returns to her Mire,
And the Burnt Fool's bandaged finger goes wabbling back to the
    Fire.

But if Nature and History are the same, how can Nature and Man, the Jungle and the City, be opposed to each other, as Kipling is clearly certain that they are? If one asks him "What is civilization?" he answers, "The People living under the Law, who were taught by their fathers to discipline their natural impulses and will teach their children to do the same":

> This we learned from famous men,
>   Knowing not its uses,
> When they showed, in daily work
> Man must finish off his work—
> Right or wrong his daily work
> And without excuses

in contrast to the barbarian who is at the mercy of his selfish appetites. But if one asks him "What is this Law and where does it come from?" he refers one back to Nature, to the Darwinian law of the Jungle, "Be Fit," or to the Newtonian law of the Machine:

We are not built to comprehend a lie
We can neither love nor pity nor forgive.
If you make a slip in handling us, you die.

One might almost say that Kipling had to concentrate his attention and ours upon the special emergency in order to avoid the embarrassment of this paradox, for it is precisely when We are threatened by Them that we can naturally think of the ethical relation between Me and You as one of self-sacrifice, and the ethical relation between Us and Them as one of self-interest. It is precisely when civilization is in mortal danger that the immediate necessity to defend it has a right to override the question of just what it is we are defending.

It may not be too fanciful, either, to see in the kind of poetry Kipling wrote, the aesthetic corollary of his conception of life. His virtuosity with language is not unlike that of one of his sergeants with an awkward squad:

Said England unto Pharaoh: "You've had miracles before
    When Aaron struck your rivers into blood,
But if you watch the sergeant he can show you something more
    He's a charm making riflemen from mud."
It was neither Hindustani, French or Coptics,
    It was odds and ends and leavings of the same
Translated by a stick (which is really half the trick)
    And Pharaoh harked to Sergeant Whatsisname.

Under his will, the vulgarest words learn to wash behind their ears and to execute complicated movements at the word of command, but they can hardly be said to learn to think for themselves. His poetry is arid; personally, I prefer this to the damp poetry of self-expression, but both are excesses.

His poems in their quantity, their limitation to one feeling at a time, have the air of brilliant tactical improvisations to overcome sudden unforeseen obstacles, as if, for Kipling, experience were not a seed to cultivate patiently and lovingly, but an unending stream of dangerous feelings to be immediately mastered as they appear.

No doubt his early experiences of India gave him a sense of the danger of Nature which it is hard for a European to realize (though easier perhaps for an American), but these are not sufficient to explain the terror of demons, visible and invisible, which gives his work its peculiar excitement, any more than the English Civil War expresses Hobbes's terror of political disorder. Nor does it matter particularly what the real cause may have been. The "mirror" that Kipling holds out to us is one in which, if we see anything, we see vague, menacing shapes which can be kept away by incessant action but can never be finally overcome:

> Heart may Fail, and Strength outwear, and Purpose turn
>   to Loathing
> But the everyday affair of business, meals and clothing
> Builds a bulkhead 'twixt Despair and the Edge of Nothing.

>> I get it as well as you—oo—oo
>> If I haven't enough to do—oo—oo
>> We all get hump,
>> Camelious hump,
>> Kiddies and grown-ups too.

UN HOMME D'ESPRIT

To discuss literature written in any tongue other than one's own is a questionable undertaking, but for an English-speaking writer to discuss a French writer borders on folly, for no two languages could be more different.

To discover the essential and unique qualities of a language, one must go to its poetry for it is the poet, as Valéry says, who attempts to remove all the noises from speech leaving only the sounds. The conventions of a poetry, its prosodic rules, the kinds of verbal ornamentation, rhymes, alliterations, etc., which it encourages or condemns can tell us much about the way in which a native ear draws this distinction. I very much doubt whether a Frenchman can ever learn really to hear a line of English verse—think of Baudelaire and Poe—and I am perfectly certain that no Englishman can learn to hear French poetry correctly. When I hear a native recite German or Spanish or Italian poetry, I believe, however mistakenly, that I hear more or less what he hears, but if the reciter is French, I know I am hearing nothing of the sort. I know, in an academic way, the rules of Classical French verse, but the knowledge does not change my habit of hearing. For example, to my ear, trained on English verse, the prevailing rhythm of the French alexandrine sounds like the anapaestic rhythm of

The Assyrian came down like a wolf on the fold

thus

Je suis belle, | o mortels! | comme un rêve | de pierre

I know this is all wrong but it is what I hear.* Further, most unfortunately, the nature of the English language forbids the use of anapaests for tragic subjects. I am convinced that, when he goes to hear *Phèdre* at the Comédie Française, an Englishman, however well he may know French, however much he admire the extraordinary varied and subtle delivery of the cast, cannot help finding Racine comic.

I have known Valéry's poem *Ebauche d'un serpent* for over twenty-five years, reread it often with increasing admiration and, as I thought, comprehension, only to discover the other day, on reading a letter by the poet to Alain, that I had missed the whole point, namely, that the tone of the poem is burlesque, that the assonances and alliterations are deliberately exaggerated, and that the serpent is intended to sound like Beckmesser in *Die Meistersinger*.

How could I, to whose ear all French verse sounds a bit exaggerated, hope to get this?

In prose, the difficulties of communication, though not so formidable, are still serious enough. It is not just a matter of the obvious translator's headaches, that there is no English equivalent to *esprit,* for instance, or that *amour* and *love* are not synonymous, but of the entirely different rhetorical structure of French and English prose, so that an English reader may entirely ignore some important effect and be over-impressed by another.

In writing about Valéry, therefore, I can only console myself with the thought that, if the Valéry I admire is in large measure a creation of my own, the man who wrote—"the proper object of thought is that which does not exist"—would be the first to appreciate the joke.

From the age of twenty, Valéry made it his daily habit to rise

---

* Another difficulty for my ear is the caesura; an English poet works just as hard to vary its position from line to line as a French poet works to keep it in the same few places.

before dawn and spend two or three hours studying the interior maneuvers of his freshly awoken mind. This habit became a physiological need so that, if circumstance made him miss these hours of introspection, he felt out of sorts for the rest of the day. The observations he made during this period he wrote down in notebooks, without a thought, he says, of their ever being read by another. From time to time, however, he was persuaded to publish selections. The reluctance he expresses seems more prima-donna-ish than real.

> I never dreamt that one day I would have these fragments printed as they stood. Dr. Ludo van Bogaert and M. Alex-andre Stols had the idea for me. They tempted me to do so by pointing out the "intimate" quality of this little ven-ture, and by the typographical perfection of the sample pages they showed me.

> There are times when one has to give way to the pre-posterous desires of lovers of the spontaneous and ideas in the rough.

This does not ring quite true, especially when one finds him writ-ing privately to a friend (Paul Souday) that he considers his note-books his real *œuvre*.

In any case, we may be very glad that he overcame his reluc-tance, for, taken together, these notes form one of the most interest-ing and original documents of "the inner life" in existence.

Most of such documents are concerned with the so-called personal, that is, with the confession of sins and vices, memories of childhood, the feelings of the subject about God, the weather, his mistress, gossip, self-reproach, and the ordinary motive for producing them is a desire to demonstrate that their author is more interesting, more unique, more *human* than other folks.

For the personal in this sense, Valéry had nothing but con-tempt. It is in what they show, he believed, that men differ, what they hide is always the same. Confession, therefore, is like undress-ing in public; everyone knows what he is going to see. Further, a man's secrets are often much more apparent to others than to himself.

One of Gide's most obvious traits, for example, was his tight-fistedness; after reading his journals, one is curious to know if he was aware of this.

A cultivation of memory for its own sake, as in Proust, was incomprehensible to Valéry, who preferred to forget everything in his past that was just a picture, retaining only what he could assimilate and convert into an element of his present mental life. As for confiding one's sufferings to paper, he thought it responsible for all the worst books.

The task which Valéry set himself was to observe the human mind in the action of thinking; the only mind that he can observe is, of course, his own, but this is irrelevant. He is not a philosopher, except in the etymological meaning of that word, nor a psychologist insofar as psychology is concerned with hidden depths—for Valéry, humanity is confined to the skin and consciousness; below that is physiological machinery—but an amazingly keen and *rusé* observer of conscious processes of thinking. For this neither a special talent, like a talent for mathematics, nor esoteric learning is required, but only what might be called intellectual virtue, which it is possible for every man to develop, if he chooses.

For the cultivation of such an *Ethique sportive,* as Valéry once called it, one must develop a vigilance that immediately distinguishes between fictions and real psychic events, between the seen, the thought, the reasoned and the felt, and a precision of description that resists all temptation to fine literary effects. Hence Valéry's repeated attacks on the popular notion of "profundity." A thought, he says, can properly be called profound only if it profoundly changes a question or a given situation, and such a thought is never found at the bottom of the mind which contains only a few stock proverbs. Most people call something profound, not because it is near some important truth but because it is distant from ordinary life. Thus, darkness is profound to the eye, silence to the ear; what-is-not is the profundity of what-is. This kind of profundity is a literary effect, which can be calculated like any other literary effect, and usually deplorable. For Valéry, Pascal's famous remark about the silence of the eternal spaces is a classic instance of literary vanity passing itself off as observation. If Pascal was genuinely interested in stating a truth, then why, Valéry maliciously asks, did he not also write: "The intermittent hubbub in the small corners where we live reassures us."

After reading his notebooks, we know no more about Valéry as a person than before—we are not told, for example, that he suffered from depressions—he has only shown us that he was a good observer and that he expressed his observations in precise language. To judge if his observations are true or false, we have only to repeat the experiment on ourselves. For instance, he says that it is impossible consciously to put a distance between oneself and an object without turning round to see if one is succeeding. I try, and I find that Valéry is right.

Valéry's attitude to life is more consistent than he admits, and begins with a conviction of the essential inconsistency of the mind and the need to react against it. The following three notes might be taken as mottoes for all his work.

Cognition reigns but does not rule.

Sometimes I think; and sometimes I *am*.

I invoke no inspiration except that element of chance, which is common to every mind; then comes an unremitting toil, which wars against this element of chance.

Valéry's observations cover a wide range of subjects. As one might expect, the least interesting, the ones in which he sounds least like Valéry and most like just one more French writer of mordant aphorisms, are those concerned with love, self-love, good, and evil.

He has extremely interesting things to say about our consciousness of our bodies, about those curious psycho-physical expressions, laughing, crying, and blushing, about the physical behavior of people when they are concentrating on a mental problem. He is excellent on dreams—he observes, for instance, that in dreams there is "practically no present tense." But for poets, naturally, and for many others too, I believe, his most valuable contributions are his remarks on the art of poetry. A critic who does not himself write poetry may be an admirable judge of what is good and bad, but he cannot have a first-hand knowledge of how poetry is written, so that not infrequently he criticizes, favorably or unfavorably, some poem for achieving or failing to achieve something that the poet was not interested in doing. Many poets have written defenses of poetry against charges that it is untrue or immoral, but surprisingly few have told us how they wrote. There are two reasons for this: the poets are more interested in writing more poems and, less laudably, they, like lawyers and doctors, have a snobbish reluctance to show the laity the secrets of their mystery. Behind this snobbery, of course, lies the fear that, if the general public knew what goes on, that a poem is not sheer logomancy, for instance, or that an intensely expressive love poem does not necessarily presuppose a poet intensely in love, that public would lose even the little respect for poets that it has.

It is unfortunate that one of Valéry's few predecessors, Poe, should have used as his case history of composition a poem, "The Raven," which does strike the reader as "contrived" in a bad way, which means that it is not contrived enough. The form Poe employed for the poem, which demands many feminine rhymes, has in English a frivolous effect out of key with the subject. A reader, who wishes to cling to a more magical view of the poetic process, can find reasons to confirm his illusion. Valéry's achievements as a poet make his critical doctrines harder to wish away. His statements are obviously intended to be polemical. He dislikes two kinds of writers, those who try to impress with sonorous or violent vagueness, and naturalistic writers who would simply record what the camera sees or their stream of accidental thoughts. For Valéry, all loud and violent writing is comic, like a man alone in a room, playing a trombone. When one reads Carlyle, for instance, one gets the impression that he had persuaded himself that it takes more effort, more *work,* to write *fortissimo* than *piano,* or *universe* than *garden.*

Of the Zola school of naturalism Valéry disposes very neatly, by asking what kinds of scents perfumers would bottle if they adopted this aesthetic.

For Valéry, a poem ought to be a festival of the intellect, that is, a game, but a solemn, ordered, and significant game, and a poet is someone to whom arbitrary difficulties suggest ideas. It is the glory of poetry that the lack of a single word can ruin everything, that the poet cannot continue until he discovers a word, say, in two syllables, containing P or F, synonymous with *break-*

ing-up, yet not too uncommon. The formal restrictions of poetry teach us that the thoughts which arise from our needs, feelings, and experiences are only a small part of the thoughts of which we are capable. In any poem some lines were "given" the poet, which he then tried to perfect, and others which he had to calculate and at the same time make them sound as "natural" as possible. It is more becoming in a poet to talk of versification than of mysterious voices, and his genius should be so well hidden in his talent that the reader attributes to his art what comes from his nature.

Needless to say, Valéry found very little in the French poetry of his age which seemed to him anything more than a worship of chance and novelty, and concluded that poetry was a freak survival, that no one today would be capable of arriving at the notion of verse if it were not already there.

In his general principles I am convinced that Valéry is right past all possibility of discussion, but I cannot help wondering if I should also agree in daily practice as much as I do, if I were a Frenchman trying to write French poetry. For polemical reasons, probably, Valéry overstresses, I think, the arbitrariness of poetic formal restrictions, and overdramatizes the opposition between them and the "Natural." If they really were purely arbitrary, then the prosodies of different languages would be interchangeable, and the experience which every poet has had, of being unable to get on with a poem because he was trying to use the "wrong" form for this particular poem until, having found the right form, the *natural* form, composition proceeded freely, would be unknown. While it is true that nothing which is without effort and attention is likely to be of much value, the reverse proposition is not true: it would take an immense effort, for example, to write half a dozen rhopalic hexameters in English, but it is virtually certain that the result would have no poetic merit.

To an English poet, French poetry seems to suffer from a lack of formal variety, as did English poetry between 1680 and 1780. Any form, be it the French alexandrine or the English heroic couplet, however admirable a vehicle originally, tends to exhaust its possibilities in the hands of two or three masters, and their successors must either find quite different forms or be doomed to remain epigoni. If it is rare to find a modern French poem that is not written in free verse (and one must not forget that Valéry himself wrote quite a lot of what he called *poésie brute*), while formal poems are still common in modern English poetry, the lack of resilience in the official forms of French verse may be partly responsible.* By comparison with French, English seems an anarchic amateur language, but this very anarchy, if it stimulates the proper revolt against it, can give rise to new and living structures. Would Valéry, I sometimes patriotically wonder, have finished his poetic career so soon if he had had the vast resources of *our* tongue, with all the prosodic possibilities which its common syllables permit, to play with?

But then, of course, we might not have got the notebooks. It is fitting that the man whose critical banner might well have carried the device *Vade retro, Musa,* should have written *Tes pas, enfants de mon silence,* one of the most beautiful invocations to the Muse in any language. His worshipped Muse, whom he sometimes called Laura, was not, perhaps, the Muse of poetry or, if so, only accidentally, but the Muse of insight and self-renewal whom he daily expected in the dawn hours.

> My mind thinks of my mind,
> My past is foreign to me,
> My name surprises me,
> My body is a pure idea.
> What I was is with all other selves
> And I am not even what I am going to be.

Aside from the money, literary success can give but small satisfaction to an author, even to his vanity. For what does literary success mean? To be condemned by persons who have not read his works and to be imitated by persons devoid of talent. There are only two kinds of literary glory that are worth winning but the writer who wins either will never know. One is to have been the writer, perhaps a quite minor one, in whose work some great

---

* About some things it would seem that French taste is more indulgent than English. Thus Valéry, while admitting that De Vigny's line *J'aime la majesté des souffrances humaines* is nonsense, allows it, nevertheless, because of its beautiful sound. An English poet could never get away with a similar line.

master generations later finds an essential clue for solving some problem; the other is to become for someone else an example of the dedicated life,

> being secretly invoked, pictured, and placed by a stranger
> in an inner sanctum of his thoughts, so as to serve him as
> a witness, a judge, a father, and a hallowed mentor.

It was this role, rather than that of a literary influence, which Mallarmé played in Valéry's life, and I can vouch for at least one life in which Valéry does likewise. Whenever I am more than usually tormented by one of those horrid mental imps, *Contradiction, Obstination, Imitation, Lapsus, Brouillamini, Fange-d'Ame,* whenever I feel myself in danger of becoming *un homme sérieux,* it is on Valéry, *un homme d'esprit* if ever there was one, more often than on any other poet, I believe, that I call for aid.

ONE OF THE FAMILY

I never enjoy having to find fault with a book, and when the author is someone I have met and like, I hate it. Lord David Cecil possesses all the qualifications for writing a first-class biography of Max Beerbohm—an understanding love of his hero, the industry and scholarship to insure that the facts are both correct and complete— but his *Max* is not nearly so good a book as it could have been. What he has published should, I feel, have been his first draft, which he should then have spent another six months condensing to at least half its present volume. As it is, he has given us a ponderous, repetitious Victorian tome of four hundred and ninety-six densely printed pages. So expansive a commemoration is singularly unsuited to the man who once counseled a prospective biographer thus:

> My gifts are small. I've used them very well and discreetly, never straining them; and the result is that I've made a charming little reputation. But this reputation is a frail plant. Don't over-attend to it, gardener Lynch! Don't drench it and deluge it! The contents of a quite small watering-can will be quite enough. This I take to be superfluous counsel. I find much reassurance and comfort in your phrase, "a little book." Oh, keep it little!—in due proportion to its theme.

With my other objection, I have learned, I can expect very few people in this age to agree, but I must state it, however eccentric it may seem. I consider the publication of long extracts from Max's letters to Florence a violation of personal privacy for which I can see no justification whatever. Max seems to have destroyed all her letters to him—an indication, surely, that he wished their correspondence to remain private. There may be some excuse for disregarding the wishes of a dead man—though I do not myself consider it valid—if the contents of his private papers reveal important aspects of his life and character, hitherto unsuspected, but Max's letters to Florence tell us nothing we could not learn from public sources. Furthermore, to a detached reader, nearly all love letters are either boring or embarrassing. Letters between friends who share the same interests and jokes can be most entertaining, as are Max's letters to Reggie Turner, superbly edited by Mr. Rupert Hart-Davis, and published, incidentally, with Max's consent on condition that certain excisions be made. But the noises of erotic devotion, however musical they may sound in the ears of the couple concerned, can seldom stir a third party's. As one would expect, there is nothing scandalous or shameful about Max the lover, only a certain kittenishness, harmless enough—but to me, at any rate, shy-making.

One more criticism, or, rather, suggestion. When I read biographies, I find myself constantly having to turn back and hunt for the date of the event I am reading about. I wish that when they print a biography publishers would make it their practice to set at the top of each page at least the year with which it is concerned.

Mr. S. N. Behrman's *Portrait of Max,* published some five years ago, in three hundred and four pages of widely spaced print, is a better book than Lord David Cecil's, but since he confined himself to describing his encounters with Beerbohm and made no attempt at a full biography, his task was of course a very much easier one. I am astonished to find both Mr. Behrman and Lord David Cecil talking of Max as a man who deliberately adopted and cultivated a mask. To say that a man wears a mask is to say that the person as he appears to be to others, perhaps even to himself, differs from the person he really is. He may wear one for various reasons. He may simply be a crook, like the man who professes love to lonely spinsters in order to swindle them out of their savings. He may be someone who is afraid or ashamed of certain aspects of his nature, which he therefore tries to hide from others and himself. Young people, who are still uncertain of their identity, often try on a succession of masks in the hope of finding the one which suits them—the one, in fact, which is not a mask. Another possibility is described in Beerbohm's story "The Happy Hypocrite": in order to win the heart of a nice girl, a rake assumes a mask of virtue, but ends up by becoming in reality what at first he had only pretended to be. Lastly, among artists of all kinds— though here the use of the word "mask" is questionable—it is not uncommon for their artistic *persona* to express but a limited area of their total experience.

Max Beerbohm falls into none of these categories. He was certainly no crook. At an astonishingly early age he knew exactly the sort of person he was, and he never showed the slightest desire to be anyone else. Lucky enough to be equally gifted in two artistic media, and without any ambition to transcend his limitations, he made his caricatures and his writings between them say everything that was in him to say. The behavior and conversation of most people vary a little according to the company they happen to be in, but Max's were the same wherever he was. Indeed, if there does seem something not quite human about him, something elfish, it is because, as an adult, he retained the transparency of a child. Intentionally or unintentionally, Oscar Wilde's wisecrack about him is acute: "Tell me, when you are alone with Max, does he take off his face and reveal his mask?"

Late in his life, Max told a journalist that he had been lucky once—when he was born. And one cannot read about his family without agreeing with him. His father, a corn merchant from Memel, who took up the study of Anglo-Saxon when he was over sixty, married Constantia Draper, an absent-minded lady with literary interests, by whom he had three sons and a daughter. On her death, he married her sister, efficient but affectionate and humorous, and begot three daughters and one more son, Max. Max was four years younger than his next sister and twenty-two years younger than his eldest half brother. Eccentricity and charm ran in both families. Ernest became a sheep farmer in the colonies and married a colored lady, Herbert became the famous actor-manager Herbert Tree, Julius turned into a passionate dandy and compulsive gambler whose hopes of making his fortune were never dimmed by his repeated failures to do so. Constance helped her stepmother run the house and came out with such remarks as:

> Mr. X tells me he has a wonderful parrot. It can judge the year of wine vintages. I want to write an article about it for the papers.

(Actually, Mr. X had said "palate.") Agnes, a beauty, was "always very gay," even after her marriage went on the rocks. Dora, the person to whom Max felt closest all his life, became a nun and wrote a music-hall song:

> Left, right, left, right.
> The girl that I left
> Is the girl that is right.

And Max became Max.

This seems a good point at which to dispose of the ladies. Since his half brothers were already out in the world, Max grew up in a mainly feminine society, the adored baby boy. Such a situation encourages imaginative precocity and an unconscious selfishness, which takes it for granted that one will always be loved and looked after. The assumption, oddly, is usually justified, and at no time in his life was Max without some woman—his mother, Florence, his secretary Miss Jungmann—who was delighted to look after him. As he himself admitted:

> I can only stand life when it is made pleasant for me. Usually it *is* made pleasant for me. I have really been rather pampered than otherwise. So I have been all right, on the whole. But I do not like life when it does not offer me something nice every day. And if it ever offered me something *not* nice I should feel myself very aggrieved.

One can very well understand why he was pampered, for few people can have been by nature so adapted to a life of cozy domesticity. He was charming, affectionate, intensely loyal, good-tempered; and none of the common threats to a happy home life, like promiscuity, the bottle, or the race track, seem ever to have tempted him.

His first two attempts to find an exogamous substitute for his sister Dora ended in failure. In the case of Grace Conover—Kilseen, as he called her—the fault was his: he was evidently more fascinated by the idea of being in love than interested in her, and she was perhaps the only person in his life whom he could be accused of having treated badly. In the case of Constance Collier, the fault was mostly hers: she needed the kind of hot-blooded passion which she must have known it was not in Max to provide. When his friends learned of his engagement to Florence Kahn, they must have felt great misgivings. He, one of the most popular men-about-town, a wit, a caricaturist and writer with an established reputation; she, socially gauche, without any sense of humor, an actress who had not quite made it: how could such a union be expected to last? Had they set up house in London, it probably wouldn't have lasted, and it seems that Max himself realized this, for he did not propose until he had decided, six years after they became acquainted, to leave England and make his home abroad.

To Reggie Turner he wrote:

> . . . we *may* live in Italy. One thing is certain: we shan't live in London, but somewhere that is uncomplicated and pleasant and un-fussy and lets one be oneself. . . . Of all my charming and un-charming acquaintances I want to get rid: they are a charming or un-charming nuisance, taking up one's time—clogs and drags. Henceforth I am going to be as exclusive as the Duchess of Buccleuch. There will be no one but Florence, and my people, and *you*—one or two others perhaps, such as the Nicholsons, but I am not sure.

One part of him had dreamed of such a life for a long time. As early as 1893, when he was only twenty-one, he had written:

> I would make myself master of some small area of physical life, a life of quiet, monotonous simplicity, exempt from all outer disturbances.

Edwardian High Society had amused him and given him copy, but at the same time living in it exhausted him:

> If I were naturally a brilliant and copious talker, I suppose that to stay in another's house would be no strain on me. I should be able to impose myself on my host and hostess and their guests without any effort, and at the end of the day retire quite unfatigued, pleasantly flushed with the effect of my own magnetism. Alas, there is no question of my imposing myself. I can repay hospitality only by strict attention to the humble, arduous process of making myself agreeable. When I go up to dress for dinner, I have always a strong impulse to go to bed and sleep off my fatigue; and it is only by exerting all my will-power that I can array myself for the final labours. . . . It's a dog's life.

Again, although at no time in his life well off, he never envied the rich their style of living:

> The great English country houses are built for gods; an exaggerated conception of the human being led to their scale. It is nightmarish to think of living in those terribly big rooms.

His natural taste was for a family kind of social life, intimate and on a small scale. And his imaginative life was not of the kind that needs constant outside stimulus or even an audience. He retained the child's capacity to be happily absorbed, playing games by itself or with one other. And so, though his friends sometimes found Florence difficult, the marriage was a success. He was happy and, for him, productive:

> It is no news merely to say that I am consciously happy during sixteen hours out of the daily twenty-four, and unconsciously happy during the other eight; and yet that is the only news I have. . . . Absolutely nothing "happens." Florence and I "see" nobody. . . . The sun shines, and the sea shines under it, and I eat a good deal twice a day, and the camellias are just beginning to bloom, and the oranges and lemons are ripe, and I do a great deal of work.

If one says that the ladies—and the men, too—were not very important in Max's life, one means that neither his character nor his art was decisively affected by his relationships with them. The decisive events in his life had already occurred at home, long before he ever met them. Important as our childhood years are to all of us, most of us cannot become ourselves without in one way or another reacting against them. Not only did Max never rebel against the values and habits of his family; he lived happily with them until the age of thirty-eight.

By the time he was eight, the adult Max begins to be visible:

> Somehow, mysteriously, when I was eight years old or so, the soldiery was eclipsed for me by the constabulary. Somehow the scarlet and the bearskins began to thrill me less than the austere costume and calling of the Metropolitan police. . . . It was not the daffodils that marked for me the coming of the season of Spring. It was the fact that policemen suddenly wore short tunics with steel buttons. It was not the fall of the leaf nor the swallows' flight that signalled Autumn to me. It was the fact that policemen were wearing long thick frock-coats with buttons of copper. . . .
>
> By the time I was eleven years old I despised the Force. I was interested only in politicians—in Statesmen, as they were called at that time.

From this interest in the clothes of others, Max soon developed, stimulated by the example of his half brother Julius, a fastidiousness about his own. He never seems to have passed through an inky-schoolboy stage (a Max with pimples is unimaginable), and by the time he was fifteen he was already a dandy:

> My new black trousers are beautifully stripey and well made, perhaps a little loose about the knee but *very* nice. . . . I am still wearing my flower which has lasted wonderfully.

So at fifteen. At twenty-four, we find him dressed for Sunday in "flannel coat, white waistcoat, purple tie with turquoise pin, duck trousers and straw hat" and possessing "a smoking suit of purple silk with dark red facings," and at eighty, when Mr. Behrman first met him:

> He wore a double-breasted suit of gray flannel with a primrose sheen, and a low-cut vest that had wide soft la-

pels. On his head was a stiff straw hat set at a rakish angle. . . . Also, he was wearing neat, well-fitting patent-leather pumps, and white socks.

Being one of those persons who generally look like an unmade bed, I have always felt a certain resentment when confronted by an impeccable turnout. I am therefore as delighted as I am surprised to learn that Max's was not always faultless. According to a fellow-dandy, William Nicholson, "The perfection of his toilet was occasionally marred by a missing button or a split glove."

Growing up in the society of siblings so much older than himself, his imaginative fantasies were directed very early toward grown-up life:

> I disbelieved in fairies, was not sure about knight errants, was glad to hear that the sea had been cleared of pirates and that Indians were dying out. . . . After dark, I was simply a man-of-the-world. . . . I dined at my club on chicken and cherry-tart and went to a party. . . . I cannot imagine what happened at the party except that I stayed late and was the guest of someone I had heard of in grown-up conversation.

A boy who on the football field wishes he were playing hunt-the-slipper and at the swimming pool looks forward to returning to the latest novel by Miss Braddon might be expected to have a hard time at his boarding school. But it was not so for Max at Charterhouse. Adolescent boys are conformists and inclined to persecute the odd individual, but only if the latter, as he usually does, shows fear; the fearlessly peculiar they leave alone and even respect. Having always at home been encouraged to be himself, Max the schoolboy had a self-confidence which made him invulnerable. He continued to draw caricatures and began also to write. In his last year at Charterhouse, he printed his first literary effort—a parody of the footnotes of Classical Scholarship of which any adult humorist could be proud. As an undergraduate, he first displayed his talent for hoaxes when he succeeded in sending no less august a personage than Professor Furnivall, the Shakespeare scholar, trotting off to the British Museum to trace down an Elizabethan heraldic device invented by Max himself. Professor Furnivall was not to be his last victim. Bernard Shaw, to mention only one, was to be bewildered:

> Max discovered a volume of photographs of Shaw in youth. Carefully he altered each for the worse; in one amplifying the nose, in another diverting the eyes into a squint. He then had these new versions rephotographed and sent them to various friends in England accompanied by a request to post them back to Shaw along with a letter from some imaginary admirer stating that he had found the enclosed photograph of Mr. Shaw and would so much like him to sign and return it. The friends obeyed. Max was delighted to learn that as one monstrous likeness after another arrived by post, Shaw grew steadily more baffled.

Though his character and tastes were fully formed by the time he was twenty-one, it naturally took Max a little longer to find the style, visual and verbal, in which to express them. But not much longer. His first exercises in wit are modeled on Oscar Wilde's. For example:

> What is your favourite day? Tuesdays make me feel very gentlemanly, Wednesdays bring out my cleverness. . . .
> On Saturdays I am common, have you noticed that?

This was written in 1893, but four years later, in a review of a volume of verses by a Mr. Clement Scott, he has already found his own voice. After quoting a stanza by that unfortunate gentleman containing the lines "You meet me with your beauty unimpaired" and "You sit and laugh at men who loved your hair," Max gets down to work:

> It is possible that a careless reader would imagine that the lines were really addressed to some lady. We prefer to think—indeed, we are sure—that they were addressed to some seaside resort, whose identity is cunningly concealed under the pseudonym of "Violet," lest Cromer or another should wax jealous. Surely it would be rather prosaic to speak of a lady's beauty as being "unimpaired." On the other hand, if we take it that, say, Broadstairs is apostrophised, then "not built over" would be the meaning, and the phrase would be felicitous and pretty. Surely, again, no

lady, worthy of the name, would sit down on a chair and guffaw at men who had loved her hair, even though their proceeding had seemed ridiculous. We are sure that the *h* in "hair" is a conversational sort of *h,* dropped in to hide a sly reference to ozone. A popular seaside resort, moreover, can afford to "laugh" at the defection of a few visitors more or less.

Similarly, while his first published caricatures show the influence of Pellegrini, the "Edwardyssey" series of 1899 could have been drawn by nobody else.

To Max, caricature was an objective art:

When I draw a man, I am concerned simply and solely with the physical aspect of him. I don't bother for one moment about his soul. . . . I see all his salient points exaggerated (points of face, figure, port, gesture and vesture), and all his insignificant points proportionately diminished. . . . In the salient points a man's soul does reveal itself, more or less faintly. . . . Thus if one underline these points, and let the others vanish, one is bound to lay bare the soul.

In literature, on the other hand, his ideal was a subjective one:

True style is essentially a personal matter . . . in fact, not a mere spy-hole to things in general, but a spy-hole to things as they are reflected in the soul of the writer. . . . To express through printed words all the little side-lights of thought and fine shades of meaning that are in him is the task of the modern stylist; and the tricks and formalities which must be gone through in accomplishing that task carry him further and further away from his ordinary manner in colloquy. . . . Modern prose style is further removed from colloquialism than was the prose style of the eighteenth century, for this paradoxical reason: that colloquialism is its model.

This difference between his conceptions of the two arts, together with the fact that he began drawing as a child and started to write only in adolescence, may account for the curious contrast between his working methods in each. For caricatures he had to be in the mood, but when the mood came he drew with great rapidity and ease, almost as if in a trance. Writing, on the other hand, he always found a slow and difficult business, not only when he was faced with a journalistic chore but even when he was writing *con amore.* The initial conception of *Zuleika Dobson,* for example, came to him many years before he succeeded in realizing it.

To mature so early, to be certain of one's identity, tastes, and talents at an age when most people are still floundering around, confers many blessings—a happy, contented life is practically guaranteed—but a price has to be paid for them. Biologists tell us that much of the achievement of our species may be put down to the fact that in comparison with other animals we are so slow in reaching physical maturity, and it would appear that in most fields of human activity—music and mathematics are exceptions—the greatest achievements are attained by those who, emotionally and intellectually, are late developers. The price which Max paid was that after about the year 1910 he became incapable of responding imaginatively to anything happening about him, whether in society or the arts. That he should have felt a nostalgia for the "good old days" is not unusual; anyone who has had the luck to have been born into a home where there existed love and good things to eat feels the same. And Max the man, though a Tory and at times a frightened one, was too intelligent and too just to become a Colonel Blimp:

> Where are all the gentlefolk of the world gone to? Not a sign of them in London (barring in the private houses one went to). Not a sign of them in the train or on the boat or anywhere. Only this rabble of dreadful creatures—who aren't of course dreadful at all, except from the standpoint of a carefully-brought-up person who remembers the days when enjoyment of life was a thing reserved for a few other carefully-brought-up persons.

What is peculiar is that in his thirties Max should as an artist have ceased to be able to transmute his current experiences into art. Another kind of caricaturist might have agreed with him that the notables of the nineties and early nineteen-hundreds were easier to draw:

] 377 [

They walked, and they walked slowly, so you could observe them. There were whiskers without mustaches and mustaches without whiskers. . . . Men wore beards of different shapes and different cuts; they wore their hair in varied styles; and they took much more care about their dress, and there were so many *ways* of dressing.

But another kind of artist would have felt the clean-shaven, uniform, and informal figures of the younger generation as a challenge, and studied them until he had learned how to bring out their comic points.

For many of us, some of our most important "new" experiences are discoveries about the hitherto unknown past. Max's favorite authors in his youth were Thackeray, the early George Meredith, the later Henry James. That he should have found few younger authors to add to his list is less strange than his apparent inability to add any older ones. More seriously, he never learned to see the experiences which did matter to him in any light but that in which he had first seen them. Consequently, if one compares two drawings or two books of his, it is almost impossible, on the evidence of the works themselves, to date them. Despite this lack of development, his work doesn't "date," as one would expect, and as the work of so many of his contemporaries does. If one asks why this should be so, the answer is, I believe, that in him the aesthetic sensibility was never divorced, as it was in many of his colleagues, from the moral feelings. Fashions in what is considered beautiful or interesting are always changing, but the difference between a man of honor and a scoundrel is eternal. Reggie Turner introduced Max into one of his novels under the fictional name Hans Branders, of whom he says:

> There was a strain of cruelty in him, not harshness nor brutality, but cruelty simple and isolated. But there was no malice in him, no pettiness, and he had the kindest of hearts.

What Turner means, I think, is that an artist whose eye immediately detects moral failings in his subjects and whose hand instinctively reveals them is bound to seem cruel. It was not personal animosity which made the drawings of Oscar Wilde and the Prince of Wales so deadly (Wilde, indeed, was his friend); he

simply could not help revealing the moral truth about them both—
that Wilde was a man "whose soul had swooned in sin and revived
vulgar" and that the First Gentleman of Europe was an ineffable
bounder. It is this immediate clarity of insight, free from all malice
or prejudice, which makes Max superior to most caricaturists, even
to Daumier. Even his most devastating portraits never strike one
as unjust; one never feels that for personal or ideological reasons
he had decided to uglify his victim before he looked at him.

While we are on the subject, I wish either Mr. Behrman or
Lord David Cecil had taken advantage of our morally permissive
culture and included among his illustrations a cartoon of Frank
Harris which few persons can have seen but many must be dying
to see:

> During a moment of silence Harris's voice was heard
> booming out. "Unnatural vice!" he was saying, "I know
> nothing of the joys of unnatural vice. You must ask my
> friend Oscar about them. But," he went on, with a reveren-
> tial change of tone, "had Shakespeare asked me, I should
> have had to submit!" Max went home and drew a cartoon
> of Harris, stark naked and with his moustache bristling,
> looking coyly over his shoulder at Shakespeare who shrinks
> back at the alarming prospect. Underneath was written,
> "Had Shakespeare asked . . ."

As in his caricatures, so in his literary judgments. His adverse
criticisms of other writers, whether in table talk or parody, are
directed against their moral defects—the sadism in Kipling, the
caddishness in Wells, Shaw's indifference to individual human lives
—and when he tries to explain his admiration for Henry James, it
is of James as a moralist that he speaks:

> Greater than all my aesthetic delight in the books is my
> moral regard for the author. . . . Despite his resolute self-
> suppression for his "form's" sake, Mr. Henry James, through
> his books, stands out as clearly to me as any preacher I
> have ever seen perched up in a pulpit. And I do not happen
> to have heard any preacher in whom was a moral fervour,
> or one whose outlook on the world seemed to me so fine
> and touching and inspiring, so full of reverence for noble
> things and horror of things ignoble.

Though Max was certainly underestimating his appeal when he said that he had an audience of fifteen hundred, much that he wrote is unlikely now to be widely read. His drama reviews will be read in bulk only by historians of the drama. For the ordinary reader, the only journalism which remains readable after the occasion which caused it has been forgotten is a piece of comic attack. Jerome K. Jerome's play *The Passing of the Third Floor Back* has sunk without trace, but Max's review of it remains afloat; Duse is now a mere name to all but a few elderly fogies, but Max's comment on her acting is remembered by many: "Age cannot wither her nor custom stale her endless uniformity."

A good deal that he wrote took the form of the "pure" essay, written, as Lord David Cecil says, "not to instruct or edify but only to produce aesthetic satisfaction." I do not know why it should be so, but today the "pure" essay is a literary genre to which no reader under sixty can bring himself to attend. We expect an essay to instruct or edify; for aesthetic satisfaction we turn to poetry or fiction.

As a literary critic, Max was wise to confine himself for the most part to literary parodies of the few writers he knew well. Of poetry, as of music, he had no understanding—Henley's "Invictus" was one of his favorite pieces—and both his taste and his reading in fiction were too limited to make him a critic of note. His table-talk criticism is sound enough as far as it goes: he is never mean—though he should have spotted the difference between Virginia Woolf's handling of "the stream of consciousness" and Joyce's—and even in writers whom he finds antipathetic he is always ready to admit their virtues. If his admiration for "Eminent Victorians" now seems excessive, one can understand it: he recognized that Strachey's literary ideal was akin to his own. In noting the authors whom he singles out for praise, I am puzzled by one thing. Had I been Max, there would have been two persons, both living, of whom I should have felt wildly envious—Ronald Firbank and James Thurber. I have searched through the Turner *Letters, Max,* and *Portrait of Max* and have found but one slight reference to Thurber and none to Firbank. Can it have been that he was?

As a parodist, he is probably the finest in English. His only rivals are James and Horace Smith, the authors of *Rejected Ad-*

dresses. Unfortunately, literary parodies can never appeal to more than a limited and highly sophisticated public, for they can be appreciated only by a reader who is intimately acquainted with the authors parodied. Caricature, or visual parody, is much more accessible, since to "get" a caricature it is not necessary to have seen the subject oneself. Thus, while Max's caricatures should delight almost everybody, the only writings of his which are likely to reach a wide public are the stories—*Zuleika Dobson, Seven Men, A Variety of Things.*

Greatly as I admire both the man and his work, I consider Max Beerbohm a dangerous influence—just how dangerous one must perhaps have been brought up in England to know. His attitude both to life and to art, charming enough in him, when taken up by others as a general cultural ideal becomes something deadly, especially for the English, an intelligent but very lazy people, far too easily bored, and persuaded beyond argument that they are the *Herrenvolk.* One may be amused—though not very—that after living in Italy for forty-five years Max still could not speak Italian, but such insularity is not to be imitated. "Good sense about trivialities," he once wrote, "is better than nonsense about things that matter." True enough, but how easily this can lead to the conclusion that anyone who attempts to deal with things that matter must be a bore, that rather than run the risk of talking nonsense one should play it safe and stick to charming trifles.

> How many charming talents have been spoiled by the instilled desire to do "important" work! Some people are born to lift heavy weights. Some are born to juggle with golden balls.

True enough again, one thinks at a first reading; at a second, one notices the insidiousness of the metaphor. In the circus, the juggler is superior to the weight lifter, for juggling is an art and lifting heavy weights primarily a matter of brute strength. Had Max written that some are jugglers, some (shall we say?) lion-tamers, the comparison might have been just. As it is, he slyly suggests that minor artists may look down their noses at major ones and that "important" work may be left to persons of an inferior kennel, like the Russians, the Germans, the Americans, who, poor dears, know no better. The great cultural danger for the English is, to my mind, their tendency to judge the arts by the values appropriate to the conduct of family life. Among brothers and sisters it is becoming to entertain each other with witty remarks, hoaxes, family games and jokes, unbecoming to be solemn, to monopolize the conversation, to talk shop, to create emotional scenes. But no art, major or minor, can be governed by the rules of social amenity. The English have a greater talent than any other people for creating an agreeable family life; that is why it is such a threat to their artistic and intellectual life. If the atmosphere were not so charming, it would be less of a temptation. In postwar Britain, the clothes, accents, and diction of the siblings may have changed, but, so far as I can judge, the suffocating insular coziness is just the same. Suffocating for nine artists out of ten; it so happened that Max was the exceptional tenth man, whose talents were fostered by family life and exactly tailored to its tastes.

Twice in his life—in 1894, with an essay in the first number of *The Yellow Book,* entitled "A Defence of Cosmetics," which caused *Punch* to call him a popinjay, and in 1923, when his cartoons of the Royal Family caused one newspaper to conclude that their author must be "either a shameless bounder or a stealthy Bolshevist"—he succeeded in shocking Philistia. (Characteristically, when he heard the cartoons had caused offense, he withdrew them from exhibition.) But in literary and artistic circles, from the start of his career until his death, he was a sacred cow. Never once, so far as I know, was he attacked by any critic worth listening to, and this is not a healthy sign. The only person who seems to have realized the danger was Reggie Turner, who wrote to Max in 1911:

> A caricaturist such as you, a satirist of the first and purest water, is not properly treated when people say that "his work can never give offence." "Amiability" is not the most outstanding quality in your work, any more than "gentleness" was in Napoleon's. And I see signs now that "the old country" is waking up to the danger of having you about. I rejoice, I rejoice, I rejoice.

Turner's rejoicing proved premature, and the man who had poured scorn on John Bull, mocked at Queen Victoria's prose, savaged Edward VII, and written a double ballade about George V and Queen Mary with its alternating refrain:

> King   Queen
> The   is duller than the
> Queen   King

ended up with a knighthood and a grave in St. Paul's Cathedral.

Of course, Max was not, or only a teensy bit, to blame for this. His charm was, and still is, irresistible, and, which is unlike many charmers, there was nothing phony about him, because, as Chesterton perceived, he did not "indulge in the base idolatry of believing in himself." He had three ambitions in life: "to make good use of such little talent as I had, to lead a pleasant life, to pass muster." He achieved them all. How many of us will be able to say as much?

WALTER DE LA MARE

As an introduction to the best of all anthologies for the young, *Come Hither,* Mr. de la Mare wrote a parable. A schoolboy named Simon has heard from his mother about a wonderful place of "trees, waters, green pastures, rare birds and flowers" called East Dene. Setting out one morning to look for it, he comes to an old stone house in a hollow called Thrae, and makes the acquaintance of its owner, Miss Taroone. When he asks her about East Dene, she gives him a strange look but does not answer. She tells him, however, that Thrae is not her only house, and speaks of Sure Vine "as a family mansion, very ancient and magnificent." She also tells him about a great traveler, Mr. Nahum.

> I could not at first make head or tail of Mr. Nahum. Even now I am uncertain whether he was Miss Taroone's brother or her nephew or a cousin many times removed; or whether perhaps she was really and truly Mrs. Taroone and he her only son; or she still Miss Taroone and he an adopted one. I am not sure whether she had much love for him, though she appeared to speak of him with pride. What I do know is that Miss Taroone had nurtured him from his cradle and had taught him all the knowledge that was not already his by right of birth. . . . Strangely enough, by the looks on her face and the tones of her voice, Mr. Taroone was inclined

] 384 [

to mock a little at Mr. Nahum because of his restlessness.
She didn't seem to approve of his leaving her so much—
though she herself had come from Sure Vine.

The names are easy to translate and the general drift of the parable is clear. Because of his peculiar position as a traveler in search of
a joy which he has yet to find and can only imagine in terms of an
innocent happiness which is no longer his, every man, whether
as a writer or a reader of poetry, demands two things which,
though not absolutely incompatible with each other, are not easy
to reconcile completely. On the one hand, we want a poem to be a
beautiful object, a verbal Garden of Eden which, by its formal
perfection, keeps alive in us the hope that there exists a state of
joy without evil or suffering which it can and should be our
destiny to attain. At the same time, we look to a poem for some
kind of illumination about our present wandering condition, since,
without self-insight and knowledge of the world, we must err
blindly with little chance of realizing our hope. We expect a poem
to tell us some home truth, however minor, and, as we know, most
home truths are neither pretty nor pleasant. One might say that,
in every poet, there dwells an Ariel, who sings, and a Prospero,
who comprehends, but in any particular poem, sometimes even in
the whole work of a particular poet, one of the partners plays a
greater role than the other. Thus Campion, one of de la Mare's
favorite poets, is an example of an Ariel-dominated poet in whose
work verbal beauty is *almost* everything, and what is said matters
very little. In Wordsworth's *The Prelude,* on the other hand,
Prospero dominates and Ariel contributes very little; it might
almost have been written in prose.

Though the role of Prospero in de la Mare's poetry is much
greater than one may realize on a first reading, it would not be
unfair, I think, to call him an Ariel-dominated poet. Certainly, his
most obvious virtues, those which no reader can fail to see
immediately, are verbal and formal, the delicacy of his metrical
fingering and the graceful architecture of his stanzas. Neither
in his technique nor his sensibility, does he show any trace of
influences other than English, either continental, like Eliot and
Pound, or Classical, like Bridges. The poets from whom he seems
to have learned most are the Elizabethan songwriters, Christina

Rossetti and, I would rashly guess, Thomas Hardy. Like Christina Rossetti, he is a master of trisyllabic substitution and foot inversion; the reader's ear is continually excited by rhythmical variations without ever losing a sense of the underlying pattern. In the predominantly anapaestic movement of the following stanza, for example, how surprising and yet convincing is the sudden shift to a trochaic movement in the fifth line and to a spondaic in the sixth.

> Wicket out into the dark
>   That swings but one way;
> Infinite hush in an ocean of silence
>   Aeons away—
> *Thou* forsaken!—even thou!—
>   The dread good-bye;
> The abandoned, the thronged, the watched, the unshared—
>   Awaiting me—I!

Like Hardy, he is a great inventor of stanzas and in command of every effect which can be obtained from contrasts between lines of different lengths, lines with masculine endings and lines with feminine endings, rhymed and unrhymed lines.

> 'Tis strange to see young children
>   In such a wintry house;
> Like rabbits on the frozen snow
>   Their tell-tale foot-prints go;
> Their laughter rings like timbrels
> 'Neath evening ominous.

* * *

> He drew each pure heart with his skill;
>   With his beauty,
>   And his azure,
>   And his topaz,
>   Gold for pleasure,
> And his locks wet with the dew of April.

*   *   *

Once gay, now sad; remote—and dear;
Why turn away in doubt and fear?
I search again your grieved self-pitying face;
Kindness sits clouded there. But, love? No, not a trace.

Many poets have some idiosyncrasy or tic of style which can
madden the reader if he finds their work basically unsympathetic,
but which, if he likes it, becomes endearing like the foibles of an
old friend. Hardy's fondness for compound and Latinate words is
one example, de la Mare's habit of subject-verb inversion another

> Leans now the fair willow, dreaming
> Amid her locks of green.

In his later work such inversions become much rarer. One can
observe also a change in his diction. Though this continues to
come from what one might call the "beautiful" end of the verbal
spectrum—he never, like Yeats and Eliot, uses a coarse or brutal
word, and seldom a slang colloquialism—a chronological study of
his poems shows a steady, patient and successful endeavor to
eliminate the overly arty diction which was a vice of his Pre-
Raphaelite forebears, and to develop a style which, without ceasing
to be lyrical, has the directness of ordinary speech. What a distance there is, for example, between these two extracts, one from
an early poem, one from a late.

> Slowly, silently, now the moon
> Walks the night in her silver shoon;
> This way, and that, she peers, and sees
> Silver fruit upon silver trees;
> One by one the casements catch
> Her beams beneath the silvery thatch;

*   *   *

What, do you suppose, we're in this world for, sweet heart?
What—in this haunted, crazy, beautiful cage—

Keeps so many, like ourselves, poor pining human creatures,
As if from some assured, yet golden heritage?
Keeps us lamenting beneath all our happy laughter,
Silence, dreams, hope for what may *not* come after,
While life wastes and withers, as it has for mortals,
    Age on to age, on to age.

His late long poem, *Winged Chariot,* is a surprising performance. He still writes as a lyric poet, not as an epic or dramatic,
and it is better read, perhaps, like *In Memoriam,* as a series of
lyrics with a meter and theme in common, but readers who are
only familiar with his early poetry will find something they would
never have predicted, a talent for metaphysical wit.

The dwindling candle with her pensive light
Metes out the leaden watches of the night.
And, in that service, from herself takes flight.

*   *   *

Fate was appalled. Her See-Saw would not stir.
Man sat dead-centre and grimaced at her.
Her prizes? None could shine where none could err;
So every dunce was a philosopher.

*   *   *

Cowed by the spectre for which 'no man waits',
Obsequious hirelings of the witless Fates,
Time pins down ev'n Dictators to their 'dates'.

De la Mare wrote many poems with an audience of children
specifically in mind, and, in his collected works, these have been
published in a volume by themselves. This has a practical con-
venience, but it must never be forgotten that, while there are some
good poems which are only for adults, because they presuppose
adult experience in their readers, there are no good poems which
are only for children. Human beings are blessed with the power
to remember; consequently, to grow old means for us not to
discard but to accumulate; in every old man, there still lives a

child, an adolescent, a young man and a middle-aged one. It is commonly believed that children are, by nature, more imaginative than adults, but this is questionable. It is probably the case only in cultures like our own which put a higher social and economic value upon practical and abstract thinking than upon wonder and images; in a culture which put a high value on imagination and a low one on logic, children might well appear to be more rational than adults, for a child is not, by nature, more *anything*. In all cultures, however, there is one constant difference between children and adults, namely, that, for the former, learning their native tongue is itself one of the most important experiences in their lives, while, for the latter, language has become an instrument for interpreting and communicating experience; to recapture the sense of language as experience, an adult has to visit a foreign country.

What the child, and the child-in-the-adult, most enjoys in poetry, therefore, is the manipulation of language for its own sake, the sound and rhythm of words. There is a deplorable tendency in the United States, which I hope and pray has not spread to the United Kingdom, to think that books for children should use a very limited vocabulary, and that verses for them should be written in the simplest and most obvious meters. This is utter nonsense. The surest sign that a child has a feeling for language is that he talks like an affected adult and always uses a polysyllabic word when a monosyllabic one would do.

As a revelation of the wonders of the English Language, de la Mare's poems for children are unrivaled. (The only ones which do not seem to me quite to come off are those in which he tries to be humorous. A gift, like Hilaire Belloc's for the comic-satiric is not his; he lacks, perhaps, both the worldliness and the cruelty which the genre calls for.) They include what, for the adult, are among his greatest "pure" lyrics, e.g., *Old Shellover* and *The Song of the Mad Prince,* and their rhythms are as subtle as they are varied. Like all good poems, of course, they do more than train the ear. They also teach sensory attention and courage. Unlike a lot of second-rate verse for children, de la Mare's descriptions of birds, beasts, and natural phenomena are always sharp and accurate, and he never prettifies experience or attempts to conceal from the young that terror and nightmare are as essential characteristics of human existence as love and sweet dreams. There is another respect in which, as all writers of good books for them know, children differ from grown-ups; they have a far greater tolerance for didactic instruction, whether in facts or morals. As Chesterton observed:

> The child does not know that men are not only bad from good motives, but also often good from bad motives. Therefore the child has a hearty, unspoiled, and unsatiable appetite for mere morality, for the mere difference between a good little girl and a bad little girl.

Without ever being tiresome, de la Mare is not afraid to instruct the young. What could be more practically useful than his mnemonic rhyme *Stars,* or more educative, morally as well as musically, than *Hi!*?

> Hi! handsome hunting man
> Fire your little gun.
> Bang! Now the animal
> Is dead and dumb and done.
> Nevermore to peep again, creep again, leap again,
> Eat or sleep or drink again. Oh, what fun!

In considering the work of any poet, it is always easier and safer to discuss the role of Ariel than that of Prospero. There is only one Ariel to a language, but there are as many Prosperos as there are poets. We can describe what one poet does with the language and compare it with what another poet has done, but we cannot compare the perspective on life of any poet with that of any other because each is unique. That is why poets themselves hate being asked what their poems "mean" because, in order to answer such a question, they would have to know themselves which, as Thoreau said, is as impossible as seeing oneself from the back without turning one's head. Every poet will second de la Mare's statement in his prefatory note to *O Lovely England.*

> What a writer has to say *about* his "poems" and their subterranean waters, is often dangerous, and may be even scientifically inaccurate. Verbal and metrical craftsmanship is another matter. . . .

But, as readers of poetry, we can no more help asking, "What is it about this poem, aside from its formal beauties or defects, which makes it sympathetic or unsympathetic to me?", than we can help trying to analyze the qualities of a fellow human being to whom, positively or negatively, we respond. What we "see" in a person or a poem may be quite wrong and is certainly only part of the truth but, if we talk about either, we can only say what we see.

Though all poetry is, ultimately, about human nature, many poems do not look at man directly, but at what he is not, the non-human part of creation which, by convention, we call "Nature" (though it may also contain human artifacts). In the work of certain poets, and de la Mare is one of them, the landscape speaks. His personal landscape is derived from two sources. Firstly, there is the countryside of pre-industrial England, so beautiful in an unspectacular way, and so kindly in climate. (Perhaps, having never suffered from bronchitis, I am biased.) The setting of one poem is a railway-junction, in another the lyric "I" rides a bus, there are a few references to water-mills, but otherwise there is no machinery and no modern building.

As the work of some of the Georgian poets bears witness, the danger of the English landscape as a poetic ingredient is that its gentleness can tempt those who love it into writing genteely. De la Mare was protected from this, firstly by his conviction that what our senses perceive of the world about us is not all there is to know, and, secondly, by his sense of the powers of evil. This does not mean that he is a Buddhist who regards the sensory world as illusion, or that he would call what we normally are blind to *super-natural*. His view, I take it, is that our eyes and ears do not lie to us, but do not, perhaps cannot, tell us the whole truth, and that those who deny this, end up by actually narrowing their vision.

> What is called realism is usually a record of life at a low
> pitch and ebb viewed in the sunless light of day—so often
> a drab waste of gray and white, and an east wind blowing.

What we would see, if our senses and imagination were keener, might be more beautiful than anything we have known.

> It seemed to be a house which might at any moment vanish
> before your eyes, showing itself to be but the outer shell or

hiding place of an abode still more enchanting. . . . If you ever sat and watched a Transformation Scene in a pantomime, did you suppose, just before the harlequin slapped with his wand on what looked like a plain brick-and-mortar wall, that it would instantly after dissolve into a radiant coloured scene of trees and fountains and hidden beings— growing lovelier in their own showing as the splendour spread and their haunts were revealed? Well, so at times I used to feel in Thrae.

On the other hand, the most beautiful object might turn out to be hiding something neither beautiful nor friendly.

> Masked by that brilliant weed's deceitful green,
> No glint of the dark water can be seen
> Which, festering, slumbers, with this scum for screen.
> It is as though a face, as false as fair,
> Dared not, by smiling, show the evil there.

*　*　*

> Darkness had fallen. I opened the door:
> And lo, a stranger in the empty room—
> A marvel of moonlight upon wall and floor. . . .
> The quiet of mercy? Or the hush of doom?

Nor, whatever it might turn out to be, can we be certain that, were we mortals to be confronted by the truth, we could endure it.

> Might that secret, if divulged, all we value most bewray!
> > Make a dream of our real,
> > A night of our day. . . .

The other element, more romantic and more disturbing, in the de la Mare landscape is partly derived from Grimm's Maerchen and similar folk-tales, and partly from dreams.

> Still and blanched and cold and lone
> > The icy hills far off from me
> With frosty ulys overgrown
> > Stand in their sculptured secrecy.

No path of theirs the chamois fleet
　Treads with a nostril to the wind;
O'er their ice-marbled glaciers beat
　No wings of eagles to my mind.

Again, the overestimation of dreams and the subjective life shown by some of the lesser Romantic poets, can become boring, for most people are even less original in their dreaming than in their waking life; their dreams are more monotonous than their thoughts and oddly enough, more literary. Fortunately, de la Mare, as those who have read *Behold This Dreamer* will have learned, was one of those uncommon persons whose dreams are really original. Like Blake, he possessed the rare gift of having visions while awake. (Mescaline and lysergic acid can, it now seems, confer it on us dullards.) He tells, for instance, how once, after dreaming that the Flora of Primavera herself was at that moment passing beneath his bedroom window, he woke up, went to the window, and there, sure enough, she was in the street.

> She sat, uplifted, ethereally lovely, surrounded by her attendant nymphs and *amorini,* and crowned and wreathed with flowers. It was with ropes of flowers, also, that her nymphs were drawing slowly on her low flat Car on its wide clumsy wooden wheels, like gigantic cotton-reels.

"Every artist," said Santayana, "is a moralist though he needn't preach," and de la Mare is one who doesn't. His poems are neither satirical nor occasional; indeed, I cannot recall coming across in his work a single Proper Name, whether of a person or a place, which one could identify as a real historical name. Nor, though he is a lyric, not a dramatic, poet, are his poems "personal" in the sense of being self-confessions; the *I* in them is never identical with the Mr. de la Mare one might have met at dinner, and none are of the kind which excite the curiosity of a biographer. Nevertheless, implicit in all his poetry are certain notions of what constitutes the Good Life. Goodness, they seem to say, is rooted in wonder, awe, and reverence for the beauty and strangeness of creation. Wonder itself is not goodness—de la Mare is not an aesthete— but it is the only, or the most favorable, soil in which goodness can grow. Those who lose the capacity for wonder may become clever but not intelligent, they may lead moral lives themselves, but they will become insensitive and moralistic towards others. A sense of wonder is not something we have to learn, for we are born with it; unfortunately, we are also born with an aggressive lust for power which finds its satisfaction in the enslavement and destruction of others. We are, or in the course of our history we have become, predatory animals like the mousing cat and the spotted flycatcher. This lust for power, which, if we surrender completely to it, can turn us into monsters like Seaton's Aunt, is immanent in every child.

> Lovely as Eros, and half-naked too,
> He heaped dried beach-drift, kindled it, and, lo!
> A furious furnace roared, the sea-winds blew . . .
> Vengeance divine! And death to every foe!
> Young god! and not ev'n Nature eyed askance
> The fire-doomed Empire of a myriad ants.

It is only with the help of wonder, then, that we can develop a virtue which we are certainly not born with, compassion, not to be confused with its conceit-created counterfeit, pity. Only from wonder, too, can we learn a style of behavior and speech which is no less precious in art than in life; for want of a better word we call it good-manners or breeding, though it has little to do with ancestry, school or income. To be well-bred means to have respect for the solitude of others, whether they be mere acquaintances or, and this is much more difficult, persons we love; to be ill-bred is to importune attention and intimacy, to come too close, to ask indiscreet questions and make indiscreet revelations, to lecture, to bore.

Making a selection from the work of any poet one admires is a job which cannot be done satisfactorily because one is always conscious that everything he wrote, even the second best, should be read. De la Mare has, in my opinion, been very shabbily treated by anthologists; in their selections, most have been content to copy each other, and few have included poems he wrote after 1920. This is a gross injustice to a poet who continued to mature, both in technique and wisdom, till the day of his death.

G. K. CHESTERTON'S
NON-FICTIONAL PROSE

I have always enjoyed Chesterton's poetry and fiction, but I must admit that, until I started work on a selection for a publisher, it was many years since I had read any of his non-fictional prose.

The reasons for my neglect were, I think, two. Firstly, his reputation as an anti-Semite. Though he denied the charge and did, certainly, denounce Hitler's persecution, he cannot, I fear, be completely exonerated.

> I said that a particular kind of Jew tended to be a tyrant and another particular kind of Jew tended to be a traitor. I say it again. Patent facts of this kind are permitted in the criticism of any other nation on the planet: it is not counted illiberal to say that a certain kind of Frenchman tends to be sensual. . . . I cannot see why the tyrants should not be called tyrants and the traitors traitors merely because they happen to be members of a race persecuted for other reasons and on other occasions.

The disingenuousness of this argument is revealed by the quiet shift from the term *nation* to the term *race*. It is always permissible to criticize a nation (including Israel), a religion (including Orthodox Judaism), or a culture, because these are the creations of human thought and will: a nation, a religion, a culture can always reform themselves, if they so choose. A man's ethnic heritage, on the other hand, is not in his power to alter. If it were true, and there is no evidence whatsoever to suppose that it is, that certain moral defects or virtues are racially inherited, they could not become the subject for moral judgment by others. That Chesterton should have spoken of the Jews as a race is particularly odd, since few writers of his generation denounced with greater contempt racial theories about Nordics, Anglo-Saxons, Celts, etc. I myself am inclined to put most of the blame on the influence of his brother and of Hilaire Belloc, and on the pernicious influence, both upon their generation and upon the succeeding generation of Eliot and Pound, exerted by the *Action Française* Movement. Be that as it may, it remains a regrettable blemish upon the writings of a man who was, according to the universal testimony of all who met him, an extraordinarily "decent" human being, astonishingly generous of mind and warm of heart.

My second reason for neglecting Chesterton was that I imagined him to be what he himself claimed, just a "Jolly Journalist," a writer of weekly essays on "amusing" themes, such as *What I found in my Pockets, On Lying in Bed, The Advantage of having one Leg, A Piece of Chalk, The Glory of Grey, Cheese* and so forth.

In his generation, the Essay as a form of *belles-lettres* was still popular: in addition to Chesterton himself, there were a number of writers, Max Beerbohm, E. V. Lucas, Robert Lynd, for example, whose literary reputations rested largely upon their achievements in this genre. Today tastes have changed. We can appreciate a review or a critical essay devoted to a particular book or author, we can enjoy a discussion of a specific philosophical problem or political event, but we can no longer derive any pleasure from the kind of essay which is a fantasia upon whatever chance thoughts may come into the essayist's head.

My objection to the prose fantasia is the same as my objection to "free" verse (to which Chesterton also objected), namely, that, while excellent examples of both exist, they are the exception not the rule. All too often the result of the absence of any rules and restrictions, of a meter to which the poet must conform, of a definite subject to which the essayist must stick, is a repetitious and self-indulgent "show-off" of the writer's personality and stylistic mannerisms.

Chesterton's insistence upon the treadmill of weekly journalism after it ceased to be financially necessary seems to have puzzled his friends as much as it puzzles me. Thus E. C. Bentley writes:

> To live in this way was his deliberate choice. There can be no doubt of that, for it was a hard life, and a much easier one lay nearby to his hand. As a writer of books, as a poet, he had an assured position, and an inexhaustible fund of ideas: the friends who desired him to make the most of his position were many. But G. K. Chesterton preferred the existence of a regular contributor to the Press, bound by iron rules as to space and time. Getting his copy to the office before it was too late was often a struggle. Having to think of a dead-line at all was always an inconvenience.

Whatever Chesterton's reasons and motives for his choice, I am quite certain it was a mistake. "A journalist," said Karl Kraus, "is stimulated by a dead-line: he writes worse if he has time." If this is correct, then Chesterton was not, by nature, a journalist. His best thinking and best writing are to be found, not in his short weekly essays, but in his full-length books where he could take as much time and space as he pleased. (In fact, in my selection, I took very little from his volumes of collected essays.) Oddly enough, since he so detested them, Chesterton inherited from the aesthetes of the eighties and nineties the conviction that a writer should be continuously "bright" and epigrammatic. When he is really enthralled by a subject he is brilliant, without any doubt one of the finest aphorists in English literature, but, when his imagination is not fully held he can write an exasperating parody of himself, and this is most likely to happen when he has a dead-line to meet.

It is always difficult for a man as he grows older to "keep up" with the times, to understand what the younger generation is thinking and writing well enough to criticize it intelligently; for an overworked journalist like Chesterton it is quite impossible, since he simply does not have the time to read any new book carefully enough.

He was, for example, certainly intelligent enough and, judging by his criticisms of contemporary anthropology, equipped enough, to have written a serious critical study of Freud, had he taken the time and trouble to read him properly: his few flip remarks about dreams and psycho-analysis are proof that he did not.

Chesterton's non-fictional prose has three concerns, literature, politics and religion.

Our day has seen the emergence of two kinds of literary critic, the documentor and the cryptologist. The former with meticulous accuracy collects and publishes every unearthable fact about an author's life, from his love-letters to his dinner invitations and laundry bills, on the assumption that any fact, however trivial, about the man may throw light upon his writings. The latter approaches his work as if it were an anonymous and immensely difficult text, written in a private language which the ordinary reader cannot hope to understand until it is deciphered for him by experts. Both such critics will no doubt dismiss Chesterton's literary criticism as out-of-date, inaccurate and superficial, but if one were to ask any living novelist or poet which kind of critic he would personally prefer to write about his work, I have no doubt as to the answer. Every writer knows that certain events in his life, most of them in childhood, have been of decisive importance in forming his personal imaginative world, the kinds of things he likes to think about, the qualities in human beings he particularly admires or detests. He also knows that many things which are of great importance to him as a man, are irrelevant to his imagination. In the case of a love-poem, for example, no light is thrown upon either its content or its style by discovering the identity of the poet's beloved.

This Chesterton understands. He thought, for example, that certain aspects of Dickens' novels are better understood if we remember that, as a child, Dickens was expected to put on public performances to amuse his father, so he informs us of this fact. On the other hand, he thought that we shall not understand the novels any better if we learn all the details about the failure of Dickens' marriage, so he omits them. In both cases, surely, he is right.

Again, while some writers are more "difficult" than others and cannot therefore hope to reach a very wide audience, no writer thinks he needs decoding in order to be understood. On the other hand, nearly every writer who has achieved some reputation complains of being misunderstood both by the critics and the public, because they come to his work with preconceived notions of what they are going to find in it. His admirers praise him and his detractors blame him for what, to him, seem imaginary reasons. The kind of critic an author hopes for is someone who will dispell these preconceived notions so that his readers may come to his writings with fresh eyes.

At this task of clearing the air, Chesterton was unusually efficient. It is popularly believed that a man who is in earnest about something speaks earnestly and that a man who keeps making jokes is not in earnest. The belief is not ill-founded since, more often than not, this is true. But there are exceptions and, as Chesterton pointed out, Bernard Shaw was one. The public misunderstood Shaw and thought him just a clown when, in fact, he was above all things a deadly serious preacher. In the case of Browning, Chesterton shows that many of his admirers had misunderstood him by reading into his obscurer passages intellectual profundities when in fact the poet was simply indulging his love of the grotesque. Again, he shows us that Stevenson's defect as a narrator was not, as it had become conventional to say, an over-ornate style but an over-ascetic one, a refusal to tell the reader anything about a character that was not absolutely essential. As a rule, it is journalism and literary gossip that is responsible for such misunderstandings; occasionally, though, it can be the author himself. Kipling would certainly have described himself as a patriotic Englishman who admired above all else the military virtues. In an extremely funny essay, Chesterton convincingly demonstrated that Kipling was really a cosmopolitan with no local roots, and he quotes in proof Kipling's own words:

> If England were what England seems,
> How soon we'd chuck her, but She ain't.

A patriot loves a country because, for better or worse, it is his. Kipling is only prepared to love England so long as England is a Great Power. As for Kipling's militarism, Chesterton says:

> Kipling's subject is not that valour which properly belongs
> to war, but that interdependence and efficiency which be-
> longs quite as much to engineers, or sailors, or mules, or
> railway engines. . . . The real poetry, the "true romance"
> which Mr. Kipling has taught is the romance of the division
> of labour and the discipline of all the trades. He sings the
> arts of peace much more accurately than the arts of war.

Chesterton's literary criticism abounds in such observations which,
once they have been made, seem so obviously true than one cannot
understand why one had not seen them for oneself. It now seems
obvious to us all that Shaw, the socialist, was in no sense a democrat but was a great republican; that there are two kinds of
democrat, the man who, like Scott, sees the dignity of all men, and
the man who, like Dickens, sees that all men are equally interesting and varied; that Milton was really an aesthete whose greatness
"does not depend upon moral earnestness or upon anything con-
nected with morality, but upon style alone, a style rather unusually
separated from its substance"; that the Elizabethan Age, however
brilliant, was not "spacious," but in literature an age of conceits, in
politics an age of conspiracies. But Chesterton was the first critic
to see these things. As a literary critic, therefore, I rank him very
high.

For various reasons I selected very little from his writings on
historical and political subjects. Chesterton was not himself an
historian, but he had both the gift and the position to make known
to the general public the views of historians, like Belloc, who were
challenging the Whig version of English History and the humanists' version of cultural history. It must be difficult for anyone
under forty to realize how taken for granted both of these were,
even when I was a boy. Our school textbooks taught us that, once
the papist-inclined and would-be tyrants, the Stuarts, had been got
rid of, and the Protestant Succession assured, the road to Freedom,
Democracy and Progress lay wide open; they also taught us that
the civilization which had ended with the fall of the Roman Empire was re-born in the sixteenth century, between which dates lay
twelve centuries of barbarism, superstition and fanaticism. If today
every informed person knows both accounts to be untrue, that
the political result of the Glorious Revolution of 1688 was to hand

over the government of the country to a small group of plutocrats, a state of affairs which certainly persisted until 1914, perhaps even until 1939, and that, whatever the Renaissance and the Reformation might signify, it was not a revolt of reason against fanaticism —on the contrary, it might be more fairly described as a revolt against the over-cultivation of logic by the late Middle Ages— Chesterton is not the least among those persons who are responsible for this change of view. The literary problem about any controversial writing is that, once it has won its battle, its interest to the average reader is apt to decline. Controversy always involves polemical exaggeration and it is this of which, once we have forgotten the exaggerations of the other side, we shall be most aware and critical. Thus, Chesterton's insistence, necessary at the time, upon all that was good in the twelfth century, his glossing over of all that was bad, seems today a romantic day-dream. Similarly, one is unconvinced by Belloc's thesis in *The Servile State,* that if, when the monasteries were dissolved, the Crown had taken their revenues instead of allowing them to fall into the hands of a few of its subjects, the Crown would have used its power, not only to keep these few in order, but also for the benefit of the common people. The history of countries like France where the Crown remained stronger than the nobility gives no warrant for such optimism. Absolute monarchs who are anxious to win glory are much more likely to waste the substance of their country in wars of conquest than plutocrats who are only interested in making money.

Chesterton's negative criticisms of modern society, his distrust of bigness, big business, big shops, his alarm at the consequences of undirected and uncontrolled technological development, are even more valid today than in his own. His positive political beliefs, that a good society would be a society of small property-owners, most of them living on the land, attractive as they sound, seem to me open to the same objection that he brings against the political ideas of the Americans and the French in the eighteenth century: "Theirs was a great ideal; but no modern state is small enough to achieve anything so great." In the twentieth century, the England he wanted would pre-suppose the strictest control of the birth-rate, a policy which both his temperament and his religion forbade him to recommend.

On the subject of international politics, Chesterton was, to put it mildly, unreliable. He seems to have believed that, in political life, there is a direct relation between Faith and Morals: a Catholic State, holding the true faith, will behave better politically than a Protestant State. France, Austria, Poland were to be trusted: Prussia was not. It so happened that, in his early manhood, the greatest threat to world peace lay, as he believed, in Prussian militarism. After its defeat in 1918, he continued to cling to his old belief so that, when Hitler came to power in 1933, he misread this as a Prussian phenomenon. In fact, aside from the economic conditions which enabled it to succeed, the National Socialist Movement was essentially the revenge of Catholic Bavaria and Austria for their previous subordination to Protestant Bismarckian Prussia. It was not an accident that Hitler was a lapsed Catholic. The nationalism of the German-speaking minority in the Hapsburg Empire had always been racist, and the hot-bed of anti-Semitism was Vienna not Berlin. Hitler himself hated the Prussian Junkers and was planning, if he won the war, to liquidate them all.

Chesterton was brought up a Unitarian, became an Anglican and finally, in 1922, was converted to Roman Catholicism. Today, reading such a book as *Heretics,* published in 1905, one is surprised that he was not converted earlier.

If his criticisms of Protestantism are not very interesting, this is not his fault. It was a period when Protestant theology (and, perhaps, Catholic too) was at a low ebb, Kierkegaard had not been re-discovered and Karl Barth had not yet been translated. Small fry like Dean Inge and the ineffable Bishop Barnes were too easy game for a mind of his caliber. Where he is at his best is in exposing the hidden dogmas of anthropologists, psychologists and their ilk who claim to be purely objective and "scientific." Nobody has written more intelligently and sympathetically about mythology or polytheism.

Critical Judgment and Personal Taste are different kinds of evaluation which always overlap but seldom coincide exactly. On the whole and in the long run, Critical Judgment is a public matter; we agree as to what we consider artistic virtues and artistic defects. Our personal tastes, however, differ. For each of us, there are writers whom we enjoy reading, despite their defects, and others who, for all their virtues, give us little pleasure. In order for us to find a writer "sympathetic," there must be some kinship between his imaginative preferences and our own. As Chesterton wrote:

> There is at the back of every artist's mind something like a pattern or a type of architecture. The original quality in any man of imagination is imagery. It is a thing like the landscape of his dreams; the sort of world he would wish to make or in which he would wish to wander; the strange flora and fauna of his own secret planet; the sort of thing he likes to think about.

This is equally true of every reader's mind. Our personal patterns, too, unlike our scale of critical values, which we need much time and experience to arrive at, are formed quite early in life, probably before the age of ten. In "The Ethics of Elfland" Chesterton tells us how his own pattern was derived from fairy-stories. If I can always enjoy reading him, even at his silliest, I am sure the reason is that many elements in my own pattern are derived from the same source. (There is one gulf between us: Chesterton had no feeling for or understanding of music.) There are, I know, because I have met them, persons to whom Grimm and Andersen mean little or nothing: Chesterton will not be for them.

LAME SHADOWS

Anyone who offers a fresh translation of a prose work—poetry is another matter—is in duty bound to justify his undertaking by explaining why he thinks that earlier versions are unsatisfactory, a task which can only be congenial to the malicious. Dr. Luke has felt, quite rightly, obliged to cite some of the errors made by Mrs. Lowe-Porter, and anybody who knows German will agree with him that many of these are serious. But he does so with obvious reluctance and concludes by paying her a just tribute.

> Her task, as the exclusive translator of [Mann's] entire work, was, of course, Herculean, and her mistakes were probably as much due to understandable haste as to an inadequate knowledge of German. Her achievement deserves credit for its sheer volume, and it would be churlish to deny that her renderings are often by no means infelicitous. My own method in retranslating these six stories was to avoid consulting the existing versions of them until I had at least decided on my first draft for a given sentence or paragraph. The corresponding passage in Mrs. Lowe-Porter would then occasionally suggest second thoughts.

Dr. Luke had already demonstrated his extraordinary gifts as a translator in his versions of three *Novellen* by Adalbert Stifter, an author who is probably more difficult to "english" than Thomas Mann. Of his latest offering, I can only say that I cannot imagine anybody thinking the job must be done a third time. His brilliant introduction, too, puts a reviewer in an awkward spot: what on earth is he to say about these six stories which Dr. Luke has not already said better?

Five of them are variations on the same theme, the incompatibility of "Life," that is to say, unreflective vitality, innocence, happiness, a "normal" existence, with alienating self-consciousness. The sixth, *"Gladius Dei,"* deals with the difference between healthy and decadent art.

In all of them, the chief character feels himself, with a mixture of pride and shame, to be an Outsider. In "The Joker" and "Tristan," he is a contemptible dilettante who imagines that a refined sensibility gives him the right to think of himself as "artistic," though he never gets down to fabricating a satisfactory art object. Before "Tonio Kröger" ends, however, its hero has justified his claim by producing good work. In the farcical and cruel "The Road to the Churchyard," he is simply a drunken failure, in "Little Herr Friedemann," the first written of the stories, a cripple.

This story does not, in my opinion, quite come off. Mann seems to be using the feeling of isolation felt by a cripple as a symbol for that felt by an artist. But cripples and artists both exist in the world and their reasons for feeling isolated are quite different. The cripple's physical deformity is a visible fact, patent to all. He knows this, and is therefore absolutely certain that he can never hope to win the love of a young, beautiful, and "normal" girl. At the age of sixteen, Herr Friedemann, after watching a flirtation between two of his contemporaries, realizes this:

> "Very well," he said to himself, "that is over. I will never again concern myself with such things. To the others they mean joy and happiness, but to me they can only bring grief and suffering. I am done with it all. It is finished for me. Never again."

That he should fail to keep his resolution and fall madly in love with Frau von Rinnlingen is not surprising, but I find it incredible that he should have openly declared his passion. What could he possibly have expected to happen except what did happen—to be rejected with scorn and laughter? An artist's problems, on the other hand, are private to himself unless he chooses to disclose them. He may be, for example, by temperament incapable of falling in love or of fidelity, but if he does fall in love and is reasonably personable to look at, he stands a perfectly good chance of marrying the girl he loves: and a number have.

If I call these stories "dated," I do not mean that they are out-of-date, only that, like most works of art, they could only have been produced at a particular period in social and cultural history. The notion of the alienated artist is a phenomenon of the second half of the nineteenth century. In earlier times we do not find it and, in our own, alienation has become almost a universal problem. The causes for it were, I think, three. Firstly, after the disappearance of patronage, artists ceased to have a professional social status. Individual artists might become famous public figures but, collectively, they ceased to have status in the way that doctors, lawyers, businessmen, farmers, etc., have, whether famous or obscure, successful or unsuccessful.

Secondly, European society in the nineteenth century and, indeed, until the First World War, was still a class-stratified society, in which almost everybody was born into an identifiable "station" and would spend his life in it. (It is to be noticed what a pride Mann's heroes take in their upper bourgeois background, and their feelings of guilt at having chosen "art" instead of going into Father's business.) The artist, that is to say, was a special case. Earlier, this had not been so. In an oral culture, a poet has a social importance irrespective of the aesthetic merit of his work, as the man who makes immortal the great deeds of the past; in a polytheistic culture, as the recounter of its myths, he is a theologian as well as an artist. Then, in any society where the rich and powerful, whether out of genuine love of the arts or because they think it enhances their prestige, include artists in their retinue, the latter have the status of an Upper Servant. Haydn wore the Esterhazy livery.

Lastly, until the Industrial Revolution, writers, composers, and painters were not the only kinds of artists. Cobblers, blacksmiths, carpenters, etc., were equally craftsmen, concerned in giving the objects they made a gratuitous aesthetic value as well as a necessary utility value. In such a society, therefore, it was taken for granted, even by those who never read a book or looked at a picture or listened to music, that beauty was as valuable as utility. But, by the end of the nineteenth century, machine production had reduced most worker-craftsmen to the status of laborers, whose only interest in their labor was as a means of earning their livelihood, and beauty came more and more to be regarded as a social luxury, making both the creators of beautiful things and their specialized public objects of social suspicion.

When a man finds himself a social oddity, he is very apt to alternate between feelings of guilt—there must be something wrong with me—and megalomania—the fact that I am an oddity proves that I am superior to the average mass. Polar opposites as in appearance they look, the two literary doctrines of Naturalism and Art-for-Art's-Sake, as propounded by Zola and Mallarmé, are really both expressions of the same megalomania. The aesthete is, at least, frank about this. He says: "Art is the only true religion. Life has no value except as material for a beautiful artistic structure. The artist is the only authentic human being: all the rest, rich and poor alike, are *canaille.*"

The naturalist is more disingenuous. Officially, he says: "Down with all art that prettifies life. Let us describe human life and nature as they really are." But his picture of life "as it really is" is a picture of human beings as animals, enslaved to necessity, who can only manifest behavior and are incapable of personal choice or deeds. But if human beings are really as the naturalist describes them, then they cannot be loved or admired. Who can be? Only the naturalist himself for his accurate clinical observations. Like all kinds of behaviorists, he does not apply his dogmas to himself. He does not say: "My books are examples of behavior, conditioned by blind reflexes." The hidden link between the naturalist and the aesthete is revealed by the total absence in both of any sense of humor.

Aestheticism, as Mann saw very clearly, has an even more pernicious effect upon art lovers than upon the artists themselves. The latter must, at least, work hard in order to win their own self-respect, but their public is passive and does nothing, yet feels itself superior to the Philistines. The nineteenth-century respectable bourgeoisie imagined that a "moral" novel meant one in which the good were rewarded for their virtues by coming into money and a happy marriage, while the bad were punished for their vices by ending in penury and disgrace. This was silly of them, but they were nearer the truth than the aesthetes who, in reaction, denied any relation between art and morality. In "*Gladius Dei*," Mann describes a decadent picture:

> It was a Madonna, painted in a wholly modern and entirely unconventional manner. The sacred figure was ravishingly feminine, naked and beautiful. Her great sultry eyes were rimmed with shadow, and her lips were half-parted in a strange and delicate smile. Her slender fingers were grouped rather nervously and convulsively round the waist of the Child, a nude boy of aristocratic, almost archaic slimness, who was playing with her breasts and simultaneously casting a knowing side-long glance at the spectator.

Now it is possible to argue that pornography has a legitimate social function, but only on condition that it claims to do nothing except act as a sexual stimulus. If, as in this case, it claims to be not only a work of art but also a religious work of art, then Hieronymus is right: it should be burnt.

In his treatment of the self-conscious sensitive artist vis-à-vis "the bright children of life, the happy, the charming and the ordinary," Mann's irony and humor reveal that, however much he may have been influenced by Nietzsche, he took him with a grain of salt. As an analyst of Pride, the primal sin of self-consciousness, Nietzsche is the greatest of all psychologists, but he should have accepted it as an unchangeable factor in the human condition. His Super-Man, who combines the self-consciousness of a man with the self-assurance of an animal, is a chimera.

In these stories Mann describes very convincingly the nostalgia felt by his "sensitive" characters for the "normal," but he makes it clear that their conception of the "normal" is subjective and not objective. In clarifying this, he amusingly makes use of an auto-biographical fact: he was born with dark hair in Northern Germany where blond hair is the norm. So Tonio (and, incidentally, Spinell in "Tristan") is dark-haired and dark-complexioned. Now, it is natural enough for a person to be attracted by his physically opposite type, as Tonio is by Hans, but if he identifies physical appearance with character traits, he is clearly indulging in a private fantasy. Nobody, for instance, could possibly contend that only fair-haired people are athletes, only dark-haired ones writers. Mann never lets us know what Hans or Ingeborg think of themselves, only what Tonio thinks about them.

Toward the end of the story the following sentence is italicized: *Hans Hansen and Ingeborg Holm walked through the dining-room.* By this device, Mann informs the reader that the sentence is, in fact, untrue: they are not Hans and Ingeborg, but another couple belonging to the same type. It was as types not as persons that Tonio had admired them. To make sure that the reader gets the point, Mann gives us Tonio's verdict on Italy. It is well-known that artists and intellectuals from Northern Europe have often fallen in love with Mediterranean countries, finding them, in contrast to their own, the home of unreflecting happiness and vitality. Not so Tonio:

> All that *bellezza* gets on my nerves. And I can't stand all that dreadful southern vitality, all those people with their black animal eyes. They've no conscience in their eyes, these Latin races.

Though Tonio Kröger is the only representative of the aesthetic in these stories whom one can respect, he is not the most interesting to read about: he talks far too much. Of them all, the one I like best is "Tristan." The title is clearly ironic. Anybody who is familiar with Wagner's opera will recognize at once that Spinell is not Tristan but Melot, the malevolent troublemaker, in disguise. He will also relish the contrast between the aged, melancholic, probably impotent figure of King Mark, and the exuberant, gourmandising Philistine to whom Frau Klöterjahn is married.

My, how times have changed since these stories were written! Less than seventy years ago, it was still possible to raise the question: Is a love for racehorses more "normal," more *echt* than a love for poetry? Today the question would be: Are these different loves the truthful manifestation of personal taste and choice, or have they been assumed in order to be popular in the social circle in which the individual happens to move? (Personal choice and taste do not, of course, exclude learning from other persons: they do exclude group influence.) In all technologically "advanced" countries, fashion has replaced tradition, so that involuntary membership in a society can no longer provide a feeling of community. (The family, perhaps, can still provide it, but families are temporary societies which dissolve when the children grow up.)

In consequence, the word "normal" has ceased to have any meaning. Community still means what it always has, a group of persons united by a love of something other than themselves, be it racehorses or poetry, but today such a love has to be discovered by each person for himself; it cannot be acquired socially. Society can only teach conformity to the momentary fashion, either of the majority or of its mirror-image, the rebellious minority. To belong to either is to be a member, not of a community, but of a "public" in the Kierkegaardian sense. Today, all visible and therefore social signs of agreement are suspect.

A CONSCIOUSNESS OF REALITY

*

It is, probably, already too late to hope that someone will write a definitive history of Bloomsbury, that fascinating cultural milieu which formed itself around 1910, exercised its greatest influence during the twenties, and came to an end with the death of Virginia Woolf. There is an excellent account of the intellectual influences from which it was born in a posthumous essay by Maynard Keynes; for its later history we shall have to rely upon the memoirs of David Garnett, which are now appearing in England, and the journals of Virginia Woolf, of which *A Writer's Diary* is, we hope, only the first installment.

Bloomsbury was not a "school" in any literary sense—there is no common Bloomsbury style or subject—nor was it centered on any one salon, like the Holland House set of the nineteenth century, or the Garsington set, to which many of its members also belonged. It included novelists, critics, painters, college dons but, curiously, no important poet (if one counts Virginia Woolf as a novelist) or composer. Nearly all its members had been to Cambridge and came from distinguished upper-middle-class families; i.e., without being aristocrats or large landowners, they were accustomed to efficient servants, first-rate meals, good silver and linen, and weekends in country houses. In rebellion against the rhetoric and conventional responses of their Victorian parents, hating dogma, ritual, and hypocritical expressions of unreal feelings, they, nevertheless, inherited from the Victorians a self-discipline and fastidiousness that made bohemian disorder impossible. "I have," writes Virginia Woolf—and most of them could have written the same—"an internal, automatic scale of values; which decides what I had better do with my time. It dictates 'This half hour must be spent on Russian,' 'This must be given to Wordsworth.' Or 'Now I'd better darn my brown stockings,'" and it is characteristic that the word she should find to express her critical reservations about *Ulysses* is "underbred." Politically a little to the left of center, they all shared a deep distrust of Parties and the State, believing passionately in the supreme importance of personal relations: "If I had to choose between betraying my country and betraying my friend, I hope I should have the guts to betray my country," wrote E. M. Forster, and during the spring of 1940, when invasion seemed imminent, Virginia Woolf refused to be distracted from writing her life of Roger Fry: "It's the vastness, and the smallness, that makes this possible. So intense are my feelings (about Roger); yet the circumference (the war) seems to make a hoop round them. No, I can't get the odd incongruity of feeling intensely and at the same time knowing that there's no importance in that feeling. Or is there, as I sometimes think, more importance than ever?"

It was, I feel, a very happy idea to confine the selections from her diary to her reflections on her own career as a writer. Henry James in his notebooks, letters, and prefaces may have said more interesting things about literary technique, but I have never read any book that conveyed more truthfully what a writer's life is like, what are its worries, its rewards, its day-by-day routine. Some readers, apparently, have been shocked to find how anxious and sensitive Virginia Woolf was about reviews, and how easily commendation of others could make her envious, but most writers, if they are honest, will recognize themselves in such remarks as "No creative writer can swallow another contemporary. The reception of living work is too coarse and partial if you're doing the same thing yourself. . . . When Desmond praises 'East Coker,' and I am jealous, I walk over the marsh saying, I am I," and even in her reflection on her father's death: "Father . . . would have been 96 . . . and could have been 96, like other people one has known: but mercifully was not. His life would have entirely ended mine."

Some of us keep up an air of stoic indifference to reviews, some avoid distress by refusing to read them, but we all care, and for good reasons. Every writer who is original is often doubtful about the value of a work; praise from a critic whom he respects is a treasured reassurance, silence or blame a confirmation of his worst fears: "So I'm found out and that odious rice pudding of a book is what I thought it—a dank failure." Then there are those critics who have made up their minds, for reasons of jealousy or fashion, about his work before they have read it, and the readers of those critics—rival contemporaries or the ambitious young— who are glad to hear that his work is bad: "I dislike the thought of being laughed at: of the glow of satisfaction that A., B., and C. will get from hearing V. W. demolished." In Virginia Woolf's case, the fact that she was a woman was a further aggravation. She belonged to a generation in which a woman had still to fight to be taken seriously as a writer. For her, therefore, good notices and brisk sales meant financial independence and masculine admission of her sex as a literary equal; when she writes, "I'm out to make £300 this summer by writing and build a bath and hot-water range at Rodmell," she is thinking of the satisfaction it will give her, as a wife, to contribute substantially to the family budget.

Sensitive as she was to attacks, she was never too vain to deny any truth there might be in even the most prejudiced: "The thing to do is to note the pith of what is said—that I don't think—then to use the little kick of energy which opposition supplies to be more vigorously oneself. . . . To investigate candidly the charge; but not fussily, not very anxiously. On no account to retaliate by going to the other extreme—thinking too much."

These selections from Virginia Woolf's diary begin in the last year of World War I, when, in spite of it, England still seemed to be pretty much the same country it had been before 1914, and end, a few days before her death, in the darkest days of World War II, when her London house had been destroyed by bombs and the future of England was problematic: "A kind of growl behind the cuckoos and t'other birds. A furnace behind the sky. It struck me that one curious feeling is, that the writing 'I' has vanished. No audience. No echo. . . . We live without a future. That's what's queer: with our noses pressed to a closed door." ˙

At the beginning, her literary reputation is just established— "I get treated at great length and solemnity by old gentlemen." During the twenties, she is universally admired; then, in the thirties, the wiggings start—she is bourgeois, oversensitive, out of date, and so on—and then she dies before she could become (what may well be the most painful fate of all) a sacred cow of whom everyone speaks in tones of hushed and bored reverence, but not before she has finished *Between the Acts,* which in my opinion, is her masterpiece.

With the exception of a description of an eclipse of the sun, which is as beautiful as any of the best pages in her novels, and an occasional comment, usually rather malicious, on people she knew, these selections are devoted to her thoughts upon the work in hand. Like every other writer, she was concerned about what particular kind of writer she was, and what her unique contribution could and should be. "My only interest as a writer lies, I begin to see, in some queer individuality; not in strength, or passion, or anything startling. Peacock for example: Borrow; Donne. . . . Fitzgerald's Letters." This is true if strength and passion are taken to mean what they conventionally mean when speaking of novelists. What she felt and expressed with the most intense passion was a mystical, religious vision of life, "a consciousness of what I call 'reality': a thing I see before me: something abstract; but residing in the downs or sky; beside which nothing matters; in which I shall exist and continue to exist. . . . How difficult not to go making 'reality' this and that, whereas it is one thing. Now perhaps this is my gift: this perhaps is what distinguishes me from other people: I think it may be rare to have so acute a sense of something like that—but again, who knows? I would like to express it too." Moreover, as is true of most mystics, she also experienced the Dark Night when "reality" seemed malignant—"the old treadmill feeling, of going on and on and on, for no reason . . . contempt for my lack of intellectual power; reading Wells without understanding. . . . society; buying clothes; Rodmell spoilt; all England spoilt: terror at night of things generally wrong in the universe."

What is unique about her work is the combination of this mystical vision with the sharpest possible sense for the concrete, even in its humblest form: "One can't," she observes, "write directly about the soul. Looked at, it vanishes; but look at the ceiling, at Grizzle, at the cheaper beasts in the Zoo which are exposed to walkers in Regent's Park, and the soul slips in." In preserving this balance, her sex was probably a help; a man who becomes interested in the Ground of Being all too easily becomes like Lowes Dickinson—"Always live in the whole, life in the one: always Shelley and Goethe, and then he loses his hot-water bottle; and never notices a face or a cat or a dog or a flower, except in the flow of the universal." A woman who has to run a house can never so lose contact with matter. The last entry in Virginia Woolf's diary is typical: "And now with some pleasure I find that it's seven; and must cook dinner. Haddock and sausage meat. I think it is true that one gains a certain hold on sausage and haddock by writing them down."

Though she took extraordinary pains over each book, she was a born spontaneous writer who never seems to have known periods when she was without a fresh idea; even while she was in the middle of writing one book, she got ideas for the next, and her output shows a greater variety than she is sometimes credited with. Each book set its particular problem and provoked in the author its particular psychosomatic reactions: "While I was forcing myself to do *Flush* my old headache came back—for the first time this autumn. Why should *The Pargiters* [*The Years*] make my heart jump; why should *Flush* stiffen the back of my neck?"

Within the years covered by this diary, Virginia Woolf wrote what her husband believes to be, and I agree with him, her three best books, *To the Lighthouse, The Waves,* and *Between the Acts,* and the fortunate reader is able to follow the writing of each. Here, for example, is the history of *The Waves:*

1926 [*She is finishing* To the Lighthouse]:

SEPTEMBER 30. It is not oneself but something in the universe that one's left with. It is this that is frightening and exciting in the midst of my profound gloom, depression, boredom, whatever it is. One sees a fin passing far out. What image can I reach to convey what I mean?

1927 [*the year of* Orlando]:

FEBRUARY 21. Why not invent a new kind of play; as for instance: Woman thinks . . . He does. Organ plays. She writes. They say: She sings. Night speaks. They miss.

JUNE 18. A man and a woman are to be sitting at a table talking. Or shall they remain silent? It is to be a love story; she is finally to let the last great moth in.

1928:

NOVEMBER 28. The poets succeeding by simplifying: practically everything is left out. I want to put practically everything in: yet to saturate. . . . It must include nonsense, fact, sordidity: but made transparent.

1929:

JUNE 23. I think it will begin like this: dawn; the shells on a beach: I don't know—voices of cock and nightingale; and then all the children at a long table—lessons. . . . Could one not get the waves to be heard all through?

[*On September 10th, she begins writing.*]

SEPTEMBER 25. Yesterday morning I made another start on *The Moths,* but that won't be its title. . . . Who thinks it? And am I outside the thinker?

DECEMBER 26. I wish I enjoyed it more. I don't have it in my head all day like *The Lighthouse* and *Orlando.*

1930:

JANUARY 12. I can now hardly stop making up *The Waves.* . . . What is essential is to write fast and not break the mood.

MARCH 17. The test of a book (to a writer) is if it makes a space in which, quite naturally, you can say what you want to say. As this morning I could say what Rhoda said.

APRIL 9. It is bound to be very imperfect. But I think it possible that I have got my statues against the sky.

APRIL 29. The greatest stretch of mind I ever knew. . . .

I suspect the structure is wrong. Never mind.

[*She begins her second version of* The Waves.]

AUGUST 20. *The Waves* is I think resolving itself into a series of dramatic soliloquies.

DECEMBER 22. . . . merge all the interjected passages into Bernard's final speech and end with the words O solitude.

1931:

[*On January 20th, she gets the idea, in her bath, for Three Guineas.*]

FEBRUARY 7. I wrote the words O Death fifteen minutes ago, having reeled across the last ten pages with some moments of such intensity and intoxication that I seemed only to stumble after my own voice, or almost, after some sort of speaker. . . . Anyhow it is done; and I have been sitting these fifteen minutes in a state of glory, and calm, and some tears. . . . How physical the sense of triumph and relief is! . . . I have netted that fin in the waste of water which appeared to me over the marshes out of my window at Rodmell.

I do not know how Virginia Woolf is thought of by the younger literary generation; I do know that by my own, even in the palmiest days of social consciousness, she was admired and loved much more than she realized. I do not know if she is going to exert an influence on the future development of the novel—I rather suspect that her style and her vision were so unique that influence would only result in tame imitation—but I cannot imagine a time, however bleak, or a writer, whatever his school, when and for whom her devotion to her art, her industry, her severity with herself—above all, her passionate love, not only or chiefly for the big moments of life but also for its daily humdrum "sausage-and-haddock" details—will not remain an example that is at once an inspiration and a judge. If I had to choose an epitaph for her, I would take a passage from *The Waves,* which is the best description of the creative process that I know:

There is a square: there is an oblong. The players take the square and place it upon the oblong. They place it very accurately; they make a perfect dwelling-place. Very little is left outside. The structure is now visible; what is inchoate is here stated; we are not so various or so mean; we have made oblongs and stood them upon squares. This is our triumph; this is our consolation.

PRIVATE POET

How can it happen, I ask myself, that a book of such extraordinary merit as *Rhymes of a Pfc* should have been turned down by publisher after publisher, and is now available only because its author could afford to pay the expenses of publication?

I can think of two possible reasons. One is related to our modern passion for labeling people. Lincoln Kirstein has long been the name of an impresario, the promoter of *Hound & Horn,* the Director of a Ballet Company who, by giving George Balanchine the opportunity to exercise his genius, has done as much as anyone alive for the cause of Classical Ballet. An impresario is, by definition, someone who does not himself "create"; should he, by any chance, produce a work of his own, one assumes that it must be the trifle of a dilettante, unworthy of serious attention. The other reason is a side-effect of the instantaneous communication of news which the telegraph and the radio have made possible. During a war, day after day, night after night, we read and hear of little else but war, and our anxiety to learn what is really happening is exacerbated by our knowledge that what we are being told is, at best, but half of the truth, couched, furthermore, in the nauseating clichés of journalese. Consequently, when peace comes, one of the greatest blessings it brings is freedom from war-news, and the last thing we feel like reading is a war book. It is now, however, over nineteen years since V-J Day, time enough, surely, for us to have gotten over our feelings of satiety. As for Mr. Kirstein the impresario, I can only implore the reader to forget his existence and approach these poems as if they were anonymous.

Despite all changes in values, interests, sensibility, the basic assumptions governing the treatment of warfare in poetry remained pretty well unchanged from Homer's time down until the Napoleonic Wars. These assumptions may be summarized as follows. 1) The Warrior is a Hero, that is to say, a numinous being. 2) War is pre-eminently the sphere of public deeds of heroism by individual persons; in no other sphere can a man so clearly disclose to others who he is. 3) Since his deeds are public, the warrior himself does not have to relate them. That duty falls to the professional poet who, as the legend of Homer's blindness indicates, is not himself a combatant. 4) The poet's job is to take the known story and sing of it in a style worthy of its greatness, that is to say, in a "high" style.

It was not until the eighteenth century that, under the influence of the Enlightenment, men began to question the numinous nobility of the Warrior, and, then, the scale of the Napoleonic Wars, involving huge armies and the whole continent of Europe, made it impossible to think of war in terms of individuals and choice. Stendhal, and Tolstoy after him, depict war as an irrational form of human behavior to which men are driven by forces quite outside their conscious control, and a battle as an unholy mess in which nothing happens as the commanders on either side intend. Irrational behavior cannot be sung of in a high style; the notes it calls for are the macabre, the ironic, the comic; and it cannot be truthfully described except by an eye-witness. Since 1800, no poet has been able to "sing" of war, and war poems written by civilians from a safe distance, like "The Charge of the Light Brigade" have been worthless. At the beginning of World War I, for a generation which had never experienced it, war was still felt to be glamorous, but by 1916, it was known to be, not merely irrational, but an obscene inexcusable nightmare.

It must be admitted, I think, that the Second World War has produced, so far at any rate, less literature of outstanding merit, whether in verse or prose, than the First. For this I can see three possible reasons. The more mechanized warfare becomes, the fewer the number of soldiers directly engaged in combat compared to the number engaged in services behind the firing-line; fewer, that is, are directly confronted by the "naked face" of war. Then, remembering the reckless waste of human lives in the First, the military authorities in the Second were determined to save as many lives as possible and to assign the individual soldier to a post which matched his character and talents. As a result, a draftee with the education and sensibility required to become a writer was very unlikely to find himself among the combat troops; most probably he would end up as a Tec Sergeant with a desk job. (Luckily for us, Mr. Kirstein had the misfortune to have a black mark against him in the records—I have never understood exactly what it was, except that it was something political—and on that account never rose above the rank of Pfc.) Lastly, the emotional attitude of an Englishman or an American to the Second World War was more complicated. In 1914 the nations of Europe had blundered into a war none of them wanted and without the faintest notion of what a modern war would be like. Whatever their politicians and generals might think, by 1916 no common soldier on either side could see a reason why they should be fighting each other. Consequently, what Wilfred Owen called "The pity of war, the pity war distilled," was a simple emotion of compassion for one's fellow sufferers in the common nightmare, which made no distinction between friend and foe. In 1939, on the other hand, it was obvious that the German Reich had fallen into the hands of very wicked men who offered the rest of Europe only the alternative of war or capitulation. The compassion which an English or American soldier might feel for his German fellow-sufferer was complicated by his conviction that the latter was suffering in an evil cause. It would have been impossible to write such a poem as Owen's "Strange Meeting."

The problem for a poet in writing about modern war is that, while he can only deal with events of which he has first-hand knowledge—invention, however imaginative, is bound to be fake— his poems must somehow transcend mere journalistic reportage. In a work of art, the single event must be seen as an element in a universally significant pattern: the area of the pattern actually

illuminated by the artist's vision is always, of course, more or less
limited, but one is aware of its extending beyond what we see
far into time and space.

For any American, this raises special difficulties. Until 1922,
when immigration quotas were imposed, the United States was the
New World, and to leave the Old for it expressed a decision to
make a complete break with the past and begin history afresh. In
trying to envision the present *sub specie aeternitate,* it is natural
for a poet of the Old World to make use of whatever mythical and
historical past is closest to him, as David Jones made use of Celtic
Mythology in his great war book *In Parenthesis.* An American
cannot. For Mr. Kirstein, History began in 1848 when his German-
Jewish grandparents emigrated from the Rhineland: even had they
been Aryan, he could not have used German mythological material,
the *Niebelungen Lied* for example, without being false to them and
to himself. For any American, the mythical war is the Civil War.

Yet my civil war's nearer than that war over the blue;
    World War II.
Which means zero to me save for drab facts which inspire me to
    fear,
    I'm absurdly quiet here
Trying hard to pretend our crack halfback lieutenant, Bill Beady
    Eye
Risks a charge under raking cross fire to let fly
    Carbines and a thin cheer.

At the same time, for all American intellectuals, the Old World
had a fascination, an exotic cultural glamour. (Had. The States are
no longer new, Europe no longer cultured.) For some it was
France, for others, like Mr. Kirstein, England.

    Often Hamlet was Jim;
We got drunk on Shakespeare's iambics and Britain's dynastic rain-
    bow.
    I most remember him
Flipping the pages of portraits vignetted from the *London News*—
    The First War's English dead,

Glorious young men all, each a university graduate.
  Fate haloed every head,
All officers, baron or baronet, not one a mere private;
  History was alive.

Lacking a common mythological past, every American artist has, in weaving his pattern, to make use of a personal mythology which means that, in order to make this intelligible to others, he has to provide many more autobiographical facts than a European would need to. Pfc. Lincoln Kirstein is, as he tells us, a member of three minorities (To a western European, the term *minority* has no emotional significance.) Firstly he is a Jew in a society which was, and still is, more anti-Semitic than it cares to admit. Secondly, his parents were assimilated enough and rich enough to send him to Exeter and Harvard, institutions almost exclusively Wasp; he has never known either the ghetto home life of New York Jews or the heterogeneous society of a State High School and University. Lastly, he is an intellectual aesthete who in childhood was, or believed himself to be, a sissy (again a term with no real European equivalent): consequently, his Lame Shadow, half worshipped, half despised, is a gentile inarticulate warrior-athlete. In peace time, relations between people of different educational backgrounds and cultural tastes are impossible or artificial; in war the only compensation for its discomforts and horrors is that such relations become possible, for in war there is only one significant social-psychological division, the one between officers and enlisted men. Mr. Kirstein relates his experiences in a roughly chronological order. He undergoes Basic Training in the States; for himself and his fellow draftees, the war still seems pretty remote, but mothers and wives are already beginning to receive regretful telegrams. He is shipped over to England, where he is billeted in a Manchester suburb and finds himself assigned to the Third Army. More training for the Invasion, the prospect of which looms steadily more menacing. He crosses the Channel twenty days after D Day, and is in the real terrifying thing. Though he never himself fires a shot, he is in close contact with combat troops, he comes under shell-fire, and he gets wounded, even if only in a jeep accident. With the Third Army, commanded by General Patton, whom he greatly admires, he enters Germany where he makes his one big contribution to the war effort. By a fantastic stroke of luck, he learns where the bulk of the art treasures looted by the Germans from all over Europe have been hidden.

His principal literary influences are, I should guess, Browning, Hardy, and Kipling. From the first he learns how to write a dramatic monologue, from Hardy and Kipling a fondness for complicated stanzas, which he handles with great virtuosity. How effective, for example, is the rhyming and the sudden lack of rhyme in the following:

> We woke up early one morning. My! what a gorgeous day!
> We'd crossed Germany's borders to capture a German May;
> Strawberries-in-wine was the weather. All outdoors smelled
> of fresh heather,
> And my captain has a lousy toothache.

The characters he meets and the stories he has to tell are of all kinds. Some are comic, like the Major who builds himself a fireplace out of liberated bricks which turn out to be made of dynamite. Others are ghastly, like the drunken Captain who kills an innocent civilian but, when it comes to his Court-Martial:

> The charge was not murder, mayhem, mischief malicious,
> Yet something worse, and this they brought out time and
> again:
> Clearly criminal and caddishly vicious
> Was his: Drinking With Enlisted Men.

Others, again, are concerned with sex, depicting it as the grubby activity which in wartime it usually is.

From Kipling, too, I think, he got the idea of trying to let his G. I.'s speak in their own low—very low—style, and in this he is brilliantly successful as Kipling was not: Kipling's Tommies speak stage Cockney. Not being a born American and, therefore, not quite trusting my own conviction that Mr. Kirstein had gotten the speech right, I have tried the poems out on a number of people born and bred in the States, and they have all confirmed it. Again, as a born Englishman, I am astounded at his success. In England, during the nineteenth century, it was possible for writers like Barnes and Hardy, who were brought up in the country and lived all their lives there, to reproduce accurately their local rustic dialect, but no English writer who has had the equivalent of Mr. Kirstein's education—Winchester and New College, let us say—can ever hope to imitate the speech of another class.

That Mr. Kirstein should succeed is a credit, I think, not only to his ear, but to American culture; whatever its faults, it is at least not bedeviled by accent-consciousness. Not only can Mr. Kirstein reproduce "low" American speech; he also catches the subtle variations of vocabulary and intonation within it which distinguish one kind of character from another. Here are three examples.

I thought: Gloria, if Ize in some Christless spot
Who'd I turn to? Fred, natch. So the Least poor I could do—
Try and help Himm. Hotel room in Norfolk with Whooo
    but a marine guard. Get the picture? I had to get permis-
    sion from his commandant before they'd let
me innn. They left the door Open so they could listen and
needn't Buggg it. Now I begin to
    Understand
it's a Court-Martial offenssse: but—they better Be Sure
    and Prove it. Just get us a good lawyer, but your
Sainted Mother now found that Some people are just Viiile.

*　*　*

Program formally opens as Fatso (tenor M.C.)
    Brays "Rose Marie,"
Shoots two lousy flat jokes. A fruity trombone introduces
    La Tony,
Who grabs at her cue. Dialogue goes
Sorta like this: "Hey you gotta fulla bag there, Rose
    Marie sweetheart; what's (rolling her eyes) you got in it?"
    "Just like you, sista: it's fulla shit."
(Groans.) Now: the chorus. In tutus, six boys:
Indescribable noise.

] 425 [

* * *

We had 75's, 88's, 101's, evry fuckin gun you kin think of
In hills back of this town, listenin fer one shot.
They hear this one shot.
Christ: we start to fire, just at roof level:
One, two, three.
Then we hit a leetle lower, a leetle lower—an lower.
Special, we pick out any tall tower, like a church steeple.
One, two, three.
Man, was this cute! Like a typewriter:
One, two,
Three.

I shall not pretend that Mr. Kirstein's poetry is without faults. Any reader will notice passages which are clumsy, or prolix, or overloaded with adjectives, or too defiantly unfashionable. I cannot believe, however, that any poet, no matter how accomplished, will read these poems without admiration and envy. As a picture of the late war, *Rhymes of a Pfc* is by far the most convincing, moving, and impressive book I have come across.

*

A VOICE OF IMPORTANCE

*

I can see no reason why the fact that Mr. Kallman and I have been close friends for over thirty years should debar me from reviewing him. In my experience, one's feelings about a writer as a person and one's aesthetic judgment of his work affect each other very little, if at all. I have met three poets whose poems I admire enormously whom I thought poor human beings: vice versa, I can think of a number whom I like personally, but whose verses I cannot, alas, appreciate.

Mr. Kallman has previously published two volumes of poetry, *Storm at Castelfranco* (1956) and *Absent and Present* (1963). These, most unjustly, received almost no attention, and this neglect I should like to rectify.

The Sense of Occasion is divided into three sections. The first, *Winter's Journey,* consists of nine poems about, if not an unhappy, at least a very difficult, love affair. Such a theme is very treacherous: all too easily it tempts the writer into indulging in egocentric self-pity, whining, and fuss.

Mr. Kallman has managed to resist these temptations, firstly, thanks to his sense of humor that never deserts him, even in the most tense moments, and, secondly, thanks to his command of linguistic technique, both metrical and rhetorical. He is a difficult poet to quote from because his poems are so tightly knit that any passage depends for its full effect upon its place in the whole. Here, however, is an example:

> Another
> One in the morning. Good God.
>   Only One.
> My change-point. At the bare
> Thought of you, thought of you,
>   just nightmare,
> Ends ends ends ends
> For the mere worse, and all
>   comparison:
> There are no likes of you and none
> Whose love makes more demands.
> Forgive me your injuries to me.
>   Care.
> God help us both if we are in his
>   hands.

The second section, *Theaters,* is a miscellany of poems, long and short, on various topics. One of the long ones, "Delphi," seems to be about some mystical vision the author had on that historic spot; I cannot, I must confess, make head or tail of it, but I am sure that the difficulty is not due to the author's incompetence. But no reader, I'm sure, will have any trouble with the charming "The Body's Complaint to the Soul," based, obviously, on Marvell's poem, but in no way an imitation.

> Miss Skylark! titivated in
> The touchy dungeon of my skin,
> Foreseeing, and yet hardly loath,
> That morning-after for us both
> When I must in the mirror meet
> A face unfocused, indiscreet,
> And you no longer think you'll fly
> To bloodless orders when I die.
> For though you wilfully admit—

In order to charge me with it—
Our time for rousing love is past,
You will possess me in one last
Elusive vanity: to prove
A pleasure while intending love.

Nor will he have any problems over "Griselda Sings" with its surprise shock ending.

Even as you swear
You loved and love me:
Would that move me
If anything could
For good now, for ill?
Try if you like,
Act as you will;
I do not know, I know
Only that should
I move I would strike,
Strike to kill.

And this, surely, is a fine example of the "pure" lyric:

SALOME DANCE

There was no theme but this;
There was no other meaning.

There was a dark dream. This.

There was no gleam but this
Sickle sharpened for gleaning.

Heads will fall, it would seem,

The final section, *The African Ambassador,* is a very remarkable achievement indeed. To begin with, it is a technical tour de force. All sixteen of the poems are written in lines of six syllables, yet this never becomes monotonous. Most of them use a strict syllabic count, but in a few contiguous vowels are elided. Stanzas vary in length: some have pure rhymes, some half-rhymes, and, by varying their placing, Mr. Kallman reproduces, in a six-syllable form, various traditional forms, such as the ballade and terza rima; there is even a triolet:

> He knows his place; he knew
> No place entirely
> A home. Seedy here, nothing new
> He knows. His place he knew
> Of old with the handsome few;
> Now in the majority
> He knows his place. He knew
> No place entirely.

Secondly, Mr. Kallman has succeeded in what is one of the most difficult of all tasks, namely, in inventing a myth, or rather, perhaps, a metaphor, that does not remain private to the author but is accessible to all.

As an epigraph to the poem, there is a quotation from Graham Greene:

> . . . to me . . . Africa will always be the Africa of the Victorian atlas, the blank unexplored continent the shape of the human heart.

I can think of two other quotations that are relevant:

> The poet has no identity—*Keats*

> . . . though our words be such,
> Our lives do differ from our lines
> by much—*Herrick*

The Ambassador is both black and Jewish, and so doubly an outsider, and, like all ambassadors, in a sense an exile from his homeland. His job is to represent the interests of the Heart in the country of Consciousness. The "language" of the Heart is non-verbal, but he can only speak to Consciousness in words, and all translation inevitably means transmutation. In every poem, that is, *Wahrheit* is transmuted into *Dichtung*.

> Scanning my lines you see
> You are what you would be
> Were I like you: i.e.
> To say a questing bee
> Wrings a morning-glory
> As a nervous lady
> The edge of her hanky
> Is to say exactly
> Nothing of each. For me
> Love appears unlikely.

And this is how he addresses the Patron Goddess of Poetry, the Moon:

> I smile, I give no tongue
> To my heart-throbs that punctuate
> The secrets of a state
>
> They shrink from knowing and you,
> Enforcer of the deep,
> Serve naught to voice, one night
> With asterisks for light
> Past appetite and song.

But no quotations can do the poem justice. It must be read in its entirety. I have no hesitation in saying that, in my opinion, *The African Ambassador* is one of the most original and significant poems written in the past twenty years.

A TRIBUTE

Though I have always loved his music—when I was sixteen I bought his *Easy Piano Duets*—I must leave it to others, better professionally qualified than I, to estimate Stravinsky's achievement as a composer. I can, however, I think, speak with some authority about Stravinsky as a paradigm of the creative artist, a model and example from whom younger men, be they composers, painters or writers, can derive counsel and courage in an age when the threats to their integrity seem to be greater than ever before.

First let them pay attention to his conception of artistic fabrication.

> I am not a mirror, struck by my mental functions. My interest passes entirely to the object, the thing made.

An artist, that is to say, should think of himself primarily as a craftsman, a "maker," not as an "inspired" genius. When we call a work "inspired," all we mean is that it is better, more beautiful than we could possibly have hoped for. But this is a judgment for the public to make, not the artist himself. True, there have been artists, Hugo Wolf, for example, who could only create during periods of intense emotional excitement, but this is a personal accident—most such artists have probably been manic-depressives. It has nothing to do with the value of what they produced in this state. Nearly all persons in a manic phase believe that they are inspired, but very few of them produce anything of artistic value.

Valéry, surely, was right when he said: "Talent without genius isn't much, but genius without talent isn't anything at all." The difference between a pure craft, like carpentry, and art is that when the carpenter starts work he knows exactly what the finished product will be, whereas the artist never knows just what he is going to make until he has made it. But, like the carpenter, all he can or should consciously think about is how to make it as well as possible, so that it may become a durable object, permanently "on hand" in the world.

As an illustration of Stravinsky's professional attitude, let me speak from personal experience. When Chester Kallman and I were offered the opportunity to write the libretto of *The Rake's Progress,* we felt, of course, immensely honored, but at the same time rather alarmed. We had heard that, during the composition of *Persephone,* there had been great friction between the composer and André Gide over the setting of the French text. Furthermore, Stravinsky had on more than one occasion expressed the view that, in setting words to music, the words themselves do not matter, only the syllables.

Though, as lovers of opera, we both knew that musical and spoken rhythmical values cannot be identical, we were afraid, particularly since Stravinsky had never set English before, that he might distort our words to the point of unintelligibility. But, from the moment we started working with him, we discovered that our fears were groundless. Going through our text, he asked for and marked into his copy the spoken rhythmical value of every word. In one instance, only one, did he make a mistake. He thought that, in the word *sedan-chair,* the accent in *sedan* fell on the first syllable. When we pointed this out to him, he immediately altered his score. In one number in the opera, The Auctioneer's aria in Act III, scene I, it is dramatically essential that the sung rhythms conform pretty closely to the spoken. They do. In the rest of the work, whatever occasional liberties he took, none of them struck our English and literary ears as impermissible.

Second, Stravinsky's career as a composer is as good a demonstration as any that I know of of the difference between a major and a minor artist. In the case of a minor artist, A. E. Housman, for example, if presented with two of his poems, both of equal artistic merit, one cannot, on the basis of the poems themselves, say which was written first. The minor artist, that is to say, once he has reached maturity and found himself, ceases to have a history. A major artist, on the other hand, is always re-finding himself, so that the history of his works recapitulates or mirrors the history of art. Once he has done something to his satisfaction, he forgets it and attempts to do something new which he has never attempted before. It is only when he is dead that we are able to see that his various creations, taken together, form one consistent *oeuvre*. Moreover, it is only in the light of his later works that we are able properly to understand his earlier.

> The chief problem in being 85 is the realisation that one may be powerless to change the quality of one's work. The quantity can be increased, even at 85, but can one change the whole? I, at any rate, am absolutely certain that my *Variations* and *Requiem Canticles* have altered the picture of my whole work.

Last, and most important of all, Stravinsky, in his attitude towards Past and Present, Tradition and Innovation, has set an example which we should all do well to follow.

When I contemplate the contemporary artistic scene, I realize how extraordinarily lucky those whom we think of as the founders of "modern" art, Stravinsky, Picasso, Eliot, Joyce, etc., all were in being born when they were, so that they reached manhood before 1914. Until the First World War European society was in all significant aspects still what it had been in the nineteenth century. This meant that, for these artists, the need they all felt to make a radical break with the immediate past was an artistic, not a historical, imperative, and therefore unique for each one of them. None of them would have dreamed of asking: "What kind of music or painting is 'relevant' in the year 1912?" Nor did they think of themselves collectively as the avant-garde, a term of which Baudelaire, who was certainly himself a great innovator, quite rightly said:

> This use of military metaphor reveals minds not militant but formed for discipline: minds born servile, Belgian minds, which can only think collectively.

What each of them felt, I believe, was rather: "It is only by creating something 'new' that I can hope to produce a work which in due time will take its permanent place in the tradition of my art." They were also lucky in their first audiences who were honest enough to be shocked. Those, for instance, who were scandalized by *Le Sacre du Printemps* may seem to us now to have been old fogies, but their reaction was genuine. They did not say to themselves: "Times have changed so we must change in order to be 'with it.'"

In times of rapid social change and political crisis, there is always a danger of confusing the principles governing political action and those that govern artistic fabrication. Thus Plato, dismayed by the political anarchy of the Athens of his day, tried to take artistic fabrication as the model for a good society. Such a theory, if put into practice, must, as we have learned to our cost, result in a totalitarian tyranny, involving, among other things, the most rigid censorship of the arts.

Today in the so-called "free" societies of the West, the most widespread error is the exact opposite of Plato's, namely, to take political action as the model of artistic fabrication. To do this is to reduce art to an endless series of momentary and arbitrary "happenings," and to produce in artists and public alike a conformism to the tyranny of the passing moment which is far more enslaving, far more destructive of integrity and originality, than any thoughtless copying of the past.

Once more, Stravinsky:

> What, may I ask, has become of the idea of universality—
> of a character of expression not necessarily popular but
> compelling to the highest imaginations of a decade or so
> beyond its time?

This, as we all know, his own compositions have achieved. If any young artist hopes to do the same, let him begin by forgetting all about "historical processes," an awareness of which, as the Master has said, "is probably best left to future and other kinds of wage-earners."

*

MARKINGS

*

To the symmetrical natures religion is indeed a crown of glory; nevertheless, so far as this world is concerned, they can grow and prosper without it. But to the unsymmetrical natures religion is a necessary condition of successful work even in this world.

—Lord Acton

A reader of *Markings* may well be surprised by what it does *not* contain—that Dag Hammarskjöld should not make a single direct reference to his career as an international civil servant, to the persons he met, or the historical events of his time in which he played an important role—but if he is surprised by what it does contain, then he cannot have read the credo which, shortly after his appointment as Secretary General, Hammarskjöld wrote for a radio program of Edward Murrow's.

From generations of soldiers and government officials on my father's side I inherited a belief that no life was more satisfactory than one of selfless service to your country—or humanity. This service required a sacrifice of all personal interests, but likewise the courage to stand up unflinchingly for your convictions.

From scholars and clergymen on my mother's side I inherited a belief that, in the very radical sense of the Gospels, all men were equals as children of God, and should be met and treated by us as our masters.

Faith is a state of the mind and the soul. . . . The language of religion is a set of formulas which register a basic spiritual experience. It must not be regarded as describing in terms to be defined by philosophy, the reality which is accessible to our senses and which we can analyze with the tools of logic. I was late in understanding what this meant. When I finally reached that point, the beliefs in which I was once brought up and which, in fact, had given my life direction even while my intellect still challenged their validity, were recognized by me as mine in their own right and by my free choice . . . the explanation of how man should live a life of active social service in full harmony with himself as a member of the community of the spirit, I found in the writings of those great medieval mystics for whom "self-surrender" had been the way to self-realization, and who in "singleness of mind" and "inwardness" had found strength to say Yes to every demand which the needs of their neighbors made them face, and to say Yes also to every fate life had in store for them. . . . Love—that much misused and misinterpreted word—for them meant simply an overflowing of the strength with which they felt themselves filled when living in true self-oblivion. And this love found natural expression in an unhesitant fulfillment of duty and an unreserved acceptance of life, whatever it brought them personally of toil, suffering—or happiness.

In *Markings,* Hammerskjöld records his gradual discovery of what saying Yes to his neighbor and to Fate would mean and involve, and the various tribulations and temptations, of the Flesh, the World, and the Devil, which made this so hard for him, as they do for all of us, to say.

Had the responsibility for the decision to publish the diary been mine, I should have been inclined to omit his covering letter to Leif Belfrage on account of one sentence in it which seems to me both false and misleading.

These entries provide the only true "profile" that can be drawn.

Even if the book were as extensive and detailed a "confession" as those of Boswell or Rousseau or Gide, this statement would still be false. No man can draw his own "profile" correctly because, as Thoreau said: "It is as hard to see oneself as to look backwards without turning round." The truth is that our friends—and our enemies—always know us better than we know ourselves. There are, to be sure, a few corrective touches to their picture of us which only we can add, and these, as a rule, are concerned with our vulnerabilities and our weaknesses.

It is, for example, axiomatic that we should all think of ourselves as being more sensitive than other people because, when we are insensitive in our dealings with others, we cannot be aware of it at the time: conscious insensitivity is a self-contradiction.

Secondly, we can hardly avoid thinking that the majority of persons we meet have stronger characters than we. We cannot observe others making choices; we only know what, in fact, they do, and how, in fact, they behave. Provided their actions are not criminal, their behavior not patently vicious, and their performance of their job in life reasonably efficient, they will strike us as strong characters. But nobody can honestly think of himself as a strong character because, however successful he may be in overcoming them, he is necessarily aware of the doubts and temptations that accompany every important choice. Unless he is a crook or has made an utter mess of his life, he will recognize the truth of Cesare Pavese's observation: "We can all do good deeds, but very few of us can think good thoughts."

If we read *Markings* without remembering all the time that it was written by a man who was a great "worldly" success, we shall fail to grasp the meaning of the sadness and "unworldliness" of many of the entries. What we read here needs, for example, to be complemented by reading his public speeches—there is an excellent selection from them, made by Mr. Wilder Foote, formerly Director of Press and Publications at the U. N., and published by Harper & Row under the title *Servant of Peace* (1962)—and accounts by others of the impression Hammerskjöld made on them.

Mr. Foote, for instance, writes:

He was sustained and inspired by pure and firmly founded beliefs and ideals about life and human relationships to which he was true in word and act. To these he joined a very brilliant, orderly, pragmatic and subtle mind, capable of lightning speed in both comprehension and construction, yet strictly disciplined. He always had a firm grip on realities and he could be as disappointed by wishful thinking or shallow optimism as by cynicism or self-serving.

He was infinitely careful in the planning and execution of all he attempted, in calm acceptance and understanding of human limitations—including his own—and of the often harsh realities with which he must work. At the same time his courage was that of the medieval mystics to whom he refers in his confession of faith. . . . This, combined with his natural mental and physical endurance, carried him through 18 and 20 hour working days for weeks on end in times of crisis.

The Danish diplomat, Eyvind Bartels, in a mainly hostile review of *Markings,* testifies to Hammarskjöld's powers of foresight:

It was shortly after the war, at a meeting between the Danish Government and the Swedish, that I first saw Hammarskjöld. He was introduced by his friends in the Swedish Government as a prodigy and impressed us as such. In a long speech he discussed problems of economic policy in relation to the United States which, to us, who had lived in another more brutal world than the Swedish one, seemed pretty remote. And yet in retrospect one can see that Hammarskjöld had formulated the economic-political problems which were later to dominate the Atlantic debate.

The next time I saw him was in Paris in 1947 during the discussion of the Marshall Plan. He brushed aside Dollar Aid as of secondary importance and raised the central question, the consequence for national sovereignty of this new co-operation. At the time this seemed to us a too theoretical point of view, but, here again, one can see in retrospect that Dag Hammarskjöld had sensed a European problem which today is as burning as ever, and has not yet found its solution.

Particularly interesting, in the light of his diary, is the impression he made on a fellow student at Uppsala, P. O. Ekelöf, with whom he went on camping trips in Lapland.

His sense of duty and his industriousness did not weigh heavily on him. On the contrary, he seemed to have a happy nature. . . . Amidst all his intellectualism, sense of responsibility, and idealistic enthusiasm, there was in the young Dag Hammarskjöld something of the playful lad. (*Ergo International,* Uppsala, 1963)

My own testimony is unimportant, but I want to give it. Brief and infrequent as our meetings were, I loved the man from the moment I saw him. His knowledge and understanding of poetry, the only field in which I was competent to judge the quality of his mind, were extraordinary, and, presumptuous as it sounds, I felt certain of a mutual sympathy between us, of an unexpressed dialogue beneath our casual conversation. The loneliness and the religious concern which his diary records, I sensed: indeed, I think the only two things which, while translating it, came as a real surprise, were his familiarity with the Anglican Psalter, and his fascination with the haiku as a poetic form.

As regards the earlier entries, the question arises: "When were they written?" Before 1953 no entry is precisely dated. In the Swedish edition there are four pages dated 1925–30, five dated 1941–42, thirteen dated 1945–49, after which the entries are grouped by single years. Writing in December 1956, Hammarskjöld says:

These notes?—They were signposts you began to set up after you had reached a point where you needed them, a fixed point that was on no account to be lost sight of.

And it is presumably this "fixed point" to which he refers in the entry for Whitsunday, 1961.

But at some moment I did answer *Yes* to Someone—or Something—and from that hour I was certain that existence is meaningful and that, therefore, my life, in self-surrender, had a goal.

Whenever this fixed point was reached, it must have been later than the entry, dated 1952, where he says:

What I ask for is absurd: that life shall have a meaning.
What I strive for is impossible: that my life shall acquire a
meaning.

If these three statements are to be taken literally, then one would
have to conclude that the whole book was composed after the
1952 entry, and this seems highly improbable. On the other hand,
however they are interpreted, it makes it difficult to believe that
many of the earlier entries, in the exact form in which we have
them, are contemporary with the events and experiences they describe. The most plausible guess, I should say, is that Hammarskjöld had kept some sort of a diary for a long time and that, after
the crucial moment in his life when he said Yes, he went through
it, cutting a lot, rewriting many entries, and, perhaps, adding some
entirely new ones.

The book, for example, opens and closes with a poem, both
poems depicting a *paysage moralisé*. It is hard to believe that this
is a mere temporal accident. Further, in the opening poem, Hammarskjöld speaks of a man

> Ready at any moment to gather everything
> Into one simple sacrifice.

I simply cannot believe that, at the age of twenty, he thought in
exactly the same terms as he was to think in thirty years later. It
even seems to me doubtful whether the last entry for 1949 was
written at the time.

> O Caesarea Philippi: to accept condemnation of the Way
> as its fulfillment, its definition, to accept this both when it
> is chosen and when it is realized.

Some people, no doubt, will condemn such retrospective revisions
(assuming that they were made) as dishonest, but such criticisms
are unjust. I am sure it is everyone's experience, as it has been
mine, that any "discovery" we make about ourselves or the meaning of life is never, like a scientific discovery, a coming upon something entirely new and unsuspected: it is, rather, the coming to
conscious recognition of something which we really knew all the
time, but, because we were unwilling or unable to formulate it

correctly, we did not hitherto know we knew. If we desire to re-write things we wrote when we were younger, it is because we feel that they are false, and were false at the time we wrote them: what, in fact, our real experience was, we were at the time unwilling or unable to say. To all experiences, other than purely sensory ones, the maxim *credo ut intelligam* applies.

To the outward eye, Dag Hammarskjöld's career was, from the very beginning, one of uninterrupted success. He does brilliantly at college. After a short spell of teaching, he enters government service. By the age of thirty-one he has become Under-Secretary of State for Financial Affairs, and by thirty-six, Chairman of the National Bank of Sweden. In addition to the success which his talents and industry win for him, his life, to the outward eye, is exceptionally fortunate. He has never known poverty, he enjoys excellent health, and, as a citizen of a neutral country, he is spared the privations, sufferings, and horrors inflicted by the war upon the majority of people in Europe. Inwardly, however, in spite of all these advantages—in part, perhaps, because of them—there is great spiritual distress. The portrait of the up-and-coming young man that emerges from the earlier pages of *Markings* is one of those "unsymmetric" natures which can all too easily come to grief.

An exceptionally aggressive superego—largely created, I suspect, by his relation to his father—which demands that *a* Hammarskjöld shall do and be better than other people; on the other hand, an ego weakened by a "thorn in the flesh" which convinces him that he can never hope to experience what, for most people, are the two greatest joys earthly life has to offer, either a passionate devotion returned, or a lifelong happy marriage. Consequently, a feeling of personal unworthiness which went very far, for it led him, it would seem, to undervalue or even doubt the reality of the friendship and sympathy which must always have been offered him in plenty. Consequently, too, a narcissistic fascination with himself. In two of his sharpest aphorisms, he points out that Narcissus is not the victim of vanity; his fate is that of someone who responds to his sense of unworthiness with defiance.

Further, though endowed with many brilliant gifts, not, I think, a genius, not, that is to say, a person with a single overwhelming talent and passion for some particular activity—be it poetry or physics or bird-watching—which determines, usually early in life, exactly what his function on earth is to be.

Excellent economist as he was, I do not imagine that his fellow economists would consider Hammarskjöld an original genius in this field, like Keynes, for example. Geniuses are the luckiest of mortals because what they must do is the same as what they most want to do and, even if their genius is unrecognized in their lifetime, the essential earthly reward is always theirs, the certainty that their work is good and will stand the test of time. One suspects that the geniuses will be least in the Kingdom of Heaven—if, indeed, they ever make it; they have had their reward.

To be gifted but not to know how best to make use of one's gifts, to be highly ambitious but at the same time to feel unworthy, is a dangerous combination which can often end in mental breakdown or suicide and, as the earlier entries show, the thought of suicide was not strange to Hammarskjöld. He describes two actual suicides, presumably witnessed by him personally, with fascination. When he has an automobile accident, his last thought before losing consciousness is, he tells us, a happy thought: "Well, *my* job's done."* And, as late as 1952, he admits that suicide is a real temptation to him.

> So! *that* is the way in which you are tempted to overcome
> your loneliness—by making the ultimate escape from life.
> No! It may be that death is to be your ultimate gift to life:
> it must not be an act of treachery against it.

Long before he discovered a solution, Hammarskjöld knew exactly what his problem was—if he was not to go under, he must learn how to forget himself and find a calling in which he could forget himself—and knew that it was not in his own power to do this. The transition from despair over himself to faith in God seems to have been a slow process, interrupted by relapses. Two themes came to preoccupy his thoughts. First, the conviction that no man can do properly what he is called upon to do in this life unless he can learn to forget his ego and act as an instrument of God. Second, that for him personally, the way to which he was called would

---

* I am informed that this accident must have happened to somebody else.

] 443 [

lead to the Cross, i.e., to suffering, worldly humiliation, and the physical sacrifice of his life.

Both notions are, of course, highly perilous. The man who says, "Not I, but God in me" is always in great danger of imagining that he *is* God, and some critics have not failed to accuse Hammarskjöld of precisely this kind of megalomania, and to cite in evidence such entries as the following:

> If you fail, it is God, thanks to your having betrayed Him, who will fail mankind. You fancy you can be responsible *to* God: can you carry the responsibility *for* God?

This accusation cannot be disproved by anything Hammarskjöld said or wrote, because humility and demonic pride speak the same language.

"By their fruits," however, "you shall know them." The man who has come to imagine he is God may be unaware of it himself, but he very soon starts to behave in a way which makes it obvious enough to others. One minor symptom, for example, is a refusal to listen to or tolerate the presence of others unless they say what he wishes to hear. And it is not long before he develops a paranoid suspicion of everyone else, combined with a cynical contempt for them. Had this been true of Hammarskjöld, those who worked or had dealings with him would have recorded it. But, in fact, his close colleagues in the Secretariat have all commented upon his exceptional patience in listening to what others had to say, and, even when the Russians were most bitterly attacking him over the Congo, calling him a murderer, they attacked him as an agent of imperialism, not as a self-appointed dictator, serving his personal interests.

His preoccupation with sacrifice in a literal physical sense is, maybe, a little more vulnerable. Though he was well aware of the masochistic element in his nature.

> The *arrêt* that leads to the summit separates two abysses: the pleasure-tinged death wish (not, perhaps, without an element of narcissistic masochism), and the animal fear arising from the physical instinct for survival.

I am not sure that it did not color and, to some degree, distort his thinking about the subject. "Just how," I find myself thinking, "did he envisage his end? Did he expect to be assassinated like Count Bernadotte? To be lynched by an infuriated General Assembly? Or simply to drop dead from a heart attack brought on by overwork?" As we all know, he *was* killed in the course of duty, but it is difficult to think of an airplane crash as an "act of sacrifice" in the sense in which Hammarskjöld uses the term. It could happen to any of us, regardless of any "commitment."

On the other hand, I do not think he is exaggerating in his portrayal of his life as Secretary General, despite its excitements and moments of joyous satisfaction, which he gratefully admits, as a *via crucis*. To be Secretary General of the U. N., he once jokingly told me, is like being a secular Pope, and the Papal throne is a lonely eminence. As the head of an international organization, the Secretary General cannot afford to show personal preferences for one person in it to another, for favoritism will arouse the suspicion of undue influence. As for friends in private walks of life, he simply hasn't the time to see them. In addition to the spiritual suffering of loneliness, of having to leave behind him "the world which had made him what he was," Hammarskjöld had to endure, and all the more severely because of his extreme conscientiousness, the plain physical suffering of constant nervous strain and overwork. If, as the reader goes through the entries between 1953 and 1957, he finds himself becoming impatient—and I must confess that I sometimes did—with their relentless earnestness and not infrequent repetitiousness, let him remember that most of them must have been written by a man at the extreme limits of mental and physical exhaustion. A man who has had only four or five hours sleep a night for weeks can hardly be expected to show levity or the strictest concern for stylistic niceties. Let him remember, too, that a man who, like Hammarskjöld, deliberately sets out to eliminate all selfish or self-regarding motives from his work, to act solely for the good of others and the glory of God, thereby deprives his "flesh" of the only consolations, like the prospect of money or fame, which can alleviate the pains of toil. As Simone Weil has written:

The same suffering is much harder to bear for a high motive than for a base one. The people who stood motionless, from one to eight in the morning, for the sake of having an

] 445 [

egg, would have found it very difficult to do in order to save a human life.

Last, I do not think that, for a man of Hammarskjöld's temperament, political life was the "natural" milieu. By training, he was a civil servant, that is to say, someone whose job it is to carry out a policy, not to decide one. He may, on the basis of his experience or convictions, advise for or against a given policy, but it is for his Minister to decide, and for him to execute that decision. This meant that, though he is in public service, he does not enter the arena of public life and public controversy. Ideally, the post of Secretary General of the U. N. should be that of an international civil servant, but so long as the world is politically organized as a number of sovereign nations, often at odds with each other, it is inevitably a political post as well. On a number of occasions Hammarskjöld found himself in the position of taking a political decision, either because he was instructed to or because a deadlock between the great powers left him no option. His conception of what, in such a historical situation, should be meant by the "neutrality" of the Secretary General is best given in his own words.

> He is not requested to be a neuter in the sense that he has to have no sympathies or antipathies, that there are no interests which are close to him in his personal capacity or that he is to have no ideas or ideals that matter to him. However, he is requested to be fully aware of those human reactions and meticulously to check himself so that they are not permitted to influence his actions. This is nothing unique. Is not every judge professionally under the same obligation? . . .
>
> In the last analysis, this is a question of integrity, and if integrity in the sense of respect for law and respect for truth were to drive him into positions of conflict with this or that interest, then that conflict is a sign of his neutrality and not of his failure to observe neutrality—then it is in line, not in conflict, with his duties as an international civil servant. (*Lecture delivered to Congregation at Oxford University, May 30, 1961*)

And, of course, such conflicts arose.

] 446 [

The milieu of the politician is the arena of public debate, and, to feel at home in it, calls for a very tough hide indeed, invulnerable to all arrows of criticism, however sharp or venomous. One gets the impression from this book that Hammerskjöld not only failed to develop such a hide, but remained more thin-skinned than most men. He seems to have felt any criticism, no matter how obviously motivated by party or national interests, as a reflection upon his personal integrity, and this sensitivity must have made life exceptionally difficult for him when he was involved in highly controversial political issues.

It makes me very happy to see that, in the last three years of his life, he took to writing poems, for it is proof to me that he had at last acquired a serenity of mind for which he had long prayed. When a man can occupy himself with counting syllables, either he has not yet attempted any spiritual climb, or he is over the hump.

Judged by purely aesthetic standards, the entries are of varying merit. Hammarskjöld, it seems to me, was essentially an "occasional" writer; that is to say, Hammarskjöld on Hammarskjöld, his personal experiences, feelings, doubts, self-reproaches, is always interesting, but when he is making general statements about the nature of the spiritual life or the "noughting" of the self, one feels one has read it all before somewhere, in Meister Eckhart, St. John of the Cross, *The Cloud of Unknowing,* or Juliana of Norwich. He lacks the originality of insight into general problems displayed by such contemporaries as Simone Weil, for example, or Charles Williams.

Markings, however, was not intended to be read simply as a work of literature. It is also an historical document of the first importance as an account—and I cannot myself recall another— of the attempt by a professional man of action to unite in one life the *via activa* and the *via contemplativa*. Most of the famous mystics were members of one contemplative Order or another: from time to time they might give advice, bidden or unbidden, to princes temporal and spiritual, but they did not think of giving advice or taking part in the affairs of this world as their function.

There are cases of men, like Lancelot Andrewes, holding positions of high authority in the Church, who have left behind them records of their private devotions, but their life of actions was in the ecclesiastical, not the secular sphere. Certainly, both mystic monk or nun and pious bishop would be startled by Hammarskjöld's statement:

> In our era, the road to holiness necessarily passes through
> the world of action.

As the records of the mystics show, the great temptation of the contemplative life—many of them passed through periods when they succumbed to it—is some form or other of Quietism, an indifference to and impatience with, not only "works" in the conventional sense, but also all the institutional and intellectual aspects of human life. As a professional civil servant, the head of a complex institution, and an economist, Hammarskjöld was, in his public secular life, protected from this temptation and exposed only to the usual "worldly" ones, which, because they are much easier to recognize, are less dangerous. In his personal religious life, I am not sure that he altogether escaped it. Professor Whitehead was a very wise man, but he once said a very silly thing: "Religion is what a man does with his solitude." Hammarskjöld's religion as revealed in *Markings* seems to me to be more of a solitary and private thing than it should have been. He understood very well and tried his best to practice such Gospel injunctions as "When thou doest alms, let not thy left hand know what thy right hand doeth" and "When thou fastest, anoint thy head and wash thy face, that thou appear not unto men to fast," but he does not seem to have pondered much upon such a saying as "Where two or three are gathered together in my name, I will grant their request" and he was, perhaps, a little overly impatient with doctrinal formulations: dogmatic theology may, like grammar, seem a tiresome subject, except to specialists, but, like the rules of grammar, it is a necessity. It is possible that his lack of participation in the liturgical and sacramental life of a church was a deliberate act of self-sacrifice on his part, that, as Secretary General, he felt any public commitment to a particular Christian body would label him as too "Western," but he gives no evidence in his diary of desiring such a commitment. In any case, I am sorry for his sake, because it is precisely the introverted intellectual character who stands most in need of the ecclesiastical routine both as a discipline and as a refreshment.

But how frivolous all such misgivings look in the light of the overall impression which the book makes, the conviction when one has finished it, that one has had the privilege of being in contact with a great, good, and lovable man.

PAPA WAS A WISE OLD SLY-BOOTS

✳

My first reason for wishing to review this book* is that it gives me an opportunity to make public acknowledgment of a debt which not only I but many writers of my generation owe to Mr. Ackerley. He informs us that he became Literary Editor of *The Listener* in 1935, but of his work there he says not a word. Those of us, however, who were starting our literary careers at the time have very good cause to remember how much he did for us: *The Listener* was one of our main outlets. More surprisingly, he says nothing about his intimate friends in the literary world, of whom there were many, including E. M. Forster. He says that he went to work for the BBC because he felt he had failed in his ambition to become a writer himself. On first reading this statement seems absurd: though he published only four books in his lifetime, all were enthusiastically received by the reviewers, and are just as good reading today as when they first appeared. I think, though, I understand what he means, namely, that he discovered that he could not create imaginary characters and situations: all his books were based on journals, whether written down or kept in his head.

In *My Father and Myself,* Mr. Ackerley strictly limits himself to two areas of his life, his relations with his family and his sex-

* *My Father and Myself,* by J. R. Ackerley.

] 450 [

life. His account of the latter, except for its happy ending, is very sad reading indeed. Few, if any, homosexuals can honestly boast that their sex-life has been happy, but Mr. Ackerley seems to have been exceptionally unfortunate. All sexual desire presupposes that the loved one is in some way "other" than the lover: the eternal and, probably, insoluble problem for the homosexual is finding a substitute for the natural differences, anatomical and psychic, between a man and a woman. The luckiest, perhaps, are those who, dissatisfied with their own bodies, look for someone with an Ideal physique; the ectomorph, for example, who goes for mesomorphs. Such a difference is a real physical fact and, at least until middle age, permanent: those for whom it is enough are less likely to make emotional demands which their partner cannot meet. Then, so long as they don't get into trouble with the police, those who like "chicken" have relatively few problems: among thirteen- and fourteen-year-old boys there are a great many more Lolitas than the public suspects. It is when the desired difference is psychological or cultural that the real trouble begins.

Mr. Ackerley, like many other homosexuals, wanted his partner to be "normal." That in itself is no problem, for very few males are so "normal" that they cannot achieve orgasm with another male. But this is exactly what a homosexual with such tastes is unwilling to admit. His daydream is that a special exception has been made in his case out of love; his partner would never dream of going to bed with any other man. His daydream may go even further; he may secretly hope that his friend will love him so much as to be willing to renounce his normal tastes and have no girl friend. Lastly, a homosexual who is, like Mr. Ackerley, an intellectual and reasonably well-off is very apt to become romantically enchanted by the working class, whose lives, experiences, and interests are so different from his own, and to whom, because they are poorer, the money and comforts he is able to provide can be a cause for affectionate gratitude. Again, there is nothing wrong with this in itself. A great deal of nonsense has been spoken and written about the sinfulness of giving or receiving money for sexual favors.

No, the real difficulty for two persons who come from different classes is that of establishing a sustained relationship, for, while a sexual relationship as such demands "otherness," any permanent relationship demands interests in common. However their tastes and temperaments may initially differ, a husband and wife acquire a common concern as parents. This experience is denied homosexuals. Consequently, it is very rare for a homosexual to remain faithful to one person for long and, rather curiously, the intellectual older one is more likely to be promiscuous than his working-class friend. The brutal truth, though he often refuses to admit it, is that he gets bored more quickly.

For many years, Mr. Ackerley was a compulsive cruiser:

In spite of such adventures, if anyone had asked me what I was doing, I doubt if I should have replied that I was diverting myself. I think I should have said that I was looking for the Ideal Friend. Though two or three hundred young men were to pass through my hands in the course of years, I did not consider myself promiscuous. It was all a run of bad luck . . . What I meant by the Ideal Friend I doubt if I ever formulated, but now, looking back, I think I can put him together in a negative way by listing some of his disqualifications. He should not be effeminate, indeed preferably normal. I did not exclude education, but did not want it, I could supply all that myself and in the loved one it always seemed to get in the way; he should admit me but no one else; he should be physically attractive to me and younger than myself—the younger the better, as closer to innocence; finally he should be on the small side, lusty, circumcised, physically healthy and clean: no phimosis, halitosis, bromidrosis. . . . The Ideal Friend was always somewhere else and might have been found if only I had turned a different way. The buses that passed my own bus seemed always to contain those charming boys who were absent from mine; the ascending escalators in the tubes fiendishly carried them past me as I sank helplessly into hell. . . . In the "thirties" I found myself concentrating my attention more and more upon a particular society of young men in the metropolis which I had tapped before and which, it seemed to me, might yield, without further loss of time, what I required. His Majesty's Brigade of Guards had a long history in homosexual prostitution. Perpetually short of cash, beer, and leisure occupations, they were easily to be found of an evening in their red tunics standing about in the various pubs they frequented, over the

only half-pint they could afford or some "quids-in" mate
had stood them. Though generally larger than I liked, they
were young, they were normal, they were working-class,
were drilled to obedience; though not innocent for long, the
new recruit might be found before someone else got at him;
if grubby they could be bathed, and if civility and consideration, with which they did not always meet in their liaisons,
were extended to them, one might gain their affection.

Frank as he is, Mr. Ackerley is never quite explicit about what
he *really* preferred to do in bed. The omission is important because
all "abnormal" sex-acts are rites of symbolic magic, and one can
only properly understand the actual personal relation if one knows
the symbolic role each expects the other to play. Mr. Ackerley
tells us that, over the years, he learned to overcome certain repug-
nances and do anything to oblige but, trying to read between the
lines, I conclude that he did not belong to either of the two commonest classes of homosexuals, neither to the "orals" who play
Son-and/or-Mother, nor to the "anals" who play Wife-and/or-
Husband. My guess is that at the back of his mind, lay a daydream
of an innocent Eden where children play "Doctor," so that the acts
he really preferred were the most "brotherly," Plain-Sewing and
Princeton-First-Year. In his appendix, he does tell us, however,
that he suffered, and increasingly so as he got older, from an
embarrassing physical disability—premature ejaculation with the
novel and impotence with the familiar. O dear, o dear, o dear.

But then, when he was nearly fifty, a miracle occurred. He
acquired an Alsatian bitch named Tulip. (Had Fate sent him an
Aureus dog instead of a *Lupus,* there would have been no miracle.)

> She offered me what I had never found in my sexual
> life, constant, single-hearted, incorruptible, uncritical de-
> votion. She placed herself entirely under my control. From
> the moment she established herself in my heart and my
> home, my obsession with sex fell wholly away from me.
> The pubs I had spent so much of my time in were never
> revisited, my single desire was to get back to her, to her
> waiting love and unstaling welcome. I sang with joy at the
> thought of seeing her. I never prowled the London streets
> again, nor had the slightest inclination to do so. On the
> contrary, whenever I thought of it, I was positively thank-

ful to be rid of it all, the anxieties, the frustrations, the wastage of time and spirit. The fifteen years she lived with me were the happiest of my life.

Very fittingly, *My Father and Myself* is dedicated to her.

In considering the story of his relationship to his father, let me begin by making two chronological lists.

ROGER ACKERLEY			JOE ACKERLEY		
Date	Event	Age	Date	Event	Age
1863	Born in Liverpool.		1896	Born.	
			c.1906	At school at Rossal.	10
75	Father financially ruined.	12			
76	Leaves school and goes to work as a clerk.	13			
79	Runs away to London and enlists in the Royal House-Guards. Makes friends with Fitzroy Paley Adams (aged 33) who starts to educate him.	16			
			1914	World War One, Enlists.	18
82	Service in Egypt where he may have contracted syphilis. Discharged.	19			
83	Adams dies, leaving him a legacy of £500. Re-enlists in the Life Guards. Makes friends with Comte James Francis de Gallatin (aged 30).	20	16	Wounded.	20
84	Discharged. Goes to work for a wine-merchant in Liverpool. Lends his legacy to de Gallatin at 20 percent interest.	21			
85	Father dies. Makes friends with Arthur Stockley (aged 20).	22	18	Again wounded and a P.O.W. Soon after interned in Switzerland. (Copy for *Prisoners of War*.) Peter Ackerley killed in action.	22

ROGER ACKERLEY		JOE ACKERLEY	
86 de Gallatin engages him to run a pony farm. They travel together in Italy.	23	19 Cambridge.	23
		21	25
88 At de Gallatin's house, meets Louise Burkhardt, a visitor from Switzerland. They become engaged. Quarrel with de Gallatin, ending in a law-suit.	25	21 Lives at home on an allowance of £350 a year.	25
		25	29
		23 Visits India (Copy for *Hindu Holiday*)	27
		24	
89 Marries L.B.	26		
92 His wife dies. Receives an allowance from her parents of £2000 a year. Meets the future mother of Joe (a legitimate actress, aged 28) on a Channel boat. Goes into a fruit business, started by Arthur Stockley.	29	25 Leases flat in Hammersmith from Arthur Needham, an old acquaintance of de Gallatin.	29
95 Peter "Ackerley" born.	32	28 Joins Talks Department of B.B.C.	32
96 Joe born.	33	29 Father dies.	33
98 A daughter by Joe's mother.	35		
		34 Takes Flat in Maida Vale.	38
		35 Becomes Literary Editor of *The Listener*.	39
1910 Twin daughters by another woman, Muriel.	47		
12 A third daughter by Muriel.	49		
		45 Acquires *Tulip*. (Copy for *My Dog Tulip* and *We Think the World of You*.)	50
		or	
		46	
19 Marries Joe's mother.	56		
		59 Retires from B.B.C.	63
29 Dies from the effects of tertiary syphilis.	66	c.1960 *Tulip* dies.	64
		67 Dies in his sleep of a coronary.	71

] 455 [

Needless to say, it was only by degrees that the son discovered some of the more startling facts about the father's life. He tells us that he learned of his illegitimacy (curiously enough, his maternal grandmother was also illegitimate) from his sister, who had heard it from his mother, but he does not say if this discovery was made before or after the marriage. There was, on the face of it, no reason to suspect such a thing. The children were given the name Ackerley and even Roger's business partner, Stockley, believed there had been a registry-office marriage. Though for the first few years, he seems to have been "a week-end father," who only paid them occasional visits, he set up house with them in 1903 and was as attentive and generous to both the children and their mother as they could possibly have wished.

Of his father's second family, Mr. Ackerley only learned from a letter he left to be opened after his death, requesting his son to make certain financial provisions for them. For Muriel's children he had shown less paternal concern.

> The birth of the twins was registered by him under an assumed name, he borrowed the name of his mistress; the youngest girl was never registered at all. They were all stowed away in a house near Barnes Common in care of a Miss Coutts. Through dietary ignorance or a desire to save his pocket, she fed them so frugally and injudiciously that they all developed rickets. They had no parental care, no family life, no friends. Their mother whom they did not love or even like, for she had less feeling for them than for her career and reputation, seldom appeared; the youngest girl does not remember to have seen her at all until she was some ten years old. But three or four times a year a relative of theirs, whom they knew as Uncle Bodger and who jokingly called himself William Whitely, the Universal Provider, would arrive laden with presents. This gentleman, almost their only visitor, they adored. He would come in a taxi with his load of gifts (sometimes with a dog named Ginger, who had perhaps provided him with a pretext for the visit: "I'm taking the dog for a walk," and who, since he was *our* dog, was also therefore another conspirator in my father's affairs, had he but known it.

Then, even after learning from his landlord, Arthur Needham, that the Comte de Gallatin was not only queer but a bold cruiser of Guardsmen, it was only after his father's death that he began to wonder about this friendship and its break-up. It must have been odd to realize that, had some Time Machine monkeyed with their time-spans, it might well have been a thirty-year-old Joe who picked up a twenty-year-old Roger in a bar, and for a short while believed he had found the Ideal Friend.

The Fruit Business did extremely well, so that the household enjoyed every comfort. There was a butler, a gardener, and, evidently, a very good table. Ackerley Senior had an Edwardian appetite in food and drink with all the risks to health which that implies. Like King Tum-Tum, he had to take the waters every year, in his case at Bad Gastein.

As a father, aside from a distressing habit of telling dirty stories, for which he must be excused because it was the convention among his business colleagues, he seems to have been all that a son could reasonably hope for. To begin with, he was good-tempered.

> Even in family quarrels, he seldom intervened, he did not take sides and put people in their places. Whatever he thought, and it was easily guessed, for the faults were easily seen, he kept to himself until, later, he might give it private expression to me in some rueful comment.

Unintellectual businessmen who find they have begotten a son who wants to become a writer are apt to be bewildered and resentful, but he gave his own a liberal allowance and never attempted to make him go into the family business or even take some regular job.

Then he was unshockable. In 1912 he told his two sons that

> in the matter of sex there was nothing he had not done, no experience he had not tasted, no scrape he had not got into and out of.

At the same time, and this seems to me to have been his greatest virtue, he was never nosy. It is quite obvious, for example, that he knew perfectly well what his son's sexual tastes were. In view of some of the characters the latter brought to the house, he could hardly have helped knowing.

] 457 [

There was a young actor who rendered my father momentarily speechless at dinner one evening by asking him, "Which do you think is my best profile, Mr. Ackerley"— turning his head from side to side—"this, or this?"; there was an Irishman with a thin, careful curled cylindrical fringe of a moustache and black paint around the lower lids of his eyes, who arrived in a leather jacket with a leopard-skin collar and pointed purple suede shoes; and an intellectual policeman. "Interesting chap," said my father afterwards, adding, "It's the first time I've ever entertained a policeman at my table."

I don't think Mr. Ackerley ever fully appreciated this aspect of his father's character. Speaking for myself, I would say that between parents and their grown-up children, the happiest relation is one of mutual affection and trust on the one hand, and of mutual reticence on the other; no indiscreet confidences on either side. In the following dialogue, it is the father, surely, who shows the greater wisdom and common sense.

> "I've got something to tell you, Dad. I lied to you about Weybridge. I didn't go there at all."
> "I know, old boy, I knew you were lying directly I asked you about the floods."
> "I went to Turin."
> "Turin, eh? That's rather farther. I'm very sorry to have mucked up your plans."
> "I'm very sorry to have lied to you. I wouldn't have done so if you hadn't once said something about me and my waiter friends. But I don't mind telling you. I went to meet a sailor friend."
> "It's all right, old boy. I prefer not to know. So long as you enjoyed yourself, that's the main thing."

Like all of us, Mr. Ackerley had his cross to bear, but I simply do not believe he was as unhappy as his habit of glooming led him to imagine. How many people have had so understanding a father? How many have found their Tulip? How many have written four (now five) good books? How many have been in the position to earn the affectionate gratitude of a younger literary generation? No, he was a lucky man.

THE JUSTICE OF DAME KIND

I have never read a book or an article by a naturalist without feeling that the author must be a very nice person, an unusually superior specimen of the human race. By a naturalist, I mean someone who studies the ways of creatures in their natural habitat and, if he interferes at all, confines his interference to establishing a personal relation with them. Professors of animal psychology and behavioral scientists are a very different story. By such I mean those who subject animals to abnormal conditions of their own contriving, usually disagreeable, overcrowding them, providing them with mechanical surrogate mothers, giving them electric shocks, removing portions of their brains, etc., etc.—those, in other words, who perform experiments on animals which they would never dream of performing on themselves or their children. Even when the results of their researches are surprising and interesting, and often elementary common sense could have predicted their findings, I rarely read an article by one of them without feeling I should hate to sit next to him at dinner. His work may be necessary or valuable, but I have no more wish to know him socially than I wish to know the public executioner.

Mr. and Mrs. Milne, thank goodness, are naturalists who are interested in animals for their own sake. They are pleased and grateful, as we all should be, when knowledge gained by the study of animal behavior, anatomy, or physiology, turns out to have practical uses for man; but human appetite and ambition are not the prime motives for their investigations. *The Senses of Animals and Men* offers the reader a variety of pleasures. To begin with, it is full of curious facts. "Quiz" knowledge may not be a very exalted form of learning, but who does not enjoy acquiring some? I am delighted to have learned, for example, that male yellow fever mosquitoes are attracted most strongly by vibrations of 500 to 550 per second, that the song of the winter wren has 130 notes, that a blowfly's front feet are five times as sensitive to some sugars as its mouth, that the "ink" ejected by squids and octopuses is not just a protective visual screen, but also an anesthetic which dulls the senses of possible predators, that the male and female luna moth which to our eyes both look green are, in their own, a brunette and a blonde respectively.

More important, of course, are the general impressions and tentative conclusions which begin to emerge as the facts about individual species accumulate. There is a certain neo-Darwinian nightmare which haunts the minds of writers of science fiction, based on the assumption that any given species of life would, if it could, be the only kind of life in existence. In this science-fiction nightmare, some species, a fungus, say, undergoes a mutation which enormously increases its powers of growth or even endows it with intelligence. At once, absolute catastrophe threatens the earth, for unless the scientific hero can discover how to destroy it in time, it will obliterate every other kind of life on the planet. (What it would live on when it had is not explained.)

Any reader of the Milnes' book will realize that this terror is imaginary. Phrases like "the struggle for survival" and "the survival of the fittest" only have meaning when applied to the competition between members of the same species, and even there their application is limited. A creature is "fit" if it is adequately adapted to its particular world, and there are as many worlds as there are species. Each of these worlds must overlay with at least one other, usually with two—the world of that which it eats, and the world of that by which it is eaten. But with the vast majority of worlds in existence, it never comes into contact at all.

One of the most striking characteristics of Nature, as this book keeps demonstrating, is the extraordinary elaboration of the precautions she takes to ensure to each species its privacy. To many, for example, she allots their own frequency bands on the visual and aural spectrum; only such frequencies have "meaning" for them, and they have no meaning for others. The noise in our ears which to us means "a cricket," means nothing to crickets; what they attend to are the supersonic sounds which are inaudible to us, but which accompany what we hear.

Particularly striking are ways by which she guarantees privacy of sexual response and prevents random mating of different species. Some 700,000 species of insects have been identified, but each is able to breed true because the mating partners can only cooperate when each presses the other at definite spots sensitive to vibration, and the number and pattern of these areas differ from one species to the next. Occasionally mistakes are made:

> The female firefly perched on a leaf-tip can summon a passing mate by flashing at the correct time interval after he has broadcast a luminous message. Occasionally the flash from a leaf-tip invites the flying male to a female that is not of its own kind. She has winked too early or too late. Usually the ardent male pays for her mistake with his life, for a firefly that cannot become a suitor is merely a meal for her.

The question of survival is a mutual one. No species could survive unless its powers in one direction were balanced by a lack of power in another. If hawks, for example, were as prolific as mice, they would perish from starvation after they had exterminated their diet. Again, from time to time, the ecological balance is upset. In origin, the lamprey is a marine creature; in fresh water, which is more turbid and a poorer conductor of electricity than sea, it becomes too efficient at capturing fish. For the fishermen of the Great Lakes this has been a serious matter, the lamprey having ruined their business, but, in the long run, it would destroy the lamprey too.

Man, one might say, is the only creature who will not mind his own business, nor obey Nature's Game Laws. It is a commonplace that man has been able to develop as he has because, physically, he is an unspecialized, childish creature who has learned to master all environments precisely because he is perfectly adapted to none. After reading what Mr. and Mrs. Milne have to say about the human senses, however, I am surprised to learn how efficient our sensory endowment is. For a creature that is not by nature nocturnal, our night vision is remarkably good, and the sensitivity of our fingers to differences of touch much greater than is practically necessary. Even in the case of smell and taste, where our inferiority to many animals seems most obvious, we have not been prevented from developing an *haute cuisine,* in comparison with which any animal's taste in food seems crude. Our chief trouble, indeed, seems to be our deliberate abuse, either by neglect or overstimulus, or our inborn sensory gifts, and it is difficult to see a remedy without making changes in our life which seem economically impossible. In any modern city, a great deal of our energy has to be expended in *not* seeing, *not* hearing, *not* smelling. An inhabitant of New York who possessed the sensory acuteness of an African Bushman would very soon go mad.

As for the future, Mr. and Mrs. Milne hope for the best that somehow "every new understanding of the nervous mechanisms in animals is likely to lead to fresh expansion of man's own world." But they are naturalists and, therefore, nice people. I wish I could feel as sanguine, and that certain passing remarks they make did not haunt my mind more than they seem to haunt theirs.

The noises of civilization match progress. If their deafening sounds double again in intensity, as they have in the recent past, we may all need to wear protective ear stopples and give up trying to talk to one another.

Perhaps all these misunderstood senses will prove to operate through a "pleasure center" located recently in the brain, found by exploring the deeper portions with electrical probes. Direct stimulation of the pleasure center seems to substitute for food and sex and companionship, to the point where the scientists who discovered the center fear the consequences for mankind if unscrupulous people should find a way to market a self-stimulator reaching this region of the brain.

From such Huxley-Orwell nightmares may God protect us! At present, if we are not able ourselves to study fiddler-crabs, bats, megapodes, we can still read about such enchanting children of Nature in the books of those who, like Mr. and Mrs. Milne, have given their lives to it.

CONCERNING THE UNPREDICTABLE

> In creation there is not only a Yes but also a No; not
> only a height, but also an abyss; not only clarity but also
> obscurity; not only progress and continuation but also im-
> pediment and limitation . . . not only value but also worth-
> lessness. . . . It is true that individual creatures and men
> experience these things in most unequal measure, their lots
> being assigned by a justice which is curious or very much
> concealed. Yet it is irrefutable that creation and creature
> are good even in the fact that all that is exists in this con-
> trast and antithesis.
>
> —Karl Barth, in *Church Dogmatics.*

Rather oddly, I first heard of Dr. Loren Eiseley not in this country
but in Oxford, where a student gave me a copy of *The Immense
Journey,* since which time I have eagerly read anything of his I
could lay my hands on. His obvious ancestors, as both writers and
thinkers, are Thoreau and Emerson, but he often reminds me of
Ruskin, Richard Jefferies, W. H. Hudson, whom, I feel sure, he
must have read, and of two writers, Novalis (a German) and Adalbert Stifter (an Austrian), whom perhaps he hasn't. But I wouldn't
be sure. Some of the quotations in his latest book, *The Unexpected
Universe,* surprised me. I would not have expected someone who is
an American and a scientist to have read such little-known literary

works as the *Völuspá,* James Thomson's *The City of Dreadful Night,* and Charles Williams' play *Cranmer.*

I have one slight criticism of his literary style, which I will get over with at once. Like Ruskin, he can at times write sentences which I would call "woozy"; that is to say, too dependent upon some private symbolism of his own to be altogether comprehensible to others. For example:

> We refuse to consider that in the old eye of the hurricane we may be, and doubtless are, in aggregate, a slightly more diffuse and dangerous dragon of the primal morning that still enfolds us.

To this objection he has, I know, a crushing reply:

> One of Thoreau's wisest remarks is upon the demand scientific intellectuals sometimes make, that one must speak so as to be always understood. "Neither men," he says, "nor toadstools grow so."

Dr. Eiseley happens to be an archeologist, an anthropologist, and a naturalist, but, if I have understood him rightly, the first point he wishes to make is that in order to be a scientist, an artist, a doctor, a lawyer, or what-have-you, one has first to be a human being. No member of any other species can have a special "field." One question his book raises is: "What differences have recent scientific discoveries, in physics, astronomy, biology, etc., made to man's conception, individually or collectively, of himself?" The answer is, I believe, very little.

We did not have to wait for Darwin to tell us that, as physical creatures, we are akin to other animals. Like them, we breathe, eat, digest, excrete, copulate, are viviparously born, and, whatever views we may have about an "afterlife," must certainly suffer physical death in this. Indeed, one result of urbanization has been that, despite what we now know about our ancestry, we feel far less akin and grateful to the animal kingdom than did primitive tribes, with their totem systems and animal folktales.

Speaking of the recognition of Odysseus by his dog Argos, Dr. Eiseley says:

> The magic that gleams an instant between Argos and Odysseus is both the recognition of diversity and the need

] 465 [

for affection across the illusions of form. It is nature's cry to homeless, far-wandering, insatiable man: "Do not forget your brethren, nor the green wood from which you sprang. To do so is to invite disaster. . . . One does not meet oneself until one catches the reflection from an eye other than human."

Before Descartes, such a warning would have been unnecessary. On the other hand, nothing Darwin and the geneticists have to tell us can alter the fact that, as self-conscious beings who speak (that is to say, give Proper Names to other beings), who laugh, who pray, and who, as creators of history and culture, continue to change after our biological evolution is complete, we are unique among all the creatures we know of. All attempts to account for our behavior on the basis of our prehuman ancestors are myths, and usually invented to justify base behavior. As Karl Kraus wrote:

> When a man is treated like a beast, he says, "After all, I'm human." When he behaves like a beast, he says, "After all, I'm only human."

No; as Dr. Eiseley says, "There is no definition or description of man possible by reducing him to ape or tree-shrew. Once, it is true, the shrew contained him, but he is gone." Or, as G. K. Chesterton said, "If it is not true that a divine being fell, then one can only say that one of the animals went completely off its head." What modern science has profoundly changed is our way of thinking about the non-human universe. We have always been aware that human beings are characters in a story in which we can know more or less what has happened but can never predict what is going to happen; what we never realized until recently is that the same is true of the universe. But, of course, its story is even more mysterious to us than our own. When we act, we do know something about our motives for action, but it is rarely possible for us to say why anything novel happens in the universe. All the same, I do not personally believe there is such a thing as a "random" event. "Unpredictable" is a factual description; "random" contains, without having the honesty to admit it, a philosophical bias typical of persons who have forgotten how to pray. Though he does use the term once, I don't think Dr. Eiseley believes in it, either:

The earth's atmosphere of oxygen appears to be the product of a biological invention, photosynthesis, another random event that took place in Archeozoic times. That single "invention," for such it was, determined the entire nature of life on this planet, and there is no possibility at present of calling it preordained. Similarly, the stepped-up manipulation of chance, in the shape of both mutation and recombination of genetic factors, which is one result of the sexual mechanism, would have been unprophesiable.

I must now openly state my own bias and say that I do not believe in Chance; I believe in Providence and Miracles. If photosynthesis was invented by chance, then I can only say it was a damned lucky chance for us. If, biologically speaking, it is a "statistical impossibility" that I should be walking the earth instead of a million other possible people, I can only think of it as a miracle which I must do my best to deserve. Natural Selection as a negative force is comprehensible. It is obvious that a drastic change in the environment, like an Ice Age, will destroy a large number of species adapted to a warm climate. What I cannot swallow is the assertion that "chance" mutations can explain the fact that whenever an ecological niche is free, some species evolves to fit it, especially when one thinks how peculiar some such niches—the one occupied by the liver fluke, for example—can be. Dr. Eiseley quotes George Gaylord Simpson as saying:

> The association of unusual physical conditions with a crisis in evolution is not likely to be pure coincidence. Life and its environment are interdependent and evolve together.

Dr. Eiseley has excellent things to say about the myth of the Survival of the Fittest:

> A major portion of the world's story appears to be that of fumbling little creatures of seemingly no great potential, falling, like the helpless little girl Alice, down a rabbit hole or an unexpected crevice into some new and topsy-turvy realm. . . . The first land-walking fish was, by modern standards, an ungainly and inefficient vertebrate. Figuratively, he was a water failure who had managed to climb ashore on a continent where no vertebrates existed. In a time of crisis he had escaped his enemies. . . . The wet fish

gasping in the harsh air on the shore, the warm-blooded mammal roving unchecked through the torpor of the reptilian night, the lizard-bird launching into a moment of ill-aimed flight, shatter all purely competitive assumptions. These singular events reveal escapes through the living screen, penetrated, one would have to say in retrospect, by the "overspecialized" and the seemingly "inefficient," the creatures driven to the wall.

The main theme of *The Unexpected Universe* is Man as the Quest Hero, the wanderer, the voyager, the seeker after adventure, knowledge, power, meaning, and righteousness. The Quest is dangerous (he may suffer shipwreck or ambush) and unpredictable (he never knows what will happen to him next). The Quest is not of his own choosing—often, in weariness, he wishes he had never set out on it—but is enjoined upon him by his nature as a human being:

> No longer, as with the animal, can the world be accepted as given. It has to be perceived and consciously thought about, abstracted, and considered. The moment one does so, one is outside of the natural; objects are each one surrounded with an aura radiating meaning to man alone.

> Mostly the animals understand their roles, but man, by comparison, seems troubled by a message that, it is often said, he cannot quite remember or has gotten wrong. . . . Bereft of instinct, he must search continually for meanings. . . . Man was a reader before he became a writer, a reader of what Coleridge once called the mighty alphabet of the universe.

For illustrations of his thesis, Dr. Eiseley begins with an imaginary voyage—Homer's epic the *Odyssey*—and goes on to two famous historical voyages, that of Captain Cook in the *Resolution,* during which he discovered not the Terra Incognita he was sent to find—a rich and habitable continent south and westward of South America—but what he described as "an inexpressibly horrid Antarctica," and Darwin's voyage in the *Beagle,* during which he found the data which led him to doubt the Fixity of Species. Lastly, Dr. Eiseley tells us many anecdotes from his own life voyage, and these are to me the most fascinating passages in the book. Of the *Odyssey* he says:

> Odysseus' passage through the haunted waters of the eastern Mediterranean symbolizes, at the start of the Western intellectual tradition, the sufferings that the universe and his own nature impose upon homeward-yearning man. In the restless atmosphere of today all the psychological elements of the Odyssey are present to excess: the driving will toward achievement, the technological cleverness crudely manifest in the blinding of Cyclops, the fierce rejection of the sleepy Lotus Isles, the violence between man and man. Yet, significantly, the ancient hero cries out in desperation, "There is nothing worse for men than wandering."

Dr. Eiseley's autobiographical passages are, most of them, descriptions of numinous encounters—some joyful, some terrifying. After reading them, I get the impression of a wanderer who is often in danger of being shipwrecked on the shores of Dejection—it can hardly be an accident that three of his encounters take place in cemeteries—and a solitary who feels more easily at home with animals than with his fellow human beings. Aside from figures in his childhood, the human beings who have "messages" for him are all total strangers—someone tending a rubbish dump, a mysterious figure throwing stranded starfish back into the sea, a vagrant scientist with a horrid parasitic worm in a bottle, a girl in the Wild West with Neanderthal features. As a rule, though, his numinous encounters are with non-human objects—a spider, the eye of a dead octopus, his own shepherd dog, a starving jackrabbit, a young fox. It is also clear that he is a deeply compassionate man who, in his own words, "loves the lost ones, the failures of the world." It is typical of him that, on recovering consciousness after a bad fall, to find himself bleeding profusely, he should, quite unselfconsciously, apologize to his now doomed blood cells—phagocytes and platelets—"Oh, don't go. I'm sorry, I've done for you." More importantly, he reveals himself as a man unusually well trained in the habit of prayer, by which I mean the habit of listening. The petitionary aspect of prayer is its most trivial because it is involuntary. We cannot help asking that our wishes may be granted, though all too many of them are like wishing that two and two may make five, and cannot and should not be granted. But the serious part of prayer begins when we have got our begging over with and listen for the Voice of what I would call the Holy Spirit, though if others prefer to say the Voice of Oz or the Dreamer or Conscience, I shan't quarrel, so long as they don't call it the Voice of the Super-Ego, for that "entity" can only tell us what we know already, whereas the Voice I am talking about always says something new and unpredictable—an unexpected demand, obedience to which involves a change of self, however painful.

At this point, a digression. Last September, I attended a symposium in Stockholm on "The Place of Value in a World of Fact." Most of those present were scientists, some of them very distinguished indeed. To my shock and amazement, they kept saying that what we need today is a set of *Ethical Axioms* (italics mine). I can only say that to me the phrase is gibberish. An axiom is stated in the indicative and addressed to the intellect. From one set of axioms one kind of mathematics will follow, from another set another, but it would be nonsense to call one of them "better" than the other. All ethical statements are addressed to the will, usually a reluctant will, and must therefore appear in the imperative. "Thou shalt love thy neighbor as thyself" and "A straight line is the shortest distance between two points" belong to two totally different realms of discourse.

But to return to Dr. Eiseley. As a rule, the Voice speaks to him not directly but through messengers who are unaware of the message they bear. In the following dream, however, he is spoken to without intermediaries:

> The dream was of a great blurred bear-like shape emerging from the snow against the window. It pounded on the glass and beckoned importunately toward the forest. I caught the urgency of a message as uncouth and indecipherable as the shape of its huge bearer in the snow. In the immense terror of my dream I struggled against the import of that message as I struggled also to resist the impatient pounding of the frost-enveloped beast at the window.
>
> Suddenly I lifted the telephone beside my bed, and through the receiver came a message as cryptic as the mes-

sage from the snow, but far more miraculous in origin. For I knew intuitively, in the still snowfall of my dream, that the voice I heard, a long way off, was my own voice in childhood. Pure and sweet, incredibly refined and beautiful beyond the things of earth, yet somehow inexorable and not to be stayed, the voice was already terminating its message. "I am sorry to have troubled you," the clear faint syllables of the child persisted. They seemed to come across a thinning wire that lengthened far away into the years of my past. "I am sorry, I am sorry to have troubled you at all." The voice faded before I could speak. I was awake now, trembling in the cold.

I have said that I suspect Dr. Eiseley of being a melancholic. He recognizes that man is the only creature who speaks personally, works, and prays, but nowhere does he overtly say that man is the only creature who laughs. True laughter is not to be confused with the superior titter of the intellect, though we are capable, alas, of that, too: when we truly laugh, we laugh simultaneously *with* and *at*. True laughter (belly laughter) I would define as the spirit of Carnival.

Again a digression, on the meaning of Carnival as it was known in the Middle Ages and persisted in a few places, like Rome, where Goethe witnessed and described it in February of 1788. Carnival celebrates the unity of our human race as mortal creatures, who come into this world and depart from it without our consent, who must eat, drink, defecate, belch, and break wind in order to live, and procreate if our species is to survive. Our feelings about this are ambiguous. To us as individuals, it is a cause for rejoicing to know that we are not alone, that all of us, irrespective of age or sex or rank or talent, are in the same boat. As unique persons, on the other hand, all of us are resentful that an exception cannot be made in our own case. We oscillate between wishing we were unreflective animals and wishing we were disembodied spirits, for in either case we should not be problematic to ourselves. The Carnival solution of this ambiguity is to laugh, for laughter is simultaneously a protest and an acceptance. During Carnival, all social distinctions are suspended, even that of sex. Young men dress up as girls, young girls as boys. The escape from social personality is symbolized by the wearing of masks. The oddity of the human animal expresses itself through the grotesque—false noses, huge bellies and buttocks, farcical imitations of childbirth and copulation. The protest element in laughter takes the form of mock aggression: people pelt each other with small, harmless objects, draw cardboard daggers, and abuse each other verbally, like the small boy Goethe heard screaming at his father, "*Sia ammazzato il Signore Padre!*" Traditionally, Carnival, the days of feasting and fun, immediately precedes Lent, the days of fasting and prayer. In medieval carnivals, parodies of the rituals of the Church were common, but what Lewis Carroll said of literary parody—"One can only parody a poem one admires"—is true of all parody. One can only blaspheme if one believes. The world of Laughter is much more closely related to the world of Worship and Prayer than either is to the everyday, secular world of Work, for both are worlds in which we are all equal, in the first as individual members of our species, in the latter as unique persons. In the world of Work, on the other hand, we are not and cannot be equal, only diverse and interdependent: each of us, whether as scientist, artist, cook, cabdriver, or whatever, has to do "our thing." So long as we thought of Nature in polytheistic terms as the abode of gods, our efficiency and success as workers were hampered by a false humility which tried to make Nature responsible for us. But, according to Genesis, God made Adam responsible for looking after the Garden of Eden on His behalf, and it now seems as if He expects us to be responsible for the whole natural universe, which means that, as workers, we have to regard the universe *etsi deus non daretur:* God must be a hidden deity, veiled by His creation.

A satisfactory human life, individually or collectively, is possible only if proper respect is paid to all three worlds. Without Prayer and Work, the Carnival laughter turns ugly, the comic obscenities grubby and pornographic, the mock aggression into real hatred and cruelty. (The hippies, it appears to me, are trying to recover the sense of Carnival which is so conspicuously absent in this age, but so long as they reject Work they are unlikely to succeed.) Without Laughter and Work, Prayer turns Gnostic, cranky, Pharisaic, while those who try to live by Work alone, without Laughter or Prayer, turn into insane lovers of power, tyrants who would enslave Nature to their immediate desires—an attempt which can only end in utter catastrophe, shipwreck on the Isle of the Sirens.

Carnival in its traditional forms is not, I think, for Dr. Eiseley any more than it is for me. Neither of us can enjoy crowds and loud noises. But even introverted intellectuals can share the Carnival experience if they are prepared to forget their dignity, as Dr. Eiseley did when he unexpectedly encountered a fox cub:

> The creature was very young. He was alone in a dread universe. I crept on my knees around the prow and crouched beside him. It was a small fox pup from a den under the timbers who looked up at me. God knows what had become of his brothers and sisters. His parent must not have been home from hunting.
>
> He innocently selected what I think was a chicken bone from an untidy pile of splintered rubbish and shook it at me invitingly. There was a vast and playful humor in his face. . . . Here was the thing in the midst of the bones, the wide-eyed, innocent fox inviting me to play, with the innate courtesy of its two forepaws placed appealingly together, along with a mock shake of the head. The universe was swinging in some fantastic fashion around to present its face, and the face was so small that the universe itself was laughing.
>
> It was not a time for human dignity. It was a time only for the careful observance of amenities written behind the stars. Gravely I arranged my forepaws while the puppy whimpered with ill-concealed excitement. I drew the breath of a fox's den into my nostrils. On impulse, I picked up clumsily a whiter bone and shook it in teeth that had not entirely forgotten their original purpose. Round and round we tumbled for one ecstatic moment. . . . For just a moment I had held the universe at bay by the simple expedient of sitting on my haunches before a fox den and tumbling about with a chicken bone. It is the gravest, most meaningful act I shall ever accomplish, but, as Thoreau once remarked of some peculiar errand of his own, there is no use reporting it to the Royal Society.

Thank God, though, Dr. Eiseley has reported it to me. *Bravo!* say I.

THE MEGRIMS

There screen'd in shades from
day's detested glare,
Spleen sighs for ever on her
pensive bed,
Pain at her side, and megrim at
her head.

—Pope

Dr. Sacks's primary purpose in writing this book* was, no doubt, to enlighten his fellow practitioners about a complaint of which most of them know all too little. As Dr. Gooddy says in his Foreword:

> The common attitude is that migraine is merely a form of mainly non-disabling headache which occupies far more of a busy doctor's time than its importance warrants. . . . Some tablets and the current inelegant cliché of "learning to live with it" are advised by the physician, who hopes he will not be on duty the next time the patient comes for advice. . . . Many doctors are only too pleased when a patient, in desperation, takes himself off to the practitioners of

* *Migraine,* by Oliver Sacks.

"fringe medicine," almost hoping that the results will be both disastrous and very costly.

I am sure, however, that any layman who is at all interested in the relation between body and mind, even if he does not understand all of it, will find the book as fascinating as I have.

It has been estimated that migraine afflicts at least 10 percent of the human race and the true percentage may well be higher, since probably only those who suffer severe attacks consult a doctor. Even if, like myself, one has had the good fortune never to have experienced an attack, we all have known some relative or friend who has had them, so that we can compare their character traits and symptoms with Dr. Sacks's detailed descriptions.

Unlike contagious diseases and genetic disabilities such as hemophilia on the one hand, and hysterias on the other, migraine is a classic example of a psychosomatic illness in which physiological and psychological factors play an equal role. As physical organisms we are pretty much the same, that is to say, our bodies have a limited repertoire of symptoms. This makes it possible to diagnose a case of migraine, to distinguish it from, say, epilepsy or asthma. But as conscious persons who can say *I,* each of us is unique. This means that no two cases of migraine are identical; treatment that succeeds with one patient can fail with another.

> A migraine is a physical event which may also be from the start, or later become, an emotional or symbolic event. A migraine expresses both physiological and emotional needs: it is the prototype of a psychophysiological reaction. Thus the convergence of thinking which its understanding demands must be based simultaneously, both on neurology and on psychiatry. . . . Finally, migraine cannot be conceived as an exclusively human reaction, but must be considered as a form of biological reaction specifically tailored to human needs and human nervous systems.

The first part of Dr. Sacks's book consists of a series of detailed clinical observations. He distinguishes between three types of migraine: common migraine, popularly called "a sick headache"; classical migraine, in which, as in epileptic attacks, there is frequently a distortion of the visual field; and migrainous neuralgia, or "cluster headache," so called because attacks are closely grouped. These descriptions, interesting as I found them, I do not feel qualified to discuss.

I will mention two curious observations Dr. Sacks makes. He tells us that the "Nightmare Song" in *Iolanthe* mentions no fewer than twelve migraine symptoms, and that the visions of the medieval nun, Hildegard of Bingen, were clearly visual auras caused by classical migraine.

Part Two is devoted to the questions: "What circumstances trigger off a migraine attack?" and "Is there a migraine personality?" The evidence is bewilderingly diverse. Thus, migraine often runs in families, but Dr. Sacks believes this is probably learned from the family environment, not genetically inherited, for many patients have no such family history.

Though classical migraine more commonly attacks young people and males, this is not invariable, and the first attack of common migraine may occur after the age of forty, among women, for example, during their menopause. Classical migraine and cluster headache tend to occur for no discernible reason at regular intervals, varying from two to twelve weeks; common migraine seems more dependent upon external and emotional situations. Some cases resemble allergies: an attack can be caused by bright lights, loud noises, bad smells, inclement weather, alcohol, amphetamines. Others suggest a hormonal origin: migraine is not uncommon among women during their menstrual periods, but very rare during pregnancy.

Such a diversity naturally produces an equal diversity of theories as to the basic cause of migraine. The somatically orientated physician looks for a chemical or neurological solution, the psychiatrist for an exclusively psychological answer. Dr. Sacks thinks that both are only half-right. Of the psychological theories the two most accepted are those of Wolff (1963) and Fromm-Reichmann (1937).

> Migraineurs are portrayed by Wolff as ambitious, successful, perfectionistic, rigid, orderly, cautious, and emotionally constipated, driven therefore, from time to time, to outbursts and breakdowns which must assume an indirect somatic form. Fromm-Reichmann is also able to arrive at a

clear-cut conclusion: migraine, she states, is a physical expression of unconscious hostility against consciously beloved persons.

Dr. Sacks's experiences with his patients have led him to conclude that while many are, as Wolff says, hyperactive and obsessional, there are others who are lethargic and sloppy, and that while, as Fromm-Reichmann says, most migraine attacks are a somatic expression of violent emotions, usually rage, this may be a reaction to an intolerable life situation of which the patient is quite aware, and may also be self-punitive.

> We find, in practice, that sudden *rage* is the commonest precipitant, although *fright* (panic) may be equally potent in younger patients. Sudden *elation* (as at a moment of triumph or unexpected good fortune) may have the same effect. . . . Nor should one claim that all patients with habitual migraine are "neurotic" (except in so far as neurosis is the universal human condition), for in many cases the migraines may replace a neurotic structure, constituting an alternative to neurotic desperation and assuagement.

In Part Three, Dr. Sacks discusses the physiological, biological, and psychological factors in migraine. His theories about its biological basis I found particularly interesting and suggestive. Among all animals are to be found two possible reactions to a situation of threat or danger, fight-or-flight and immobilization. He quotes Darwin's description of the second:

> The picture of passive fear, as Darwin portrays it, is one of passivity and prostration, allied with splachnic and glandular activity (". . . a strong tendency to yawn . . . death-like pallor . . . beads of sweat stand out on the skin. All the muscles of the body are relaxed. The intestines are affected. The sphincter muscles cease to act, and no longer retain the contents of the body. . . ."). The general attitude is one of cringing, cowering, and sinking. If the passive reaction is more acute, there may be abrupt loss of postural tone or of consciousness.

He believes that, despite the association between migraine and rage, it is from this passive reaction, tailored to human nature, that migraine is biologically derived. This seems to me very plausible. Before he invented weapons, primitive man must have been one of the most defenseless of all the creatures, being devoid of fangs or claws or tusks or hooves or venom, and a relatively slow mover. It seems unlikely, therefore, that aggression or rage can have been a basic biological instinct in man as it is in the predator carnivores. Human aggression must be a secondary modification of what was originally a feeling of terror and helplessness. As Coleridge said: "In all perplexity there is a portion of fear, which disposes the mind to anger."

Dr. Sacks concludes his chapter on psychological approaches to migraine by saying that three kinds of psychosomatic linkage may occur.

> . . . first, an inherent physiological connection between certain symptoms and effects; second, a fixed symbolic equivalence between certain physical symptoms and states of mind, analogous to the use of facial expressions; third, an arbitrary, idiosyncratic symbolism uniting physical symptoms and phantasies, analogous to the construction of hysterical symptoms.

The last part is devoted to the problems of therapy. As in all cases of functional disorders, the personal relation between doctor and patient is of prime importance. "Every sickness is a musical problem," said Novalis, "and every cure a musical solution." This means, as Dr. Sacks says, that, whatever method of treatment a physician may choose or be forced to choose, there is only one cardinal rule:

> . . . one must always *listen* to the patient. For if migraine patients have a common and legitimate complaint besides their migraines, it is that they have not been listened to by physicians. Looked at, investigated, drugged, charged; but not listened to.

Dr. Sacks recognizes that there are drugs, notably Ergotomine Tartrate and Methysergide, which can relieve the pain of an acute attack, and which it would be heartless to refuse a patient, unless he has other physiological conditions which counter-indicate their use, but he regards them as somewhat dangerous palliatives which cannot effect a permanent cure.

His own bias, he tells us, is toward psychotherapy, but he is modest in his claims. He does not think, for example, that the only solution to migraine is depth analysis, for which few patients have either the money or the time. Further, he admits that some patients find a psychotherapeutic approach unacceptable.

> Severely affected patients should be seen on a regular basis, at intervals—approximately of two to ten weeks. The early interviews must be long and searching, in order to expose for both patient and physician the general situation and specific stresses which are involved, while establishing the foundations of the physician's authority and the patient-physician relationship; later consultations may be briefer and more limited in scope, and will chiefly be concerned with the discussion of current problems as these are experienced by the patient and expressed in his migraines. Cursory medical attention in disastrous, and an important cause of allegedly "intractable" migraine.

He also recommends the keeping of two calendars, a migraine calendar and a calendar of daily events, which may reveal unsuspected circumstances as provocative of attacks.

"Cure," in his opinion, means finding for each particular patient the best *modus vivendi for him*. This can mean, in certain cases, allowing the patient to "keep" his headaches.

> The attempt to dislodge severe habitual migraines in a pathologically unconcerned or hysterical personality may force the patient to face intense anxieties and emotional conflicts which are even less tolerable than the migraines. The physical symptoms, paradoxically, may be more merciful than the conflicts they simultaneously conceal and express.

Such patients would agree with Marx: "The only antidote to mental suffering is physical pain."

*

DEBORAH

*

I wonder if the psychologists can explain why it is that mountaineering should so strongly appeal to the intellectual, the book-loving, the introvert, persons for whom conventional athletics, like football or baseball, have no interest. Whatever the reason, one consequence has been that the books written about mountaineering have been of an unusually high literary standard. The first historical account of ascending a mountain for its own sake (no rock-climbing, of course) is by Petrarch, and from the middle of the nineteenth century when serious rock-climbing became popular until the present day, a succession of vivid accounts of expeditions have appeared, starting with Edward Whymper's account of climbing the Matterhorn. David Roberts has already written one excellent book, *The Mountain of My Fear; Deborah,* in my opinion, is even finer.

It tells of the attempt by two friends from Harvard—henceforth I shall call them, as they are in the book, Dave and Don—to climb the East Face of Mount Deborah, Alaska, in the summer of 1964. (The Western, and easier, face had been climbed in 1954.) The expedition, that is to say, the time they spent alone together in the wilderness, lasted six weeks.

There are two threads to the narrative. Firstly, it is a detailed factual account of what all mountain climbers have to do and suffer, of carrying heavy loads, being storm-bound for days in a tiny tent, aware all the time of the possibility of being killed by an avalanche or by falling into a crevasse. On the way down, Don twice fell into one with nearly fatal results: the first time it took four hours to get him out, the second time he suffered severe facial injuries. And then of course whoever the climbers are, there is the excitement and worry of wondering: "Shall we succeed?" In this case, they did not. From a high col Dave saw the East Face for the first time at close range.

"The crumbly brown rock towered, flat and crackless, a few degrees less than vertical. A thin splotchy coating of ice overlay most of the rock. Where the rock overhung, great icicles grew. . . . And above, blocking out half the sky, was the terrible black cliff, the six-hundred-foot wall that we had once blithely, back in Cambridge, allowed three days to climb. At its upper rim, nearly a thousand feet above me, hovered monstrous chunks of ice, like aimed cannons at the top of a castle wall. As I watched, one broke off, fell most of the six hundred feet without touching anything, then smashed violently on a ledge to my left and bounced out of sight down the precipice."

Curiously, they felt less disappointed than one might have expected. "Of course we were sad. But as we turned down, we were almost light-hearted, too. The mountain had been fair to us; it had unequivocally said Stop, instead . . . of forcing the decision of failure on us. . . . The mountain had allowed us pride."

During the ascent, both Dave and Don had suffered from anxiety dreams. (As one would expect, neither had sexual dreams.) Thus Dave: "I would be a guest at a buffet dinner where every imaginable delicacy was heaped in inexhaustible piles on a huge table. There would be scores of other guests . . . But each time I started to eat, someone would interrupt me with a question." After their defeat, the anxiety disappeared, and now he dreamed that "this time I was the host and friend after friend kept showing up and complimenting me on the food."

The second thread of the story is of the greatest psychological interest, a day-by-day account of the personal reactions to each other of two young men united by a love of climbing at which both are equally gifted, but of very different temperaments, living at very close quarters under conditions of great stress.

Of course, we only hear Dave's side of the story, but I don't think Don's would contradict it.

Long before they decided to climb Deborah (it was actually Don who suggested making it a two-man show), Dave had begun to reflect on the differences between them. Dave was quick and impatient, Don slow and methodical. "I loved conversations, but Don preferred to think by himself." Then there was the contrast between their attitudes towards their academic studies. Dave, majoring in mathematics, took exams in his stride; Don, majoring in philosophy, would panic at the prospect almost to the point of a nervous breakdown.

Even their attitudes towards their common love, climbing, were not the same. Dave was approaching their expedition as "an arduous adventure to be got through with, a thing to be conquered, a place to visit for the sake of the wonder and beauty, but from which to return when it began to wear thin." For Don, it was just the opposite, "an adventure to be lived as long as possible, a place to go where he could be at home and relax."

Their first angry argument broke out as they were approaching base camp. "Don had used the phrase 'well-behaved' four or five times to describe the glacier's lack of crevasses . . . we irritably argued the merits of the word 'well-behaved.' What had really provoked the quarrel, I suppose, was the boredom of the hiking. I had started to notice some of Don's mannerisms and, for lack of a better preoccupation, had picked on one of them to vent my frustrations. It was the first time that I recognized a trait of my own. . . . I could not stand for things to go well for too long a stretch; it was as if I needed a regular exercise of hostility."

Since a person's eating habits are always a manifestation of his character, it is not surprising that these were a frequent source of irritation. "I got mad at his deliberate way of spooning his breakfast cereal because it was indicative of his methodicalness, which was indicative of a mental slowness, which was why he disliked and opposed my impatience." For one cause of annoyance, Dave was entirely to blame: he should never have tried to play chess, which he played well, with Don, who did not. No game is any fun unless both sides are equally matched.

To avoid ill-feelings, they found that they had to obey strict rules when it came to dividing things between them, like food and weights. "The pound was not a fine enough unit; we haggled over ounces. . . . We vacillated between the roles of the accuser ('Come on now, the stove's easily two and a half pounds') and martyr ('It's all right, I'll take it anyway')."

Such incidents in isolation can make it sound as if their expedition was a disastrous failure, which it clearly wasn't. As Dave gratefully acknowledges, there were many good moments of warmth, joy and brotherhood. The difficulty for a writer about such moments is that it seems to be a law of language that happiness, like goodness, is almost impossible to describe, while conflict, like evil, is all too easy to depict.

THE KITCHEN OF LIFE

Though it contains a number of recipes, *The Art of Eating* is a book for the library rather than the kitchen shelf. If it were simply a manual of culinary technique, I could not discuss it because, much as I enjoy reading recipes, they remain for me mysterious magical spells; like most people who cannot cook, I cannot combine the various ingredients in my imagination so as to guess what the dish will taste like. When, for example, I read Mrs. Fisher's recipe for *Prune Roast,* though I have no doubt that it is delicious, I can only taste the prunes in isolation and shudder.

For the benefit of readers who are also cooks and therefore in a position to judge, I asked a friend upon whose authority I rely to select three recipes as examples of her taste and skill. He chose *Hot Winter Borscht, Hindu Eggs 1949* and *Hamburgers à la Mode de Moi-même*. All three are simple well-known dishes. A comparison of her versions with what is generally served demonstrates the truth of Countess Morphy's dictum: "Plain cooking cannot be entrusted to plain cooks."

Cooking is an art and its appreciation, therefore, is governed by the law which applies to all artistic appreciation. Those who have been subjected too long and too exclusively to bad cooking become incapable of recognizing good cooking if and when they encounter it. Nobody can afford to keep a good professional cook any more and, though there are still good restaurants, their prices are geared to people with expense accounts. For most of us, the possibility of eating well depends upon the skill and passion of the amateur cook, and learning the art should now be regarded as essential to an educated man or woman. At Oxford and Cambridge, for example, I should like to see a stove installed in every undergraduate's room and the College dining-halls transformed into supermarkets and liquor-stores. In the meantime, I would recommend all parents (and godparents) to present their children of both sexes on their sixteenth birthday with a copy of *The Art of Eating*. It will not teach them how to cook, but I cannot think of any other reading-matter which is more likely to inspire them with the desire to learn.

The Art of Eating is about Food and People. For such a theme Mrs. Fisher is singularly well qualified. In the first place, cooking is her avocation not her profession. Several famous chefs have published their reminiscences but, in describing their clients, they are at the disadvantage of having only known them as diners, but Mrs. Fisher has also known her guests as friends, lovers, husbands, so that she is able to relate their gastronomical habits to the rest of their personalities. Again, since she is not a professional tied to a kitchen, she is free to dine in restaurants and at the tables of others and is immune from professional jealousy.

In the second place, though she is an amateur by status, she is a practicing cook, not a member of some Wine and Food Society. The difference between an expert cook and a professional gourmet is the difference between an artist and a connoisseur: because he does not work for his pleasure but only pays for it, the connoisseur can, and only too often does, divorce pleasure from love. There is a kind of gourmet who writes about eating in the same way that an elderly roué talks about sex and the effect on me is the same—he makes all pleasure sound disgusting: after listening to him holding forth about some exquisite meal he had in 1910, I feel like living on capsules for the rest of my life.

Last but not least, Mrs. Fisher is as talented a writer as she is a cook. Indeed, I do not know of anyone in the United States today who writes better prose. If a reader wishes to test this assertion, let him turn to the first three pages of the section in *An Alphabet for Gourmets* entitled *I is for Innocence.*

It is extraordinary how little attention has been paid by either historians or novelists to the eating habits of nations, generations and individuals. Nobody, so far as I know has seriously tackled the history of cooking, which is full of fascinating problems. For instance, neither the potato nor pasta were native to Europe and must, when first introduced, have been exotic foods. How did they become staple diets? Why did the northern peoples take to the potato and the Italians to pasta? Today, when no nation can live in isolation and mass travel has become possible, such questions have assumed great political importance. The average man is more conservative in his gastronomical habits than in any others; at the same time, the greatest insult one can offer to another is to refuse the food he provides. Americans intending to travel abroad now receive a letter from the President reminding them that, even as tourists, they are emissaries of their country. Food, I am sorry to say, is not mentioned. Every tourist ought to be warned that, if he refuses to eat the typical food of the country he is visiting, he is doing more to create ill will than if he stole it.

Such adaptation is, of course, not always easy. "What is patriotism," wrote Lin Yutang, "but the love of the good things we ate in our childhood?" But it is also true that one reason why we find certain dishes good is *because* we ate them in childhood. Having grown up in England, I belong to a class of persons for whom Mrs. Fisher feels an exasperated pity, those who desire potatoes twice a day. When I started to read her description of *The Perfect Dinner,* my mouth watered but, presently, I came to the main meat course with which she serves noodles and I salivated no more. I *can* eat noodles or spaghetti or even rice, but they *say* nothing to me, whereas I can hear a song in any overboiled elderly spud. There are certain tastes which those who have never experienced them as children can neither understand nor cure: who but an Englishman, for example, can know the delights of stone-cold leathery toast for breakfast, or the wonders of *Dead Man's Leg?*

It is no accident that the central rite of the Christian religion, its symbol for agape, love untainted by selfish desire or self-projection, should be the act of eating bread and drinking wine. For such a symbol, a sexual rite would never do. In the first place, since it presupposes two different sexes, it divides as well as unites; in the second, it is not intrinsically selfish enough. Though it is necessary to the survival of the race, the sexual act is not necessary to the survival of the individual so that, even at its crudest, it contains an element of giving. Eating, on the other hand is a pure act of taking. Only the absolutely necessary and absolutely self-regarding can stand as a symbol for its opposite, the absolutely voluntary and self-forgetful. From watching the way in which a person eats, one can learn a great deal about the way in which he loves himself and, consequently, about the way he will probably love or hate his neighbor. The behavior towards others of the gobbler will be different from that of the pecker, of the person who eats his titbit first from the person who leaves his to the last.

Mrs. Fisher gives us a whole gallery of portraits. Here, for example, is Madame Biarnet.

> She ate like a madwoman, crumbs falling from her mouth, her cheeks bulging, her eyes glistening and darting about the plates and cups and her hands tearing at chunks of meat and crusts of bread. Occasionally she stopped long enough to put a tiny bite between the wet delicate lips of her little terrier Tango, who sat silently on her knees through every meal. . . . She drank only in Lent, for some deeply hidden reason. Then she grew uproarious and affectionate and finally tearful on hot spiced *Moulin à Vent* in which she sopped fried pastries called *Friandaises de Carême*. They immediately became very limp and noisy to eat, and she loved them; a way to make long soughings which irritated her husband and satisfied her bitter insistence that we are all beasts.

And here is a horrible young American blonde.

> She smoked all through the meal, which none of us was doing, and once, when she let her pretty arm fall towards Chexbres and the fingers unfold commandingly, I saw him pick up the cigarette box and offer it to her, so that she had to lift her hand again and choose one for herself, and I knew that he was deeply angry with her, in spite of his wisdom and tolerance.

The rest of us were disjointing our little brown birds and eating them in our fingers, as is only proper on a summer night among friends in a friendly room. But the girl cut one little piece off one side of the breast, one little piece off the other, and then pushed the plump carcase almost fretfully away. She picked a few late summer peas from the vegetables on her plate, and ate a little bread, and then asked Chexbres for coffee.

The portrait which Mrs. Fisher draws of herself interests me very much. On her own showing, she believes in and practices equality of the sexes: there is nothing of the Little Woman about her. The male wolf neither frightens nor shocks her—she sounds as if she were quite capable of playing the wolf herself—she knows how to handle waiters and can dine alone in a restaurant with perfect composure.

If this self-portrait is accurate, it confirms a theory of mine that in most women who develop a passion for cooking, their *animus,* their unconscious masculine side, is unusually strong, while in men who show the same passion, it is their *anima* which is stronger than normal. One might put it like this. The male who loves cooking as an art owes this love to the fact that he has no breasts; in his female colleague, the origin of such a love is the wish that her status as a human person shall not depend upon her possessing them. (I wish some psychologist would provide a convincing explanation of why murder is commoner among cooks than among the members of any other profession.)

By social custom, in all households except those rich enough to afford a professional chef, it is the woman not the man who does the cooking, but there is no reason to suppose that an avocation for cooking is commoner among women than among men. One can generally spot the woman who does not love cooking for its own sake by two symptoms. If she is cooking for somebody she likes, she may cook very well but she almost always serves too much; if, on the other hand, she dislikes or is angry with the person she is obliged to feed, no matter how good a cook she can be, she almost always cooks badly. Men are not socially obliged to cook, so that a man for whom cooking is not a passion seldom prepares a meal except for a girl he is trying to make. His characteristic culinary defect is due to the self-centeredness of the masculine imagination; he tends to plan his meal in terms of what he imagines would seduce him if he were a woman.

Mrs. Fisher has attended a number of such Bachelor Dinners and has some shrewd observations to make.

> I have found that most bachelors like the exotic, at least, culinarily speaking: they would rather fuss around with a complex recipe for Le Hochepot de Queue de Bœuf than a simple one called Stewed Oxtail, even if both come from Andre Simon's *Concise Encyclopedia of Gastronomy*. . . . The drink is good. He pops discretely in and out of his gastronomical workshop, where he brews his sly receipts, his digestive attacks upon the fortress of her virtue. She represses her natural curiosity, and if she is at all experienced in such wars, she knows fairly well that she will have a patterned meal which has already been indicated by his ordering in restaurants. More often than not it will be some kind of chicken, elaborately disguised with everything from Australian pine-nuts to herbs grown by the landlady's daughter.

In the reverse situation when it is the Spinster—or shall we say the Merry Widow?—who is giving the dinner, men are so transparent that she can hardly go wrong. If he is shy, the right kind and right amount of alcohol may be important, but the food is unlikely to affect his intentions. The only mistake she can make is to serve her Desirable Guest with some dish to which he happens to have a profound aversion, rooted in childhood. No matter how charming the server, I should have to be very much in love indeed to survive Cold Shape or Sago Pudding. But, being a woman, this is a mistake the Merry Widow scarcely ever makes. Her problem is more likely to be one of trying to avoid having to say No and thus spoiling a pleasant evening. If she can cook, she has only to follow Mrs. Fisher's recipe, which is guaranteed to reduce the most ardent wooer to a clumbering mass of masculine inactivity.

> I would serve one too many Martinis, that is, about three. Then while his appetite raged, thus whipped with alcohol, I would serve generous, rich, salty Italian hors d'œuvres: prosciutto, little chilled marinated shrimps, olives stuffed

with anchovy, spiced and pickled tomatoes—things that would lead him on. Next would come something he no longer wanted but couldn't resist, something like a ragout of venison, or squabs stuffed with mushrooms and wild rice, and plenty of red wine, sure danger after the cocktails and the highly salted appetisers. I would waste no time on a salad, unless perhaps a freakish rich one, treacherously containing truffles and new potatoes. The dessert would be cold, superficially refreshing and tempting, but venomous; a chilled bowl of figs soaked in kirsch with heavy cream. There would be a small bottle of Sauterne, sly and icy, or a judicious bit of champagne, and then a small cup of coffee so black and bitter that my victim could not down it, even therapeutically.

On every social aspect of eating, beginning with the gastronomic education of children, Mrs. Fisher shows wisdom and common sense.

Gastronomical perfection can be reached in these combinations: one person dining alone, usually upon a couch or a hillside; two persons, of no matter what sex or age, dining in a good restaurant; six people of no matter what sex or age, dining in a good home. . . . A good combination would be one married couple, for warm composure; one less firmly established, to add a note of interrogation to the talk; and two strangers of either sex, upon whom the better acquainted could sharpen their questioning wits.

Only on the subject of the Family dinner do I find her shocking. However psychologically beneficial it may prove to shift Father's position at table and serve untraditional food, it still seems to me blasphemous. What is the use of pretending one can treat the members of one's own family as ordinary human beings?

As an observer of the human condition, Mrs. Fisher has led a varied life. She came from what must have been a happy family and has children of her own. She has lived in many places, Alsace, Dijon, Switzerland, Italy, Mexico, and met all kinds of persons from peasants to Hollywood film-stars. She has lived in boarding-houses, rented apartments and homes. She has known poverty and relative affluence. She has had several husbands, with one of whom she had to live in the knowledge that he was doomed to die presently from an incurable disease.

Of her many stories and anecdotes, some are hilarious, some macabre, some tragic. If most of them are bitter-sweet, she is never saccharine nor acid. *The Art of Eating* is a book which I think Colette would have loved and wished she had written.

AS IT SEEMED TO US

Mr. Evelyn Waugh opens the first volume of his autobiography with the words

> Only when one has lost all curiosity about the future has one reached the age to write an autobiography.

If I believed that Mr. Waugh meant this literally, I should feel very sorry for him and, as one of his readers, for myself, since it would mean that he had no intention of writing another line, that all he desired was a speedy death. I am certain, however, that all he means is that a person should not write an autobiography until he is sufficiently sure of his identity to know that, whatever he may do or write from now on, it will not come as a dramatic surprise to him or to others. At sixty-one, Mr. Waugh knows that, however many more years of life may be granted him, he will not run away with a housemaid, become a Plymouth Brother, or compose an epic in Spenserian stanzas; in other words, the rest of his life, aside from any novels he may write, is unlikely to be of much interest to anyone except himself, his family, and his friends.

For an autobiography, like any story, to be really interesting, it is not enough that the reader should be wondering what is going to happen next; its hero must be equally in the dark. As Mr. Leonard Woolf rightly says, apropos of some reviewer:

He . . . is really assuming that because a thing happened it and nothing else had to happen. Because Desmond [MacCarthy] never did write a novel, he never could have written a novel. This simplifies life, history, and people, and, if it were true, it would be unnecessary to write or review biographies or autobiographies.

The principal motive for writing an autobiography, says Mr. Waugh, is a desire to understand the immediate past. I agree. Consequently, no one can read an autobiography which describes a time, a country, a class familiar to him without starting to compose his own, and I can review Mr. Woolf's *Beginning Again* and Mr. Waugh's *A Little Learning* only as I have read them; that is to say, as a participant. In doing so, I can find this justification for my self-indulgence: I do not know whether Mr. Woolf and Mr. Waugh have ever met, but I cannot imagine such a meeting being a success; the aversion of the one to God and of the other to the Lib.-Lab. *Weltanschauung* would make a dialogue very diffy. If not in complete accord with either, I feel myself sufficiently close to Mr. Waugh theologically and to Mr. Woolf politically to act as a moderator.

The names Leonard Woolf and Evelyn Waugh are known to the public, and whoever acquires a public name also acquires a public legend. Some legends magnify their victim, others diminish him. To those who do not know Leonard Woolf personally, the name conjures up the image not of a person but of a shadow— the husband of Virginia Woolf, a partner in the Hogarth Press, a *New Statesman* "type" who must, of course, be passionately devoted, like its first editor, Clifford Sharp, to the causes of Collectivization and Drainage. In 1908, he won six hundred and ninety pounds in a sweepstake, and this, he tells us, gave rise to the legend that he and Virginia started the Hogarth Press on sweepstake money; it is characteristic of *his* legend that by the time the story reached me, it was Virginia who had been the winner.

The legendary Mr. Waugh, on the other hand, is as exaggeratedly visible as a character in Dickens—a fantastic choleric snob in country-squire tweeds, who, though a Christian, is conspicuously lacking in Christian charity. Now that they have both published their autobiographies, however, no reader is ever again going to be able to take their legends seriously. Mr. Woolf turns out to be real flesh and blood, and no collectivist; Mr. Waugh to be generous, just, and modest. In reading them, I have come across only two remarks—one in each—that seem to have been uttered by their legendary rather than their real selves:

> It was, I still believe, touch and go whether the movement towards liberty and equality—political and social—and towards civilisation, which was strong in the first decade of the 20th century, would become so strong as to carry everything before it. *Its enemies saw the risk and the result was the war of 1914; they postponed the danger of our becoming civilised for at least a hundred years.* [Italics mine.]

Such a suggestion of conscious malevolent conspiracy is an imaginary New Statesman's paranoia.

> Today (instead of men of letters) there are the reporters of the popular papers who interview authors rather than review their work; there are the charmers of Television; *there are the State-trained professional critics with their harsh jargon and narrow tastes.* [Italics mine.]

I do not care for the kind of critic Mr. Waugh is referring to any more than he does, but to suggest that such critics are all offspring of the Lower Orders is a snobbish fantasy.

One of the fascinations of reading about the recent past lies in observing the steady foreshortening of time. In 1911, when Mr. Woolf's third volume begins, Mr. Waugh and I were both already on earth, but, as a man of thirty, a boy of nearly eight, and a child of four, respectively, the three of us inhabited three different universes. Today, Mr. Waugh and I are contemporaries, and the age difference between us and the eighty-four-year-old Mr. Woolf is less than the three and a half years that separated the two of us in 1919, when Mr. Waugh was going on sixteen and I was twelve. A century from now, nobody will know or care which of the three of us was born first.

I can see no way to compare our several experiences except by classifying them under various aspects. Since our school experiences were important to us, I should perhaps at this point remind American readers of a confusing difference between British and American nomenclature. British preparatory—or prep—school is the equivalent of American private school for boys from seven to fourteen; British public school is the equivalent of American private preparatory school.

Preliminary Chronicle

1880. L. W. born in Kensington, London. Arthur Waugh, aged 14, a public-school boy in his first year at Sherborne, Dorset. George Auden, aged 8, in his first year at prep school in Repton, Derbyshire.

1885. Arthur Waugh goes up to New College, Oxford. Reads Mods and Greats.

1890. George Auden goes up to Christ's College, Cambridge. Reads Natural Science as a preliminary to studying medicine.

1892. L. W.'s father, Sidney Woolf, dies suddenly.

1892–94. L. W. a boarder at Arlington House School, near Brighton.

1893. Arthur Waugh marries Catherine Raban.

1894–99. L. W. a day boy at St. Paul's School, London. During these years, George Auden becomes an interne at St. Bartholemew's Hospital. 1898, Alec Waugh born. 1899, George Auden marries Constance Bicknell and sets up practice in York.

1899–1904. L. W. at Trinity College, Cambridge. Reads Classics, then stays up an extra year to read for the Civil Service Examination. 1900, Bernard Auden born. 1902, Arthur Waugh becomes managing director of Chapman & Hall, publishers. 1903, E. W. born, in Hampstead, London. John Auden born.

1904. L. W. leaves for Ceylon with ninety volumes of Voltaire and a wire-haired terrier.

1904–11. L. W. a civil administrator in Ceylon. 1907, Arthur Waugh builds a house in North End, Hampstead (postal address later altered to Golders Green). W. H. A. born. 1908, George Auden gives up his practice in York to become the School Medical Officer of Birmingham. 1910, E. W. becomes a day boy at Heath Mount School, Hampstead, and writes his first novel.

Heredity

Ethnically, Mr. Woolf is a Jew, Mr. Waugh and I are Gentiles
—in his case, a mixture of Scotch, Irish, Welsh, English, and
Huguenot; in mine, as far as I know, pure Nordic. Mr. Woolf does
not mention any occasion, either at school or later, when he was
taunted with being a Jew. I hope this means that there was none.
Among middle-class Gentiles of the time, a mild and for the most
part quite unthinking anti-Semitism was very common. (It is
singularly unfortunate that, in a rhyme-poor language, the words
"Jew" and "Jews" should have so many more rhymes than most,
for this has facilitated the composition in English of cheap comic
verses about the race.) I am proud to say that when the advent of
Hitler compelled my parents to think, they immediately took in a
succession of German refugees.

Socially, we were all born into the professional middle class:
Mr. Woolf's father was a barrister, Mr. Waugh's a publisher, mine
a physician. The Woolf family had only recently entered this class,
Mr. Woolf's grandfathers having been a successful bespoke tailor
and a diamond merchant; Mr. Waugh's family and mine had belonged to it for several generations. It was a common game among
children of this class to attempt to divine their future careers by
counting the plum stones on their plates and chanting "Army,
Navy, Law, Church." My father, like Mr. Waugh's paternal grandfather, was a doctor, and the social status of the doctor remained
uncertain until near the end of the nineteenth century. When my
mother became engaged to my father, in 1898, one of her sisters,
married to a clergyman, told her, "If you marry this man, you
know nobody will call on you." The typical snobberies of this
professional middle class were their contemptuous attitudes toward
businessmen, or "persons in trade," as they were called—for some
mysterious reason, book publishing was not a trade—and toward
Dissenters; Roman Catholics might be eccentric, or even immoral,
but, thanks to the existence of old Catholic families like the Nor-
folks, they could not be regarded as socially inferior. A third
snobbery, which, if less reprehensible morally, had more serious
practical consequences, was their disdain for science. The only

education befitting a gentleman was, so they believed, the study, both at school and at the university, of Latin and Greek. Mr. Waugh gives us some excellent illustrations of this attitude from his own experience:

> One of the most profitable connections of Chapman & Hall's was an American firm of technical publishers for whom they acted in England. He [my father] regarded this association as something almost shady, and its representatives as much less worthy of attention than a minor poet. . . . The visits of these valuable American clients were strictly confined to an exchange of politeness in his office and a swift relegation to the hands of a young man of scientific education whom he regarded as a subordinate rather than a colleague. He never asked to his house the men who had come 3,000 miles to bring him business. . . .
>
> In school we demonstrated our contempt for "stinks" and our resentment that we, on the classical side, should be required to study them once or twice a week. Scientists were regarded as a socially inferior race and we treated our masters in these subjects superciliously. . . .
>
> Mathematicians were respected but were thought to be out of their proper milieu; they should have been at Cambridge. There was said to be a laboratory somewhere near Keble, but I never met anyone who dabbled there. No Fellow of Hertford, when I went up, had any connection with the National Sciences.

This snobbery, at least, I was mercifully spared. In my father's library, scientific books stood side by side wtih works of poetry and fiction, and it never occurred to me to think of one as being less or more "humane" than the other. I am very glad that, as was true for Mr. Woolf and Mr. Waugh, my first six years of schooling were devoted largely to Latin and Greek, for I fully share Mr. Waugh's conviction of the value of this:

> Today I remember no Greek. I have never read Latin for pleasure and should now be hard put to it to compose a simple epitaph. But I do not regret my superficial classical studies. I believe that the conventional defence of them is valid; that only by them can a boy fully understand that a

sentence is a logical construction and that words have basic inalienable meanings, departure from which is either conscious metaphor or inexcusable vulgarity.

On the other hand, although I soon realized that I was not cut out to be a scientist, I am equally glad that I spent my last two years at school in the exclusive study of chemistry, zoology, and botany.

Genealogies are admirable things, provided they do not encourage the curious delusion that some families are older than others. I wish Mr. Woolf had given us more information about his ancestry, and that I knew as much about my forebears as Mr. Waugh knows about his. Who would not feel happy at being able to claim descent from William Morgan, F.R.S. (1750–1833), a clubfooted Unitarian, Jacobin, and mathematician who was the first man to introduce actuarial techniques into the insurance business, or from Thomas Gosse (1765–1844), an itinerant portrait painter who, after a vision of the risen Christ, "evinced a confidence in his eternal salvation which rendered him indifferent to his own worldly prosperity and, later, to that of his family"? On my mother's side of the family, for instance, I should like to know more about the Reverend Dr. Birch who for a time was tutor to the young Prince of Wales, the future Edward VII—a thankless job which he lost when the Queen discovered he had Puseyite sympathies—and about the Miss Bicknell who, to the dismay of her parents, married Constable. As it is, my certain knowledge does not go further back than my grandparents, but my twelve uncles and aunts, six on each side, have given me some understanding of the difference between the Auden-Hopkins and Bicknell-Birch strains in my character. Both my grandfathers were Church of England clergymen and both died of heart attacks in early middle-age. My maternal grandfather was evidently a sadist, like Mr. Waugh's paternal one, for his sons danced round the table for joy when they heard he was dead. Neither Mr. Woolf nor Mr. Waugh seems to have encountered a phenomenon which cannot have been uncommon in large Victorian families: I had an uncle on my father's side and an aunt on my mother's who were what is now euphemistically called "mentally retarded." Uncle Lewis was looked after by a housekeeper, Aunt Daisy by Anglican nuns.

On the whole, the members of my father's family were phleg-
matic, earnest, rather slow, inclined to be miserly, and endowed
with excellent health; my mother's were quick, short-tempered,
generous, and liable to physical ill health, hysteria, and neuroti-
cism. Except in the matter of physical health, I take after them.

Parents and Home Life

All three of us started off life with the enormous advantage of
being born to parents who genuinely loved us and treated us gently.
Moreover, our adult judgment tells us that, whatever their little
peculiarities and failings, they were lovable and admirable human
beings.

I don't know if it is a universal habit of children, but everybody whom I have asked about the matter tells me that he classified
his parents as I did: one parent stood for stability, common sense,
reality, the other for surprise, eccentricity, fantasy. In my case, it
was Father who stood for the first, Mother for the second. Mr.
Woolf lost his father at the age of eleven, and from his descriptions
of his parents I am not quite certain of his classification, but I
suspect it was the same as mine:

> He was certainly intelligent, reserved, and quick-tem-
> pered, but also very nervous and highly strung, and, though
> normally very kind, more intolerant of fools and their folly
> than almost any other man whom I have known. Though
> not an orthodox Jew, his ethical code of conduct was ter-
> rific, but he was not, in my recollection of him, either pas-
> sionately on the side of righteousness or violently against
> sin. . . .
> [My mother] lived in a dream world which centered in
> herself and her nine children. It was the best of all possible
> worlds, a fairyland of nine perfect children worshipping a
> mother to whom they owed everything, loving one another,
> and revering the memory of their deceased father. Nothing
> that actually happened, no fact, however black, however
> inconsistent with the dream, made her doubt its reality and
> its rosiness. That anyone, particularly one of her own chil-
> dren, should doubt or throw doubt on it was the one thing
> in life which really distressed her.

In Mr. Waugh's mind, the classification is quite clear. It was Mama who stood for sanity, Papa for oddity:

> My mother was small, neat, reticent and, until her last decade, very active. . . . She would have preferred to live in the country and from her I learned that towns are places of exile where the unfortunate are driven to congregate in order to earn their livings in an unhealthy and unnatural way. She had to be content with walking her dog on Hampstead Heath and working in the garden. She spent hours there, entirely absorbed; not merely snipping off dead heads but potting, planting, watering, weeding. . . . Her flowers did not interest her more than her fruit and vegetables. . . . I associate her less with lilies than with earthy wash-leather gloves and baskets of globe artichokes and black and red currants. . . .
>
> [My father] always excelled in the charades which were an essential part of our family life, especially at Christmas. I think he was, by amateur standards, genuinely gifted, but it was in the daily routine of his private life that he acted with the greatest virtuosity. In greeting visitors he was Mr. Hardcastle; in deploring the ingratitude of his sons, Lear. Between these two extremes all the more likeable of Dickens's characters provided him with roles which from time to time he undesignedly assumed. . . . He never sulked. He was mercurial, and a word of humour or appreciation would win him in an instant from the blackest depression. Even in his coughing and wheezing, genuine and distressing as they were, he put his voice into the production, interspersing his bouts with quotations calling on death for release. His sighs would have carried to the back of the gallery at Drury Lane.

I did not, like Mr. Woolf, lose my father physically by death, but to some degree I lost him psychologically. I was seven—the age at which, as Mr. Waugh says, a son begins to take serious notice of his father and needs him most—when he enlisted in the R.A.M.C., and I didn't see him again until I was twelve and a half. I think this is probably the reason that, although we got on amicably enough (all my rows were with my mother), we never really came to know each other. He was the gentlest and most unselfish man I have ever met—too gentle, I used sometimes to think, for as a husband he was often henpecked. My mother, whom I understood very well, could be very odd indeed. When I was eight years old, she taught me the words and music of the love-potion scene in *Tristan,* and we used to sing it together.

Mr. Woolf's childhood seems to have been less happy than the unclouded childhoods that Mr. Waugh and I remember. His father's death brought him grief, and though he did not feel unloved by his mother, he felt that she loved him less than her other children. When he speaks of his first numinous experiences, the two he remembers most vividly were visions not of joy but of dread:

> I stood by myself in the patch of scurfy grass and contemplated the spiders; I can still smell the smell of sour earth and ivy; and suddenly my whole mind and body seemed to be overwhelmed in melancholy. I did not cry, though there were, I think, tears in my eyes. . . .
>
> I do not know how long I had sat there when, all at once, I felt afraid. I looked up and saw that an enormous black thunder cloud had crept up and now covered more than half of the sky. It was just blotting out the sun, and, as it did so, the newts scuttled back into their hole. It was terrifying and, no doubt, I was terrified. But I felt something more powerful than fear, once more that sense of profound, passive, cosmic despair, the melancholy of a human being, eager for happiness and beauty, powerless in the face of a hostile universe.

Many of Mr. Waugh's early numinous experiences were, like mine, associated with a house—in his case, his three maiden aunts', and, in mine, my maternal grandmother's, both houses very mid-Victorian in their smells and furnishings. Mr. Waugh says of his enchantment:

> I am sure that I loved my aunts' house because I was instinctively drawn to the ethos I now recognise as mid-Victorian; not, as perhaps psychologists would claim, that I now relish things of that period because they remind me of my aunts.

I doubt whether either his or the psychologists' explanation is correct. For an object or an atmosphere to enchant us, there must, of course, be some psychological affinity between it and us, but I suspect that in childhood the mere chance of priority plays a greater role than such explanations suggest. What happens, I believe, is akin to "imprinting" in birds, who fall in love with the first large object they see after hatching, whether suitable or unsuitable. I am certain, at least, that the feelings aroused in a child by an enchanting artifact—my joy, for example, in contemplating a gas-works—have little, if anything, in common with the feelings of the adults who made it.

Neither Mr. Woolf nor Mr. Waugh seems to have indulged in a kind of daydreaming that was of immense importance to my childhood. Between the ages of six and twelve, I spent a great many of my waking hours in the construction and elaboration of a private sacred world, the basic elements of which were a landscape, northern and limestone, and an industry, lead mining. In construc-ing it, fantasy had to submit to two rules. In deciding what objects were to be included, I was free to select this and reject that, on condition that both were real objects (two kinds of water turbine, for instance, which could be found in textbooks on mining ma-chinery or a manufacturer's catalogue); I was not allowed to invent one. In deciding how my world was to function, I could choose between two practical possibilities (a mine could be drained either by an adit or by a pump), but physical impossibilities and magic means were forbidden. It is no doubt psychologically significant that my sacred world contained no human beings. However, though this world was constructed for and inhabited by myself alone, I needed the help of others—my parents, in particular—in collecting the raw materials for its construction. Others had to procure for me the necessary textbooks, maps, catalogues, guidebooks, and photo-graphs, and, when occasion offered, take me down real mines— tasks they performed with unfailing patience and generosity. It sounds more than a little mad now, but I enjoyed myself enor-mously and never felt lonely or bored.

One last point. Mr. Waugh was the younger of two sons, I the youngest of three and the youngest of quite a number of grand-children. I should be curious to know if this ordinal position in the family has had the same effect upon him that it has had upon me. It implanted in me the lifelong conviction that in any company I am the youngest person present—a conviction quite unaffected by the fact that now, at fifty-eight, I am often the oldest.

War

On August 4, 1914, Mr. Woolf was standing outside the post office in Lewes, Sussex, waiting for the news; Mr. Waugh was at his aunts' house, in Midsomer Norton, near Bath, having just completed his fourth year at school; I was in my home, in King's Norton, near Birmingham, and was due to go away to prep school the following month. On November 11, 1918, Mr. Woolf was writing in his room in Richmond, London (Virginia celebrated the occasion by a visit to the dentist); Mr. Waugh was "idling in the Classical Middle Fifth under an exceedingly dull form master"; I was in a school sanatorium in Surrey, out of bed for the first time since coming down with the Spanish flu. During the four years between these dates, one of Mr. Woolf's brothers had been killed and one severely wounded; Mr. Waugh's only brother had been reported "missing" for a time after the Ludendorf offensive; my father was overseas, first in the Middle East and then in France, and my eldest brother had been called up, though he was still in training camp when the war ended.

For Mr. Woolf, the war was as real as it was horrible. Though exempted from military service on account of a hereditary hand tremor, he could imagine exactly what trench warfare must be like, he could read the casualty lists, and he was sufficiently educated politically to know that in 1914—as opposed to 1939—war could have been avoided:

> The horror of the years 1914 to 1918 was that nothing seemed to happen, month after month and year after year, except the pitiless, useless slaughter in France. Often if one went for a walk on the downs above Asham one could hear the incessant pounding of the guns on the Flanders front. And even when one did not hear them it was as though the war itself was perpetually pounding dully on one's brain, while in Richmond and Sussex one was enmeshed in a cloud

] 503 [

of boredom, and when one looked into the future, there was nothing there but an unending vista of the same boredom.

In addition, Mr. Woolf had to endure great personal affliction. From the summer of 1913 to the summer of 1914, his wife had been insane, and early in 1915 the insanity returned. He does not indulge in self-pity, but from his dispassionate description of her symptoms one can guess something of what he must have gone through:

> In the first stage she was in the depths of depression, would hardly eat or talk, was suicidal. In the second she was in a state of violent excitement and wild euphoria, talking incessantly for long periods of time. In the first stage she was violently opposed to the nurses and they had the greatest difficulty in getting her to do anything; she wanted me to be with her continually. . . . In the second stage of violent excitement, she was violently hostile to me, would not talk to me or allow me to come into her room. . . .
>
> When the time for a meal came, she would pay no attention whatsoever to the plate of food put before her and, if the nurses tried to get her to eat something, she became enraged. I could usually induce her to eat a certain amount, but it was a terrible process. Every meal took an hour or two; I had to sit by her side, put a spoon or fork in her hand, and every now and again ask her very quietly to eat and at the same time touch her arm or hand. Every five minutes or so she might automatically eat a spoonful.

Mr. Waugh says that after a few weeks of excitement he lost interest in the war and accepted it as a condition of life. To me, it was not even a condition; it had no reality of any kind. During most of the war, fortunately, my father was behind the firing line, but even when he was taking part in the Gallipoli campaign the thought never entered my head that he might be in danger. At school one morning, Christopher Isherwood appeared wearing a black armband; I knew this meant that his father was dead, but the words "killed in action" brought no image to my mind.

One change in my life, indirectly caused by the war, seemed a great improvement. At the time my father enlisted, the lease of our house was just about to expire, and my mother did not renew it. When our school holidays came round, she took furnished rooms for my brothers and me, each time in some new and exciting part of the country. Our only "war work" consisted in collecting sphagnum moss, when there was any, and knitting mufflers in the evening while she read aloud to us. At school, we drilled with wooden rifles and had "field days" when we took cover behind bushes and twirled noisemakers to represent machine-gun fire. Assistant masters, young and old, came and went, becoming more peculiar each year. The oddest had a name to match—Captain Reginald Oscar Gartside-Bagnell. He had written a play, *The Waves*—a barefaced crib, I later discovered, from *The Bells*—which he used to read aloud in a Henry Irving voice to his awed and astonished favorites.

Curiously, I do not remember, as Mr. Waugh so vividly does, that the food at school was particularly nasty or insufficient. There were dishes, like the boiled cod on Fridays, that I hated, but they might have turned up on any school menu in peacetime. The honey sugar he mentions I remember—it was reputedly made by treating potatoes with weak sulphuric acid—but found quite edible. I also remember that when I once took a second slice of bread and margarine, which was permitted, a master remarked, "Auden, I see, wants the Huns to win."

I can only attribute the difference between our gastronomic memories of this time to the fact that I was still a little boy and Mr. Waugh was an adolescent, with an adolescent's appetite.

School

Mr. Woolf spent two years with a private tutor, then two years as a boarder at a prep school, then his five years of public school as a day boy; Mr. Waugh spent his seven prep-school years as a day boy, his five public-school years as a boarder; I spent the whole eleven years of my schooling as a boarder. Whether boarding schools are a good or a bad thing I don't know, but from personal experience, both as a boy and as a teacher, I am certain that if a boy is to be sent away to school at all, it is kinder to send him at an early age. A boy of seven or eight seems to get over his homesickness very quickly; the ones who really suffer are those who, like Mr. Waugh, are over eleven when they are first deprived of the warmth and protection of family life.

Mr. Woolf describes his prep school as "a sordid brothel," but he was fortunate in its games master:

> I learned from Mr. Woolley the seriousness of games, the importance of style, the duty when you go in to bat of making every stroke with the concentration which an artist puts into every stroke of his brush in painting a masterpiece. Since those days I have played nearly every kind of game from fives and bowls to golf and rugger, and I have played them each and all of them with the greatest pleasure.

What life for such an intellectual as Mr. Woolf would have been like in the colonial society of Ceylon without Mr. Woolley's inspiration and his own aptitude for games doesn't bear thinking about.

Mr. Waugh was happy at his prep school and got on well with the other boys, but from his account it seems that the standard of teaching was below average for such establishments, and that means pretty poor. I was fortunate in the headmaster of mine, who taught Latin and Greek. He could be brutal, but he was a born teacher. If he was in a bad temper, one might get beaten on the spot for an error in syntax, but when this happened to me, I never felt it was unjust, because I knew the error was due to my carelessness, not to his faulty instruction.

In describing the ethos of school life in his day, Mr. Woolf keeps harping on the hostility of both boys and masters toward intellectual interests of any kind—a hostility so strong that, until his last year at St. Paul's, he did not dare speak of this to a single soul. If this was so, then I must say that by the time Mr. Waugh and I went to school, the climate had greatly improved. Athletics were still the normal road to popularity and social prestige, and, for that reason, as Mr. Waugh perceived, not so much fun as they could and should have been:

> I think few associated games with pleasure. They were a source of intense competition, anxiety and recrimination to those who excelled; of boredom and discomfort to those who were bad at them.

Intellectuals and persons with unusual hobbies like bird-watching were in the minority, as they are in any society, but at

the schools I went to they were tolerated; I could always find someone with whom I could talk freely, and with the rest I never felt
that I must either conceal an interest or feign one.

Mr. Waugh describes himself as being "fond of solitude." If
that is true today, then he has changed greatly from the boy and
the young man he portrays in *A Little Learning,* whose need for
company seems to have been greater than most people's. The
bitterest memory of his school days is not of being bullied but of
being left alone on an Ascension Day school holiday:

> That first year I knew no one and had nowhere to go.
> The whole place was emptied as though by plague. Inquiry
> elicited the information that there was no dinner that day.
> The steward gave me some slices of bread and a ghastly
> kind of sausage meat. Rain came on. The House Room, as
> on Sundays, was locked. The library was out of bounds to
> me. I wandered out with my damp packet of food and after
> a time took shelter among the trees called Lancing Ring, ate
> a little and, for the first and last time for many years, wept.
> It was with comfort that late that afternoon I heard the
> noisy return of the holiday-makers.

In my first year at public school, I should have been enchanted
to have the whole place to myself and listened to the holiday-
makers returning with a sinking of the heart.

Mr. Waugh's natural sociability is revealed by his reaction at
that time to the experience of being unpopular:

> I did not admire the other boys. I did not want to be
> like them. But, in contradiction, I wanted to be one of them.
> I had no aspirations to excel, still less to lead; I simply
> longed to remain myself and yet be accepted as one of this
> distasteful mob.

This is a longing I have never felt; nor, I suspect, has Mr.
Woolf. The difference is partly a matter of temperament and partly
one of early experience. Mr. Waugh says:

> Odium was personal and something quite new to me.
> For thirteen years I had met only people who seemed dis-
> posed to like me.

I, too, experienced nothing but affection at home, but I was not equally fortunate with my uncles, aunts, and cousins. Most of them thought me—with justice, I'm sure—a precocious, insolent little monster; I thought most of them either hysterical or stupid, which they probably were. The only one I got on with was Uncle Harry, my father's younger bachelor brother, who was an authority on sulphuric acid.

As far back as I can remember, I knew that the things of greatest interest to me were of no interest to most people I met, whether grownups or contemporaries. Some things, like my lead-mining world, were unsharable with anybody; others, like music and archeology, could be shared with some persons but not very many. I think I can honestly say I never thought that my minority concerns were superior to the concerns of the majority. At school, my total lack of interest in and aptitude for games of any kind did not make me despise athletes; on the contrary, I greatly admired them, as I have always admired anybody who does something well, but I did not envy them, because I knew that their skill could never be mine. (I was, however, insufferably superior with anybody who, when speaking about matters in which I was interested, said something I thought stupid.) Consequently, I have never, I think, wanted to "belong" to a group whose interests were not mine, nor have I resented exclusion. Why should they accept me? All I have ever asked is that others should go their way and let me go mine. If I did not enjoy my first year at public school, though I cannot say I was particularly ill-treated, this was because boys in early adolescence find it very difficult to let each other alone. Being, like Mr. Woolf and Mr. Waugh, a bright boy, I was usually the youngest in my form, so that nearly all my friends were older than I, and when it came to my last year, they had left school. During that year, I went for long solitary walks, played the organ, hardly spoke to anyone unless I had to, and was extremely happy.

In all the reminiscences of their school days which I have read, the authors remember at least one master with pleasure and gratitude, either because he stimulated their minds or because he treated them as human beings like himself. At St. Paul's, Mr.

Woolf found a Mr. A. M. Cook; at Lancing, Mr. Waugh found a Mr. J. F. Roxburgh; at Gresham's, I found a Mr. W. Greatorex, the music master. Many boys, too, can remember some adult, neither a schoolmaster nor a relative, who took an interest in them and taught them something not in the school curriculum. Behind this interest there is usually an element of homosexual feeling, sublimated or overt. Some of the most fascinating pages in Mr. Waugh's autobiography are devoted to a Mr. Crease, with whom he studied script. The corresponding figure in my life I had to meet clandestinely—my housemaster having forbidden me to see him, and not without reason, for he was a practicing homosexual and had, I think, been to prison. Why he should have taken a shine to me I cannot imagine, since I was a very plain boy. He made advances, which I rejected, not on moral grounds but because I thought him unattractive. Instead of dropping me, however, he continued to give me books and write me long letters full of encouraging and constructive criticism of my juvenile verses. I owe him a great deal.

University

In Mr. Robert Graves' historical novel *Wife to Mr. Milton,* the future Mrs. Milton's brother, after reading *Comus* for the first time, remarks, "This smacks to me of Cambridge, where they tune their viol strings always a little sharp." An acute observation, I think, and a fair one, since it permits the retort "At Oxford they always play a little flat."

The difference between Cambridge at the turn of the century, as it is described by Mr. Woolf, and Oxford in the twenties, as it is described by Mr. Waugh, cannot be attributed solely to the passage of time. In "Sinister Street," Sir Compton Mackenzie portrays an Oxford more or less contemporary with Mr. Woolf's, and it seems more like Oxford twenty-five years later than its eastern rival of the same date.

Though, like all undergraduates, Mr. Woolf and his friends laughed and made jokes, they strike me as having been extremely serious-minded young men, passionately and puritanically concerned for the True and the Good. Also, both then and later, when they turned into Bloomsbury, they seem to have been much more of a homogeneous group, all holding the same tastes and convictions, than any I can imagine Oxford producing. As both Mr. Woolf and Maynard Keynes (in *Two Memoirs*) have testified, this was in large measure due to the influence of one man, then nearing thirty—the philosopher G. E. Moore, who acted as a sort of guru to them all. Mr. Woolf writes:

> Moore was not witty; I do not think that I ever heard him say a witty thing; there was no scintillation in his conversation or his thought. But he had an extraordinary profundity and clarity of thought, and he pursued truth with the tenacity of a bulldog and the integrity of a saint. . . . On the surface and until you got to know him intimately, he appeared to be a very shy, reserved man, and on all occasions and in any company he might fall into profound and protracted silence. When I first got to know him, the immensely high standards of thought and conduct which he seemed silently to demand of an intimate, the feeling that one should not say anything unless the thing was both true and worth saying, the silences which would certainly envelop him and you, tinged one's wish to see him with some anxiety, and I know that standing at the door of his room, before knocking and going in, I often took a deep breath just as one does on a cool day before one dives into the cold green sea. . . .
>
> Talking to him one lived under the shadow of the eternal, though silent, question: "What exactly do you mean by that?" It is a menacing question, particularly when you know that muddle and not knowing "exactly what you mean by *that*" will cause to Moore almost physical pain which he will show involuntarily in his eyes.

There have been other philosophers, like Wittgenstein—also, by the way, at Cambridge—who have attracted disciples, but these were professionals. Of the group around Moore, only Bertrand Russell was a professional philosopher; most of them—Lytton Strachey, Thoby Stephen, Clive Bell, E. M. Forster, Desmond MacCarthy, Leonard Woolf himself—were primarily interested in the arts.

On the whole, the mental atmosphere of Oxford in this century does not seem to have encouraged gurus. It has produced dons whose wit and manner of speaking admiring undergraduates have tried to imitate, but their influence has been social and personal rather than intellectual; it has produced no equivalent of Dr. Leavis.

By Moore standards, the Oxford of the twenties was frivolous indeed. At Cambridge in 1903, Pleasure was not, so Mr. Woolf tells us, considered a good; to us it was almost the only one. Looking back now, I find it incredible how secure life seemed. Too young for the war to have made any impression upon us, we imagined that the world was essentially the same as it had been in 1913, and we were far too insular and preoccupied with ourselves to know or care what was going on across the Channel. Revolution in Russia, inflation in Germany and Austria, Fascism in Italy, whatever fears or hopes they may have aroused in our elders, went unnoticed by us. Before 1930, I never opened a newspaper.

Since I came up to Oxford only one year after Mr. Waugh went down, I have little to add to his description. Two of his friends, Mr. Harold Acton and Mr. Tom Driberg, were still up, and the latter introduced me to the poetry of T. S. Eliot. The lunch parties were still going on. The George Restaurant was still crowded. Panache and elegance were still much admired. Making friends was still of much greater importance than the academic studies we were ostensibly there to pursue. "It was a male community," says Mr. Waugh. "Undergraduettes lived in purdah." This was still the rule, but I knew of exceptions to it. There were three or four girls in my day who had somehow managed to get out and, like token Jews in a Wasp community, were accepted by us. Not every lunch party was stag, but at a mixed one the female faces were always the same.

Mr. Woolf says nothing about the drinking habits at Cambridge, but he tells us he has "an intense dislike of drunkenness and almost a physical horror of drunken people." At Oxford, there was a drinking set, and Mr. Waugh soon found himself in it:

> We drank copiously but indiscriminately—and I use "copiously" in relation to our age. We were often very

drunk but the actual quantities we consumed in our orgies were far less than I now regularly enjoy in complete sobriety. A few glasses of sherry, half a bottle of burgundy, claret or champagne, a few glasses of port, threw us into transports. A glass or two of brandy or whisky on top of them rendered us unconscious.

If at Oxford and for many years afterward I drank little, this was a matter of chance (none of my friends drank heavily) and of money (I could not afford to drink much or often). As far as taste and temperament are concerned, I might just as well have acquired a thirst then as later, for today my average alcohol intake is, I should guess, equal to Mr. Waugh's. What really surprises me when I compare his life with mine is his astonishing gregariousness and range of social activities. He can hardly have been alone for a second:

> Terence and I formed the nucleus of a coterie which we used to call "the Hertford underworld." . . . We used, unless any of us was giving a luncheon party or going to one, to have our commons together in my rooms. This soon developed into my keeping open house for men from other colleges; sometimes as many as a dozen collected. . . . We drank large quantities of beer and made a good deal of noise. Few of us could sing. We used to recite verse in unison.

In addition to entertaining and being entertained, he joined club after club, from the highly respectable Carlton to the highly unrespectable Hypocrites; he spoke at the Oxford Union; he wrote for the *Isis* and the *Cherwell;* he designed countless headpieces and covers for these magazines, and also designed bookplates, O.U.D.S. programs, and caricatures. Such a life would have driven me crazy. I preferred then, as I do now, to see my friends one at a time; I never entered the doors of the Union; the only club I belonged to was a Christ Church Essay Club; and though I was just as academically idle as Mr. Waugh, I spent a good deal of time by myself reading.

Mr. Waugh read History, and he and his tutor, Mr. Cruttwell, detested each other. After coming up to Christ Church as a science exhibitioner, I got permission in my first year to switch to the English School. I had no intention of studying English literature academically, but I wanted to read it, and the English School would give me official license to do so. At that time, Christ Church was far too snooty to have an English tutor, so I was farmed out to Mr. Nevill Coghill, at Exeter, who became a lifelong friend. He was not a guru of the Moore kind; I never took a deep breath before knocking on his door. On the contrary, he put me so at my ease that I felt I could say anything to him, however silly, whether about literature or my personal life, without fear of being laughed at or rebuked.

Of his emotional life as an undergraduate, Mr. Woolf writes:

> I have never again been quite so happy or quite so miserable as I was in the five years at Cambridge from 1899 to 1904. One lived in a state of continual excitement and strong and deep feeling. . . . We lived in extremes—of happiness and unhappiness, of admiration and contempt, of love and hate.

Mr. Waugh says nothing explicit on this subject, but I do not think that if he were asked he would speak of deep feeling or extremes of happiness and unhappiness; he would say, I think, that he lived in a state of continuous mild euphoria, having fun without a conscious care in the world. In my own case, intense emotion was a state I had experienced earlier in life and was to experience again later, but it was absent from my undergraduate years. Despite the pleasures of friendship and intellectual discovery, I do not look back on them with any nostalgia. Beneath the fun I was always conscious of a dull, persistent, gnawing anxiety. To begin with, I felt guilty at being so idle. I was not taken in, as Mr. Waugh hints he was, by the F. E. Smith legend, according to which "a man of parts could idle for eight terms and at the end sit up with black coffee and master the required subjects in a few weeks." I knew very well what sort of degree I was going to get and what a bitter disappointment this was going to be to my parents. More important than guilt, however, was ambition. Unlike Mr. Waugh, who does not seem to have realized until after he went down that his vocation was to write novels—at Oxford he was more interested in the visual arts—I had been quite certain since the age of fifteen of what I wanted to do. At nineteen, I was self-critical enough to know that the poems I was writing were still merely derivative, that I had not yet found my own voice, and I felt certain that in Oxford I should never find it, that as long as I remained there, I should remain a child.

I said earlier that we were politically ignorant and indifferent. There were, of course, individual undergraduates who were neither—those I met personally were all Socialists—but they were intending to enter politics as a career, and the rest of us thought of their social concern as a professional specialty in which we could not be expected to share. One event which Mr. Waugh was not in Oxford to experience, the General Strike of 1926, deserves a note, because it reveals so clearly our political innocence. Neither Marx nor any other social anatomist had spotted that it was the daydream of almost every middle-class English boy to drive a train or a bus, to do something which his social position normally forbade, like loading a ship or directing traffic. The hundreds of undergraduates who responded to the Government's appeal did so not out of class consciousness in the Marxist sense—none of them felt any hostility, personal or ideological, toward the strikers—but because, suddenly, here was a heaven-sent opportunity to realize their daydream. Out of sheer contrariness, I did not, like most of my friends, volunteer to help the Government; instead, I volunteered to drive a car for the T.U.C. The only quarrel this led to was not in Oxford. One day, I had driven R. H. Tawney to his house in Mecklenburgh Square. It happened that a first cousin of mine, married to a stockbroker, lived a few doors away, so I paid a call. The three of us were just sitting down to lunch when her husband asked me if I had come up to London to be a Special Constable. "No," I said. "I am driving a car for the T.U.C." Whereupon, to my utter astonishment, he ordered me to leave his house. It had never occurred to me that anybody took the General Strike seriously.

Money

As children, none of us knew real poverty, or real affluence, either. The financial situation in the Woolf family was the most precarious. Mr. Woolf's father, a successful barrister, had earned a great deal of money, but he had saved none by the time he died, at the age of forty-seven, leaving his widow with nine children to bring up:

> She determined to spend the whole of her capital on educating her nine children, in the hope that by the time the money was exhausted they would be in positions in which they could maintain her and themselves. The gamble came off, but it would not have done so unless four of us had got scholarships at St. Paul's School and three of us scholarships at Cambridge. From my twelfth to my twenty-fourth year the menace of money hung over us all always and we had to be extremely careful of every penny.

My father's practice in York had been lucrative, and abandoning it to enter the Public Health Service meant a considerable financial loss. Mr. Waugh's father was, I should imagine, the best off, but after the war he, too, began to feel the pinch.

In their behavior when they were confronted with bills, there is a curious resemblance between Mr. Waugh's father and Virginia Woolf's father, Leslie Stephen. Mr. Woolf writes:

> . . . this fortunate man, whose bank balance was virtually impregnable, never stopped worrying himself and his children about money. . . . Every Monday morning Vanessa brought to him the household books in order that he might give her a cheque to cover the previous week's expenditure. Then for ten minutes or more he sighed and groaned over the enormous sums which they were spending on food, wages, light, coal—at this rate ruin stared them in the face and they would soon all be in the workhouse. . . .
>
> He [Arthur Waugh] was never even momentarily straitened financially, but he would not sign a cheque without crying: "How can I possibly find the money? They will ruin me. They will bring me to a pauper's grave."

I never remember hearing my father complain about money. It was only later in life that I realized what a moral effort this must have cost him—that by nature, like many in his family, he was one of those persons who cannot disburse even the smallest sums without mental anguish.

All three of us won scholarships to the university, but no

college scholarship was sufficient to live on without a parental contribution. At Cambridge, Mr. Woolf received £120 per annum and managed to keep out of debt. At Oxford, I received £250 and almost managed, but only by staying at home during the vacations; I went down owing some fifty pounds to Blackwell's for books. From friends who have sons at Oxford, I am told that to live as I did would now cost £800. Mr. Waugh had £350, plus small sums he earned by journalism and book-jacket designing, and did not manage; he went down owing two hundred pounds to tradesmen and about the same sum to friends.

England in 1912 was, as Mr. Woolf says, "economic paradise for the bourgeoisie." Very comfortable rooms in Brunswick Square —a good address—with first-class cooking cost him between eleven and twelve pounds a month. When he married Virginia Stephen, she had a private annual income of something less than four hundred pounds; he, aside from six hundred pounds he had saved while he was in Ceylon, had no money and no job. For the next ten years, he tells us, both of them had to work very hard and budget carefully to make ends meet. Their expenditure for the year 1917 was £697; on this they maintained a house in London and a house in Sussex, and employed a cook and a house-parlor-maid, whose joint wages per annum amounted to £76. 1s. 8d. In that year, they started the Hogarth Press, on a capital of £41. 15s. 3d.:

> This sum was made up of £38. 8s. 3d., which we spent on a small printing machine and type, and £3. 7s. 0d., which was the total cost of production of the first book which we printed and published. We made a profit of £6. 7s. 0d. in the first year on the first publication and that "went back into the business," so that at the end of 1917 the total capital which we had put into the Hogarth Press was £35. After that the business financed itself out of profits and we never had to "find capital" for it.

I hope that in the next volume of his autobiography Mr. Waugh will tell us something about the economics of novel writing since he began his career. A poet's earnings qua poet are too paltry to be worth discussing. When I returned from Berlin and had to find a job, I became, like Mr. Waugh, a prep-school master. Unlike him, I found, rather to my surprise, that I enjoyed teaching very much, and I continued in that profession for the next five years.

Religion

L. W.: Grandfather Woolf, an Orthodox Jew; parents, Reformed. 1894, declares himself an atheist. Has remained one ever since.

E. W.: Great-Grandfather Waugh, brought up a Presbyterian, becomes a clergyman of the Church of England; parents, Anglo-Catholic. 1914, period of ecclesiastical *Schwärmerei.* 1921, discovers that he has lost his faith. 1930, received into the Roman Catholic Church.

W. H. A.: Grandfathers, clergymen of the Church of England; parents, Anglo-Catholic. 1920, period of ecclesiastical *Schwärmerei.* 1922, discovers that he has lost his faith. 1940, returns to the Anglican Communion.

There is nothing of pagan indifference or frivolity about Mr. Woolf's atheism. In him, as, I think, in most of his Bloomsbury friends, it is a religious passion. To believe in God, especially the Christian God, is for him not merely silly but morally and intellectually wicked. (In the Woolfian vocabulary, "sin" and "original sin" are taboo words but one may speak freely of "wickedness" and "instinctive nastiness.") How he is able to reconcile his life-long unflagging passion for righteousness, personal and social, with his conviction that the universe is meaningless—even, maybe, malevolent—I do not quite understand, and he makes one remark which, coming from an atheist, strikes me as most peculiar. Speaking of a Cambridge friend who was a clergyman, he says:

> I feel sure that, if he and I had been walking down Piccadilly and had suddenly come face to face with Jesus Christ, I should have recognised him instantly, but Leopold, if he noticed him at all, would have dismissed him as merely another queer-looking person.

However, this is no business of mine. Who knows what, on Judgment Day, our real standings will turn out to be, except that for lucidity and elegance of verbal expression Mr. Waugh will be way ahead?

Every Christian has to make the transition from the child's "We believe still" to the adult's "I believe again." This cannot have been easy to make at any time, and in our age it is rarely made, it would seem, without a hiatus of unbelief. Looking back later, one asks oneself, of course, why it was so. Could not the period of unbelief have been avoided, or at least shortened? What difference would it have made, Mr. Waugh asks, if at eighteen he had been given a book of Christian philosophy to read or had met a person of holy life? The answer, I fear, is that probably it would have made none. Theology and "Christian philosophy" are written by and for believers—persons, that is, to whom God is already a subject of prayer, even if only subconsciously. Except in the context of prayer they are meaningless, for to talk *about* God, as one talks about the weather or bimetallism, is to take His name in vain. As for holy persons, Mr. Waugh did meet one—Friedrich von Hügel's niece Gwen Plunket-Greene—and he has recorded his impression:

> At the age of twenty-one I merely accepted her with the same incurious enjoyment as my contemporaries afforded.

Events and Acts

No matter what stage of the author's life an autobiography is concerned with, a great deal of it will be a record of events which befell him, by chance or by the will of providence. All events are comparable, and as long as we are reading about what happened to *a* person, to some degree we can identify ourselves with him and ask the same questions we put in regard to the events in our own lives. What would X's life have been if he had met not A but B, or fallen in love with M instead of N? Would Mr. Woolf, for example, have become interested in the co-op movement and gone on from that to the cause of international government if he hadn't happened to meet Margaret Llewelyn Davies, evidently a very remarkable woman? Would Mr. Waugh's political convictions be exactly what they are today if he had not first encountered "progressive" thought in the persons of Barbara Jacobs and her mother, who, from his description of them, seem to have been well meaning but very silly? As for myself, I have often wondered what my life would have been if, on a Sunday in March 1922, a friend, Robert Medley, who is now a painter, had not suggested to me that I write poetry: the thought had never entered my head before.

But no adult life is a record of events only; it also includes the author's personal acts—the things he chooses to do, whatever the consequences may be, and for which he holds himself responsible. Unlike events, acts are incomparable and unrepeatable; they disclose a unique person, the exact like of whom has never existed before and never will again.

The first important act in Mr. Woolf's life that he records was his decision to accept a job in the Ceylon Civil Service. He had done worse in the Civil Service Examination than he had expected:

> The best that I could hope for was a place in the Post Office or Inland Revenue. I was over age for India. I felt that I could not face a lifetime to be spent in Somerset House or in the Post Office, so I decided to take an appointment in the Colonial Service, then called Eastern Cadetships. I applied for Ceylon, which was the senior Crown Colony, and I was high enough up on the list to get what I asked for. I found myself to my astonishment and, it must be admitted, dismay in the Ceylon Civil Service.

The prospect of putting thousands of miles between himself and all his friends cannot have been pleasant; that, nevertheless, he chose Ceylon rather than the Post Office reveals him as a man prepared to live up to his belief that intellectuals should be "engaged," as today's jargon has it. He had really meant what he wrote a year previously:

> While philosophers sit outside the cave, their philosophy will never reach politicians or people, so that after all, to put it plainly, I *do* want Moore to draft an Education Bill.

Ceylon turned out to be much more interesting than he had expected, he proved to be a very efficient administrator, and when he returned to England on leave in 1911, he had good reason to suppose that he would rise to the top in the career he had chosen. Nevertheless, he did not feel altogether happy in the Colonial

Service. His discontent at the time was more aesthetic than moral:
he had not yet asked himself if it was just that a people should
be ruled by aliens, but he did know that he disliked the white
society in Colombo. Shortly after his return, he fell in love with
Virginia Stephen and realized that he was confronted by a choice:

> 1) If Virginia would marry me, I would resign from
> Ceylon and try to earn my living by writing; 2) If Virginia
> would not marry me, I did not want to return to Ceylon and
> become a successful civil servant in Colombo and end even-
> tually with a governorship and K.C.M.G. But if I could go
> back and immerse myself in a District like Hambantota for
> the remainder of my life . . . I might welcome it as a final
> withdrawal, a final solitude, in which, married to a Sin-
> halese, I would make my District or Province the most effi-
> cient, the most prosperous place in Asia.

Fortunately, Virginia accepted his proposal, he resigned, and
they married. The marriage was to bring him great sorrows, but it
is clear that he never for one moment regretted it.

In 1917, the two of them started the Hogarth Press. Mr.
Woolf's initial motive for this act is curious and touching:

> The difficulty with Virginia was to find any play suffi-
> ciently absorbing to take her mind off her work. We were
> both interested in printing and had from time to time in
> a casual way talked about the possibility of learning to
> print. It struck me that it would be a good thing if Virginia
> had a manual occupation of this kind which, in say the
> afternoons, would take her mind completely off her work.
> Towards the end of 1916 we definitely decided that we
> would learn the art of printing.

The venture proved a success, financially as well as artistically,
and relieved them of the money worries which had been theirs since
their marriage.

Naturally, since Mr. Waugh is writing of his youth, he has no
decisions to record of such crucial importance to his future, but he
does mention two acts and one attempted act which are self-
revelatory. The first was in 1921:

> My father's hope was that, like him, I should go to New
> College. Two or three other colleges were in the same

group, among them Hertford. When the time came to fill up the application form, I found that the senior Hertford scholarship was considerably the most valuable. My father was not well off—worse off in fact, like most men of his position, than he had been ten years before. I knew that . . . he would find the financial emolument very convenient. I knew, too, I was not up to a New College scholarship. . . . The motive of the very strenuous work I did in my last six months was primarily the wish to leave school at the earliest possible date. Both these considerations prompted me to an act which was to make a great difference to my university life. I put down the Hertford scholarship as my first preference.

The second was in 1924, when he decided that, rather than continue living on an allowance from his father, he would take a post as a master in a prep school. He found teaching most uncongenial, so when he was given to understand that there was a job as a private secretary waiting for him in Pisa, he gave notice. No sooner had he done so than two blows fell. He had sent some chapters of a novel to Mr. Harold Acton; the letter he received in return and the comments it contained made him burn the thing. Then he learned that the Pisa job was off. Feeling at the end of his tether, he attempted to drown himself—an attempt foiled, fortunately for his soul and for English Letters, by a school of jellyfish.

The first personal choice I can remember making was my decision, when my father offered me a year abroad after I had gone down from Oxford, to spend it in Berlin. I knew no German and no German literature, but I felt out of sympathy with French culture, partly by temperament and partly in revolt against the generation of intellectuals immediately preceding mine, which was strongly Francophile. It is a decision I have been very thankful ever since that I took.

Most of us have known bad periods when we humiliated ourselves before some idol or other, and in adolescence the most common idol is Popularity, or Social Power. The mature Mr. Waugh writes of the diaries he kept during his last two years at Lancing:

> If what I wrote was a true account of myself, I was conceited, heartless and cautiously malevolent. I should like to

believe that even in this private journal I was dissembling a more generous nature; that I absurdly thought cynicism and malice the marks of maturity. I pray it may be so. But the damning evidence is there, in sentence after sentence on page after page, of consistent caddishness. I feel no identity with the boy who wrote it. I believe I was a warm-hearted child. I know that as a man my affections, though narrow, are strong and constant. The adolescent who reveals himself in these pages seems not only cold but quite lacking in sincerity.

He goes on to describe the effects of such a mental attitude upon his outward behavior:

There were frequent small shifts in the kaleidoscope of personal importance, but in the House my friends and I practically controlled the founts of popularity and capriciously stopped them or let them flow. In all these nasty manoeuvres there lay hidden the fear that I myself might at any moment fall from favour and become, as I had been in my first year, the object of contempt.

Change

Among Mr. Woolf's friends at Cambridge, the admired modern novelists were Thomas Hardy, Meredith, and Henry James, and the admired poet was Swinburne. Of the older novelists, Jane Austen and Peacock were in, Dickens and Thackeray were out. Out, too, was Tennyson. Neither Marx nor Freud had been heard of. The *annus mirabilis* was 1903, which saw the publication of *The Way of All Flesh, Principles of Mathematics,* and *Principia Ethica.* Close friends still addressed each other by their surnames.

In 1911 and 1912, the great artistic events in London were the Russian Ballet and the Post-Impressionist Exhibition. In 1914, Mr. Woolf, who was later to become Freud's English publisher, reviewed his "Psychopathology of Everyday Life." During the war years, the great literary figures, against whom Bloomsbury felt the need to react, were Shaw, Wells, and Arnold Bennett. Conrad was admired for his prose style but was considered too "respectable."

The year 1917 saw the publication of *Prufrock,* 1919 *Poems,* by T. S. Eliot, the latter issued by the Hogarth Press, as was *The Waste Land* in 1923. The Woolfs would have published *Ulysses* as well if they had been able to find a printer willing to set it up, though they did not themselves care much for the book. Virginia Woolf recorded in her diary the occasion when Miss Harriet Weaver brought them the manuscript:

> Her neat mauve suit fitted both soul and body; her grey gloves laid straight by her plate symbolised domestic rectitude; her table manners were those of a well bred hen. We could get no talk to go. Possibly the poor woman was impeded by her sense that what she had in the brown paper parcel was quite out of keeping with her own contents. But then how did she ever come in contact with Joyce and the rest? Why does their filth seek exit from her mouth? Heaven knows.

I wish Mr. Waugh had told us more about the books he read—his likes and dislikes, his literary ancestors. The only information he offers is that at the age of seven he had as his literary models *Chums* and *The Boys' Friend;* that when he was thirteen his favorite books were *Le Morte d'Arthur* and *Sinister Street;* that at fourteen he was taken by Samuel Butler's *Notebooks;* and that at Oxford he cherished E. M. Forster's *Pharos and Pharillon.*

I know too little about fiction to be able to give any accurate picture of undergraduate taste and fashions in that medium during my time. Henry James, if I recall rightly, had gone into the shadows, awaiting his triumphal reëntry in the nineteen-forties. Meredith the novelist was no longer read; on the other hand, Meredith the poet, author of *Modern Love,* who seems to have gone unnoticed twenty-five years before, was greatly admired. As for the poets of the past, the most striking change in our ranking of them had resulted from the rediscovery of the metaphysical poets of the seventeenth century. The modern stars were, of course, Eliot, the early-later Yeats, Wilfred Owen, and I would add the names of two who, though they had lived in the nineteenth century, had only recently been published—Emily Dickinson and Gerard Manley Hopkins. I don't think any of my friends shared my enthusiasm for Thomas Hardy, Robert Frost, and Edward Thomas, whom I had discovered at school.

The world as we now know it, created by the automobile, the airplane, the phonograph, radio, television, and social conscience, was only just beginning to take shape—a world without earth privies, oil lamps, gas jets, horses, domestic pianos, maids, governesses, and silence, and it would seem, soon to be without open space. Whatever the differences between Mr. Woolf, Mr. Waugh, and myself, we all three react in the same way to an overcrowded planet.

> No sane man would walk to Peacehaven from Asham today for on the way he would see lovely downs spattered with ugly buildings and, when he got there, he would find all round him, as far as the eye can see, miles of disorderly ugliness, shoddiness, and squalor. [L. W.]

> More than once already in the preceding pages mention has been made of the obliteration of English villages. . . . This is part of the grim cyclorama of spoliation which surrounded all English experience in this century and any understanding of the immediate past . . . must be incomplete unless this huge deprivation of the quiet pleasures of the eye is accepted as a dominant condition. . . . [E. W.]

It is possible to hope against hope for many things—that science may learn how to provide us with an unending supply of synthetic foodstuffs, that intelligence and good will may solve all our economic and political problems—but no human agency can increase the surface area of the earth. If the effects of overcrowding on rats can be as deleterious as experiments have shown them to be, what can we expect will happen to human beings? "Every two men should shoot a third," said Sydney Smith in the eighteen-forties. Today, such a step would not be nearly drastic enough. How can we contemplate the not so distant future with anything but alarm when no method both morally tolerable and practically effective has as yet been discovered for reducing the population of the world to a tenth of its present size and keeping it there?

A Note on the Text

*

For the present edition the author has made some minor corrections and changes. Otherwise, the essays are reprinted from the original appearances listed below. The compiler is grateful to the author for advice in preparing the selection.

The Greeks and Us. Editor's introduction to *The Portable Greek Reader* (New York: Viking Press, 1948). Copyright 1948 by The Viking Press, Inc. Reprinted by permission of The Viking Press, Inc.

Augustus to Augustine. A review of *Christianity and Classical Culture,* by Charles Norris Cochrane, *The New Republic,* 25 September 1944.

Heresies. A review of *Pagan and Christian in an Age of Anxiety,* by E. R. Dodds. *The New York Review of Books,* 17 February 1966.

The Protestant Mystics. Introduction to *The Protestant Mystics,* edited by Anne Freemantle (Boston: Little, Brown, 1964; London: Weidenfeld and Nicolson, 1964). Copyright © 1964 by W. H. Auden and Anne Freemantle. Reprinted by permission of Little, Brown and Company.

Greatness Finding Itself. A review of *Young Man Luther,* by Erik Erikson. *The Mid-Century,* June 1960.

Shakespeare's Sonnets. Introduction to the Signet Classic edition of the *Sonnets,* edited by William Burto (New York: New American Library, 1964). Copyright © 1964 by W. H. Auden. Reprinted by arrangement with The New American Library, Inc.

A Civilized Voice. A review of *Alexander Pope: The Education of a Genius 1688–1728,* by Peter Quennell. *The New Yorker,* 22 February 1969.

Werther *and* Novella. Foreword to a translation by Elizabeth Mayer and Louise Bogan of Goethe's *The Sorrows of Young Werther and Novella* (New York: Random House, 1971).

Italian Journey. Introduction to a translation by Auden and Elizabeth Mayer of Goethe's *Italian Journey* (London: Collins, 1962; New York: Pantheon, 1962).

Mr. G. A review of *Goethe: Conversations and Encounters,* edited by David Luke and Robert Pick. *The New York Review of Books,* 9 February 1967.

Portrait of a Whig. Introduction to *Selected Writings of Sydney Smith* (New York: Farrar, Straus and Cudahy, 1956). Reprinted by permission of Curtis Brown, Ltd. Copyright © 1956 by W. H. Auden.

Søren Kierkegaard. Introduction to *The Living Thoughts of Kierkegaard* (New York: David McKay, 1952). This book was also published in England as *Kierkegaard: Selected and Introduced by W. H. Auden* (London: Cassell, 1955). Copyright 1952 by David McKay Company, Inc. Reprinted by permission of the publisher.

A Knight of Doleful Countenance. A review of Kierkegaard's *Journals and Papers,* vol. I, edited by Howard and Edna Hong. *The New Yorker,* 25 May 1968.

Grimm and Andersen. Introduction to *Tales of Grimm and Andersen* (New York: Modern Library, 1952).

Edgar Allan Poe. Introduction to *Edgar Allan Poe: Selected Prose, Poetry, and Eureka* (New York: Rinehart, 1950). Introduction copyright 1950 by W. H. Auden. Reprinted by permission of Holt, Rinehart and Winston, Inc.

Tennyson. Introduction to *A Selection From the Poems of Alfred, Lord Tennyson* (New York: Doubleday, Doran, 1944). This book was also published in England as *Tennyson: An Introduction and a Selection by W. H. Auden* (London: Phoenix House, 1946).

A Very Inquisitive Old Party. A review of a reissue of *London Labour and the London Poor,* by Henry Mayhew. *The New Yorker,* 24 February 1968.

The Greatest of the Monsters. A review of *Richard Wagner: The Man, His Mind, and His Music,* by Robert Gutman. *The New Yorker,* 4 January 1969.

A Genius and a Gentleman. A review of *Letters of Giuseppe Verdi,* edited by Charles Osborne. *The New York Review of Books,* 9 March 1972.

A Poet of the Actual. A review of *Anthony Trollope,* by James Pope Hennessy, *The New Yorker,* 1 April 1972.

George Macdonald. Introduction to *The Visionary Novels of George Macdonald,* edited by Anne Fremantle (New York: Noonday Press, 1954).

A Russian Aesthete. A review of *Against the Current,* by Konstantin Leontiev. *The New Yorker,* 4 April 1970.

Lewis Carroll. First published as "Today's 'Wonder-World' Needs Alice" in *The New York Times Magazine,* 1 July 1962.

Calm Even in the Catastrophe. A review of *The Complete Letters of Vincent van Gogh. Encounter,* April 1959. Published in an abridged form in *The Mid-Century,* September 1959 and May 1960.

An Improbable Life. A review of *The Letters of Oscar Wilde,* edited by Rupert Hart-Davis. *The New Yorker,* 9 March 1963.

A Worcestershire Lad. A review of *The Letters of A. E. Housman,* edited by Henry Maas. *The New Yorker,* 19 February 1972.

C. P. Cavafy. Introduction to *The Complete Poems of Cavafy,* translated by Rae Dalven (New York: Harcourt, Brace and World, 1961; London: Hogarth Press, 1961). Copyright © 1961 by W. H. Auden. Reprinted by permission of Harcourt Brace Jovanovich, Inc.

A Marriage of True Minds. A review of *The Correspondence Between Richard Strauss and Hugo von Hofmannsthal;* published in America under the title *A Working Friendship.* Reproduced by permission from *The Times Literary Supplement,* 10 November 1961. Also published in *The Mid-Century,* March 1962.

The Poet of the Encirclement. A review of *A Choice of Kipling's Verse,* made by T. S. Eliot. *The New Republic,* 24 October 1943.

A Note on the Text

Un Homme d'Esprit. Introduction to *Analects,* by Paul Valéry, from *The Collected Works of Paul Valéry,* edited by Jackson Mathews (Princeton: Princeton University Press, Bollingen Series XLV, vol. 14, 1970; London: Routledge and Kegan Paul, 1970). Copyright © 1970 by Princeton University Press. Also published in *Hudson Review,* Autumn 1969.

One Of the Family. A review of *Max,* by Lord David Cecil. *The New Yorker,* 23 October 1965.

Walter de la Mare. Introduction to *A Choice of de la Mare's Verse* (London: Faber and Faber, 1963).

G. K. Chesterton's Non-Fictional Prose. Introduction to *G. K. Chesterton: A Selection From His Non-Fictional Prose* (London: Faber and Faber, 1970).

Lame Shadows. A review of *Tonio Kröger and Other Stories,* by Thomas Mann. *The New York Review of Books,* 3 September 1970.

A Consciousness of Reality. A review of *A Writer's Diary,* by Virginia Woolf. *The New Yorker,* 6 March 1954.

Private Poet. A review of *Rhymes of a Pfc,* by Lincoln Kirstein. *The New York Review of Books,* 5 November 1964.

A Voice of Importance. A review of *The Sense of Occasion,* by Chester Kallman. *Harper's Magazine,* March 1972.

A Tribute. First published as "Craftsman, Artist, Genius" in *The Observer,* 11 April 1971.

Markings. The introduction to *Markings,* by Dag Hammarskjöld (New York: Alfred A. Knopf, 1964).

Papa Was a Wise Old Sly-Boots. A review of *My Father and My-self,* by J. R. Ackerley. *The New York Review of Books,* 27 March 1969.

The Justice of Dame Kind. A review of *The Senses of Animals and Men,* by Loris J. and Margery Milne. *The Mid-Century,* Mid-summer 1962.

Concerning the Unpredictable. A review of *The Unexpected Universe,* by Loren Eiseley. *The New Yorker,* 21 February 1970.

The Megrims. A review of *Migraine,* by Oliver Sacks. *The New York Review of Books,* 3 June 1971.

Deborah. A review of *Deborah,* by David Roberts. *The New York Times Book Review,* 7 February 1971.

The Kitchen of Life. Introduction to *The Art of Eating,* by M. F. K. Fisher (London: Faber and Faber, 1963).

A Note on the Text

As It Seemed to Us. A review of *A Little Learning,* by Evelyn Waugh, and *Beginning Again,* by Leonard Woolf. *The New Yorker,* 3 April 1965.

ABOUT THE AUTHOR

WYSTAN HUGH AUDEN was born in York, England, in 1907. He came to the United States in 1939, and became an American citizen in 1946. Educated at Gresham's School, Holt, and at Christ Church, Oxford, he was associated with a small group of young writers in London—among them Stephen Spender and Christopher Isherwood—who became recognized as the most promising of the new generation in English letters. He collaborated with Isherwood on the plays *The Dog Beneath the Skin, The Ascent of F6,* and *On the Frontier,* as well as on *Journey to a War,* a prose record of experiences in China. He has edited many anthologies, including *The Oxford Book of Light Verse* and, with Norman Holmes Pearson, *Poets of the English Language.* In collaboration with Chester Kallman, he has also written the libretti for Igor Stravinsky's opera *The Rake's Progress,* and for Hans Henze's opera *Elegy for Young Lovers.* His selected essays, *The Dyer's Hand,* appeared in 1962. *Academic Graffiti,* with illustrations by Filippo Sanjust, appeared in 1972.

W. H. Auden is the author of several volumes of poetry, including *The Double Man, For the Time Being, The Age of Anxiety, Nones,* and *The Shield of Achilles,* which received the National Book Award in 1956. His most recent collections of poetry are *City Without Walls* (1969) and *Epistle to a Godson* (1972).

In 1972 Mr. Auden returned to Oxford. He now resides at Christ Church, where he is an honorary student, but he retains his U.S. citizenship.